D0919772

ALSO BY NICK TURSE

The Complex: How the Military Invades Our Everyday Lives

United States Army has never condoned wanton killing or disregard for human life."[2]

This was, and remains, the American military's official position. In many ways, it remains the popular understanding in the United States as a whole. Today, histories of the Vietnam War regularly discuss war crimes or civilian suffering only in the context of a single incident: the My Lai massacre cited by McDuff. Even as that one event has become the subject of numerous books and articles, all the other atrocities perpetrated by U.S. soldiers have essentially vanished from popular memory.

The visceral horror of what happened at My Lai is undeniable. On the evening of March 15, 1968, members of the Americal Division's Charlie Company, 1st Battalion, 20th Infantry, were briefed by their commanding officer, Captain Ernest Medina, on a planned operation the next day in an area they knew as "Pinkville." As unit member Harry Stanley recalled, Medina "ordered us to 'kill everything in the village.'" Infantryman Salvatore LaMartina remembered Medina's words only slightly differently: they were to "kill everything that breathed." What stuck in artillery forward observer James Flynn's mind was a question one of the other soldiers asked: "Are we supposed to kill women and children?" And Medina's reply: "Kill everything that moves."[3]

The next morning, the troops clambered aboard helicopters and were airlifted into what they thought would be a "hot LZ"—a landing zone where they'd be under hostile fire. As it happened, though, instead of finding Vietnamese adversaries spoiling for a fight, the Americans entering My Lai encountered only civilians: women, children, and old men. Many were still cooking their breakfast rice. Nevertheless, Medina's orders were followed to a T. Soldiers of Charlie Company killed. They killed everything. They killed everything that moved.

Advancing in small squads, the men of the unit shot chickens as they scurried about, pigs as they bolted, and cows and water buffalo

AN OPERATION, NOT AN ABERRATION

On January 21, 1971, a Vietnam veteran named Charles McDuff wrote a letter to President Richard Nixon to voice his disgust with the American war in Southeast Asia. McDuff had witnessed multiple cases of Vietnamese civilians being abused and killed by American soldiers and their allies, and he had found the U.S. military justice system to be woefully ineffective in punishing wrongdoers. "Maybe your advisors have not clued you in," he told the president, "but the atrocities that were committed in Mylai are eclipsed by similar American actions throughout the country." His three-page handwritten missive concluded with an impassioned plea to Nixon to end American participation in the war.[1]

The White House forwarded the note to the Department of Defense for a reply, and within a few weeks Major General Franklin Davis Jr., the army's director of military personnel policies, wrote back to McDuff. It was "indeed unfortunate," said Davis, "that some incidents occur within combat zones." He then shifted the burden of responsibility for what had happened firmly back onto the veteran. "I presume," he wrote, "that you promptly reported such actions to the proper authorities." Other than a paragraph of information on how to contact the U.S. Army criminal investigators, the reply was only four sentences long and included a matter-of-fact reassurance: "The

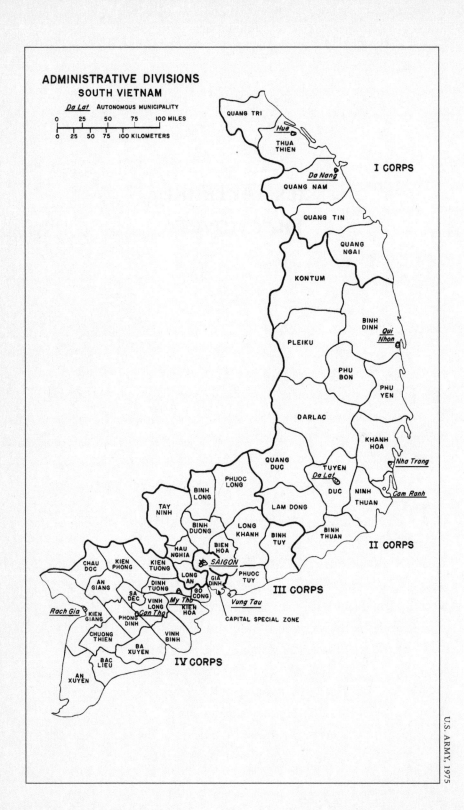

ADMINISTRATIVE DIVISIONS
SOUTH VIETNAM

Da Lat AUTONOMOUS MUNICIPALITY

0   25   50   75   100 MILES
0 25 50 75 100 KILOMETERS

QUANG TRI

Hue

THUA THIEN

I CORPS

Da Nang

QUANG NAM

QUANG TIN

QUANG NGAI

KONTUM

BINH DINH

Qui Nhon

PLEIKU

PHU BON

PHU YEN

DARLAC

KHANH HOA

QUANG DUC

TUYEN *Da Lat* DUC

Nha Trang

NINH THUAN

Cam Ranh

PHUOC LONG

BINH LONG

TAY NINH

LAM DONG

BINH DUONG

LONG KHANH

BINH TUY

BINH THUAN

II CORPS

CHAU DOC

KIEN PHONG

KIEN TUONG

HAU NGHIA

BIEN HOA

SAIGON

LONG AN

GIA DINH

PHUOC TUY

III CORPS

AN GIANG

SA DEC

DINH TUONG

GO CONG

Vung Tau

Rach Gia

KIEN GIANG

PHONG DINH

VINH LONG

My Tho

KIEN HOA

CAPITAL SPECIAL ZONE

Can Tho

CHUONG THIEN

BA XUYEN

VINH BINH

BAC LIEU

IV CORPS

AN XUYEN

U.S. ARMY, 1975

KILL ANYTHING
THAT MOVES

CONTENTS

For all those who shared their stories—
and for those with stories yet to be told.

Metropolitan Books
Henry Holt and Company, LLC
Publishers since 1866
175 Fifth Avenue
New York, New York 10010
www.henryholt.com

Metropolitan Books® and m® are registered trademarks of
Henry Holt and Company, LLC.

Library of Congress Cataloging-in-Publication Data

Turse, Nick.
  Kill anything that moves : the real American war in Vietnam / Nick Turse.—1st ed.
    p. cm.
  Includes bibliographical references and index.
  ISBN 978-0-8050-8691-1
  1. Vietnam War, 1961–1975—Atrocities. 2. Vietnam War, 1961–1975—United States.
3. Massacres—Vietnam—History—20th century. 4. War crimes—Vietnam—History—
20th century. 5. Violence—Vietnam—History—20th century. 6. Racism—Vietnam—
History—20th century. 7. United States—Military policy. I. Title.
  DS559.2.T87 2013
  959.704'34—dc23   2012020903

Designed by Kelly S. Too

Printed in the United States of America
5 7 9 10 8 6 4

KILL ANYTHING THAT MOVES

The Real American War in Vietnam

NICK TURSE

METROPOLITAN BOOKS

HENRY HOLT AND COMPANY   NEW YORK

KILL ANYTHING
THAT MOVES

lowing among the thatch-roofed houses. They gunned down old men sitting in their homes and children as they ran for cover. They tossed grenades into homes without even bothering to look inside. An officer grabbed a woman by the hair and shot her point-blank with a pistol. A woman who came out of her home with a baby in her arms was shot down on the spot. As the tiny child hit the ground, another GI opened up on the infant with his M-16 automatic rifle.

Over four hours, members of Charlie Company methodically slaughtered more than five hundred unarmed victims, killing some in ones and twos, others in small groups, and collecting many more in a drainage ditch that would become an infamous killing ground. They faced no opposition. They even took a quiet break to eat lunch in the midst of the carnage. Along the way, they also raped women and young girls, mutilated the dead, systematically burned homes, and fouled the area's drinking water.[4]

There were scores of witnesses on the ground and still more overhead, American officers and helicopter crewmen perfectly capable of seeing the growing piles of civilian bodies. Yet when the military released the first news of the assault, it was portrayed as a victory over a formidable enemy force, a legitimate battle in which 128 enemy troops were killed without the loss of a single American life.[5] In a routine congratulatory telegram, General William Westmoreland, the commander of U.S. forces in Vietnam, lauded the "heavy blows" inflicted on the enemy. His protégé, the commander of the Americal Division, added a special note praising Charlie Company's "aggressiveness."[6]

Despite communiqués, radio reports, and English-language accounts released by the Vietnamese revolutionary forces, the My Lai massacre would remain, to the outside world, an American victory for more than a year. And the truth might have remained hidden forever if not for the perseverance of a single Vietnam veteran named Ron Ridenhour. The twenty-two-year-old Ridenhour had not been among the hundred American troops at My Lai, though he had seen civilians murdered elsewhere in Vietnam; instead, he heard about the slaughter from other soldiers who had been in Pinkville that day. Unnerved, Ridenhour took the unprecedented step of carefully gathering testimony from multiple American eyewitnesses. Then, upon returning to the United States after his yearlong tour of duty, he committed himself to doing whatever was necessary to expose the incident to public scrutiny.[7]

Ridenhour's efforts were helped by the painstaking investigative reporting of Seymour Hersh, who published newspaper articles about the massacre; by the appearance in *Life* magazine of grisly full-color images that army photographer Ron Haeberle captured in My Lai as the slaughter was unfolding; and by a confessional interview that a soldier from Charlie Company gave to CBS News. The Pentagon, for its part, consistently fought to minimize what had happened, claiming that reports by Vietnamese survivors were wildly exaggerated. At the same time, the military focused its attention on the lowest-ranking officer who could conceivably shoulder the blame for such a nightmare: Charlie Company's Lieutenant William Calley.[8]

An army inquiry into the killings eventually determined that thirty individuals were involved in criminal misconduct during the massacre or its cover-up. Twenty-eight of them were officers, including two generals, and the inquiry concluded they had committed a total of 224 serious offenses.[9] But only Calley was ever convicted of any wrongdoing. He was sentenced to life in prison for the premeditated murder of twenty-two civilians, but President Nixon freed him from prison and allowed him to remain under house arrest. He was eventually paroled after serving just forty months, most of it in the comfort of his own quarters.[10]

The public response generally followed the official one. Twenty-five years later, Ridenhour would sum it up this way.

At the end of it, if you ask people what happened at My Lai, they would say: "Oh yeah, isn't that where Lieutenant Calley went crazy and killed all those people?" No, that was not what happened. Lieutenant Calley was one of the people who went crazy and killed a lot of people at My Lai, but this was an operation, not an aberration.[11]

Looking back, it's clear that the real aberration was the unprecedented and unparalleled investigation and exposure of My Lai. No other American atrocity committed during the war—and there were so many—was ever afforded anything approaching the same attention. Most, of course, weren't photographed, and many were not documented in any way. The great majority were never known outside the offending unit, and most investigations that did result were closed, quashed, or abandoned. Even on the rare occasions when the allegations were seriously investigated within the military, the reports were soon buried in classified files without ever seeing the light of day.[12] Whistle-blowers within the ranks or recently out of the army were threatened, intimidated, smeared, or—if they were lucky—simply marginalized and ignored.

Until the My Lai revelations became front-page news, atrocity stories were routinely disregarded by American journalists or excised by stateside editors. The fate of civilians in rural South Vietnam did not merit much examination; even the articles that did mention the killing of noncombatants generally did so merely in passing, without any indication that the acts described might be war crimes.[13] Vietnamese revolutionary sources, for their part, detailed hundreds of massacres and large-scale operations that resulted in thousands of civilian deaths, but those reports were dismissed out of hand as communist propaganda.[14]

And then, in a stunning reversal, almost immediately after the exposure of the My Lai massacre, war crime allegations became old hat—so commonplace as to be barely worth mentioning or looking into. In leaflets, pamphlets, small-press books, and "underground" newspapers, the growing American antiwar movement repeatedly pointed out that U.S. troops were committing atrocities on a regular basis. But what had been previously brushed aside as propaganda and leftist kookery suddenly started to be disregarded as yawn-worthy common knowledge, with little but the My Lai massacre in between.[15]

Such impulses only grew stronger in the years of the "culture wars," when the Republican Party and an emboldened right wing rose to power. Until Ronald Reagan's presidency, the Vietnam War was generally seen as an American defeat, but even before taking office Reagan began rebranding the conflict as "a noble cause." In the same spirit, scholars and veterans began, with significant success, to recast the war in rosier terms.[16] Even in the early years of the twenty-first century, as newspapers and magazines published exposés of long-hidden U.S. atrocities, apologist historians continued to ignore much of the evidence, portraying American war crimes as no more than isolated incidents.[17]

But the stunning scale of civilian suffering in Vietnam is far beyond anything that can be explained as merely the work of some "bad apples," however numerous. Murder, torture, rape, abuse, forced displacement, home burnings, specious arrests, imprisonment without due process—such occurrences were virtually a daily fact of life throughout the years of the American presence in Vietnam. And as Ridenhour put it, they were no aberration. Rather, they were the inevitable outcome of deliberate policies, dictated at the highest levels of the military.

The first official American combat troops arrived in Vietnam in 1965, but the roots of the conflict go back many decades earlier. In the nineteenth century, France expanded its colonial empire by taking control of Vietnam as well as neighboring Cambodia and Laos, rechristening the entire region as French Indochina. French rubber production in Vietnam yielded such riches for the colonizers that the latex oozing from rubber trees became known as "white gold."

The ill-paid Vietnamese workers, laboring on the plantations in harsh conditions, called it by a different name: "white blood."[18]

By the early twentieth century, anger at the French had developed into a nationalist movement for independence. Its leaders found inspiration in communism, specifically the example of Russian Bolshevism and Lenin's call for national revolutions in the colonial world. During World War II, when Vietnam was occupied by the imperial Japanese, the country's main anticolonial organization—officially called the League for the Independence of Vietnam, but far better known as the Viet Minh—launched a guerrilla war against the Japanese forces and the French administrators running the country. Under the leadership of the charismatic Ho Chi Minh, the Vietnamese guerrillas aided the American war effort. In return they received arms, training, and support from the U.S. Office of Strategic Services, a forerunner of the Central Intelligence Agency.

In 1945, with the Japanese defeated, Ho proclaimed Vietnam's independence, using the words of the U.S. Declaration of Independence as his template. "All men are created equal," he told a crowd of half a million Vietnamese in Hanoi. "The Creator has given us certain inviolable rights: the right to life, the right to be free, and the right to achieve happiness." As a young man Ho had spent some years living in the West, reportedly including stretches in Boston and New York City, and he hoped to obtain American support for his vision of a free Vietnam. In the aftermath of World War II, however, the United States was focused on rebuilding and strengthening a devastated Europe, as the Cold War increasingly gripped the continent. The Americans saw France as a strong ally against any Soviet designs on Western Europe and thus had little interest in sanctioning a communist-led independence movement in a former French colony. Instead, U.S. ships helped transport French troops to Vietnam, and the administration of President Harry Truman threw its support behind a French reconquest of Indochina.

Soon, the United States was dispatching equipment and even

military advisers to Vietnam. By 1953, it was shouldering nearly 80 percent of the bill for an ever more bitter war against the Viet Minh.[19] The conflict progressed from guerrilla warfare to a conventional military campaign, and in 1954 a Gallic garrison at the well-fortified base of Dien Bien Phu was pounded into surrender by Viet Minh forces under General Vo Nguyen Giap. The French had had enough. At an international peace conference in Geneva, they agreed to a temporary separation of Vietnam into two placeholder regions, the north and the south, which were to be rejoined as one nation following a reunification election in 1956.

That election never took place. Fearing that Ho Chi Minh, now the head of the communist Democratic Republic of Vietnam in the north, was sure to sweep any nationwide vote, the United States picked up where its French partners had left off. It promptly launched efforts to thwart reunification by arming its allies in the southern part of the country. In this way, it fostered the creation of what eventually became the Republic of Vietnam, led by a Catholic autocrat named Ngo Dinh Diem.

From the 1950s on, the United States would support an ever more corrupt and repressive state in South Vietnam while steadily expanding its presence in Southeast Asia. When President John Kennedy took office there were around 800 U.S. military personnel in South Vietnam. That number increased to 3,000 in 1961, and to more than 11,000 the following year. Officially listed as advisers involved in the training of the South Vietnamese army, the Americans increasingly took part in combat operations against southern guerrillas—both communist and noncommunist—who were now waging war to unify the country.[20]

After Kennedy's assassination, President Lyndon Johnson repeatedly escalated the war with bombing raids on North Vietnam, and unleashed an ever more furious onslaught on the South. In 1965 the fiction of "advisers" was finally dropped, and the American War, as it is known in Vietnam, began in earnest. In a televised speech, Johnson insisted that the United States was not inserting itself into a far-away civil war but taking steps to contain a communist menace. The war, he said, was "guided by North Vietnam . . . Its goal is to conquer the South, to defeat American power, and to extend the Asiatic dominion of communism."[21] To counter this, the United States turned huge swaths of the South Vietnamese countryside—where most of South Vietnam's population lived—into battered battlegrounds.

At the peak of U.S. operations, in 1969, the war involved more than 540,000 American troops in Vietnam, plus some 100,000 to 200,000 U.S. troops participating in the effort from outside the country. They were also aided by numerous CIA operatives, civilian advisers, mercenaries, civilian contractors, and armed members of the allied "Free World Forces"—South Korean, Australian, New Zealand, Thai, Filipino, and other foreign troops.[22] Over the entire course of the conflict, the United States would deploy more than 3 million soldiers, marines, airmen, and sailors to Southeast Asia.[23] (Fighting alongside them were hundreds of thousands of South Vietnamese troops: the Army of the Republic of Vietnam would balloon to a force of nearly 1 million before the end of the war, to say nothing of South Vietnam's air force, navy, marine corps, and national police.) Officially, the American military effort lasted until early 1973, when a cease-fire was signed and U.S. combat forces were formally withdrawn from the country, though American aid and other support would continue to flow into the Republic of Vietnam until Saigon fell to the revolutionary forces in 1975.

From the U.S. perspective, the enemy was composed of two distinct groups: members of the North Vietnamese army and indigenous South Vietnamese fighters loyal to the National Liberation Front, the revolutionary organization that succeeded the Viet Minh and opposed the U.S.-allied Saigon government. The NLF's combatants, officially known as the People's Liberation Armed Forces (PLAF), included guerrillas in peasant clothing as well as uniformed troops organized into professionalized units. The U.S. Information Service invented the moniker "Viet Cong"—that is, Vietnamese Communists—as a derogatory term that covered anyone fighting on the side of the NLF, though many of the guerrillas themselves were driven more by nationalism than by communist ideology. American soldiers, in turn, often shortened this label to "the Cong" or "VC," or, owing to the military's phonetic Alpha-Bravo-Charlie alphabet, to "Victor Charlie" or simply "Charlie."[24]

By 1968 the U.S. forces and their allies in the South were opposed by an estimated 50,000 North Vietnamese troops plus 60,000 uniformed PLAF soldiers, while the revolutionaries' paramilitary forces—part-time, local guerrillas—likely reached into the hundreds of thousands.[25] Americans often made hard-and-fast distinctions between the well-armed, green- or khaki-uniformed North Vietnamese troops with their fabric-covered, pressed-cardboard pith-style helmets; the khaki-clad main force PLAF soldiers, with their floppy cloth "boonie hats"; and the lightly armed, "black pajama"–clad guerrillas (all of whom actually wore a wide variety of types and colors of clothing depending on the time and place). In reality, though, they were very hard to disentangle, since North Vietnamese troops reinforced PLAF units, "local" VC fought in tandem with "hard-core" professionalized PLAF troops, and part-time farmer-fighters assisted uniformed North Vietnamese forces.

The plethora of designations and the often hazy distinctions between them underscore the fact that the Americans never really grasped who the enemy was. On one hand, they claimed the VC had little popular support and held sway over villages only through terror tactics. On the other, American soldiers who were supposedly engaged in countering communist aggression to protect the South Vietnamese readily killed civilians because they assumed that most villagers either were in league with the enemy or were guerrillas themselves once the sun went down.

The United States never wanted to admit that the conflict might be a true "people's war," and that Vietnamese were bound to the revolution because they saw it as a fight for their families, their land, and their country. In the villages of South Vietnam, Vietnamese nationalists had long organized themselves to resist foreign domination, and it was no different when the Americans came. By then, the local population was often inextricably joined to the liberation struggle. Lacking advanced technology, financial resources, or significant firepower, America's Vietnamese enemies maximized assets like concealment, local knowledge, popular support, and something less quantifiable—call it patriotism or nationalism, or perhaps a hope and a dream.

Of course, not every Vietnamese villager believed in the revolution or saw it as the best expression of nationalist patriotism. Even villages in revolutionary strongholds were home to some supporters of the Saigon government. And many more farmers simply wanted nothing to do with the conflict or abstract notions like nationalism and communism. They worried mainly about their next rice crop, their animals, their house and children. But bombs and napalm don't discriminate. As gunships and howitzers ravaged the landscape, as soldiers with M-16 rifles and M-79 grenade launchers swept through the countryside, Vietnamese villagers of every type—supporters of the revolution, sympathizers of the Saigon regime, and those who merely wanted to be left alone—all perished in vast numbers.

The war's casualty figures are staggering indeed. From 1955 to 1975, the United States lost more than 58,000 military personnel in Southeast Asia. Its troops were wounded around 304,000 times, with 153,000 cases serious enough to require hospitalization, and 75,000 veterans left severely disabled.[26] While Americans who served in Vietnam paid a grave price, an extremely conservative estimate of Vietnamese deaths found them to be "proportionally 100 times greater than those suffered by the United States."[27] The military forces of the U.S.-allied Republic of Vietnam reportedly lost more than 254,000 killed and more than 783,000 wounded.[28] And the casualties of the revolutionary forces were evidently far graver—perhaps 1.7 million, including 1 million killed in battle, plus some 300,000 personnel still "missing" according to the official but incomplete Vietnamese government figures.[29]

Horrendous as these numbers may be, they pale in comparison to the estimated civilian death toll during the war years. At least 65,000 North Vietnamese civilians were killed, mainly from U.S. air raids.[30] No one will ever know the exact number of South Vietnamese civilians killed as a result of the American War. While the U.S. military attempted to quantify almost every other aspect of the conflict—from the number of helicopter sorties flown to the number of propaganda leaflets dispersed—it quite deliberately never conducted a comprehensive study of Vietnamese noncombatant casualties.[31] Whatever civilian casualty statistics the United States did tally were generally kept secret, and when released piecemeal they were invariably radical undercounts.[32]

Yet even the available flawed figures are startling, especially given that the total population of South Vietnam was only about 19 million people. Using fragmentary data and questionable extrapolations that, for instance, relied heavily on hospital data yet all but ignored the immense number of Vietnamese treated by the revolutionary forces (and also failed to take into account the many civilians killed by U.S. forces and claimed as enemies), one Department of Defense statistical analyst came up with a postwar estimate of 1.2 million civilian casualties, including 195,000 killed.[33] In 1975, a U.S. Senate subcommittee on refugees and war victims offered an estimate of 1.4 million civilian casualties in South Vietnam, including 415,000 killed.[34] Or take the figures proffered by the political scientist Guenter Lewy, the progenitor of a revisionist school of Vietnam War history that invariably shines the best possible light on the U.S. war effort. Even he posits that there were more than 1.1 million South Vietnamese civilian casualties, including almost 250,000 killed, as a result of the conflict.[35]

In recent years, careful surveys, analyses, and official estimates have consistently pointed toward a significantly higher number of civilian deaths.[36] The most sophisticated analysis yet of wartime mortality in Vietnam, a 2008 study by researchers from Harvard Medical School and the Institute for Health Metrics and Evaluation at the University of Washington, suggested that a reasonable estimate might be 3.8 million violent war deaths, combatant and civilian.[37] Given the limitations of the study's methodology, there are good reasons to believe that even this staggering figure may be an underestimate.[38] Still, the findings lend credence to an official 1995 Vietnamese government estimate of more than 3 million deaths in total—including 2 million civilian deaths—for the years when the Americans were involved in the conflict.[39]

The sheer number of civilian war wounded, too, has long been a point of contention. The best numbers currently available, though, begin to give some sense of the suffering. A brief accounting shows 8,000 to 16,000 South Vietnamese paraplegics; 30,000 to 60,000 South Vietnamese left blind; and some 83,000 to 166,000 South Vietnamese amputees.[40] As far as the total number of the civilian war wounded goes, Guenter Lewy approaches the question by using a ratio derived from South Vietnamese data on military casualties, which shows 2.65 soldiers seriously wounded for every one killed. Such a proportion is distinctly low when applied to the civilian population; still, even this multiplier, if applied to the Vietnamese government estimate of 2 million civilian dead, yields a figure of 5.3 million civilian wounded, for a total of 7.3 million Vietnamese civilian casualties overall.[41] Notably, official South Vietnamese hospital records indicate that approximately one-third of those wounded were women and about one-quarter were children under thirteen years of age.[42]

What explains these staggering figures? Because the My Lai massacre has entered the popular American consciousness as an exceptional, one-of-a-kind event, the deaths of other civilians during the Vietnam War tend to be vaguely thought of as a matter of mistakes or (to use a phrase that would come into common use after the war) of "collateral damage." But as I came to see, the indiscriminate killing of South Vietnamese noncombatants—the endless slaughter that wiped out civilians day after day, month after month, year after year throughout the Vietnam War—was neither accidental nor unforeseeable.

I stumbled upon the first clues to this hidden history almost by accident, in June 2001, when I was a graduate student researching post-traumatic stress disorder among Vietnam veterans. One afternoon, I was looking through documents at the U.S. National Archives when a friendly archivist asked me, "Could witnessing war crimes cause post-traumatic stress?" I had no idea at the time that the archives might have any records on Vietnam-era war crimes, so the prospect had never dawned on me. Within an hour or so, though, I held in my hands the yellowing records of the Vietnam War Crimes Working Group, a secret Pentagon task force that had been assembled after the My Lai massacre to ensure that the army would never again be caught off-guard by a major war crimes scandal.

To call the records a "treasure trove" feels strange, given the nature of the material. But that's how the collection struck me then, box after box of criminal investigation reports and day-to-day paperwork long buried away and almost totally forgotten. There were some files as thick as a phonebook, with the most detailed and nightmarish descriptions; other files, paper-thin, hinting at terrible events that had received no follow-up attention; and just about everything in between. As I leafed through them that day, I knew one thing almost instantly: they documented a nightmare war that is essentially missing from our understanding of the Vietnam conflict.

The War Crimes Working Group files included more than 300 allegations of massacres, murders, rapes, torture, assaults, mutilations, and other atrocities that were substantiated by army investigators. They detailed the deaths of 137 civilians in mass killings, and 78 smaller-scale attacks in which Vietnamese civilians were killed, wounded, and sexually assaulted. They identified 141 instances in which U.S. troops used fists, sticks, bats, water torture, and electrical torture on noncombatants. The files also contained 500 allegations that weren't proven at the time—like the murders of scores, perhaps hundreds, of Vietnamese civilians by the 101st Airborne Division's Tiger Force, which would be confirmed and made public only in 2003.

In hundreds of incident summaries and sworn statements in the War Crimes Working Group files, veterans laid bare what had occurred in the backlands of rural Vietnam—the war that Americans back home didn't see nightly on their televisions or read about over morning coffee. A sergeant told investigators how he had put a bullet, point-blank, into the brain of an unarmed boy after gunning down the youngster's brother; an army ranger matter-of-factly described slicing the ears off a dead Vietnamese and said that he planned to continue mutilating corpses.[43] Other files documented the killing of farmers in their fields and the rape of a child carried out by an interrogator at an army base. Reading case after case—like the incident in which a lieutenant "captured two unarmed and unidentified Vietnamese males, estimated ages 2–3 and 7–8 years ... and killed them for no reason"—I began to get a sense of the ubiquity of atrocity during the American War.[44]

In the years that followed, with the War Crimes Working Group documents as an initial guide, I began to track down more information about little-known or never-revealed Vietnam War crimes. I located other investigation files at the National Archives, submitted requests under the Freedom of Information Act, interviewed generals and top civilian officials, and talked to former military war crimes investigators. I also spoke with more than one hundred American veterans across the country, both those who had witnessed atrocities and others who had personally committed terrible acts. From them I learned something of what it was like to be twenty years old, with few life experiences beyond adolescence in a small town or an inner-city neighborhood, and to be suddenly thrust into villages of thatch and bamboo homes that seemed ripped straight from the pages of *National Geographic*, the paddies around them such a vibrant green that they almost burned the eye. Veteran after veteran told me about days of shattering fatigue and the confusion of contradictory orders, about being placed in situations so alien and unnerving that even with their automatic rifles and grenades they felt scared walking through hamlets of unarmed women and children.

Some of the veterans I tried to contact wanted nothing to do with my questions, almost instantaneously slamming down the phone receiver. But most were willing to speak to me, and many even seemed glad to talk to someone who had a sense of the true nature of the war. In homes from Maryland to California, across kitchen tables and in marathon four-hour telephone calls, scores of former soldiers and marines opened up about their experiences. Some had little remorse; an interrogator who'd tortured prisoners, for instance, told me that his actions were merely standard operating procedure. Another veteran, whispering so that his family wouldn't overhear, adamantly insisted that, though he'd been present at a massacre of civilians, he hadn't pulled the trigger, no matter what his fellow unit members said. Then there was the veteran who swore that he knew nothing about civilians being killed, only to later recount an incident in which someone in his unit shot an unarmed woman in the back. And yet another former GI ruefully recounted how, walking through a Vietnamese village, he had spun around when a local woman chattered angrily at him (probably complaining about the commotion that the troops were causing) and driven the butt of his rifle into her nose. He remembered walking away, laughing, as blood poured from the woman's face. Decades later, he could no longer imagine how his nineteen-year-old self had done such a thing, nor could I easily connect this jovial man to that angry adolescent with a brutal streak.

My conversations with the veterans gave nuance to my understanding of the war, bringing human emotion to the sometimes dry language of military records, and added context to investigation files that often focused on a single incident. These men also repeatedly showed me just how incomplete the archives I'd come upon really were, even though the files detailed hundreds of atrocity allegations. In one case, for instance, I called a veteran seeking more information about a sexual assault carried out by members of his unit, which I found mentioned in one of the files. He offered me more details about that particular incident but also said that it was no anomaly. Men from his unit had raped numerous other women as well, he told me. But neither those assaults nor the random shootings of farmers by his fellow soldiers had ever been formally investigated.

Among the most poignant of the interviews I conducted was with Jamie Henry, a former army medic with whom I eventually forged a friendship. Henry was a whistle-blower in the Ron Ridenhour mold— the type of man that many want to be but few actually are, a courageous veteran who spent several years after his return to America trying to bring to light a series of atrocities committed by his unit. While many others had kept silent, Henry stepped forward and reported the crimes he'd seen, taking significant risks for what he believed was right. He talked to the U.S. Army Criminal Investigation Command (known as CID), he wrote a detailed article, he spoke out in public again and again. But the army left him to twist in the wind, a lone voice repeatedly recounting apparently uncorroborated tales of shocking violence, while most Americans paid little attention. Until I sought him out and showed him the documents I'd found, Henry had no idea that in the early 1970s military investigators had in fact tracked down and interviewed his fellow unit members, proving his allegations beyond any doubt—and that the army had then hidden away this information, never telling him or anyone else. When he looked over my stacks of photocopies, he was astounded.

Over time, following leads from the veterans I'd spoken to and from other sources, I discovered additional long-forgotten court-martial records, investigation files, and related documents in assorted archives and sometimes in private homes across the country. Paging through one of these case files, I found myself virtually inhaling decades-old dust from half a world away. The year was 1970, and a small U.S. Army patrol had set up an ambush in the jungle near the Minh Thanh rubber plantation in Binh Long Province, north of Saigon. Almost immediately the soldiers heard chopping noises, then branches snapping and Vietnamese voices coming toward them. Next, a man broke through the brush—he was in uniform, they would later say, as was the entire group of Vietnamese following behind him. In an instant, the Americans sprang the ambush, setting off two Claymore mines—each sending seven hundred small steel pellets flying more than 150 feet in a lethal sixty-degree arc—and firing an M-60 machine gun. All but one of the Vietnamese in the clearing were killed instantly. The unit's radioman immediately got on his field telephone and called in ten "enemy KIA"—killed in action.

Later, however, something didn't ring right at headquarters. Despite the claim of ten enemy dead, the Americans had no weapons to show for it. With the My Lai trials garnering headlines back in the United States, the commanding general of the 25th Infantry Division did something unusual: he asked the division's Office of the Inspector General, whose job it was to probe instances of alleged misconduct, to investigate. The next day, a lieutenant colonel and his team arrived at the site of the ambush, where they found the corpses of five men, three women, and two children scattered on the forest floor. None was wearing enemy uniforms, and civilian identification cards were found on the bodies. The closest thing to a weapon was a piece of paper with "a small drawing of a rifle and of an airplane." The soldiers who sprang the ambush claimed it was evidence that the dead were enemy fighters, but the lieutenant colonel noted that it looked like "something a child would do." Similarly, "the makings of booby traps" found on the bodies, and cited by the soldiers as evidence of hostile intent, turned out to be a harmless agricultural tool. As the American investigators photographed the corpses, it was apparent that the Vietnamese had been civilians carrying bags of bamboo shoots and a couple of handfuls of limes—regular people simply trying to eke out an existence in a war-ravaged landscape.

The lime gatherers' deaths were typical of the kind of operation that repeatedly wiped out civilians during the Vietnam War. Most of the time, the noncombatants who died were not herded into a ditch and gunned down as at My Lai. Instead, the full range of the American arsenal—from M-16s and Claymore mines to grenades, bombs, mortars, rockets, napalm, and artillery shells—was unleashed on forested areas, villages, and homes where perfectly ordinary Vietnamese just happened to live and work.

As the inspector general's report concluded in this particular incident, the "Vietnamese victims were innocent civilians loyal to the Republic of Vietnam." Yet, as so often happened, no disciplinary action of any type was taken against any member of the unit. In fact, their battalion commander stated that the team performed "exactly as he expected them to." The battalion's operations officer explained that the civilians had been in an "off-limits" or free-fire zone, one of many swaths of the country where everyone was assumed to be the enemy. Therefore, the soldiers had behaved in accordance with the U.S. military's directives on the use of lethal force.

It made no difference that the lime gatherers happened to live there, as their ancestors undoubtedly had for decades, if not centuries, before them. It made no difference that, as the local province chief of the U.S.-allied South Vietnamese government told the army, "the civilians in the area were poor, uneducated and went wherever they could get food." The inspector general's report pointed out that there was no written documentation regarding the establishment of a free-fire zone in the area, noting with bureaucratic understatement that "doubt exists" that the program to warn Vietnamese civilians about off-limits areas was "either effective or thorough." But that, too, made no difference. As the final investigation report put it, the platoon had operated "within its orders which had been given and/or sanctioned by competent authority . . . The rules of engagement were not violated."[45]

Seeking to connect such formal military records with the actual experience of the ordinary Vietnamese people who had lived through these events, I made several trips to Vietnam, making my way to remote rural villages with an interpreter at my side. The jigsaw-puzzle pieces were not always easy to align. In the files of the War Crimes Working Group, for example, I located an exceptionally detailed investigation of a massacre of nearly twenty women and children by a U.S. Army unit in a tiny hamlet in Quang Nam Province on February 8, 1968. It was clear that the ranking officer there had ordered his men to "kill anything that moves," and that some of the soldiers had obeyed. What was less than clear was exactly where "there" was.

With only a general location to go by—fifteen miles west of an old port town known as Hoi An—we embarked on a shoe-leather search. Inquiries with locals led us to An Truong, a small hamlet with a monument to a 1968 massacre. But this particular mass killing took place on January 9, 1968, rather than in February, and was carried out by South Korean forces allied to the Americans rather than by U.S. soldiers themselves. It was not the place we had been looking for.

After we explained the situation, one of the residents led us to another village not very far away. It, too, had a memorial—this one commemorating thirty-three locals who died in three separate massacres between 1967 and 1970. However, none of these massacres had taken place on February 8, 1968, either. After interviewing villagers about these atrocities, we asked if they knew of any other mass killings in the area. Yes, they said: not the next hamlet down the road but a little bit beyond it. So on we went. Daylight was rapidly fading when we arrived in that hamlet and found a monument that spelled out the basics of the grim story in spare terms: U.S. troops had killed dozens of Vietnamese there in 1968. Conversations with the farmers made it clear, though, that these Americans were marines, not army soldiers, and the massacre had taken place in August. Such is the nature of investigating war crimes in Vietnam. I'd thought that I was looking for a needle in a haystack; what I found was a veritable haystack of needles.

In the United States, meanwhile, the situation in the archives was often frustratingly the opposite. At one point, a Vietnam veteran passed on to me a few pages of documents from an investigation into the killing of civilians by U.S. marines in a small village in the extreme north of South Vietnam. Those pages provided just enough information for me to file a Freedom of Information Act request for court-martial transcripts related to American crimes there. The military's response to my request was an all too common one: the documents were inexplicably missing. But the government file was not entirely empty. Hundreds of pages of trial transcripts, sworn testimony, supporting documents, and the like had vanished into thin air, but the military could offer me something in consolation: a copy of the protective jacket that was once wrapped around the documents. I declined.

Indeed, an astonishing number of marine court-martial records of the era have apparently been destroyed or gone missing. Most air force and navy criminal investigation files that may have existed seem to have met the same fate. Even before this, the formal investigation records were an incomplete sample at best; as one veteran of the secret Pentagon task force told me, knowledge of most cases never left the battlefield. Still, the War Crimes Working Group files alone demonstrated that atrocities were committed by members of *every* infantry, cavalry, and airborne division, and every separate brigade that deployed without the rest of its division—that is, every major army unit in Vietnam.

The scattered, fragmentary nature of the case files makes them essentially useless for gauging the precise number of war crimes committed by U.S. personnel in Vietnam.[46] But the hundreds of reports that I gathered and the hundreds of witnesses that I interviewed in the United States and Southeast Asia made it clear that killings of civilians—whether cold-blooded slaughter like the massacre at My Lai or the routinely indifferent, wanton bloodshed like the lime gatherers' ambush in Binh Long—were widespread, routine, and directly attributable to U.S. command policies.

And such massacres by soldiers and marines, my research showed, were themselves just a tiny part of the story. For every mass killing by ground troops that left piles of civilian corpses in a forest clearing or a drainage ditch, there were exponentially more victims killed by the everyday exercise of the American way of war from the air. Throughout South Vietnam, women and children were asphyxiated or crushed to death when their bunkers collapsed on them, burying them alive after direct hits from jets' 500-pound bombs or 1,900-pound shells launched from offshore ships. Countless others, crazed with fear, bolted for safety when helicopters swooped toward their villages, only to have a door gunner cut them in half with bursts from an M-60 machine gun—and many others, who froze in place, suffered the same fate. There's only so much killing a squad, a platoon, or a company can do. Face-to-face atrocities were responsible for just a fraction of the millions of civilian casualties in South Vietnam. Matter-of-fact mass killing that dwarfed the slaughter at My Lai normally involved heavier firepower and command policies that allowed it to be unleashed with impunity.

This was the real war, the one that barely appears at all in the tens of thousands of volumes written about Vietnam. This was the war that Ron Ridenhour spoke about—the one in which My Lai was an operation, not an aberration. This was the war in which the American military and successive administrations in Washington produced not a few random massacres or even discrete strings of atrocities, but something on the order of thousands of days of relentless misery—a veritable system of suffering. That system, that machinery of suffering and what it meant for the Vietnamese people, is what this book is meant to explain.

1

THE MASSACRE AT TRIEU AI

In 2008, visiting Trieu Ai village in Quang Tri, the northernmost province in South Vietnam, meant driving down a long, winding, rutted road of crushed rock and burnt-orange mud. It was slow going, as the car rocked and pitched past shattered concrete buildings, through forests, across fields. The last mile or two had to be traversed on foot, though the worst to worry about, while slogging through the mire, was losing a shoe. Forty years before, the Americans trudging through this area had far more to fear.

On the night of October 21, 1967, members of Company B, 1st Battalion, 1st Marine Regiment, in the midst of a long, grueling patrol, found themselves on the outskirts of Trieu Ai.[1] On a hill overlooking the village, one of the Americans tripped a booby trap. A well-liked marine from the company's 1st Platoon was killed, three others were injured, and the embittered, frustrated troops hunkered down, awaiting a medical evacuation—"medevac"—helicopter.

It was a commonplace story. Vietnamese revolutionary forces, decisively outgunned by their adversaries, relied heavily on mines and other booby traps, as well as sniper fire and ambushes. Their way of war was generally to strike swiftly and immediately withdraw. Unable to deal with an enemy that overwhelmingly dictated the time, place, and duration of combat, U.S. forces took to destroying whatever they could manage. Often, civilians paid the price.

Soon after the booby trap struck his men, Lieutenant Robert Maynard held a briefing with Lieutenant John Bailey and Sergeant Don Allen of the 1st Platoon. Maynard assured them, Allen later reported, that they would get "first crack at the ville." He remembered the orders vividly: "We would take our platoons and move through the ville. When we reached the other side 'there was nothing to be left alive or unburned, as far as the children goes, let our conscience be our guide.'"[2]

When Lieutenant Bailey, who had been slightly wounded by the booby trap, returned from the briefing, he too told his platoon that they were about to be sent into the village. Lance Corporal Olaf Skibsrud recalled the orders passed on to him: "They said that we were going to kill everyone in the ville and burn it down."[3] Lance Corporal Eddie Kelly remembered Bailey's orders as "search-and-destroy everything in the village."[4] And rifleman Edward Johnson recalled a command similar to so many others handed down by Americans all over South Vietnam, year after year: "We was going to kill anything that we see and anything that moved."[5]

The marines who would need to call on their consciences concerning the children of Trieu Ai were not that far from childhood themselves. Indeed, most U.S. troops who served in Vietnam were in their teens or barely out of them. Whether they had been drafted or had volunteered (often to avoid the uncertainty of the draft), they had gone off to basic training as little more than boys.

The boot camp experience was consciously organized to reduce recruits to a psychological state akin to early childhood. Their previous eighteen or so years of learning were to be stripped away through shock, separation, and physical and psychological stress, creating a tabula rasa on which a military imprint could be stamped. For eight weeks of up to seventeen-hour days, every detail of their lives was prescribed, every action relearned in a military manner, all stringently enforced by the omnipresent authority of the drill instructor.[6] As historian Joanna Bourke puts it, a deft combination of "depersonalization, uniforms, lack of privacy, forced social relationships, tight schedules, lack of sleep, disorientation followed by rites of reorganization according to military codes, arbitrary rules and strict punishment" was brought to bear to accomplish the task.[7]

Frequent punishments, meted out for infractions as simple as not beginning and ending every sentence with "sir," were crucial to the process. They consisted of both psychological debasement and physical suffering—everything from being forced to eat garbage to being exercised to the point of collapse. At the same time, everyday training itself could be an agonizing experience. Even the best athletes were often overtaxed by the grueling workouts. "Simple exhaustion," as the historian Christian Appy points out, was a "key factor in explaining the willingness of recruits to follow orders" since they soon "learned that disobedience of any kind only brought more pain."[8]

Recruits were also indoctrinated into a culture of violence and brutality, which emphasized above all a readiness to kill without compunction.[9] Like many soldiers, the Vietnam-era draftee Peter Milord told Appy that at first he only mouthed the violent chants during his army training—"Kill! Kill! Kill! To kill without mercy is the spirit of the bayonet!"—but later found himself being overtaken by the ethos. "I didn't become a robot," Milord said, "but you can get so close to being one it's frightening."[10] Another veteran put it this way: "For eleven months I was trained to kill. For eight weeks, during basic training, I screamed 'kill,' 'kill.' So when I got to Vietnam I was ready to kill."[11] Still another told me that after having chanted "kill, kill, kill" through basic training, advanced infantry training, and long-range reconnaissance patrol instruction, he felt absolutely "brainwashed."[12]

Remorseless killing was additionally legitimized by the explicit racism that suffused the training. As army veteran Wayne Smith remembered, "The drill instructors never ever called the Vietnamese, 'Vietnamese.' They called them dinks, gooks, slopes, slants, rice-eaters, everything that would take away humanity . . . That they were less than human was clearly the message."[13] Similarly, veteran Haywood Kirkland described his experience this way.

> As soon as [you] hit boot camp . . . they tried to change your total personality . . . Right away they told us not to call them Vietnamese. Call everybody gooks, dinks. They told us when you go over in Vietnam, you gonna be face to face with Charlie, the Viet Cong. They were like animals, or something other than human . . . They wouldn't allow you to talk about them as if they were people. They told us they're not to be treated with any type of mercy . . . That's what they engraved into you. That killer instinct.[14]

This attitude was reinforced once soldiers arrived "in-country."[15] Many recall immediately being told that, whatever the official policy, in reality all Vietnamese were to be distrusted, that even women and small children were possible foes or outright enemies—a particularly sinister attitude in the context of a war that was supposedly being fought to protect Vietnamese civilians from communist aggression.[16] A child, GIs believed, might throw a grenade or be strapped with explosives. An elderly woman could help to construct booby traps. Though official military publications aimed at troops headed for Vietnam stressed discrimination between civilians and guerrillas, some of them still suggested that everyone in a conical hat or the loose-fitting Vietnamese clothes that Americans called "black pajamas" was a potential adversary.[17]

One veteran told me that his training made it clear that the "enemy is anything with slant eyes who lives in the village. It doesn't make any difference if it's a woman or child."[18] An officer summarized the prevailing mind-set: "So a few women and children get killed . . . Teach 'em a damned good lesson. They're all VC or at least helping them . . . You can't convert them, only kill them."[19]

Among the many reasons for this suspicion was that, in village after village, U.S. patrols regularly encountered women and children plus a few old men, but almost no military-age males. "All through the whole entire time that I spent out in the field, I could literally count the amount of men or boys that we saw," one veteran who spent a year in combat told me.[20] "You go into a village, and there was never a man in a village. Never," said another.[21] To Americans, the reason was obvious: the "missing" men, all the village's sons and husbands, were Viet Cong guerrillas. This was, of course, one definite possibility. But it was also quite possible that the men were serving in the U.S.-allied South Vietnamese forces; or were draft dodgers, hiding from armies of both sides; or were off working in a distant rice paddy, market, or town, trying to earn a living. In any case, most older boys and young men knew to flee whenever U.S. or South Vietnamese troops arrived, since they were prime targets for conscription, arrest, or execution. Women with children and elders couldn't move as fast and stood a somewhat better chance of being spared, so they were often left behind.

Many U.S. soldiers were also suspicious because South Vietnamese villagers always seemed to know where to walk to avoid VC booby traps. This wasn't really true; civilians were also, in fact, killed or wounded by such weapons. But to the soldiers, the fact that the peasants didn't warn them about these dangers was more clear evidence that the locals were supporting the VC, if not members themselves.

The soldiers also had trouble sorting out who was who. Troops often got only fleeting glimpses of figures dressed in the loose-fitting "black pajamas"—which, in the countryside, were actually worn by men and women, young and old, civilians and guerrillas alike. From a distance, a black-clad female farmer with a hoe could be indistinguishable from a male fighter with a rifle. Unable to readily tell friend from foe, and often unwilling to take the risk of trying to do so, many troops simply decided to fire on anyone they saw. And they often did so with the tacit support of or on explicit orders from superiors.

It was illegal to order the killing of unarmed villagers, no matter whom they supported in the war. But illegal orders were not uncommon, and how soldiers should react to them was, at best, unclear. During boot camp or in-country instruction, many soldiers were given a short lesson—generally about an hour long—on the laws of war, but it paled in comparison to the weeks of training that suggested a very different standard operating procedure.[22] As the psychiatrist and war crimes expert Robert Lifton notes, there was "a striking contrast between the formal instruction (given rotely if at all) to kill only military adversaries, and the informal message (loud and clear) to kill just about everyone."[23]

What's more, basic training emphasized that obedience to commanders was paramount. Using an instructional outline in the army's field manual, a chaplain would often put forward an Orwellian-sounding concept: "The freest soldier is the soldier who willingly submits to authority." Invoking both honor and self-interest, the chaplain would tell recruits, "When you obey a lawful command you need not fear, nor worry." However, no clear definition of an *un*lawful order was offered, and young recruits were pressed to exhibit simpleminded obedience.[24] Nor did they receive any specialized training regarding the added responsibilities and moral complexities of fighting a guerrilla war in villages filled with civilians.[25]

Meanwhile, the young officers to whom these recruits were to show blind obedience, men like Lieutenants Maynard and Bailey at Trieu Ai, had often themselves received exceptionally lackluster instruction in the laws of war. In 1965, the reporter and historian Bernard Fall surveyed American small-unit commanders in Vietnam and found that few had anything but "the vaguest idea" about the 1949 Geneva Conventions. Some even argued that, contrary to the laws of war, "VC were all 'traitors' and thus could be shot out of hand" after being taken prisoner.[26]

In 1967, Fall's findings were validated in a study of junior officers at the U.S. Army Intelligence School at Fort Holabird, Maryland, which found that even at this specialized training center there were students who showed "a lack of understanding of the provisions of the Geneva Conventions pertaining to the treatment of prisoners of war."[27] That same year, another official army report noted that even after receiving instruction on the proper treatment of prisoners, fully half the students in a class of officers-in-training about to graduate from the army's Officer Candidate School at Fort Benning, Georgia, told officials they would mistreat a "prisoner of war to obtain information"—a clear violation of the laws of war. Twenty percent blithely stated that they would readily kill prisoners as a matter of expediency if their unit was ambushed.[28]

In a similar vein, more than 60 percent of army officers surveyed in 1969 said they would employ torture or the threat of it to force prisoners to talk during interrogations. That study also found that roughly 20 percent of captains and 25 percent of lieutenants and warrant officers believed they could legally carry out summary executions of civilians caught spying or setting booby traps.[29]

This situation supposedly improved in the wake of the 1969 My Lai revelations, when a new emphasis on laws-of-war training was allegedly implemented.[30] In 1971, however, the reporter William Greider visited a class filled with young second lieutenants at Fort Benning. He watched as the instructor spelled out a scenario in which an enemy machine gunner causes six U.S. casualties but then stops firing and surrenders, walking forward, unarmed, with his hands over his head. "What do you do?" the instructor asked. "In loud unison," Greider noted, "the 200 students instantly chorused their response: 'Shoot him! Shoot him!'"—even though the Geneva Conventions explicitly prohibit violence against adversaries who have laid down their arms.[31]

Often, there was no relevant instruction in the laws of war as they related to the way Americans actually fought the conflict in Vietnam. One of the crimes detailed in the U.S. military's formal investigation of the My Lai massacre, for example, was "the burning of dwellings."[32] But for years before and after the massacre, homes, hamlets, and whole villages were regularly torched by U.S. troops— most of the time on the orders of officers—for a variety of reasons. Sometimes Americans burned homes where they found hidden war matériel or enemy propaganda literature. At other times they burned houses or hamlets in reprisal for a nearby booby trap, or if they took sniper fire, or simply because they were angry, frustrated, and looking to strike back at any Vietnamese people they could find.

Whole villages might also be set aflame as a matter of policy, to drive people from an area and thereby deny guerrillas access to food, support, and recruits. The idea was to separate the general population from the guerrillas in the most literal way possible. After being forcibly removed, villagers would often be sent to a government-run concentration area. Some of these were "New Life" hamlets—artificial villages surrounded by barbed wire and located far from the inhabitants' own fields, homes, and ancestral burial grounds. Other villagers wound up in one of the South Vietnamese government's many refugee camps, overcrowded and unsanitary stretches of barren land where dispossessed, unemployed, and hopeless peasants were expected to wait out the war in squalor.

Trieu Ai—a farming village where locals raised chickens, ducks, and cows, and supplemented Vietnam's ubiquitous rice paddies with plots of cassava and sweet potatoes—was among the thousands of villages in Quang Tri province that were attacked by the Americans. It was regularly blasted by bombs and artillery fire, and just a few days before the arrival of Company B much of the "ville" had been burned by U.S. troops.[33] Trieu Ai's surviving villagers were then relocated to a concentration area.

The younger men and older boys from Trieu Ai were forced to remain in the refugee camp, but on the afternoon of October 21, the village's women, young children, and older men were allowed to travel back to Trieu Ai for twenty-four hours to retrieve whatever belongings they could. After a trek across four miles of rugged, cratered terrain, the former residents collected what could be salvaged and went to sleep in the only place available—the underground shelters that they had dug for protection from the frequent artillery shelling and bombing in the area.[34] Such shelters were common all across the country throughout the war years. Some were nothing more than big, crude holes gouged out of hard earth. Others were A-framed structures with wooden support beams. As the years went by, villagers would build ever more complex bunkers, L- or Z-shaped with angled walls to provide protection from grenades, and some families even procured metal struts to provide extra stability.

Life became an exercise in playing the percentages. Just how long did you stay in your bunker? Long enough to avoid the artillery, of course, but not so long that you were still there when the Americans and their grenades arrived. If you left the shelter's confines too soon, some helicopter's machine gun might open up on you as you emerged, or you could get caught in a cross fire between withdrawing guerrillas and onrushing American troops. If you waited too long, those grenades might begin rolling in. Every second mattered immensely. An instant too late could mean death, but a second too early was potentially no less lethal. Guess wrong and your family might be wiped out. And such calculations went on for years on end, shaping every decision to leave the confines of a shelter, day or night, to get water or relieve oneself or work in the fields or gather vegetables for a hungry family. Life could be measured by calculating the distance from the rice paddy to the bunker against the altitude of a jet or the speed of a helicopter. Under such circumstances, existence became an endless series of risk assessments.

The Americans lived with a different reality. That October night, not long after the medevac helicopter whirled off into the sky, tired, angry, scared marines entered Trieu Ai village firing their rifles, grenading shelters, and setting fire to some of the few remaining structures as they advanced.[35] Unable or unwilling to distinguish a civilian bomb shelter from an enemy fighting position, and never knowing who might be inside, U.S. troops often simply tossed in grenades to force whoever was sheltering below to come out—or to make sure that they never did. In some hamlets, they flushed out or killed guerrillas this way. In Trieu Ai that night, there were only civilians in the subterranean bunkers, quickly measuring the odds in their latest life-or-death encounter, trying to work out just how the heavily armed foreign teenagers wreaking havoc in their village would react if they emerged or stayed put.

As the fatigue-clad Americans moved through the hamlet, rifleman Ronald Toon watched Sergeant Don Allen prevent Lance Corporal Rudolph Diener and another marine from killing a group of children. But no one apparently tried to stop the nineteen-year-old Diener when he grabbed a woman in her fifties and marched her toward a deserted field. "He turned the old lady into the rice paddy. She started walking and he just raised his rifle and started firing. He fired approximately six rounds," Toon later testified at Diener's trial.[36]

Events were unfolding rapidly and chaotically, even though there wasn't a single enemy gunshot all night. As the burning homes cast a flickering glow beneath a crescent moon that threw precious little light, the men crept forward, stopped, and fired.[37] Radioman Lester Beard heard Lieutenant Bailey tell Lieutenant Maynard that they were finding children in the shelters being grenaded. According to Beard, Maynard responded, "Tough shit, they grow up to be VC."[38] Sergeant Allen remembered it that way too.[39] Meanwhile, the Vietnamese huddled together in fear, not knowing what was happening to relatives and friends in other shelters as shots rang out, grenades exploded, fires crackled, and marines shouted incomprehensibly in English or pidgin Vietnamese.

According to rifleman Edward Johnson, the marines came across a bunker where they heard voices and could see a light. He passed the word to Lieutenant Bailey, who approached the rear entrance of the shelter and threw in a grenade. "We heard screams, rushing about, and obviously people were inside," Lance Corporal Wilson Dozier recalled. "Another grenade was tossed in and at this point, people started rushing out of the bunker." Dozier estimated that five to ten people dashed out. Then came an order to shoot.[40] As he described it, "The first several men opened up, some with automatic fire, some with semi-automatic fire."[41] Bailey said he saw two victims fall, but when another marine yelled that they were still moving, he ordered his men to open fire again.[42] Not far from the scene, Lieutenant William Steen heard a grenade explode, then a woman and children screaming, followed by gunfire and finally silence.[43] Many other unit members recalled the same sequence: horrible shrieking—which most attributed to women and children—ended by gunfire.[44]

Nguyen Van Phuoc, a young villager sheltering underground, heard the sound of the medevac helicopter landing and departing and, not long after, gunshots. His mother, fearing that they would die if they remained in the bunker, grabbed him and his two-year-old brother and fled from their shelter into the chaos above. "Racing from our bunker, we saw the shelter opposite ours being shot up," he recalled. One of the Americans then wheeled around and fired at his mother, killing her and leaving his brother covered in her blood.[45] "After they shot my mother," Phuoc remembered, "I grabbed my brother and ran back to the bunker where Pham Thi Luyen stayed."[46]

Pham Thi Luyen was just thirteen years old in 1967. The youngest of six children, she had graduated to tending the cows—a rite of passage for rural children—by the time war came to Trieu Ai, bringing with it near-daily artillery shelling. One day, the Americans burned her house to the ground. When her family tried to save some of their possessions, the marines threw what goods they had salvaged back into the fire.

On October 21, Luyen and her father, Phan Van Tuyen, an older man past military age, had taken refuge in an underground shelter like many of the other villagers. She vividly recalled seeing Phuoc running into their shelter with his brother in his arms, blood-soaked but uninjured, shouting, "My mom was killed, my mom was killed!" (Luyen didn't know it yet, but her own mother, who'd taken shelter in another bunker, had by this point also been killed by the marines.)[47] Soon, Luyen heard the Americans above. "They spoke incomprehensibly, but we were scared and walked out," she recalled. "Everyone came out."[48]

Interactions like this were commonplace. The Americans were generally ignorant of a melodic language of six subtle tones in which a one-syllable, two-letter word could have six different meanings. Most GIs shouted commands in incomprehensible, monotonal, ersatz Vietnamese: *Dung lai!* (Halt!) *Lai day!* (Come here!) *Di Di Mau!* (Run away!). Occasionally they mixed up the meanings of even these basic phrases. At other times they turned to pidgin commands cobbled together with faux-French or pseudo-Japanese slang. And not infrequently, they simply resorted to high-decibel English to question "papa-sans," "mama-sans," and "baby-sans"—men, women, and children—about the whereabouts of "boo-coo VC" (*beaucoup* or many Viet Cong). The onus was on the frightened villagers to figure it all out.[49]

Lance Corporal Wilson Dozier later testified, "As we continued on our patrol we approached another bunker, and I believe people started coming out of it . . . and a couple of the men yelled 'Lai Dai,' come out, quite a few more people came out."[50] The rest of the bunkers in the area were then grenaded, as the Vietnamese above ground huddled together in fear.[51]

As Luyen remembered it, "The Americans just pushed us ahead . . . They forced us to go to the river."[52] Terrified, she gripped her father's hand tightly, but the marines pulled him back and forced her forward with the others. As the women and children splashed through the water to the opposite bank, Tuyen was the only one left standing in front of Lieutenant Bailey and Corporal Terry Spann. The way Phuoc recalled it, Tuyen got bogged down in the mud, at which point a marine struck him and then shot him near the riverbank.[53] According to Spann's testimony, Tuyen made a sudden turn and Bailey butt-stroked him with his shotgun. Spann then tried to shoot the unarmed, wounded man, but his rifle jammed. Bailey, he reported, attempted to fire his shotgun, but that too misfired. "Then he pulled his pistol," Spann said of the lieutenant, "and fired twice."[54] Across the river, Luyen heard two gunshots and called out to her father, but there was no reply.

The marines left the women and children on the far bank, from where they filtered back to the government camp the next day.[55] At the shelter where the villagers had been gunned down en masse, Dozier testified to seeing the mangled bodies of an older man and woman. "There was quite a bit of blood and some torn flesh," he recalled. Other marines, he said, found the bodies of children and elderly people.[56] Edward Johnson saw bodies near the bunker, too. "I found that it was some children and a woman," he recalled. "There was a real small baby and another one looked like it was about two or three years old."[57]

The court-martial transcript paints a vivid picture. Lieutenant Bailey had the men shove the bodies back into the bunker.[58] Lieutenant Steen saw what he thought was a child's body being thrown in. Another marine remembered helping a fellow unit member stuff an older woman, still moaning, into the shelter with the corpses.[59] On Bailey's orders, marines then shoveled in dirt, brush, logs, and other debris to seal up the bunker.[60] Later, Vietnamese who inspected the scene found seven mangled bodies in that shelter, and Tuyen's body in the river.[61] In all, according to Vietnamese survivors, twelve unarmed civilians were killed that night in Trieu Ai village.[62]

The survivors never complained to their government about the massacre, even though it had been carried out by Saigon's allies. Nor did they seek legal action or restitution. Their country was in a state of civil war; corruption was rampant; the entire regime was beholden to the United States; and foreign military forces had been given free rein to fight a full-scale war in heavily populated rural areas. What's more, no standardized means for civilians to report war crimes existed; dissent was criminalized; and mere residence in certain areas branded villagers as de facto enemies of the state. Indeed, complaints or protests could land victims in prison.

A survivor from Trieu Ai told me that after an earlier incident in which Americans had killed a civilian, villagers did try bringing the corpse to the South Vietnamese authorities to lodge a protest. "All those who went to complain were arrested and jailed. After that, no one dared to go," he said.[63] After the October 1967 massacre, when Luyen simply tried to get the documents necessary to bury her parents, she was detained and held for a week by South Vietnamese authorities.[64]

Today, we know about the massacre in Trieu Ai village only because a single marine, Lance Corporal Olaf Skibsrud, was troubled enough by the killings to speak out. Several days after the events, he talked to a navy chaplain, whose efforts led to an official inquiry. Even though Skibsrud was transferred from the unit for his own safety after reporting the incident, he still feared retaliation. He said that a superior threatened his life, and for the rest of his tour he slept with a loaded weapon beside him.

Thanks to Skibsrud's report, Maynard, by then a captain, and Lance Corporal Diener were eventually court-martialed.[65] Maynard was apparently convicted of nothing more serious than failing to properly report the incident in the village, though the record of his court-martial, like so many other files relating to Vietnam war crimes, has since disappeared.[66] Diener, tried for the execution of the Vietnamese woman in the field, was found not guilty.[67] Years later, the unit's battalion commander said that he had been acquitted because the company was fired upon and it was impossible to distinguish civilians from combatants. Yet none of the marines had reported enemy fire or the presence of enemy forces; no weapons were found in the village; and the marines' command chronology for October 1967 states that "no significant contact" was made at any point during the operation.[68]

The killing of a dozen civilians that night in October 1967, several months before the My Lai massacre, is barely a footnote in the blood-soaked history of the Vietnam War. Yet in the story of Trieu Ai one can see virtually the entire war writ small. Here was the repeated aerial bombing and artillery fire, pounding the rural population on an almost daily basis and forcing them into underground bunkers. Here was the deliberate burning of peasant homes and the relocation of villagers to refugee camps, where their movements were strictly controlled by the government. And here, too, was the inevitable outcome of the troops' training: all the endless chants of "kill, kill, kill," the dehumanization of the "dinks, gooks, slopes, slants," and the constant insistence that even women and small children were to be regarded as potential enemies.

The key elements present at Trieu Ai recur over and over again in war crimes files and the recollections of veterans. Angry troops primed to lash out, often following losses within the unit; civilians trapped in their path; and officers in the field issuing ambiguous or illegal orders to young men conditioned to obey—that was the basic recipe for many of the mass killings carried out by army soldiers and marines over the years.

Similar scenes took place across the entire length of South Vietnam, from bomb-blasted Quang Tri in the far north to the coastal plains of Binh Dinh Province in the central region and the verdant paddies of the Mekong Delta, the country's rice bowl, in the deep south. Many of the enclaves in these and other densely populated areas had been the home of revolution for decades, if not generations, following the French invasion of the 1860s. Now, much of their population was equally committed to the struggle against Saigon and its American allies.[69]

American military planners divided the map of South Vietnam

into five sectors: a special capital zone for Saigon and four tactical zones, numbered from I Corps in the north just below the demilitarized zone (DMZ) to IV Corps in the south. I Corps began as the domain of the marines, who arrived there in March 1965 and soon distinguished themselves with the kind of cruelty shown at Trieu Ai.[70] In short order, the marines were joined in Vietnam by army units, including the 1st Cavalry Division and 173rd Airborne Brigade, as well as by allied South Korean troops serving farther to the south. The U.S. Air Force, meanwhile, initiated a campaign of strikes by massive B-52 bombers throughout the country. By the end of 1965, there were more than 184,000 U.S. military personnel in South Vietnam.[71]

As American operations began to expand into the Mekong Delta in late 1966, the number of U.S. forces in the country swelled to more than 385,000. Many expected that the delta campaign would also be led by the marines, since their history of amphibious operations seemed to lend itself well to the waterlogged IV Corps region. The army, however, won an interservice battle for the domain, and eventually its 9th Infantry Division embarked on large-scale operations in the delta instead.[72] But the substitution of one military branch for another made little difference to the South Vietnamese population. The army, like the marines, left a devastating trail of civilian casualties in its wake—thousands upon thousands of noncombatants beaten, wounded, raped, tortured, or killed in the years that followed.

The parallels between atrocities that took place in the Mekong Delta and the northern provinces, between the massacres carried out by members of the army and those perpetrated by marines, make it abundantly clear that individual soldiers and their immediate commanders were not the only ones to blame. There is, of course, no excusing the acts carried out by the American troops on the ground at Trieu Ai, but these actions did not occur in a vacuum. Rather, they were the unmistakable consequence of deliberate decisions made long before, at the highest levels of the military.

2

A SYSTEM OF SUFFERING

By the mid-1960s, the American military had turned war making into a thoroughly corporatized, quantitatively oriented system that the sociologist James William Gibson astutely calls "technowar." The philosophy behind it was simple: by combining American technological and economic prowess with sophisticated managerial capacities, the Pentagon meant to guarantee ultimate success on the battlefield. The country's unmatched military capability would allow it to impose its will anywhere in the world, with the war machine functioning as smoothly and predictably as an assembly line.[1]

This mind-set was embodied most fully in the person of Robert McNamara, the secretary of defense from 1961 to 1968. As a Harvard Business School professor, McNamara had designed statistical methods of analysis for the War Department during World War II, most famously systematizing the flight patterns and improving the efficiency of the bombers that decimated German and Japanese cities. Before answering President John Kennedy's call to return to government service, he had spent the previous decade as a top executive of the Ford Motor Company.[2] He brought to the Pentagon a corps of "whiz kids" and "computer jockeys" whose job was to transform the military establishment into a corporatized system that could, as the political commentator Tom Engelhardt put it, "be managed in the same 'scientific' and 'efficient' manner as a business."[3] McNamara seemed almost to mimic the computers that he and his staff so fervently believed in. He relied on numbers to convey reality and, like a machine, processed whatever information he was given with exceptional speed, making instant choices and not worrying that such rapid-fire decision making might lead to grave mistakes.[4] There was to be no "fog of war" for his Pentagon. McNamara and his national security technocrats were sure that, given enough data, warfare could be made completely rational, comprehensible, and controllable. And they never looked back.

In Vietnam, the statistically minded war managers focused, above all, on the notion of achieving a "crossover point": the moment when American soldiers would be killing more enemies than their Vietnamese opponents could replace. After that, the Pentagon expected, the communist-led forces would naturally give up the fight—that would be the only rational thing to do. What McNamara and the Pentagon brass failed to grasp was that Vietnamese nationalists, who had long battled foreign invaders in pursuit of independence, might not view warfare as a straightforward exercise in benefit maximization to be pursued in a "rational" manner and abandoned when the ledger sheet showed more debits than credits.[5]

The crossover point, however, proved elusive; as years went by, the conflict only escalated.[6] But though the Pentagon's expectations were not borne out on the battlefield, it failed to question the basic assumptions behind them. Instead, American officials launched study after study to further develop the principles of technowar. Statistical analyses of enemy attacks, measurements of the security status of each and every South Vietnamese community, tabulations of enemy activity rates, and reams of other numbers poured out of the U.S. military in the field to be processed by the Pentagon.[7] At the most basic level, though, everything came down to the "body count"— the preeminent statistic that served in those years as both the military's scorecard and its raison d'être. How else could you tell if the crossover point was within reach unless you tallied the enemy dead? The war managers, of course, gave little thought to what this strategy—basing the entire American military effort on such an indicator as Vietnamese corpses—might mean for Vietnamese civilians.

General William Westmoreland, who in 1964 took command of the U.S. military effort in the country (formally known as Military Assistance Command, Vietnam, or MACV), eventually attempted to distance himself and the army from the term "body count." In his postwar memoir, he claimed that in the early 1960s—before he arrived in Vietnam—the United States had been forced to add the phrase to its lexicon to appease the press's desire for accurate casualty statistics, but that he personally "abhorred" it.[8] In reality, though, the body-count concept had been employed as early as 1951 in the Korean War. There, too, KIAs—enemies killed in action—became the primary indicator of success.[9] And as McNamara and other war managers demanded a statistic that would definitively demonstrate progress in the expanding war, body count would become, in the words of Assistant Secretary of Defense Alain Enthoven, "*the* measure of success."[10]

The pressure to produce high body counts flowed from the Pentagon to Westmoreland's Saigon villa, down through the chain of command, and out to the American patrols in the Vietnamese countryside. As Gibson notes:

> Producing a high body count was crucial for promotion in the officer corps. Many high-level officers established "production quotas" for their units, and systems of "debit" and "credit" to calculate exactly how efficiently subordinate units and middle-management personnel performed. Different formulas were used, but the commitment to war as a rational production process was common to all.[11]

As a result, low-level officers, who generally had six months in the field to prove themselves and earn a promotion, and the young combat troops they led were under constant pressure to produce enemy "kills."[12]

The emphasis on body counts was everywhere: from the early 1960s through the early 1970s, from the delta to the DMZ, soldiers and marines experienced the same sort of pressures. "The term 'body count' kept popping up whenever officers talked to each other," Robert Peterson of the 25th Infantry Division remembered. "It seemed that securing or pacifying an area was secondary to 'getting some kills.'"[13] As Captain William Baker of the 4th Infantry Division recalled it, "Your success was measured by your body count. It came down through the channels."[14] According to Rion Causey, of the 101st Airborne Division, "It was all about body count. Our commanders just wanted body count."[15] Gary Nordstrom, a combat medic with the 9th Infantry Division, remembered it as a constant drumbeat: "Get the body count. Get the body count. Get the body count. It was prevalent everywhere. I think it was the mind-set of the officer corps from the top down."[16]

Whether you achieved or exceeded what were essentially killing quotas had a significant impact on what your tour of duty in Vietnam would be like. Insufficient body counts translated into fewer comforts. They also meant less support in the form of airlifts—resulting in long, hot, dangerous hikes through treacherous terrain instead of helicopter rides to or from the base.[17] Under pressure from commanders, low-level officers who hadn't met body-count expectations would keep their troops in the field longer, courting exhaustion and shattered unit morale while exposing themselves and their men to a greater chance of death or injury. "I knew," said an officer from the 9th Infantry Division, "if I went in without a body count or at least a prisoner I'd be on the shitlist, so I kept the patrol out."[18]

While officers sought to please superiors and chased promotions, the "grunts" in the field also had a plethora of incentives to produce dead bodies. These ranged from "R&R" (rest and recreation) passes, which might allow a soldier several days of fun in the sun at a beach resort, to medals, badges, extra food, extra beer, permission to wear nonregulation gear, and light duty at base camp.[19] According to Wayne Smith, a medic with the 9th Infantry Division, the body-count system led to "a real incentivizing of death and it just fucked with our value system. In our unit, guys who got confirmed kills would get a three-day in-country R and R. Those guys got sent to the beach at Vung Tau."[20] Another veteran echoed the same sentiments: "They would set up competition. The company that came in with the biggest body count would be given in-country R and R or an extra case of beer. Now if you're telling a nineteen-year-old kid it's okay to waste people and he will be *rewarded* for it, what do you think *that* does to his psyche?"[21] As the war went on, some Americans racked up huge personal body counts—up to a thousand or more for a select few who served numerous tours.[22]

Entire units were sometimes pitted against each other in body-count competitions with prizes at stake.[23] This helped make the body-count mind-set even more pervasive, lending death totals the air of sports statistics. "Box scores" came to be displayed all over Vietnam—on charts and chalkboards (also known as "kill boards") at military bases, printed up in military publications, and painted as crosshatched "kills" on the sides of helicopters, to name just a few of the most conspicuous examples.[24] "We had charts in the mess hall that told what our body count was for the week," recalled one veteran. "So as you passed through the chow line you were able to look up at a chart and see that we had killed so many."[25]

Competitions and command pressures quite naturally led to body-count inflation.[26] As Wayne Smith remembered, "If we came across four different body parts we called in four kills."[27] Yet while overestimating or simply fabricating body counts has long been acknowledged within the military and by historians, much less recognized is a different type of body-count padding: the inclusion of civilian dead. On September 1, 1969, for example, members of the 196th Infantry Brigade in Quang Tin Province spotted a group of

Vietnamese. Officers and sergeants, peering through binoculars, conferred about the situation. After about ten minutes of observation the senior officer, Captain David Janca, ordered his machine gunners to open fire and called in an artillery fire mission. A small patrol was then dispatched to the kill zone. "Upon arrival," assistant machine gunner Robert Gray said later, "we found dead and wounded Vietnamese children."[28] Patrol member Welkie Louie described the scene: "I observed about four to six Vietnamese children lying in one pile, dead. About five meters from this position were two or three wounded Vietnamese children huddled together."[29] Afterward, artillery forward observer Robert Wolz told army investigators that he saw an official document in which "the dead were listed as VC."[30] Another report even referred to them as "NVA"—that is, North Vietnamese army troops.[31] In death, this small group of children had morphed into guerrillas and then into uniformed enemy soldiers as the body count wound its way through the military's statistics generation machine.

Sometimes, when units were short of "kills," prisoners or detainees were simply murdered. On September 22, 1968, for example, members of the 82nd Airborne Division captured a wounded Vietnamese in Thua Thien Province. "I got on the radio and told the CO [commanding officer] that the man was wounded, unarmed and had surrendered," said Lieutenant Ralph Loomis. According to Loomis's testimony to an army criminal investigator, his superior officer, Captain John Kapranopoulous, replied, "Dammit, I don't care about prisoners, I want a body count." Although Loomis ordered his men not to execute the prisoner, his radioman, Specialist Joseph Mattaliano, "opened up with a burst of automatic fire from his M-16 killing the Vietnamese instantly."

At roughly the same time, a second Vietnamese man, a civilian, was also detained. He had his hands tied behind his back and was forced to kneel. The unit's forward observer recalled that Sergeant Alexander Beard called the CPT [captain] on the horn and told him the man had no papers and the CPT replied that the man was a gook or dink "and you know what to do with him." The group of GI's left the prisoner and walked away about 5–6 yards and then I heard one weapon fire a burst and I saw the prisoner fall . . . I then saw the group approach the dead prisoner, remove the rope from his arms and roll him over into a ditch.

Unit member Johnny Brinson told investigators that it had been a standing order for months not to take prisoners.

Such cold-blooded killings went on in unit after unit, all for the sake of the body count.[32] The practice of counting all dead Vietnamese as enemy kills became so pervasive that one of the most common phrases of the war was: "If it's dead and Vietnamese, it's VC."[33]

In 1970, a candid internal report commissioned by the army's acting general counsel addressed the question of whether the pressure for kills encouraged troops "to inflate the count by violating established rules of engagement."[34] The findings were damning. The report concluded that there was "a certain inescapable logic" to claims that emphasizing the body count led to violations of the laws of war.

It is common knowledge that an officer's career can be made or destroyed in Vietnam. A command tour there is much sought after and generally comes only once to an individual, who may have anywhere from six months to a year to prove himself in the "crucible of combat." The pressure to excel is inevitably tremendous . . . A primary indication of such excellence has in the past been the unit's enemy body count. One reason for this has probably been the difficulty of developing other concrete indices. Under such circumstances—and especially if such incentives as stand-downs, R&R allocations, and decorations are tied to body count figures— the pressure to kill indiscriminately, or at least report every

Vietnamese casualty as an enemy casualty, would seem to be practically irresistible.[35]

Sometimes there were even too many civilian corpses, leading to a different sort of statistical manipulation: body-count deflation.[36] After the My Lai massacre, the Americal Division claimed only 128 enemy dead, when in actuality more than 500 civilians had been slaughtered. At nearby My Khe, American troops massacred from 60 to 155 civilians, according to U.S. sources, but a body count of only 38 was reported to headquarters.[37] Similarly, at the village of Truong Khanh (2), where 63 civilians were massacred, only 13 of those bodies were counted as enemy KIAs due to combat action by ground troops, with another 18 reported as having been killed by subsequent air strikes.[38] And when marines massacred 16 unarmed women and children at Son Thang, they were reported as a body count of 6 enemy kills.[39]

Soldiers realized that small groups of civilians could be killed with impunity and logged as enemy dead, but larger numbers might raise red flags if there were no U.S. casualties or few weapons captured.[40] To avoid uncomfortable questions about skewed kills-to-weapons ratios, many patrols planted grenades, rifles, or other arms on dead civilians as a matter of standard operating procedure. They obtained these from weapons caches they discovered, or by taking arms from prisoners or enemy dead carrying more than one weapon, or sometimes even by repurposing U.S. weapons as enemy matériel.[41] As one marine explained, "When civilians got killed, no problem, just stick a chicom [Chinese communist] grenade on 'em, or an AK[-47 assault rifle], they become VC."[42]

The dark humor in the opening stanzas of a song composed by soldiers from 1st Cavalry Division caught the anything-goes attitude perfectly.

We shoot the sick, the young, the lame,
We do our best to kill and maim,

Because the kills count all the same,
Napalm sticks to kids.

Ox cart rolling down the road,
Peasants with a heavy load,
They're all VC when the bombs explode,
Napalm sticks to kids.[43]

The piling up of Vietnamese bodies to be counted—and in a sense discounted—was facilitated by the contempt that Americans generally had for the country and its people. To President Johnson, Vietnam was "a piddling piss-ant little country."[44] To McNamara, a "backward nation."[45] President Nixon's national security adviser Henry Kissinger called North Vietnam a "little fourth-rate power," later downgrading it to "fifth-rate" status.[46] Such feelings permeated the chain of command, and they found even more colorful voice among those in the field, who regarded Vietnam as "the outhouse of Asia," "the garbage dump of civilization," "the asshole of the world."[47] A popular joke among GIs went: "What you do is, you load all the friend-lies [South Vietnamese] onto ships and take them out to the South China Sea. Then you bomb the country flat. Then you sink the ships."[48] Others swore that the best solution to the conflict was to pave the country over "like a parking lot."[49] An even simpler proposal was commonly offered: "Kill 'em all and let God sort 'em out."[50]

The deeply ingrained racism that helped turn the Vietnamese countryside into a charnel house was summed up in a single word: the ubiquitous "gook." That epithet evidently entered the military vocabulary in an earlier conflict, the eerily similar campaign in the Philippines at the turn of the twentieth century, where American troops began calling their indigenous enemies "goo-goos." The pejorative term then seems to have transmuted into "gook" and was applied over the decades to racially dissimilar enemies in Haiti, Nicaragua, and Korea before returning to Southeast Asia.[51] From the beginning of the war to the end, it was uttered ad infinitum.[52] "The colonels called them gooks, the captain called them gooks, the staff all called them gooks. They were dinks, you know, subhuman," recalled one veteran.[53]

The notion that Vietnam's inhabitants were something less than human was often spoken of as the "mere-gook rule," or, in the acronym-mad military, the MGR. This held that all Vietnamese—northern and southern, adults and children, armed enemy and innocent civilian—were little more than animals, who could be killed or abused at will.[54] The MGR enabled soldiers to abuse children for amusement; it allowed officers sitting in judgment at courts-martial to let off murderers with little or no punishment; and it paved the way for commanders to willfully ignore rampant abuses by their troops while racking up "kills" to win favor at the Pentagon.[55]

Even high-ranking officers, who might never actually use the word "gook" in public, operated in an MGR world.[56] General West-moreland told the filmmaker Peter Davis: "The Oriental doesn't put the same high price on life as does the Westerner. Life is plentiful, life is cheap in the Orient. As the philosophy of the Orient expresses it, life is not important."[57] And the dismissive mind-set influenced military policy everywhere in the country.[58] As the Vietnam War correspondent Frances FitzGerald trenchantly noted in her classic book *Fire in the Lake*, the Americans' "bombing and artillery prac-tices would have been unthinkable for U.S. commanders in occupied France or Italy during the Second World War."[59]

The MGR mentality excused all manner of atrocities and encour-aged troops to kill without compunction. "Shouldn't bother you at all, just some more dead gooks. The sooner *they* all die, the sooner *we* go back to the World," one marine explained to another.[60] In this way, the MGR provided lubrication for a system of suffering that, once set in motion, churned through the countryside without pause. At the top, pursuit of the crossover point demanded body counts; in the field, that meant Vietnamese KIAs, and the mere-gook rule promised that any dead Vietnamese would do.

In a conflict where American soldiers found it almost impossible to tell the enemy from the general population, the constant emphasis on body counts made civilian deaths almost inevitable. Specific command policies instituted in Vietnam, meanwhile, further ensured widespread slaughter. Chief among these were search-and-destroy tactics, loophole-laced rules of engagement, and "free-fire" zones.

The primary mission of U.S. troops sent out into the jungles, rice paddies, valleys, and villages of South Vietnam was to search out and destroy the revolutionaries. This was how Westmoreland saw the war, and at his behest members of his staff gave the "search-and-destroy" mission its name. These operations consisted of near-ceaseless patrols by small units meant to "find, fix, and finish" enemy troops. In other words, their role was to draw or flush an enemy unit out of hiding in the countryside and hold it in place while more U.S. forces were called in, generating the sort of big battles in which air-power and heavy artillery would make all the difference.[61] By June 1967 U.S. battalions were spending 86 percent of their time on such operations.[62]

Search and destroy was "more a gestalt than a tactic, brought up alive and steaming from the Command psyche," wrote the combat correspondent Michael Herr in his fever-dream war memoir, *Dispatches*. "In action it should have been named the other way around, pick through the pieces and see if you could work together a [body] count." There was something absurd about the entire enterprise. Day after day, patrol after patrol, U.S. troops wandered around the country-side spoiling for a fight—trying to goad a lightly armed enemy to abandon all sense and stand toe-to-toe in open battle with the best-armed military in the world.[63]

U.S. troops were to be used as the "principal combat reconnaissance force," and "supporting fires as the principal destructive force,"
wrote Colonel Sidney Berry in a widely disseminated 1967 essay on
the tactic. That is, the American boys on patrol were just a lure—
"dangling the bait," as the veteran and future senator James Webb
put it in his Vietnam War novel *Fields of Fire*. When attacked, they
were supposed to back away and call in heavy firepower to destroy
their Vietnamese foes.[64]

It sounded easy enough and looked good on paper, but in the field
search and destroy proved to be a wholly defective tactic. Vietnamese
forces refused to do battle as Americans wished them to, declining
to take the lure and fight at the time and place of the U.S. military's
choosing. Tipped off by preparatory artillery, roaring helicopters, and
repetitively predictable patrolling patterns, the revolutionary forces
generally refrained from large, set-piece combat engagements where
the odds would be greatly against them.[65]

Indeed, search and destroy gave Vietnamese revolutionary forces
an overwhelming tactical advantage. They could take the "bait"
whenever and wherever it suited them, which meant that, no matter
how aggressive the patrols were, the Americans almost invariably
found themselves on the defensive. According to the Pentagon Papers,
the Viet Cong surprised U.S. forces—dictating the time, the place,
and often the duration of combat engagements—more than 78 percent of the time.[66] Another report showed that the revolutionary
forces began 73 percent of all firefights.[67] Unable to effectively engage
the enemy, U.S. soldiers sometimes took to attacking whatever they
could, which often meant that civilians ended up paying the heaviest
price.

Looking back, Westmoreland later claimed that "many Americans apparently failed to comprehend 'search and destroy.'" It was,
he insisted, anything but a "brutal" policy of "aimless searches in the
jungle" and the "random destroying of villages."[68] His troops, however, provided a far more accurate description of the tactic than their

base-bound commander. To infantrymen and field marines, the phrase "search and destroy" was shorthand for systematic destruction of hamlets and sometimes of everyone in them.[69] "It was a search-and-destroy mission," one officer with the 4th Infantry Division recalled, "which meant we searched all the hootches we found and then burned them down. Whether a single farmer's hootch or a whole village—all were burnt."[70]

A rifleman questioned about a massacre by his unit explained how the term was generally understood by troops in the field.

Q: What about this operation . . . Were you told anything—were you given any special instructions?
A: Destroy everything.
Q: Destroy it all: village, livestock, and food stocks?
A: (Witness nods in the affirmative.) That's what a search and destroy is, isn't it?

That soldier testified that his commander didn't explicitly order his troops to "kill all the people" in the village. But when the men were ordered to carry out a search-and-destroy operation, the implication was that "anything there was VC and to do away with it."[71] Another veteran had a similar assessment: "The search-and-destroy mission is just another way to shoot anything that moves."[72]

Westmoreland's idealized vision of search-and-destroy operations was typical of the way that policies on paper diverged radically from the reality of the war. For instance, the U.S. command usually issued specific rules of engagement (ROE) that detailed when, where, and under what circumstances personnel could bomb, shell, or use helicopters or ground forces to attack. Ostensibly, the ROE protected noncombatants by providing clear guidance on who could be killed and why. Telford Taylor, chief prosecutor at the Nuremberg trials of Nazi war criminals, found these rules, on their face, "virtually impeccable."[73]

In practice, though, the ROE constantly put Vietnamese civilians in impossible predicaments. Rules on which villages could be attacked and when, for example, were predicated on a fantasy belief that civilians had the ability to evict armed guerrillas. Sometimes attacks were justified by months-old announcements stating that locals had to either force out guerrillas or abandon their land. If villagers failed to heed such warnings, it was their fault in the eyes of the Americans. They had made themselves legitimate targets.[74]

Instead of providing genuine protection, the ROE often served as an exculpatory device. For example, when it came to a "target [that] involves non-combatants, such as in a hamlet or village," a South Vietnamese observer—often termed a "backseat"—had to give approval for an air strike "whenever possible."[75] The idea, as the reporter Jonathan Schell explained, was that "the province chief, or district chief . . . as a Vietnamese, is presumed to be more familiar with the surroundings than the Americans and able to restrain them from destroying populated areas." After seeing the process in action, though, Schell noted that "in the case of Binh Duong Province in January 1967 the province chief . . . was from outside the province, had taken his post only three months before and had never controlled most of the areas being bombed, so he knew less about the area than most of the Americans."[76]

Generally, the Vietnamese observers just gave U.S. forces blanket authority to do as they wished. And when they didn't, the Vietnamese were often simply ignored. As one American province senior adviser blandly noted following an incident in which U.S. helicopters killed some unarmed people, "The gunship pilots were . . . over eager and did not follow the instructions of the Vinh Binh backseat."[77]

Behind the scenes, commanders recognized that wanton attacks prohibited under an honest interpretation of the ROE were a regular occurrence. In a confidential 1967 message to his top Marine Corps generals, Lieutenant General Robert Cushman wrote: "To answer sniper fire from a hamlet or village with mortars, artillery or 90 mm gun fire will kill or injure more noncombatants than it will snipers. The rules of engagement are clear, but they are not always followed."[78] After the war, in a survey of generals who commanded troops in Vietnam, only 19 percent said that the rules of engagement were "carefully adhered to throughout the chain of command" before the My Lai massacre became public knowledge, while 15 percent admitted that that ROE weren't even "particularly considered in the day to day conduct of the war."[79] The true purpose of the various directives, regulations, and pocket-sized codes of conduct handed out to troops was not to implement genuine safeguards for noncombatants, but to give the military a paper trail of plausible deniability.[80]

At every turn, the onus was put on Vietnamese civilians to actively demonstrate that they were indeed noncombatants—by carrying identification cards certifying their loyalty to the Saigon government; by staying out of off-limits areas (the borders of which they might not know); by adhering to dusk-to-dawn curfews; by using no lights at night (which might signal guerrillas), or sometimes by displaying lights at night (to demonstrate that they were not hiding); by not running or not walking in a certain way, or not standing still and thus looking unnatural; by somehow forcing armed guerrillas from their villages but also not carrying weapons, which would automatically brand a Vietnamese as VC. If villagers did not know about any one of these or many other regulations, if an ID card was lost when a house went up in flames, if they had to leave before dawn to get to a far-off market or to make it to a rice field, if they were forced by hunger to forage in an off-limits area, it was their fault. "The claim that civilians broke the rules," the historian Christian Appy notes, "gave the American military a legal-sounding justification for both accidental and intentional slaughter."[81]

Over and over again, the killings of civilians were excused by citing such capricious, even contradictory rules. In March 1969, for example, helicopters from the 1st Cavalry Division spotted a group of nine woodcutters and their truck in a forest in Binh Long Province and hovered above them for ten minutes as the Americans grew increasingly agitated that the Vietnamese would not look up or acknowledge them. There was ample reason for such behavior, as Lieutenant Colonel Anthony Herbert would recall in his memoir. Vietnamese going about their daily work, he pointed out, "knew not to look up. By then it had become almost instinct. Each had probably known someone who had looked up who was now dead. I had actually read it in one of our so-called manuals: 'When they look up, they're VC.' Stupid, but typical."[82]

Eventually, one of the helicopter pilots ordered his door gunner to drop canisters of tear gas, one of which soon started a fire near the woodcutters' truck. With tear gas in the air and a fire raging, some of the woodcutters began to run, while one jumped into the truck and tried to drive it into a nearby clearing. In response, an order was issued in a chopper above: "They're bad guys . . . roll in and get them."[83] Rockets streamed down, blasting the truck, while machine-gun fire ripped through the area. Only one of the woodcutters survived the attack.[84]

An investigation of the incident revealed that all the dead were civilians. Three bodies were eventually identified as those of a middle-aged man, a woman, and a young boy. The others were too badly disfigured for identification.[85] In interviews with army agents, the helicopter crew members readily admitted that they had not received gunfire from the woodcutters and that the Vietnamese had exhibited no hostile behavior. Furthermore, investigators found no enemy shell casings or weapons at the site. Yet none of the troops were punished. According to the official inquiry, they had "fired in good faith convinced that they were engaging a hostile force"—which, under the ROE, automatically made their action legal.[86]

A lack of effective rules of engagement plus command-level failure to take action against obvious breaches meant that when hard decisions had to be made in the field, troops often chose their own safety over that of the civilians they had supposedly been sent to protect. For example, guerrillas might open fire from concealment and then dash into a nearby village for cover. A young U.S. officer, adrenaline coursing, thankful for a near miss or upset and enraged over a man down, now had a choice to make. He could let the guerrillas go and explain to his superior why he had no body count to report; or he could lead his young, angry, scared troops into a possibly booby-trapped village to face another attack. There was, however, a third option. Disregarding or bending the ROE, he could ring up a rear base and call in artillery, jets, or helicopter gunships, perhaps saving the lives and limbs of his troopers and getting some bodies to count, which would please command and get them off his back. The third choice, of course, was usually the easiest to justify for a twenty-something lieutenant looking to survive his six months of trigger time and keep his group of boys alive.

Hard choices became progressively easier with repetition, in part because it was soon apparent to many young officers that few at headquarters knew or cared much about the details in the field—beyond the stats, that is. Commanders regularly seemed disconnected and indifferent. It was easy enough for them to order a patrol out on a search-and-destroy mission; it was a lot harder for those on patrol to trudge mile after mile across sweltering jungles and rice paddies, through thorny hedgerows or razor-sharp elephant grass standing six feet high, up and down highland hills and valleys, all simply to serve as bait for enemy guerrillas. Generals and colonels weren't out in the field—dirty, hungry, and dehydrated—slogging through mud, muck, and water, each step an ordeal, day after day, sometimes for weeks on end, until their feet swelled and the skin painfully sloughed off in silver-dollar-sized chunks. The commanders didn't come down with constant bacterial infections, suffer oozing sores, "crotch rot," and other fungal infections; they didn't have to burn off leeches and face heat exhaustion while being bitten by fire ants and eaten alive by mosquitoes. They sat back at the base or soared high above it all in helicopters, micromanaging from the sky. Who were they to prescribe rules about firing on villages? Who were they to demand additional risks from troops who had it tough enough as it was?

After all, a young lieutenant or captain had to ask himself, didn't artillery fire already blanket the countryside? When choppering out to a landing zone to begin a patrol, he couldn't fail to notice field after field of craters and the endless burned-out villages. The artillerymen and the jet pilots—who never had to worry about tripping a booby trap or walking into a hostile village—seemingly had carte blanche to shell and bomb with impunity and were never investigated for violating the ROE. Given all this, was a young officer prepared to have his point man get hit and listen to him scream for help while enemy fire pinned the patrol in place and the medic tried to crawl out to save him? Or was he going to call in a fire mission on the village, no questions asked? Even if some REMF (rear-echelon motherfucker) at base did bring up the rules of engagement and note that the grid square to be targeted came up as a populated area on the map, all that the officer needed to do was declare "contact"—that is, enemy fire—to override it. So what if the guerrillas' attack had stopped? So what if they might have long since escaped? Was it worth the lives of his men to take the risk for rules that were written up in some air-conditioned office in Saigon or Washington?[87]

In addition, the amorphousness of the ROE allowed troops to invent almost any rationale to justify killing, from a "bouncy gait" ("those shuffling farmers don't have a gait like that," said one pilot) to killing people for the "sin of running," as the historian David Hunt termed it.[88] One adviser in the Mekong Delta surveyed forward air control pilots and helicopter crews about such acts. "Their standard reply is this—if you take evasive action you are guilty," he wrote in an official report. "It takes extrem[e] courage to stand in the middle of a rice paddy when a Cobra [helicopter gunship] buzzes you. If you live in an area that is frequented by these operations, your first instinctive reaction is to clear out and get into the nearest bunker."[89]

In many instances, as in the case of the woodcutters in Binh Long, troops took measures that frightened Vietnamese into running, and then treated them as legitimate targets.[90] William Patterson, who had served as a helicopter door gunner in the region outside of Saigon, told army criminal investigators how he'd been instructed: "If we ran across unarmed people that appeared to be civilians, I was to fire as near to them as possible. If they ran I had permission to kill them."[91]

Nguyen Thi Lam, a villager from the Mekong Delta, described to me the effect of these policies as seen from the other end of the machine gun. On the morning of May 20, 1968, she was out working in the rice paddies near her home when she and her fellow farmers heard the roar of approaching helicopters. Fearing for their lives, they ran for cover. One of the choppers then opened fire, pouring bullets down at them; a round tore through her sister-in-law's throat, killing her on the spot. As Lam dove to the ground, another bullet ripped through her left leg and she blacked out. When she came to, an American was standing over her. He took her to a U.S. hospital for medical treatment, but she lost the leg.[92]

Perhaps the purest expression of the effect of the rules of engagement I ever found was on the death certificate of Nguyen Mai, an unarmed Vietnamese man who died from a "penetrating wound" to the face. The official military paperwork in the U.S. National Archives was written up by an American medical officer. Sparse in its details— Nguyen's date of birth, marital status, religion, and next of kin are all missing—the certificate does, however, list the official "external caus[e]" of death: "Running from U.S. forces."[93]

As ill-defined and porous as the rules of engagement were, they still at least nominally required troops to distinguish civilians from combatants. Another command concept, though, did away with that distinction altogether in much of the country: the notion of the "free-fire" or "free-strike" zone, a label given to areas where everyone was assumed to be the enemy. (Later, the name would be changed for public-relations reasons to "specified strike zone," but the meaning remained the same.) In free-fire zones, an infantryman later recalled, "everyone, men, women, children, could be considered [a fair target]; you could not be held responsible for firing on innocent civilians since by definition there were none there."[94]

The effects were ruinous for the Vietnamese. On April 15, 1970, for instance, members of Company B, 1st Battalion, 5th Marines, asked their company commander whether there were "any friendlies" in the hamlet of Le Bac (2). As Sergeant Paul Cox recalled, the commander replied: "No, this is a free fire zone."[95] Immediately, there was shooting. "The first hut I got to, there was an old mama-san lying in the middle of the floor gut-shot, she was dying," Cox told me years later. At the next hut, a small group of elderly villagers and mothers with children had been gunned down. Nearby, he saw yet another similar scene.[96]

Inside the hamlet, a young girl named Ho Thi A watched in terror as the carnage unfolded. "There were three of us standing at the entrance to the bunker, me and two old women—my neighbor and my grandmother," she told me. The three had just scrambled out of their earthen bomb shelter when an American took aim and shot the two elderly women, one after the other. Ho Thi A wheeled around and clambered back into the bunker, cowering there as the Americans tossed in grenades after her. She later emerged to find that a total of fifteen villagers had been killed in Le Bac (2) that day. All of the victims, she and other survivors from the hamlet told me, were civilians.[97]

The "free-fire" label was not quite an unlimited license to kill, since the laws of war still applied to these areas. As the military legal expert and former marine prosecutor Gary Solis noted, a "free-fire zone doesn't mean a free-crime zone . . . Just because it's a free-fire zone, doesn't mean you can go in and shoot whoever you run into."[98] But many American soldiers did not make that subtle distinction. Even a U.S. Senate study acknowledged that by 1968 an estimated 300,000 civilians had been killed or wounded in free-fire zones.[99]

The horrific toll was not unforeseen. In 1962, before most Americans even knew that their nation was at war in Southeast Asia, Brigadier General H. K. Eggleston was already sounding the alarm about the military's propensity for unleashing firepower on heavily populated areas. In a "Lessons Learned" memorandum, an internal report presenting knowledge gleaned in the field, he emphatically decreed: "ALL FORMS OF FIREPOWER, FROM THE CARBINE TO THE 500 POUND BOMB, MUST HAVE POSITIVELY IDENTIFIED VC TARGETS." Eggleston noted that "since the VC have no 'rear areas,' no logistic bases and no staging or cantonment areas in the generally accepted conventional sense, the application of firepower on a 'suspected VC area' to destroy VC combat potential is of little value." Ultimately, he said, "unless targets are positively identified as enemy . . . casualties among the people, rather than the VC, will result."[100]

But the warning fell on deaf ears. A year after Eggleston issued his memorandum, Westmoreland received his orders for Vietnam. Before heading to Saigon, he met to discuss the new assignment with retired general Douglas MacArthur, who had served as a top commander in the Pacific during World War II, functionally ruled occupied Japan after its surrender, and commanded U.S. and allied forces in Korea. According to Westmoreland's memoir, MacArthur "urged me to make sure I always had plenty of artillery, for the Oriental, he said, 'greatly fears artillery,'" and suggested that Westmoreland might have to employ a "scorched earth policy" in Vietnam.[101]

As U.S. troops began to flood into the country in the mid-1960s, Eggleston's guidance quickly gave way to policies that hewed to MacArthur's advice. In September 1965, Westmoreland issued MACV Directive Number 525-3. Ostensibly concerned with "minimizing non-combatant battle casualties," it actually turned vast swaths of the South Vietnamese countryside into areas where anyone and anything was fair game for U.S. firepower. "Free strike zones should be configured to eliminate populated areas except those in accepted VC bases," the directive decreed—thus declaring open season on millions of Vietnamese. According to McNamara's 1964 figures, 40 percent of the South Vietnamese countryside was considered to be "under Viet Cong control or predominant influence." Westmoreland's policy made that entire territory theoretically open to unrestrained attack.[102]

Warnings of impending strikes were supposed to be issued "whenever possible."[103] But sometimes such announcements, broadcast from loudspeakers on aircraft, could not be heard or understood.[104] Other times, confusing leaflets would rain down on illiterate villagers.[105] Even when warned, villagers frequently had nowhere else to go or little time to do so. Often enough, no warning came at all; planes would simply flash across the skies, dropping high-explosive bombs or napalm canisters that tumbled end over end and bloomed into enormous fiery bursts. Of course, even if ample warnings were issued, firing on villages was still a violation of the laws of war, which prohibit direct attacks on civilians.[106]

Indiscriminate as bombing and artillery fire often were in Vietnam, free-fire zones took away, by definition, any need for discrimination. While serving as an assistant to Ambassador Henry Cabot Lodge, Richard Holbrooke complained to both the ambassador and Westmoreland that free-fire zones were a real danger to the war effort. "There are people living down there," he complained once as the three flew over a free-fire zone, only to be told, "Well, they're Communist-controlled areas."[107] Any villages declared hostile by South Vietnamese province chiefs were regarded as VC base camps, and the U.S. military officially considered every man, woman, and child in them Viet Cong supporters if not outright Viet Cong—and thus reasonable targets. According to Pentagon figures, in January 1969 alone, air strikes were carried out on or near hamlets where 3.3 million Vietnamese lived.[108]

Of course, peasants lived in "VC base" areas because their families had been there for generations. That's where their rice fields were, and their ancestors' graves. Many felt so deeply rooted in the land that they couldn't imagine leaving, even when bombs and shells began to fall. And many of those who contemplated moving simply couldn't afford to leave. When one peasant who did "rally" to the Saigon government—moving away from a hamlet that had been almost totally destroyed by bombing and shelling—was asked why more than one hundred of his fellow villagers still remained there, he explained: "Most of them are poor farmers. A few of them had left the village for [Saigon]-controlled areas but they had to come back since they were not able to make a living over there. Those who stayed . . . didn't have a choice."[109]

It was this kind of poverty that made Le Thi Van's family remain in their hamlet of Nhi Binh in the Mekong Delta, even though the area was hit by mortar and artillery rounds several times a day and bombed once or twice a month.[110] They paid a terrible price. On February 10, 1968, while Van was visiting relatives in another village, an artillery shell scored a direct hit on her family's bomb shelter. Seven of her relatives, including her pregnant sister-in-law, were instantly killed. Their corpses were so badly mutilated that when Van returned to Nhi Binh, she could identify them only by their legs.[111]

Aside from augmenting the body-count statistics, free-fire zones were also integral to another policy objective: driving villagers out of territory controlled by the NLF and into areas controlled by the Saigon government. These efforts were commonly known as "pacification," but their true aim was to depopulate the contested countryside. "The people are like water and the army is like fish," Mao Zedong, the leader of the Chinese Communist revolution, had famously written. American planners grasped his dictum, and also studied the "kill-all, burn-all, loot-all" scorched-earth campaigns that the Japanese army launched in rural China during the 1930s and early 1940s, for lessons on how to drain the "sea."[112] Not surprisingly, the idea of forcing peasants out of their villages was embraced by civilian pacification officials and military officers alike.

In 1964, an American officer remarked, "We must terrorize the villagers even more, so they see that their real self-interest lies with us. We've got to start bombing and strafing the villages that aren't friendly to the Government."[113] One reporter recalled an army captain in a heavily populated Mekong Delta province sweeping his hand across a couple dozen hamlets on a map and remarking that refugees were streaming out of the area. The reporter asked why. "Because it's not healthy out there," the captain replied. "We're shelling the hell out of them."[114]

U.S. commanders repeatedly denied that there was any formal policy of "generating refugees," but one U.S. official admitted in 1967 that "policy or not, they're sure doing it."[115] General William Westmoreland did, in fact, plainly state the military's thinking in a 1965 speech.

> Until now the war has been characterized by a substantial majority of the population remaining neutral. In the past year we have seen an escalation to a higher intensity in the war. This will bring about a moment of decision for the peasant farmer. He will have to choose if he stays alive.
>
> Until now the peasant farmer has had three alternatives. He could stay put and follow his natural instinct to stay close to the land, living beside the grave of his ancestors. He could move into an area under government control, or he could join the VC. Now if he stays put there are additional dangers ... Our operations have been designed to make the first choice impossible.[116]

Similarly, Robert Komer, President Lyndon Johnson's special assistant for pacification, sent a cable to Deputy Ambassador William Porter in 1966 regarding "military operations specifically designed to generate refugees." The next year, after being appointed as Westmoreland's deputy and the U.S. pacification chief, Komer suggested implementing a policy of stepping up "refugee programs deliberately aimed at depriving the VC of a recruiting base."[117] "In order to thwart the communist's [*sic*] designs," wrote Westmoreland a year later, one had to either eliminate the "fish"—which was, he noted, difficult and time-consuming—or "dry up the 'water' so that the 'fish' cannot survive."[118] Another general was even more explicit, telling the reporter R. W. Apple: "You've got to dry up the sea the guerrillas swim in—that's the peasants—and the best way to do that is to blast the hell out of their villages so they'll come into our refugee camps."[119]

When Vietnamese abandoned their villages, they were often simply shuttled into overwhelmed, underfunded, understaffed, underprovisioned, and underequipped "concentration zones"—either refugee camps or artificial villages that the refugees were sometimes forced to build themselves. These settlements, which went by many different names over the years, often made farming impossible.[120] "I had two hectares of rice in the old village," one elderly man complained. "Now it is ripe and the grain falls into the paddy mud. I cannot harvest it. There are men here with guns who tell me that we must dig a ditch . . . In the bottom of that ditch we must put sharpened bamboo stakes and on each side of the ditch there must be a fence of barbed wire. When it is finished, I can return to harvest my rice. But my rice will be gone then. Who will feed my family?"[121]

In 1962, the *New York Times* described a scene in which U.S. advisers and allied Vietnamese troops relocated hundreds of villagers as part of Operation Sunrise. The operation's cheerful title belied the fact that it involved burning the food, homes, and in some cases all the possessions of the villagers before sending them to inhospitable barracks that even the lead U.S. adviser conceded were "no happy hollow."[122] In 1969, an article in the *Times* would describe another village-clearing operation, this time with U.S. troops in the lead. The commanders had changed and the firepower had increased, but the procedures were much the same.

Twenty-four hours before the villages are razed, the inhabitants are warned by leaflets and loudspeaker broadcasts . . . to leave their homes. The inhabitants are then placed in newly constructed "resettlement villages" which are often enclosed by barbed wire . . . First the Zippo squads set fire to the thatched dwellings with their lighters . . . If the town is in a free-fire zone . . . and if the village has already been burned once before "the people who go out know that they will be dead," [Sergeant Steve Kohrt] declared.

"If it's all a free-fire zone, you can sit on the hills and see the dinks running around, so they call in big air strikes," he said.

Lieutenant [Norman] Cuttrell added: "What we try to do is to get all of the people out of the ville before we start burning . . . of course they don't want to go—that's their home and everything."

Those particular troops destroyed more than a dozen villages in just one week.[123] A few years later, an American aid worker described the Saigon-run refugee camps in the area as being "more like concentration camps than the attractive-sounding 'return to village' programs, as they are called by the Government. Conditions in these camps are appalling."[124]

For those thrust into camp life, the experience was jarring. One reporter described how what had been a thriving, well-populated farming area in Quang Tri Province was transformed into a landscape of "burned-out houses and bomb and artillery craters" after the marines arrived, with the surviving civilian population "evacuated to a resettlement area near Cam Lo."[125] An American survey of the Cam Lo refugees showed that 54 percent of them had received no advance warning of their move at all, and that of those who did get warned in advance more than half were given less than a day's notice. Nearly a quarter of the refugees lost everything they owned in the evacuation. Even after propaganda sessions with a South Vietnamese psychological warfare platoon, the villagers did not hide their displeasure from interviewers. Ninety-seven percent of them said their employment situation was worse than before; 95 percent described their resettlement house as less comfortable than their former home; and 87 percent said that their "life situation" was now worse than it had been in the war zone—where bombing, artillery strikes, and U.S. military operations were a constant threat, and where conscription and taxation by revolutionary forces were routine.[126] Within months, thousands in the camp were facing starvation.[127]

Their situation was not unusual. Take, for instance, the experience of Quang Nam resident Nguyen Van Tam. First, aircraft dropped leaflets declaring his hamlet a free-fire zone, giving the inhabitants twenty-four hours to evacuate. The bombing that followed forced his family into an underground existence, and one bomb killed his father as he worked in a rice paddy. A few days later, U.S. troops entered his village. "They pointed to the road and said we must all leave," Tam recalled. "My mother cried. They took matches and burned our house. Then they shot our buffaloes. Then we began to walk to the refugee camp outside Da Nang to find shelter and food."[128] Both would prove in short supply.

Asked about "special problems" in refugee camps, one district chief from Quang Nam Province provided a succinct list.

1. Not enough water
2. Not enough food
3. Not enough first aid station [attendants] and medical personnel
4. No arable lands, no jobs
5. Not enough schools.[129]

At the Hung-Quang Evacuee Regroupment site in the same province, 95 percent of refugees said they were worse off in terms of employment than before their resettlement.[130] Not far away, at the Ngoc Thanh Camp on the outskirts of Hoi An, 92 percent of residents complained that their current home was less comfortable than the one they'd had in their village.[131] It's not hard to imagine why.

A marine described one of the province's camps as "several hundred one-room tin shacks with no doors, and rags over the windows for curtains, all jammed in one next to the other in tight rows on bare hardpacked earth and surrounded by barbed wire and chainlink fencing. It reeked of squalor."[132] Similarly, a survey team from the U.S. General Accounting Office wrote of a Quang Nam camp:

> During our inspection, we observed there were no latrines, no usable wells, no classrooms, and no medical facilities. The shelters were crudely constructed from a variety of waste material, such as empty ammunition boxes and cardboard. We observed that the number of shelters would not adequately house these people . . . The [American] refugee advisor stated that there were no plans to improve the living conditions at this site.[133]

In October 1967, South Vietnam's commissioner for refugees noted that he often received only a day's warning before U.S. operations in I Corps swamped him with as many as 10,000 people at a time.[134] Many displaced villagers were left out of official statistics, but even a U.S. Marine Corps history put the total number of refugees in I Corps that month at 539,000. Two years later it stood at an estimated 690,000, more than half the official count of refugees in the entire country.[135]

As the war dragged on, ever less money would be devoted to refugee aid and public health programs. In 1967, the support that the U.S. Agency for International Development (USAID) gave to South Vietnam's Ministry of Health topped out at $5.9 million. The agency's total medical budget in Vietnam for the year added up to one-quarter of one percent of U.S. expenditures in the country. In effect, said one analyst, an entire year's allocation equaled what was spent in less than a day on the war effort. Two years later, USAID support for the ministry had dropped to less than $1 million.[136] In the words of the journalist Jonathan Schell:

The Americans in Vietnam liked to speak of the "military half" of what they were doing, but the "half" was in reality more like nine-tenths, and the other one-tenth—the contribution to "nation building"—was often, in the context of the war, pure mockery. For example, it frequently happened that in driving the enemy out of a village the Americans would destroy it. That was the "military half." The "civilian half" then might be to drop thousands of leaflets on the ruins, explaining the evils of the N.L.F., or perhaps introducing the villagers to some hygienic measures that the Americans thought were a good idea.[137]

U.S. and South Vietnamese officials repeatedly explained the exodus of peasants by claiming that the people were voting with their feet, fleeing VC terror, taxation, and conscription. However, both the head of the U.S. refugee division and South Vietnam's refugee commissioner admitted that most of those who fled their hamlets did so to escape bombardment and battle.[138] A 1967 U.S. study in Kien Giang Province found that nearly two-thirds of refugees cited shelling and bombing—in most cases from the United States and its allies—as their reason for fleeing. In nearby Dinh Tuong Province, more than 60 percent of the Vietnamese surveyed blamed South Vietnamese and U.S. forces for making them leave their hamlets, while only 22 percent blamed the Viet Cong.[139] Similarly, a 1970 study of refugees in Quang Nam Province found that 80 percent of refugees whose villages had been destroyed blamed U.S. and allied forces, 18 percent said that the damage had happened in firefights between the two sides, and just 2 percent blamed the revolutionary forces alone.[140]

Just how disproportionately civilians could suffer during battles, and why so many were forced to flee their homes, can be seen from the events on Ky Hoa Island, off the coast of Quang Tin Province. On July 9, 1965, when U.S. Marines fought a pitched battle against the revolutionary forces on the island, the Americans lost three men in the fighting, the guerrillas six. Among the civilian population of Ky Hoa, however, one hundred people were reportedly killed.[141] According to their official command diary, the marines also allegedly burned 185 homes and beat up many civilians, including "a middle aged Vietnamese woman and her seven month old daughter."[142]

Civilians who attempted to thwart the refugee generation system by staying in their villages often paid the price. Larry Farmer, who served with Company E of the 4th Battalion, 31st Infantry, testified about one such group of resisters in late September 1969 in the Quang Tin/Quang Nam border region.

> Our squad was running the Vietnamese women and children from the area . . . and we were burning their huts as we went to insure they wouldn't return after we left . . . That day we had burned one hut in a clearing where there were three huts and about fifteen women and children living. As we were burning the hut I told all of the people to leave the area and go to the refugee camp . . . The next day my squad returned to that same area, when we approached the clearing where we had burned the hut we found the same women and children, however, they had all moved into the two remaining huts.[143]

Finding that their orders had been disobeyed, the Americans began by shooting up a pen full of pigs. Then, according to testimony by fellow unit members, Farmer, infantryman Alter Floyd, and several others fired on the group of women and children. "I think Floyd shot one and tore his leg off—it was just hanging there by the meat," unit member Davey Hoag said in a sworn statement. Squad leader Charles Downing remembered some of them gunning down women and young children. Michael Garcia recalled the men firing on a woman holding a baby, and then turning on the infant. "They just shot the baby all up," he told army investigators. Altogether, nine or ten women and children were murdered and called in as "confirmed VC kills."[144]

The I Corps provinces of Quang Tin, Quang Ngai, Quang Nam, and Quang Tri in the north were not the only areas where U.S. forces deliberately attacked villages in order to force their residents into refugee camps. Such assaults happened throughout the country. In 1966, for instance, when U.S. and South Vietnamese troops first arrived in Thanh Son hamlet, a farming enclave in Binh Dinh Province in II Corps, many of the hamlet's young men fled. The soldiers then herded together some of the remaining villagers, beat them, and shocked them with electric cattle prods to force them to leave for a refugee center. Many other residents were brutalized or shot.

Over the following years, American and South Vietnamese troops would return to Thanh Son again and again, destroying rice crops and abusing, arresting, and sometimes killing residents. Pham Thi Hien told me that her home was destroyed at least five times during the war—a common story for villagers in free-fire zones. The Americans detained villagers and burned their homes because they wanted people to move to the "concentration area," Hien explained to me years afterward.[145] "The leaf house burned down, the soil house emerged" became a hamlet axiom during the days of these frequent home burnings, as people were reduced to living in A-framed earthen bunkers.[146]

Helicopter gunships and artillery also extracted a gruesome toll on Thanh Son residents who stayed in their ancestral hamlet. Luong Thi Oi's twelve-year-old daughter was literally torn in two by an artillery shell while tending cows; Bui Xich lost two sons when their bunker suffered a direct hit from another artillery shell.[147] Luong Dai's parents, two older brothers, a younger brother, a niece, and a nephew all died when their bunker collapsed during a U.S. bombardment.[148] When I interviewed several hamlet residents in 2008, they came up with the names of twenty-nine victims but insisted that there had been many more, too many to recall.[149] Sometimes the number of dead had overwhelmed the ability of survivors to bury them, they said, and pigs and ducks started eating the corpses.[150]

Pham Thi Hien, for her part, was captured in Thanh Son during a joint U.S.–South Vietnamese operation in 1967 or 1968. She was beaten, then stretched spread-eagle on the ground. A U.S. soldier interrogated her through an interpreter while water was poured into her nose and mouth, choking her. "Where are your husband and children? What are they doing?" demanded the American, who accused her of living in the hamlet in order to support the guerrillas. After undergoing this water torture, Hien was taken away to a military outpost, where she was put to work filling sandbags. She spent eight months there and then, like so many other Vietnamese, made her way back to her mostly destroyed village to begin her life again.[151]

The assault on Thanh Son hamlet was part of a concerted U.S. effort to pacify Binh Dinh, a region with a long history of fierce resistance to the French occupation. The campaign began with the 1st Cavalry Division's "Operation Masher," though its name struck President Johnson as so inflammatory that the softer "White Wing" was soon tacked onto it—as if one somehow canceled out the other.[152]

During the six weeks of Masher/White Wing, from late January to early March 1966, the 1st Cavalry Division fired 133,191 artillery rounds into Binh Dinh's heavily populated An Lao Valley and Bong Son Plain. The navy added 3,213 rounds from its ships. The air force launched 600 tactical air sorties, dropping more than 427 tons of general-purpose bombs, 265 tons of fragmentation ordnance, 165 tons of napalm, and 80 tons of white phosphorus, which damaged or destroyed more than 600 huts and other structures. Of course, troops on the ground also laid waste to many other homes at the same time.[153] One correspondent described the results in a village in An Lao Valley.

More than half the huts were burned down and the rice fields were pock-marked with bomb craters. The villagers assembled as the Americans marched in. They sat silently in front of their ruined huts. Women held crying children in their arms. When a young American tried to comfort a child, it began screaming while the mother stared in terror at the foreign white giant.[154]

Allied efforts yielded an estimated 5,576 enemy casualties, and a suspiciously low 354 personal weapons, even though the Americans took more than 600 prisoners, some presumably armed. "In the process," noted the reporter and historian Frances FitzGerald, U.S. and South Vietnamese forces "left hundreds of civilians dead and wounded and 'generated' so many refugees as almost to depopulate the fertile An Lao valley."[155]

As operations in Binh Dinh continued, scenes of suffering like those at Thanh Son played out over and over again throughout the province. In early 1966, for instance, Gia Huu and fifteen nearby hamlets were ravaged by artillery fire and air strikes during one three-week span. In just three of those hamlets, approximately one thousand homes were blown apart by bombs and shells or reduced to cinder by napalm, leaving the hamlets, rice paddies, and surrounding hills scorched and pockmarked with craters. Additionally, shelling from U.S. Navy ships destroyed hundreds of coconut trees, the economic lifeblood of the region. The area around Tam Quan, just south of Gia Huu, was also pummeled by the same offensive, with an estimated one hundred civilians killed there and hundreds more injured in just a few weeks. Afterward, survivors were showered with leaflets saying that the Viet Cong were responsible for the destruction, since they had dug trenches and bunkers within the hamlets.[156]

The Americans' dedication to driving villagers out of their hamlets in Binh Dinh Province was often not accompanied by much concern for what happened to the villagers who were driven out. In March 1967, for instance, members of Company A, 8th Engineer

Battalion of the 1st Cavalry Division, joined a platoon from the 1st Battalion, 8th Cavalry, on a search-and-destroy mission in the province's Hoai Nhon District. The engineers blew up the "family-style bomb shelters" that the remaining locals were using for protection, destroying the village in the process. Left homeless and with nowhere to go, twelve civilians from the village—eight women, two teenage girls, and two men over fifty years old—walked along with the patrol back to the American command post but were soon sent away.

That same afternoon, an unarmed man and a woman were spotted walking in a nearby rice paddy. From his post, one of the Company A engineers, Private First Class Richard Clark, watched the 8th Cavalry infantrymen unleash a fusillade at them. He saw the two Vietnamese fall to the ground and start crawling away as a platoon of cavalry troops swept toward them; then he heard the firing of rifles, machine guns, and grenade launchers. The next day, Clark was part of a patrol that set out in the same direction. "We passed within 50 feet of numerous bodies," he said. "At least 4 of which I could identify as the people we had taken out of the village the day before."[157]

Matthew Brennan of the 1st Cavalry recalled how his unit helped transform Binh Dinh from a "paradise" into an artillery-blasted and bomb-cratered wasteland. The soldiers, he wrote, would

> search deserted villages, many of which had beige stucco Catholic churches crowned by the one true cross, and burn every standing structure. Huts and haystacks were set aflame; rice caches were soaked with aviation fuel and burned. On some days we would burn so much rice and so many huts that in the evening our day's route would be marked by dozens of columns of rising white smoke, extending back across some silent valley or another.[158]

By May 1968, official U.S. statistics put the number of refugees in Binh Dinh at over 180,000.[159] Those who warned that this policy was counterproductive were utterly ignored. "It is a mistake," declared

Lieutenant Colonel Nguyen Be, who had served as the Republic of Vietnam's deputy province chief, "to move the people off their hallowed land. This is a political war and it must be fought by trained counterguerrillas and political cadres, not by massive, impersonal free-strike-zone bombings from the air. If we move the people from the land, we will surely lose their support; they will resent us."[160]

Nguyen Be was right. When a sample of the province's refugees were surveyed in 1969, a clear majority blamed U.S. and allied forces for destroying their villages and worsening their lives.[161] Years later, the *New York Times* correspondent Gloria Emerson summed up the results of the American efforts. "Despite the American occupation," she wrote, "Binh Dinh never became a place they could overwhelm and change to be what they wanted. The number of dead Vietnamese and the refugees grew: Binh Dinh was never pacified."[162]

3

OVERKILL

The dystopian 1980s comic book series *Watchmen* offers an alternative history of the Vietnam years, one in which the United States emerged victorious by deploying a godlike, nuclear-powered blue superhero named Dr. Manhattan. His destructive capacity and near omnipotence practically awe the Vietnamese into submission. There is simply no resisting his overwhelming power, and within three months of his arrival the conflict is over.[1]

In the real world, though, the United States already had an endless supply of superweapons at its command. Indeed, to a barefoot peasant in rural Vietnam, a 40,000-pound bomb load dropped by a giant B-52 Stratofortress bomber—silent and invisible to those on the ground—must have had an element of Dr. Manhattan in it. The American forces came blazing in with fighter jets and helicopter gunships. They shook the earth with howitzers and mortars. In a country of pedestrians and bicycles, they rolled over the landscape in heavy tanks, light tanks, and flame-thrower tanks. They had armored personnel carriers for the roads and fields, swift boats for rivers, and battleships and aircraft carriers off shore. The Americans unleashed millions of gallons of chemical defoliants, millions of pounds of chemical gases, and endless canisters of napalm; cluster bombs, high-explosive shells, and daisy-cutter bombs that obliterated everything within a ten-football-field diameter; antipersonnel rockets, high-explosive rockets, incendiary rockets, grenades by the millions, and myriad different kinds of mines. Their advanced weapons included M-16 rifles, M-60 machine guns, M-79 grenade launchers, and even futuristic technologies that would only later enter widespread use, like electronic sensors and unmanned drones. In other words, in Vietnam the American military amassed an arsenal unlike any seen before. As it faced off against guerrillas armed with old rifles and homemade grenades fashioned out of soda cans—or North Vietnamese troops with AK-47 assault rifles and rocket-propelled grenade launchers—the United States had at its disposal more killing power, destructive force, and advanced technology than any military in the history of the world.[2]

Notably, many of the weapons that Americans brought to Vietnam were designed specifically to maim and incapacitate people, on the theory that horribly wounded personnel sapped enemy resources even more than outright killing.[3] An army munitions official later described the history of these efforts.

> Early in the 1950s, the Department of [the] Army embarked on a program to develop special antipersonnel munitions for a variety of weapons systems. These munitions were characterized by a design philosophy which considered the efficient distribution of the smallest effective fragment. The definition of effectiveness was the fallout of a considerable wound ballistics program which evolved the lethal potential of small fragments at high velocity.[4]

In the period immediately preceding the Vietnam War, the army developed brand-new fragmentation munitions; the navy modernized its aircraft-delivered high explosives; and the air force worked to find new and improved ways to utilize antipersonnel weapons. These programs ushered in a new era of scientific slaughter, focused on unleashing small fragments—tiny steel pellets and razor-sharp flechettes—that did immense damage to human bodies. Removing such fragments could tax the skills of even the finest surgeons in well-appointed hospitals, to say nothing of medics triaging the wounded in swamps, jungles, or cramped underground tunnels.[5]

For more than a decade, South Vietnam became a proving ground for such advanced military technologies.[6] General Maxwell Taylor, a key war manager during the formative years of the conflict, who served as a presidential military adviser from 1961 to 1962, the chairman of the Joint Chiefs of Staff from 1962 to 1964, U.S. ambassador to Vietnam from 1964 to 1965, and a presidential consultant on the war from 1965 to 1968, was one of many who spoke of the importance of the area as a "laboratory" for new concepts and equipment.[7] General William Westmoreland, the top U.S. commander in Vietnam from 1964 to 1968, also celebrated the country as a weapons lab. His memoir devotes several pages to a laundry list of military innovations that emerged from Vietnam, such as the converted military transport planes—known as "Spooky" gunships—that could spit out thousands of bullets a minute.[8]

That such military power might not prevail against poorly armed guerrillas in an agrarian country seemed inconceivable. Even as the conflict dragged on, year after year, the Pentagon's war managers never gave up their conviction that American technological prowess would ensure victory. A full-scale invasion of North Vietnam was out of the question; that approach would have risked confrontation with China and required an enormous conscript army, a prospect that few in Washington thought they could sell to the American public. Using nuclear weapons was likewise dismissed as politically untenable. With those options closed off, the Pentagon instead decided to simply pursue technowar ever more intensely as its path to victory. The United States would not deploy its nuclear arsenal, but it would nonetheless assault Vietnam with the destructive power of hundreds of Hiroshimas. In other words, it would wage a war of overkill. A sound from the tree line? Hose it down with machine-gun fire. A sniper shot from the ville? Hit the hamlet with napalm. A hunch that an area might have enemy fighters in it? Plaster it with artillery fire. A Saigon-appointed Vietnamese official identifies a village as an enemy stronghold? Bomb it back to the stone age.

American war managers were all but certain that no Third World people, even with Soviet and Chinese support, could stand up to the mightiest nation on Earth as it unleashed firepower well beyond levels that had brought great powers like Germany and Japan to their knees. (The amount of ammunition fired per soldier was twenty-six times greater in Vietnam than during World War II.) Overkill was supposed to solve all American problems, and the answer to any setbacks was just more overkill. At its peak, the U.S. effort in Vietnam was soaking up 37 percent of all American military spending and required the fighting strength of more than 50 percent of all Marine Corps divisions, 40 percent of all combat-ready army divisions, and 33 percent of the navy. Overall, estimates of the U.S. expenditure on the war range from $700 billion to more than $1 trillion in 2012 dollars.[9]

In the end, of course, this tremendous and profligate investment in war making failed to achieve its objective. The Vietnamese revolutionary forces never yielded to American firepower. But overkill did succeed in producing misery on an epic scale, especially for Vietnamese civilians.

During the conflict, some antiwar critics predicted that North Vietnam might end up as the most bombed country in the history of the world.[10] They had good reason to fear this: on average, between 1965 and 1968, thirty-two tons of bombs per hour were dropped on the North. It turned out, however, that of the munitions unleashed by the United States in Southeast Asia during the Vietnam War—which added up to the equivalent of 640 Hiroshima-sized atomic bombs— the lion's share was dropped not on the North but on South Vietnam,

America's own ally.[11] There, around 19 million people would be subjected to the most lopsided air war ever fought. The guerrillas of
South Vietnam had no airpower at all, and North Vietnam's modest
air force fought a minimal, purely defensive battle in the skies north
of the demilitarized zone. Unchallenged in the South except by
ground fire, the United States carried out the most intense bombing
campaign in history.

In 1962, the first full year of the U.S. air war, 12,000 sorties—a
sortie being defined as one mission by one plane—were launched
against South Vietnamese targets. As American involvement escalated in 1965, airpower was unleashed on a devastating scale, and
the U.S. military equaled that number of strike sorties in September
alone.[12] At the war's height in 1969, 50 percent of American fighter-
bombers and 25 to 50 percent of the Air Force Strategic Air Command's massive B-52 Stratofortress bombers were committed to
Southeast Asia.[13] Between 1965 and 1972, U.S. and South Vietnamese aircraft flew 3.4 million combat sorties in Southeast Asia, with a
plurality of these conducted in South Vietnam.[14]

U.S. aircraft laid waste to huge swaths of rural areas. American
forces considered the spartan Vietnamese thatch-roofed huts, built
of bamboo, mud, and leaves, to be "enemy structures" and regarded
the earthen shelters beneath them as fortified "bunkers." They were
often officially classified as military targets and treated accordingly.
In September 1965, in an agrarian countryside with only the most
modest of buildings, nearly 10,000 enemy structures were blasted by
U.S. and allied aircraft. By mid-1966, some 100,000 had reportedly
been destroyed from the air.[15] All types of buildings were fair game:
homes, hospitals, temples, pagodas, and schools, in addition to actual
enemy fortifications.

Often, a few rounds from a sniper in or near a hamlet, smoke
from a cooking fire, or a glimpse of a running figure clad in "black
pajamas" was enough to warrant an aerial attack. On March 17, 1965,
for example, hostile fire drew an air strike on Man Quang, a village

governed by the National Liberation Front in I Corps. Some forty-five villagers, thirty-seven of them schoolchildren, were killed.[16] Such bombings took place the length of the country. A similar incident occurred on August 9, 1966, when—again in response to enemy fire—two U.S. Air Force jets devastated a hamlet in IV Corps with bombs and cannon fire, killing 15 civilians and wounding 182. "I assure you that we regret this action entirely. But the strike went exactly where it was scheduled to go," said a U.S. official afterward.[17]

Densely populated coastal provinces like Quang Nam, Quang Ngai, and Binh Dinh, as well as the "Iron Triangle" region near Saigon, were among the most heavily bombed areas.[18] The hardest hit was Quang Tri, the northernmost province in South Vietnam. The province's capital district, saturated with 3,000 bombs per square kilometer, was Vietnam's single most devastated area.[19] On March 2, 1967, several bombs slammed into the village of Lang Vei, killing at least 100 civilians and wounding another 175.[20] And Lang Vei was hardly exceptional. Only 11 of the province's 3,500 villages went unbombed during the war.[21]

Observing the landscape of Quang Tri in 1973, Arthur Westing, an ecologist who had worked for the U.S. Forest Service and later the Stockholm International Peace Research Institute, wrote:

> Despite a year of frontline combat experience in Korea, and despite three previous trips to Indochina to study the war zones of Cambodia and South Vietnam, I was unprepared for the utter devastation that confronted us wherever we turned. Our tour took us through much of the lowland region and some of the central hilly region. Never were we out of sight of an endless panorama of crater fields. As far as we could determine not a single permanent building, urban or rural, remained intact: no private dwellings, no schools, no libraries, no churches or pagodas, and no hospitals. Moreover, every last bridge and even culvert had been bombed to bits. The one rail line through the province was also obliterated.[22]

Three and a half decades later, the unnatural undulations of the land in Quang Tri and the potentially still lethal ordnance regularly found rusting there testify to the lasting impact of the war. In 2008, Pham Thi Luyen—the villager from Trieu Ai who was orphaned as a thirteen-year-old girl during the massacre there in 1967—recalled how by the end of the war "the land was full of bomb and artillery craters, nothing else . . . cluster bombs were everywhere." Now, her home stands just steps from a cratered expanse that serves as a grave-yard. "On this land, bomb and artillery shells are abundant," she said. "We're still scared, today."[23]

Among the aircraft that laid waste to Quang Tri were those mas-sive B-52 bombers, which, flying six in formation, could destroy everything within a strike zone two miles long and five-eighths of a mile wide.[24] The U.S. military often claimed that B-52s bombed only uninhabited areas, but this simply wasn't so. The strikes often hit vil-lages or at least struck close enough to kill.[25] In 1972, U.S. adviser Gene Niewoehner lamented that B-52s were being called in on areas known to be filled with civilians. "The B-52 targets are selected in advance," he said. "We told them about civilians in one area in Quang Tri two weeks ago, but it took about seven days before the B-52s stopped."[26]

Between 1965 and 1973, the U.S. Strategic Air Command launched at least 126,615 B-52 combat sorties, the majority of them hitting targets in South Vietnam. Deaths from these devastating B-52 strikes often left indelibly traumatic memories. One villager described how shock waves from such a bombing killed children, leaving blood gushing from their ears.[27] Villagers who had been far enough from the drop zone to survive the almost indescribable, earth-shaking explosions frequently still suffered serious injuries, and they filled hospitals across the country.[28]

B-52s were not, however, the most common strike aircraft. Sixty-six percent of air-launched munitions were unleashed by smaller fighter-bombers, such as F-4 Phantoms.[29] These planes streaked across the sky laden with high-explosive bombs, napalm canisters, and other antipersonnel weapons. The jellied incendiary napalm, engineered to stick to clothes and skin, had been modified to blaze hotter and longer than its World War II–era variant. An estimated 400,000 tons of it were dropped in Southeast Asia, killing most of those unfortunate enough to be splashed with it.[30] Thirty-five percent of victims died within fifteen to twenty minutes, according to one study. Another found that 62 percent died before their wounds healed. For those not asphyxiated or consumed by fire, the result could be a living death.[31] Noses and lips, nipples and eyelids would be burned off or melted away, while charred skin would flake off as a chemical-scented powder.[32] The Magnum photographer Philip Jones Griffiths photographed a number of such victims, and he would never forget a child he saw in the napalm ward of a Quang Ngai hospital. "He had his eyelids burned off, his nose burned off, and his lips burned off. He was halfway to becoming a skull, but he was still alive," the photographer recalled.[33]

Nguyen Van Tuan was lucky: the napalm only scorched his face. In 1964, he had taken cover in a ditch outside his school in the Mekong Delta as a napalm canister sent a wave of fire over the top of the trench. Then, for him, everything went silent. Trees were collapsing and exploding in flames, but he couldn't hear a sound. Nguyen must have been in a relatively safe spot or turned his body in just the right way. His clothes didn't catch fire, nor his hair. Others got the worst of it. "My schoolmates burned below the neck all died," he told me. In the immediate chaos, the air filled with the smell of gasoline, the heat unbearable, he bolted toward home and collapsed unconscious on arrival. His family took him to the nearest hospital, where he lay in a coma for more than two weeks. After regaining consciousness, he spent another two and a half months recovering. Decades later, this soft-spoken man with salt-and-pepper hair and piercing brown eyes still bore the scars of that afternoon. The skin on his neck was tight and striated, as if he were forever straining its muscles, and his face bore a patchwork of unnatural-looking skin discolorations. And he was one of the fortunate ones.[34]

Sometimes napalm was combined with white phosphorus, another incendiary agent. Known to troops as "Willy Peter," white phosphorus ignited when exposed to air and burned until its oxygen supply was cut off. A face touched by Willy Peter might burn up or melt into wrinkled rivulets of skin. A tiny chunk of phosphorus could become embedded and slowly burn its way right through a body. "I have seen skin and bone sizzling on a child's hand from phosphorus burns for 24 hours resisting any treatment," one Canadian aid worker recalled.[35] The U.S. Air Force procured more than 3 million white phosphorus rockets over the course of the conflict, and the American military bought 379 million M-34 white phosphorus grenades in 1969 alone.[36]

When I met him on a spring day in 2006, forty-six-year-old Tran No had fine, wispy black hair that he combed down to cover his forehead. One side of his face looked youthful for a man his age, the other resembled a stroke victim's—his mouth sagged, lips and mustache seeming to slide down toward an oddly shaped scaffold of skin that connected his face and neck. It was the legacy of an explosion that changed his life forever when he was just seven or eight years old.

That day, Tran No was sitting in the shade of a stand of bamboo in his Quang Ngai hamlet, playing with two other children, when artillery shells began to rain down. The three-year-old boy beside him was killed instantly, the little girl wounded (she would later die in another attack), and Tran was badly injured. He was too young to understand what was burning him. He still remembers, though, the relentlessness of the incendiary and the horrible pain. "Water would not stop the burning," he told me. Fortunately, an old man from the village knew what to do. He took mud from the nearby lake and slathered it on the boy's wounds—a nightmare maneuver as far as infection is concerned, but probably the only available way to cut off the oxygen supply to a fire that otherwise couldn't be quenched.

Tran's parents were scared of the Americans, so they took him to a local healer. The healer, though, threw up his hands and figured out a way to get the boy to a U.S. hospital in Chu Lai. There, Tran's clothes were cut off his body, and he was placed in a tank of water. After fifteen days of treatment by the Americans, he spent a month in a South Vietnamese hospital, followed by herbal medicine treatments at home. Only then did the pain finally subside. Someone in an American patrol later saw the disfigured little boy and, evidently shocked by the sight, sent him back to a hospital, but there was nothing more that could be done.

Tran No laughed about his predicament, but he was also clearly bitter about his fate. At the end of our conversation, he leaned across a small table as if to share a secret. "Because of the war and the American artillery," he said, "I'm less handsome and many girls didn't like me."[37]

Napalm and white phosphorus bombs were not the only diabolically destructive munitions unleashed by American airplanes. Cluster munitions were simply slaughter spring-loaded into little metal cans. The BLU-3 bomblet, for instance, better known as a "pineapple," was a small container filled with 250 steel pellets. One B-52 could drop 1,000 pineapples across a 400-yard area. As they burst open, 250,000 lethal ball bearings would tear through everything in the blast radius. For their victims, that could literally mean death by a thousand cuts.[38] The "guava" cluster bomb, officially designated CBU-24, was even deadlier. Loaded with 640 to 670 separate BLU-26 bomblets, each packing 300 steel pellets, just one guava could send 200,000 steel fragments shooting in all directions as it hit the ground.[39] A single B-52 bomber loaded with guava bomblets could saturate an area slightly smaller than a square mile with more than 7.5 million deadly steel pellets.[40] From 1964 to 1971, the U.S. military ordered at least 37 million pineapples, and between 1966 and 1971 it bought approximately 285 million guava bomblets—nearly seven for each man, woman, and child in Vietnam, Laos, and Cambodia combined.[41]

Multiple types of munitions were often used in tandem. In 1969, as fourteen-year-old Nguyen Thi Chanh and her family took cover in the shelter under their home, the house was hit by an incendiary bomb. The mud-and-thatch structure burst into flames, leaving them with little choice but to try to escape right through the inferno. As the family dashed through the fire, the teenage girl was badly burned, but they all made it out alive—emerging into the open just as an attacking plane was making another pass. This time, the aircraft unleashed a cluster bomb, spraying shrapnel throughout the area and wounding Chanh again. When I talked to her almost forty years later, she still bore the scars of both bombs.[42]

Villagers who managed to survive the initial bombing raids and napalm strikes were still in grave danger from the strafing runs that often followed the bombardment. Attack aircraft would also roar in as close air support when U.S. or allied troops were under fire or when ground troops could not or would not dislodge enemy forces from populated areas. "Enemy" hamlets—those deemed loyal to the National Liberation Front or suspected of such sympathies—were often struck with impunity, and even "friendly" villages that supported the Saigon government were not immune from attack. In July 1965, for instance, when Americans entered a friendly village in Quang Ngai Province, they were confronted with the stench of burned bodies and the wailing of women. They saw wrecked bamboo houses, shattered concrete homes, the remnants of a schoolhouse, and a church pockmarked by aircraft cannon rounds. The explanation was simple: a South Vietnamese military outpost had been overrun, and airpower had been called in to deal with the problem. "When we are in a bind like we were [here,] we unload on the whole area to try to save the situation. We usually kill more women and kids than we do Viet Cong but the government troops just aren't available to clean out the villages so this is the only answer," a U.S. Air Force officer candidly remarked afterward.[43]

Similarly, on February 26, 1969, U.S. and South Vietnamese

planes, helicopters, and artillery responding to an "attempted attack" on a U.S. air base blasted Tan Hiep hamlet in Bien Hoa Province, a resettlement area for 1,500 Roman Catholic refugees from North Vietnam. They damaged or destroyed nearly all the homes, wiped out the hamlet's livestock, and killed ten civilians.[44] And in April 1967, a U.S. F-100 Supersabre "mistakenly bombed" the Mekong Delta town of Truc Giang and a nearby village housing Viet Cong defectors and their families, killing fourteen and wounding twenty-five others.[45]

Many American "accidents" and "errors" were even more deadly than that.[46] In February 1968, for instance, the pro-Saigon Catholic village of Nhi Binh in Gia Dinh Province was decimated by a B-52 strike. According to American sources, as many as two hundred civilians were killed there and at least another seventy wounded.[47] Similarly, on August 8, 1968, the friendly village of Cai Rang in the Mekong Delta was torn apart by American firepower. "We once lived in a hamlet where there were many Viet Cong," Huynh Thi Tam lamented afterward. "We moved here because we thought it would be safe. Now my son is dead." He was just one of seventy-two killed and more than two hundred injured that night.[48]

In 1972, John Paul Vann, one of the three top-ranking Americans in the country, ruefully summarized the situation.

> In the last decade, I have walked through hundreds of hamlets that have been destroyed in the course of a battle, the majority as the result of the heavier friendly fires. The overwhelming majority of hamlets thus destroyed failed to yield sufficient evidence of damage to the enemy to justify the destruction of the hamlet. Indeed, it has not been unusual to have a hamlet destroyed and find absolutely no evidence of damage to the enemy.[49]

That same year, army captain Thomas Pugh was questioned by a military investigator concerning allegations of the "excessive" destruction of a village. Pugh replied with a matter-of-fact summary of the situation in Quang Nam Province in the early 1970s. "Sir, since I have been in this AO [area of operations] this tour," he said, "that whole area out there has had villages blown away at least three or four times a day by A-37s, by A1E's, by F4's, by AH1G's . . . it happens on a daily basis."[50]

The A-37 Dragonfly, A-1E Skyraider, and F-4 Phantom were all attack airplanes, but Pugh's mention of AH-1Gs calls attention to another lethal aspect of American airpower: the helicopter.[51] By 1966, the marines had already committed 50 percent of their helicopter strength to Vietnam, and at the conflict's peak the U.S. military would have more than 4,000 helicopters in the country. Over the course of the war, U.S. "choppers" flew more than 36 million sorties in Southeast Asia.[52] Not surprisingly, no image evokes the American conflict in Vietnam like the UH-1 "Huey," the iconic troop transport and weapons platform that came to typify the airmobile war waged by U.S. forces, with troops choppered to and from the countryside at the beginning and end of their patrols. The Huey, introduced into the conflict in 1962, and its more heavily armed cousin the AH-1G "Huey Cobra," which arrived on the scene in 1967, constantly crisscrossed the Vietnamese skies. So did numerous other rotary-wing craft, from tiny "Loach" scout choppers to large Chinook troop carriers with their tandem rotors.

The army's questioning of Captain Pugh arose from comments made by one of the men under his command, Warrant Officer Cecil Jimeson of the 48th Assault Helicopter Company, who was distraught about the unit's killing of civilians. Army investigators asked Jimeson for more details, warning him, "This can't be ignored if it is one of these My Lai things." Jimeson replied that what Pugh's unit had done completely conformed to the military's rules of engagement. "It isn't anything like a My Lai," he told them. "It was completely legal."

Jimeson then offered the investigators a vivid account of the mission in question. On April 4, 1972, he had been a gunner/copilot in a two-man Cobra, part of a contingent of five UH-1 Hueys and four Cobra gunships assigned to support South Vietnamese military operations in Quang Nam Province. Eventually, they arrived at a village where, Jimeson said, the rules of engagement meant "anything that moves dies." Jimeson was clearly uncomfortable with those rules; when the aircraft commander cleared him to fire on the Vietnamese below, he repeatedly "missed on purpose." Pressure from his commander, however, eventually drove him to join in what he called a "blood bath." Jimeson heard no ground fire but counted ten civilians killed during the mission. "I seen a lot of old ladies and kids," he told the investigators. "I seen one old man—old. He had a white long beard. That was the only man I seen."[53]

When the investigators talked to other members of the unit, the men were incredulous that anyone could possibly consider their actions to be a problem. Warrant Officer Thomas Equels, for example, emphasized to investigators that the pilots were following official orders—which called for them to destroy villages even in the absence of enemy fire. "We've blown up villages," Equels explained, "but this is with clearance . . . and that's the job to go out and destroy . . . villages."[54]

Lieutenant Phillip Manual, who had transported troops as part of the April 4 mission, described what he'd heard from the gunship pilots over the radio: "'There's people down there. I got them in sight. We are going to have some fun here . . . Okay. I'm going to roll in and kill some folks.'" Soon after, gunships attacked with cannons blazing. Asked about the destruction of houses, Manual replied with some bewilderment, "Well, they followed orders. They said there was a hootch down there with people around it, blow it away and [the pilots] always . . . replied, I understand I am cleared on the hootch down there."[55] Warrant Officer David Waldron also found the entire logic of the investigation hard to grasp. "Well, allegations against killing civilians. I think it's kind of crazy in that area . . . If they were there, Sir, they asked for it."[56]

The same brutal they-asked-for-it attitude was also on display in the south of the country, where heavily armed Cobra gunships were shuttled into service in the Mekong Delta as part of the 307th Combat Aviation Battalion's "Phantom III" program. Phantom III and similar efforts involved attacks on "targets of opportunity"—including, according to an official list, sampans, houses, and unarmed men. In short order, Phantom III and other gunship operations became notorious for killing anything that moved.[57]

On May 22, 1969, senior adviser Philip Hamilton reported a Phantom III strike in Chuong Thien Province that killed thirteen civilians and wounded six others. Later that year, in the same province, thirty-two civilians were reportedly gunned down by U.S. helicopters while they were planting rice in their fields.[58] On July 18, gunships killed two children in Ba Xuyen Province's Hoa Tu village; two days later, a helicopter killed another civilian in the area. And on July 23, helicopters gunned down four farmers in nearby Tra Canh hamlet. Such attacks finally prompted John Evans, the province senior adviser, to complain in an official report about "indiscriminate firing on civilians working outside free-fire zones."[59]

From January through October 1969, the Phantom III program officially carried out 862 strikes that damaged or destroyed 13,828 structures and 3,551 sampans, while claiming 1,698 confirmed kills.[60] According to Louis Janowski, who served as the deputy district senior adviser and then district senior adviser of Tra Cu District, Vinh Binh Province, in 1969, civilians were the predominant victims. In his official end-of-tour report, Janowski went so far as to call Phantom operations a form of "non-selective terrorism." Most missions, he said, consisted of attacks on houses, sampans, and bunkers, carried out without any knowledge or concern about who was inside. Indeed, if any enemy forces were killed, it was almost entirely by random chance. "I have flown Phantom III missions," he wrote, "and have medivaced enough elderly people and children to firmly believe that the percentage of Viet Cong killed by support assets is roughly equal to the percentage of Viet Cong in the population. That is, if 8% of the population [of] an area is VC about 8% of the people we kill are VC."[61]

The constant threat of air strikes was not the only danger facing Vietnamese civilians. Throughout the conflict, they also had to contend with seemingly omnipresent artillery fire. In embattled areas of South Vietnam, shells rained down with remarkable regularity on hamlets, gardens, rice fields, and other places where civilian life went on.[62] In 1969 alone, U.S. units fired approximately 10 million artillery rounds.[63] Over the course of the war, the Americans expended almost 15 billion pounds of artillery shells.[64]

In addition to rounds called in by ground troops on suspected or real enemy positions, the countryside was also continually pounded by "harassment and interdiction" (H&I) fire. While theoretically based on the gleanings of American and South Vietnamese intelligence, H&I often amounted to little more than the regular firing of shells into random areas simply to keep the enemy in a state of unease.[65] According to 1966 Army data, 91.2 percent of artillery fire missions were *not* employed in close support of ground forces. For the Marine Corps, the figure was 88.6 percent.[66] A July 1967 study found only a modest drop, to 85 percent and 73 percent, respectively. Although H&I use later declined, the tactic continued into the next decade.[67]

The idea behind H&I was to expend munitions, not men. And the same mind-set prevailed when it came to all types of artillery support. For instance, it was not out of the ordinary for U.S. troops in Vietnam to blast a whole village or bombard a wide area in an effort to kill a single sniper.[68] One U.S. general coined a dictum in relation to artillery use in Vietnam: "Waste ammunition like a millionaire and lives like a miser."[69] Even while commanders in the field, eager to please the Pentagon, used search-and-destroy patrols as "bait" for guerrillas, when it came to artillery the war managers in Washington focused almost exclusively on the lives of U.S. soldiers. They paid little attention to the effect of overwhelming firepower on Vietnamese civilians, despite the insistence that they were in the business of "winning hearts and minds."

The CBS News correspondent John Laurence remembered two officials from the State Department bitterly complaining to him about harassment and interdiction fire. They explained that "the targets were chosen by local South Vietnamese officials who gave grid coordinates to American artillery officers who had only a vague idea what they were shooting at. Sometimes the targets were villages whose farmers had not paid taxes to local government bureaucrats or were suspected of being sympathetic to the VC." The two officials called H&I "inhuman" and "criminal," and said that it was "killing and injuring Vietnamese who had nothing to do with the war other than being caught in it. Most shelling took place at night and it made the peasants crazy with fear."[70]

Sometimes military officers agreed.[71] In a secret communiqué to other generals, the top marine commander Lieutenant General Robert Cushman admitted that "H&I is one of the primary causes of civilian casualties."[72] Another general more bluntly called it "madness."[73]

Almost any excuse could justify artillery strikes. The commander of the 25th Infantry Division, General Ellis Williamson, explicitly rejected the principle of proportionality—a tenet of the laws of war that requires the amount of force used be proportional to the threat posed and advantage gained—and instituted a devastatingly disproportionate reprisal policy.[74] One U.S. adviser who walked through a hamlet in Hau Nghia Province near the 25th Infantry Division's post in late 1968 summed up the results.

The first area was still close to the American base and thus nearly two-thirds of the houses had burned. Several of the old women seem very bitter and talked very little . . . Apparently the 25th Division has a policy of 1,000 outgoing for every one incoming ... In this village, the people were terrified. I asked them how long things had been this way. They replied ever since the American base was built.[75]

Even more extreme, as the *New Yorker* magazine reporter Jonathan Schell noted, were policies dictating that artillery be fired at regular intervals regardless of any military justification.[76] An artillery battery commander explained, "The ammo kept coming whether or not we had targets for it, so the batteries fired their allotments every opportunity they had, whether there was actually anything to shoot at or not."[77]

In all, the United States expended close to 30 billion pounds of munitions in Southeast Asia over the course of the war.[78] At the peak of its effort, in 1970, the U.S. was using up 128,400 tons of munitions per month. (By comparison, the revolutionary forces never fired more than 1,000 tons per month.)[79] By the early 1970s, years before the war's end, South Vietnam's landscape was already pockmarked with an estimated 21 million craters, some of them twenty feet or more across.[80] Analyzing the effects of the "tremendous firepower" of U.S. forces, two South Vietnamese generals wrote, "Many villages were completely obliterated ... houses were reduced to rubble, innocent people were killed, untold numbers became displaced, riceland was abandoned, and as much as one half of the population of the countryside fled."[81]

The "cratering" of South Vietnam also produced a cascade of environmental effects. Huge numbers of rice paddies, orchards, farms, and gardens were lost to cultivation.[82] This led to rampant erosion and weed invasion, destroyed wildlife habitats, and played havoc with the countryside's intricate irrigation systems. Craters in the more tropical Mekong Delta and those in the coastal regions tended to remain flooded year-round, becoming mosquito breeding grounds and thus sources of disease.[83] What's more, according to postwar

estimates, at least 12 million acres of forest were subjected to satura-
tion bombing. Many trees crucial to Vietnam's rubber and timber
industries were destroyed; others were filled with metal fragments,
which made them more susceptible to fungal rot or unusable altogether.[84]

In addition to such environmentally devastating side effects of
the war, the U.S. military deliberately sprayed more than 70 million
liters of herbicidal agents—most notably Agent Orange—across the
countryside.[85] When plants absorbed the herbicides, their leaves rapidly shriveled and dried up. "The effects appeared overnight," wrote
a South Vietnamese colonel about defoliants that drifted across
orchards and farms in Bien Hoa Province. "Fruit fell from the trees
and the rubber trees in the large nearby plantations turned brown
and lost their leaves." He noted that the aerial spraying took an especially heavy toll on custard apples, mango, jackfruit, pineapples, and
other economically important crops.[86]

Vietnamese farmers also worried about the chemicals' effects on
their livestock and their families. They had good reason to be concerned. One American observer, who visited a village following a
defoliation mission in 1970, reported that

> of the 10,000 chickens in the hamlet, 5,000 were subsequently sick
> and about 1,000 chicks died. Of the 200 pigs, 100 pigs were sick and
> 15 died. The chickens did not eat and, upon death, they ran in
> circles. We drove to the village and saw that defoliation had taken
> place. [It must have been] five weeks ago because many dried leaves
> were still hanging on trees. About 10–20% of the trees were defoli-
> ated, all *Autocarpus integrifolia* (jackfruit) looked defoliated . . .
> Some of the lower leaves of the banana [trees] were dead, the leaves
> of mangoes were shriveled, and . . . vegetables were affected.[87]

"Only you can prevent forests," a play on the Smokey the Bear
slogan about forest fires, was the dark motto of the troops who car-

ried out "ecocide" in the previously verdant country. It was obvious to anyone who cared to look, though, that forests were only a small fraction of the story.[88] According to hamlet census data, toxic defoliants were sprayed on as many as 4.8 million Vietnamese.[89] Immediate reactions to exposure included nausea, cramps, and diarrhea. In the longer term, the defoliants have been associated with higher incidence of stillbirths as well as a variety of illnesses, including cancers and birth defects such as anencephaly and spina bifida.[90] Children born decades after the war still suffer the aftereffects.[91]

More broadly, defoliation begat hunger and privation and caused a rupture in the fabric of rural civic life. Toxic herbicides turned formerly emerald-colored areas into bare "white zones" where nothing but invasive weeds would grow for years. Lush green paddy fields where rice was cultivated—the very center of Vietnamese rural life—were deliberately targeted, in many cases severing an almost sacred connection that bound the Vietnamese to their land.[92] In 1965, 42 percent of all chemical defoliants sprayed in South Vietnam were aimed at food crops, and the country quickly went from rice exporter to rice importer.[93] A 1967 analysis by the RAND Corporation, an air force–sired think tank with strong military ties, concluded that "the civilian population seems to carry very nearly the full burden of the results of the crop destruction program; it is estimated that over 500 civilians experience crop loss for every ton of rice denied the VC."[94]

American war planners expected that this crop loss would play into the policy of "pacification," helping to drive villagers out of areas of the countryside controlled by the NLF and into areas controlled by the Saigon government. But many peasants remained in their ancestral hamlets, even as children grew rail-thin and their parents became increasingly desperate. Army veteran John Beitzel watched as defoliants blanketed valleys, and noted the human toll. His unit would dump garbage from their base camp outside a nearby village, he wrote, and the local Vietnamese would almost immediately "start eating whatever was there ... because they just didn't have enough food . . . Before we were there, they did. And now that we were there, supposedly helping them, they didn't."[95] By 1970, the food supplies of at least 600,000 people had been disrupted by the defoliation campaign, according to a report released by the American Association for the Advancement of Science.[96]

As with other facets of the American project in Vietnam, when it came to ecological destruction, "overkill" was the operative word. From 1965 to 1967, for example, massive fires set by U.S. forces reportedly wiped out about 100,000 acres of forest.[97] Powerful bulldozers, known as Rome plows, also systematically attacked the landscape.[98] In 1967, Lieutenant Colonel John Manning of the 168th Combat Engineer Battalion bragged that his "clearing blades" could flatten ten to twelve acres per day—and that was just a fraction of the heavy machinery active in Vietnam at the time.[99] In 1971, massive twenty-ton Caterpillar tractors tore into parts of the Boi Loi Woods, an area northwest of Saigon that had already been defoliated, bombed, and burned. In twenty-six days, they cleared 6,037 acres.[100] In all, American bulldozers may have torn up and plowed under as much as 2 percent of the entire land area of South Vietnam.[101]

Bulldozers, heavy tanks, and other armored vehicles were also employed to destroy orchards, paddies, individual homes, and even whole hamlets.[102] A more common way of destroying villages, though, was fire.[103] When U.S. troops took casualties near populated areas, Major General George O'Connor wrote, "the instant reaction of the troops [was] to burn the whole hamlet down."[104] "Burn the damn gooks out. Burn it. Burn it, and they can't ever come back," was the order handed down as a marine patrol on a search-and-destroy mission used their Zippo cigarette lighters to torch a hamlet filled with civilians and all their worldly possessions.[105]

The slaughter of animals was another key component of the American program of destruction. Upon entering a hamlet, U.S. soldiers often headed straight for the animal pens to liquidate the locals' livestock, killing chickens, ducks, and pigs en masse. Most

disastrous of all were the killings of expensive water buffalo. Sometimes, the "water-boo," as U.S. troops called them, were shot dead
when, enraged by the presence of outsiders, they charged soldiers
and marines. On other occasions, they were killed simply for sport
or out of spite. And frequently, destruction of the large, horned beasts
was carried out systematically as part of the larger campaign to drive
Vietnamese from their paddy fields where water buffalo functioned
as living tractors.[106]

In 1970, veteran Richard Brummett, who had served in A Troop,
1st Squadron, 1st Cavalry Regiment, wrote a letter to Secretary of
Defense Melvin Laird, calling upon him to take action against those
responsible for the wanton violence he witnessed. Brummett told
Laird that his unit

> did perform on a regular basis, random murder, rape and pillage
> upon the Vietnamese civilians in Quang Tin Province . . . with the
> full knowledge, consent and participation of our Troop Com-
> mander, a Captain David Roessler . . .
>
> These incidents included random shelling of villages with 90mm
> white phosphorus rounds, machine gunning of civilians who had
> the misfortune to be near when we hit a mine, torture of prisoners,
> destroying of food and livestock of the villagers if we deemed they
> had an excess, and numerous burnings of villages for no apparent
> reason.[107]

What seemed so senseless and shocking to the young veteran,
however, was just the overkill mind-set in action.

What seemed so senseless and shocking to the young veteran,
however, was just the overkill mind-set in action.

Even when their homes were bombarded and their rice fields
destroyed, most South Vietnamese villagers were reluctant to move
to government-run concentration zones. A significant portion of
them, instead, headed to the cities: Saigon's population nearly tripled

after the American assault on the countryside began, and squalid shantytowns sprang up on the outskirts of almost every provincial and district capital. The urban slums were filthy, overcrowded, disease-ridden, and desperately impoverished, but they did, for a while, offer one key advantage: a respite from the bombs, shells, helicopter gunships, and search-and-destroy ground patrols. In urban areas, U.S. troops still killed civilians in shootings, bar fights, and traffic accidents, but large-scale attacks were relatively rare.[108] Then came 1968.

On January 29, the eve of Tet—the Vietnamese lunar new year, a holiday so important that both North and South Vietnam traditionally declared a several-day cease-fire for the festivities—a top U.S. embassy official named George Jacobson threw a gala party on the lawn of his French villa. Jacobson's swanky digs were located in a walled, four-acre compound on Saigon's embassy row. In front of them was the new multimillion-dollar U.S. embassy, completed a few months earlier: a six-story fortress of reinforced concrete walls, solid teak doors, and a large terra-cotta sunscreen that doubled as a blast shield.[109]

On this night, Saigon's foremost citizens, South Vietnamese government officials, and U.S. civilian and military powerbrokers—including Ambassador Ellsworth Bunker—were enjoying the smooth sounds of a band and the staccato rat-a-tat of a twenty-three-foot-long string of firecrackers set off to scare away evil spirits for the new year. A gift from a top South Vietnamese government official, the noisemakers signaled a newfound confidence. For years, traditional firecrackers at Tet had been forbidden to prevent the revolutionary forces from using the sound as a cover for gunfire. Now, it seemed, there was no need to worry. More than 492,000 American troops were stationed in the country, and victory, if not yet in plain sight, seemed a foregone conclusion. "I have never been more encouraged in my four years in Vietnam," General William Westmoreland had announced just two months earlier when he and Bunker had gone to

Washington to brief President Lyndon Johnson. The ambassador had assured Johnson and the American people that the Republic of Vietnam now held sway over 67 percent of the country's population while the NLF controlled only 17 percent. And more gains were expected in 1968. Viet Cong recruitment, Bunker reported, had sagged by as much as 50 percent over the course of 1967, and Saigon's troops were performing better than ever. Westmoreland added that 45 percent of enemy forces were not fit for combat and let slip that in two years the United States might begin a "phase-out" of its troops. "We have reached an important point when the end begins to come into view," the general told the National Press Club in Washington.[110] There finally was a light at the end of the tunnel.

Before it got too late, Bunker left Jacobson's party and headed back to his own villa. Twenty-four hours later, festive fireworks again rang out across the city. But at 3 AM on January 31, Bunker's marine guards woke him with startling news: Saigon was under attack. There was no time for the ambassador to get dressed. Bunker threw on a bathrobe, hustled into an armored personnel carrier, and was driven away. Behind him, smoke poured from his study, as marines burned secret documents in case the house fell to the enemy.

Six thousand revolutionary fighters—the same guerrilla forces that had been given last rites by Bunker and Westmoreland all autumn long—had infiltrated the South Vietnamese capital and its suburbs, and a tiny commando unit had set its sights on the shiny new American embassy. "They're coming in! Help me!" a military policeman at the embassy shouted into his radio. Seconds later, he was dead. Jacobson, the party host, found himself trapped on the second floor of his villa when an injured guerrilla took refuge on the ground floor. U.S. troops tossed a pistol and a gas mask to Jacobson through a window and fired tear gas into his home. He eventually outdueled the wounded fighter and made it out alive. U.S. credibility, however, did not survive the night.

The American embassy was just one of the seemingly untouchable

Saigon landmarks attacked by the guerrillas. Revolutionary fighters similarly assaulted the Independence Palace, South Vietnam's version of the U.S. White House. Guerrillas also took over the studio of the government radio station; attacked the South Vietnamese navy's headquarters; and struck Tan Son Nhut, Saigon's mammoth air base and military complex, the nerve center of the war effort. "The enemy is inside the base!" South Vietnam's Vice President Nguyen Cao Ky, who lived at Tan Son Nhut, screamed into the phone, pleading for reinforcements. "They are less than 500 meters from my house!" The fighting in the capital would ultimately go on for more than a month.[111]

It took six and a half hours for the U.S. military to finally secure the embassy compound. During the battle, guerrillas exchanged shots with U.S. military police, while 101st Airborne Division paratroopers landed on the embassy roof. Journalists also flocked to the scene; an assault on one of the foremost symbols of American power in Vietnam was too big a story to pass up. They were shocked by what they found. The new complex, featured in puff pieces just a few months before, was now a war zone. American troops and armed personnel in civilian attire were running and crouching for cover on the manicured lawn, huddling against ornamental trees and decorative fountains. The bodies of dead U.S. troops lay sprawled in the street out front. Vietnamese corpses littered the compound lawn, there was a gaping hole in the blast wall, and bullet scars were everywhere. And then there was General Westmoreland.

With U.S. troops still blowing up unexploded grenades in the background, the general stood ready for TV cameras in neatly pressed fatigues, four silver stars on each lapel, and his olive green baseball cap on his head. Speaking as if he were at a routine stateside press conference, the bushy-eyebrowed commander castigated the enemy for "very deceitfully" taking advantage of the Tet truce. He said that their efforts were aimed at creating "maximum consternation" and claimed that attacks on Saigon and other cities were just a diversion from the real target: an isolated and long-besieged marine outpost at Khe Sanh, in the desolate northern mountains near the DMZ and the border with Laos. In reality, the exact opposite was the case: the siege of Khe Sanh had been a Vietnamese diversion designed to pin down U.S. troops at a lonely outpost while guerrillas snuck into key cities and towns. Even though guerrillas were still holding significant parts of the capital, Westmoreland sounded as confident as ever as he stood before the cameras. But after months of cheery talk about a weakened enemy and with American vulnerability on display for all the world to see, he appeared bizarrely out of touch, if not utterly delusional. As Don Oberdorfer of the *Washington Post* put it, "The reporters could hardly believe their ears. Westmoreland was standing in the ruins and saying everything was great."[112]

The attack on Saigon, it turned out, was part of a coordinated strategy. Revolutionary forces struck four other major cities, thirty-five of forty-four provincial capitals, sixty-four district seats, and fifty other locations throughout South Vietnam.[113] Hoping to spark a popular uprising, guerrillas and North Vietnamese regulars dug in wherever they could. This left the American forces with two options: fight at close quarters house by house to dislodge small bands of sappers and individual guerrillas or broadly target great swaths of cities and towns as they had long targeted the countryside. The United States chose the latter.

"We had been trying for years to get them to come out in the open so we could slaughter them, and we slaughtered them." That was how John Singlaub, the commander of a clandestine U.S. special operations force known as MACV-SOG, summed up the Tet counteroffensive. "I've never seen so many dead people stacked up."[114] The counteroffensive treated crowded cities as free-fire zones—with devastating results.[115] As the journalist Neil Sheehan observed, "Saving of the soldiers' lives was not the principal reason for the lack of restraint. It was more in the nature of a reflex to turn loose on the urban centers the 'stomp-them-to-death' firepower that had brutalized the Vietnamese countryside."[116]

U.S. troops secured their own embassy floor by floor, but they employed more sweeping methods elsewhere. Bombs, shells, and rockets pounded entire residential neighborhoods, leaving nothing but smoldering rubble.[117] In the streets, everyone was fair game. An American official recorded what happened to one South Vietnamese army veteran whose home caught fire in the fighting: "The veteran, in attempting to drag some of his belongings to safety on Nguyen Van Thoai Street, ran into American soldiers who called on him to stop, in English. The veteran failed to heed the Americans and was shot dead. He lay for three days in the entrance to Lane 177 before sanitation crews took away the body."[118]

In Saigon and its suburbs, around 6,300 civilians died and 11,000 were wounded. Some 19,000 dwellings were destroyed, more than 125,000 people were left homeless, and 206,000 Saigon residents became refugees. According to a U.S. military inspector general's report, most of the damage in the capital was caused by U.S. forces.[119]

Hue, South Vietnam's third-largest city and once the imperial capital of the country, also suffered severely. While Westmoreland had focused most of his pre-Tet attention on Khe Sanh, the revolutionary forces had quietly withdrawn two regiments that had been laying siege to the outpost and sent them over the mountains to join in the attack on Hue. For twenty-five days, they held large portions of the city and carried out one of the most notorious and well-publicized atrocities of the war: preplanned, targeted executions of select officials, military personnel, and others loyal to the Republic of Vietnam.[120] According to a captured document, during this occupation the revolutionary forces "eliminated 1,892 administrative personnel, 38 policemen, 790 tyrants, 6 captains, 2 first lieutenants, 20 2d lieutenants and many noncommissioned officers."[121] In all, 3,000 or more people may have been killed in the massacre.[122]

As U.S. and South Vietnamese forces launched a counterattack to take back the city, another bloodbath commenced. Reporting on the marines as they fought street to street, the CBS television correspondent John Laurence asked Lieutenant Colonel Ernie Cheatham what would happen to innocents trapped between them and the guerrillas. "I'm pretty sure they are civilians that we would consider bad guys right now," Cheatham replied.[123]

Navy ships lobbed 7,670 shells into Hue, and Marine Corps aircraft flew dozens of sorties, dropping napalm and five-hundred-pound bombs on residential neighborhoods. In all, U.S. forces unleashed an astonishing six hundred tons of bombs, plus barrages from artillery and tank cannons, dismantling the city in a chorus of explosions while ground troops fought street to street.[124] "We used everything but nuclear weapons on this town," said one marine.[125] Another admitted, "A great many civilians must have died in the fighting. If you saw or heard—or thought you saw or heard—movement in the house next door, you didn't stop to knock; you just tossed in a grenade."[126]

At least 3,800 of Hue's citizens were killed or reported missing as a result of the bombardment and battle, and 116,000 people were made homeless. More than three-quarters of the city's homes were destroyed or seriously damaged.[127] "Nothing I saw during the Korean War or in the Vietnam War so far has been as terrible, in terms of destruction and despair, as what I saw in Hue," wrote the correspondent Robert Shaplen.[128] Cheatham, the commander of the 2nd Battalion, 5th Marines, put it more simply: "We pretty much destroyed the place, I guess."[129]

The brutality of the Tet counteroffensive became front-page news around the world when the national police chief, General Nguyen Ngoc Loan, strode up to an unarmed, bound prisoner on a Saigon street, leveled his revolver, and put a bullet in the man's brain. The scene was captured by the Associated Press photographer Eddie Adams and by an NBC television camera, and the shockingly close-range killing—the gun just a few inches from the prisoner's temple, a grimace on his face at the moment of impact, blood spurting like a fountain in the video footage as the prisoner crumpled to the ground—became an indelible image of the war.[130] Such summary executions were commonplace. A U.S. Army investigation, for example, looked into allegations that a South Vietnamese major, Nguyen Quang Ngoc, had murdered a prisoner in Nha Trang while U.S. Special Forces officers looked on. The execution, which took place around the same time as Loan's killing of the prisoner in Saigon, was substantiated. What's more, according to War Crimes Working Group documents, an American officer claimed that it was merely the tip of the iceberg. and that Ngoc and an American major, Wilbur Lee, had decided to kill seventeen or eighteen more prisoners to "improve the body count."[131] After Hue was retaken by U.S. and South Vietnamese forces, "black teams" of South Vietnamese assassins moved in, reportedly torturing and "disappearing" those accused of collaborating with the revolutionary forces, including women and children.[132]

In the wake of the Tet counteroffensive, the NLF's Liberation Radio reported, "Many heavily populated areas in Saigon, Cholon, Ben Tre, Can Tho, My Tho and elsewhere have been completely leveled, and thousands of our compatriots, including many women, children, old men and women have been killed or seriously injured."[133] The official South Vietnamese army history largely concurs, reporting that more than 14,000 civilians were killed during the Tet Offensive—most of them by U.S. firepower. Another 24,000 were reportedly wounded and 627,000 made homeless.[134] U.S. military estimates of the civilian dead and wounded are only marginally smaller.[135]

Whenever the war returned to the cities in subsequent months and years, similar carnage followed. District 8 had been a rare bright spot in Saigon, part of a joint U.S.–South Vietnamese "nation-building in action" effort, in which fetid canals and crude shacks were replaced with thousands of new homes, a school, a market, and other public buildings. The neighborhood was intended to serve as the heart of a new capital, and a vision of what a modern Vietnam might be. In the spring of 1968, its residents—perhaps the most pro-American Vietnamese in the capital—reported that guerrillas were infiltrating the area, but the government did nothing.[136] On May 5, revolutionary forces launched a "mini-Tet" assault on Saigon, meaning to demonstrate their resilience and ability to strike anywhere at any time. Their attack was swiftly answered by five days of air strikes by American Phantom jets and helicopter gunships. "U.S. helicopters were killing everything that moved," the Magnum photographer Philip Jones Griffiths later told an interviewer.[137]

Newsweek reporter Kevin Buckley saw the devastation firsthand, later recalling the many bloody sandals that fell from the feet of residents as they fled. "By the time District 8 was 'secure,'" he wrote, "close to 8,000 houses had been destroyed and at least 100 civilians killed. Another 40,000 people, about a quarter of the district's residents, were left homeless."[138] In a secret memo to Vice President Hubert Humphrey, a top-level U.S. adviser also mentioned 2,000 wounded, and confided, "There isn't one building left intact, almost all were totally demolished by American bombs and artillery shells."[139]

John Paul Vann, then the chief of the pacification effort in the provinces surrounding Saigon, similarly wrote, "I estimate 15,000 houses destroyed—about 99 per cent of this has been the result of over-reaction on the part of US and Vietnamese units."[140] In a secret memo for Lyndon Johnson, his special adviser John Roche noted, "The communists are getting us to do in the *South* what we have refrained from doing in the North—'city busting.' Probably more 'innocent civilians' have been hit in Saigon than in Hanoi and Haiphong combined."[141] Outdoing the U.S. attacks on Hanoi and Haiphong was no small feat. The two major urban centers in North Vietnam had been spared full-scale aerial bombardment during Operation Rolling Thunder, which ultimately unleashed 640,000 tons of bombs against the North Vietnamese; nonetheless, they had still been struck by many thousands of bombing sorties during that campaign.[142]

President Lyndon Johnson halted Rolling Thunder in October 1968, but it would prove to be only a temporary respite. In spring 1972, responding to the "Easter Offensive" launched by North Vietnamese forces, President Richard Nixon ordered the start of a new aerial campaign. That April alone, North Vietnam would be slammed by seven hundred B-52 raids, including a forty-eight-hour sustained air assault on Hanoi and Haiphong.[143] The following month would bring the start of Operation Linebacker I, which escalated the bombing even further.

The massive U.S. bombing campaigns that followed the Easter Offensive were not, however, confined to north of the demilitarized zone. Forty specially designed B-52 bombers, each carrying almost thirty tons of ordnance, unloaded on Quang Tri on a daily basis, destroying up to 99 percent of all buildings in the southeastern quadrant of the province. The provincial capital, Quang Tri City, was all but obliterated by the relentless assault.[144] "Not one structure in Quang Tri [City] escaped major damage," wrote the *Los Angeles Times* reporter Jacques Leslie. "Rooms are collapsed like accordions. Odd-shaped plaster slabs that once were walls point into the air, surrounded by rubble. Here a staircase leads up to nowhere. There a house's metal frame, shed of its cement coating, holds up roofing that is still intact."[145] The few buildings in the area that were not totally pulverized—such as the Bo De School and Nha Tho Long Hung Catholic Church—survived only as bombed-out shells.[146] Another reporter on the scene described Quang Tri's capital as "no longer a city but a lake of masonry."[147] Other areas of the province suffered a similar fate, with air strikes and artillery fire wiping out homes and killing thousands of civilians.[148]

From the start of the American War to its final years, from the countryside to the cities, Americans relentlessly pounded South Vietnam with nearly every lethal technology in their arsenal short of nuclear weapons, indiscriminately spreading death across vast swaths of territory. Such supercharged killing—so often carried out from the relative safety of a jet flying thousands of feet above the ground, a helicopter gunship hovering over thatch-roofed huts, an artillery battery miles from the target zone, a ship lobbing shells from offshore—undoubtedly saved the lives of some American soldiers. But the logic of overkill exacted an immense, almost unimaginable toll on Vietnamese civilians. U.S. commanders wasted ammunition like millionaires, hoarded American lives like misers—and often treated Vietnamese lives as if they were worth nothing at all.

4

A LITANY OF ATROCITIES

In the mid-1960s, when the first American troops arrived, the densely populated coastal plains of Quang Nam and Quang Ngai provinces were renowned for their rich rice lands. The rustic landscape featured meandering rivers and streams, thick stands of bamboo, and white sand beaches on the shore of the South China Sea. But in short order, the Americans turned this peaceful countryside into a land of endless carnage. A whole village could be completely wiped off the map in minutes by a single aircraft sortie or in a few hours by ground troops on a search-and-destroy mission. Few reporters were around to witness the annihilation, so what went on in Vietnam's killing fields often stayed there. Tiny hamlets whose own inhabitants sometimes used just a numeric designation to differentiate them from their neighbors were battered in obscurity, their suffering largely unnoticed by the outside world. Still, the sheer volume of death and destruction has meant that some traces of the near-constant civilian suffering have made it into the historical record.

Even these scattered pieces of evidence are overwhelming in their totality; no one could bear to read a full listing of every village burning, hamlet bombing, cold-blooded massacre, and other atrocities that have managed to bubble up in press accounts, military documents, and personal testimonies. Think of what follows, instead, as simply a series of snapshots culled from a vast album of horrors. Selected more or less at random from incidents that took place in Quang Nam and Quang Ngai from the arrival of the American combat troops in 1965 through the Tet counteroffensive in early 1968, these accounts—just a fraction of the surviving reports I've managed to assemble from those two provinces—offer a window onto the day-to-day reality of the Vietnam War.

Quang Nam and Quang Ngai had a particularly long revolutionary history and a strong NLF presence. But a similar record could be compiled for any populous province heavily targeted by Americans during any year of the conflict. In Binh Dinh Province, south of Quang Ngai along the coast; in Hau Nghia Province, on the Cambodia border to the west of Saigon; in the verdant Mekong Delta—the story was much the same. I've chosen this particular format and these few incidents only to demonstrate that year after year, in attacks carried out by unit after unit, the atrocities were of the same type, the horrors of a similar magnitude, the miseries of the same degree.

In Quang Nam, the civilian population was unmistakably the focus of the American effort from the time that the marines landed in the city of Da Nang in March 1965. Lieutenant General Victor Krulak, commander of the Fleet Marine Force, Pacific, summarized the military's mind-set: "The real war is among the people and not among these mountains . . . If we can destroy the guerrilla fabric among the people, we will automatically deny the larger [enemy] units the food and the intelligence and the taxes, and the other support they need."[1] In practice, that meant: the fabric of rural life in Quang Nam would be torn to shreds.

To be sure, the marines performed outreach activities for the civilian population: offering vaccinations and medicines, building cribs for orphanages, handing out some school supplies, food, and clothing.

But such efforts paled in comparison with the brutal war that they brought to Quang Nam's villages, especially to the three-hundred-square-mile coastal strip running southward from Da Nang to the Nui Loc Son Basin, home to about 1 million people.[2] In the first three months of 1967, for example, the 1st Marine Division carried out close to 37,000 significant operations, patrols, and ambushes just in the region surrounding Da Nang.[3] By September 1969, the division would have 24,000 troops in the province, operating in conjunction with four South Korean battalions, seven South Vietnamese battalions, and forty platoons of local militia, most of which were assisted by U.S. Marines as part of the Combined Action Platoon program.[4] The fighting was intense: U.S. forces suffered more deaths in Quang Nam—8,084 troops killed—than in any of the South's other forty-three provinces.[5]

Philip Caputo, who would later write a best-selling memoir about his Vietnam experience, arrived in Quang Nam in March 1965 as a young marine officer.[6] The following month, a nineteen-year-old corporal in Caputo's battalion gunned down an unarmed Vietnamese man who ran from an American patrol near the village of Hoi Vuc. "I felt kind of sorry for him," said the marine as he stood over the corpse. "And he didn't even have a weapon."[7] Possibly as a result of this killing, or another in which a member of the battalion shot a farmer, Caputo received new instructions from higher headquarters: unarmed Vietnamese were not to be fired on, unless they were running. Running, however, was precisely what had led to the killing of the unarmed man near Hoi Vuc in the first place. Treating every running Vietnamese as a legitimate target was little short of an invitation to gun down any terrified peasant who panicked and fled in the face of heavily armed American troops. Momentarily bewildered, Caputo had the rules of engagement cleared up for him by a commander, who explained, "I talked to battalion and they said that as far as they're concerned, if he's dead and Vietnamese, he's VC."[8]

Moving east of Hoi Vuc, Caputo's troops passed through a series of hamlets. Outside one of them, known as Giao Tri (3), the marines walked into an ambush. A superficial hand wound was the worst injury suffered, but the hamlet paid a heavy price. Once the firefight had ended, enraged marines rushed in, firing wildly, shooting animals, grenading bunkers, and setting homes aflame. "Women are screaming, children are crying," Caputo recalled. "Panic-stricken, the villagers run out of the flame and smoke as if from a natural disaster." The marines destroyed the hamlet completely, leaving behind only ash, embers, and skeletal house frames.[9]

The heavy suffering of civilians in Giao Tri (3) was typical of the conflict. On March 17, 1965, for example, South Vietnamese Skyraiders—likely piloted by American airmen—attacked the village of Hoa Thuan, which had dared to fly the NLF flag. The raid left an estimated forty-five civilians dead, most of them children, who were killed when a bomb struck their school.[10]

On July 12, 1965, marines entered the village of Cam Ne (4) and met stiff resistance, suffering three dead and four wounded. The next month, the Americans had their revenge.[11] With the CBS correspondent Morley Safer and a cameraman in tow, the troops set out for the area in armored vehicles. "They told us if you receive one round from the village, you level it," recalled marine Reginald Edwards.[12] Safer heard much the same.

> I talked to a captain, trying to get some idea what the operation was about. And he said, "We've had orders to take out this complex of villages called Cam Ne." I'd never heard anything like that. I'd heard of search-and-destroy operations; I'd seen places ravaged by artillery or by air strikes. But this was just a ground strike going in. He said to "take out" this complex of villages. And I thought perhaps he's exaggerating . . .
> The troops walked abreast toward this village and started firing. They said that there was some incoming fire. I didn't witness it, but

it was a fairly large front, so it could have happened down the line. There were two guys wounded in our group, both in the ass, so that meant it was "friendly fire."

They moved into the village and they systematically began torching every house—every house as far as I could see, getting people out in some cases, using flame throwers in others. No Vietnamese speakers, by the way, were among the group with the flame thrower.[13]

About 150 homes in Cam Ne were burned; others were bulldozed, as marines razed two entire hamlets. Artillery was then called in on the wreckage. According to reports, one child was killed and four women were wounded.[14] In actuality, many more may have died. Edwards recalled being ordered to fire on a fleeing man and missing, only to see another marine kill the man with a grenade as he was dashing through a doorway. "But what happened," Edwards said, "was it was a room full of children. Like a schoolroom. And he was runnin' back to warn the kids that the Marines were coming. And that's who got hurt. All those little kids and people."[15] Months later, Safer learned that Cam Ne had been targeted for destruction because the government's province chief wanted to punish the village for delinquent taxes.[16]

While Cam Ne was struck first by ground troops and then by artillery, many other areas in the province were attacked in the opposite order. On August 2, 1965, for example, U.S. artillery blasted the "Vietcong-dominated" village of Chan Son with 1,000 shells. Afterward, marines advanced through the village, one of them bellowing, "Kill them. I don't want anyone moving." They found a woman lying dead with a wound in her side, while a baby next to her wailed in pain from an injured arm. Hearing enemy shots ring out, one marine threw a grenade into a bunker, ending the lives of two children. In all, twenty-five Vietnamese were killed in Chan Son that day, according to U.S. sources; NLF reports put the total at more than one hundred civilians. Acting on orders from higher command, the marines also burned all the homes in the village that they believed had been used by snipers.[17]

By the end of 1965, a U.S. adviser noted that Quang Nam's main hospital was in need of supplies "to cope with increasing numbers of wounded."[18] And the new year only brought more of the same misery. On January 13, 1966, for instance, marine jets attacked four small boats packed with civilians some twenty miles southwest of Da Nang, killing and wounding a total of twenty-five people.[19] That same month, after U.S. forces fought a small battle with guerrillas around the hamlet of Phu My, the area was plastered with heavy firepower; the shelling collapsed a particularly large and well-built bomb shelter where many villagers had congregated, killing twenty-seven civilians at once.[20] Over the course of the war, locals told me, at least one hundred people in Phu My would die from shelling alone, while others were killed by bombs or ground troops.[21]

In March 1966, after marines received heavy small-arms fire from the hamlets of Phu Tay (2) and Phu Tay (3), eight five-hundred-pound incendiary bombs sent the hamlets up in flames.[22] Around the same time, marines also entered the village of An Trach, west of Da Nang. There, Corporal Kenneth Ransbottom—one of the longest-serving field marines of the entire war—led a fire team tasked with clearing locals from the area. Marines shouted at civilians, rousting them from their homes, after which the military engineers systematically destroyed their bomb shelters. Moving through the village, Ransbottom came across a large bunker with a group of people, mostly women and children, huddling inside while others clustered at its entrance. "We could get a few of them to move who were scared, but others were so scared they wouldn't move," he later recalled.

Ransbottom's superiors and the advancing engineers were pushing him hard to clear out the villagers, and he, in turn, took out his frustrations on the sobbing civilians. He remembered a lot of screaming: "The babies were just going nuts. The women, the old men, some were down on their knees like they were praying to Buddha." Then an old man approached. Ransbottom spoke to him in pidgin Vietnamese, which was more than likely gibberish. When the man said that he didn't understand, Ransbottom knocked him to the ground. As the elderly villager struggled to get up, he grasped at Ransbottom's leg. "I took my right leg and I drove my boot . . . into his exposed left side and I caught him midway up his rib cage," the marine recalled. A spray of blood erupted from the man's nose and mouth, to which Ransbottom replied with another kick. "But this time, I buried my foot as far into his chest as it would go. He collapsed. I assume he was dead." Ransbottom took the body and shoved it into the shelter, telling the engineers, "Blow it. I'm tired of this shit." They did. Afterward, Ransbottom peered inside. In his words, "It looked like a huge beef potpie."[23]

Again and again, American operations in the Quang Nam countryside would spell doom for the local inhabitants. When Americans first arrived in the hamlet of My Luoc, for example, they ordered everyone to leave and then set the houses ablaze. Unwilling to abandon their land, the residents constructed some small huts; these, in turn, were burned whenever American patrols passed through, until the villagers gave up and took to living in their underground bunkers. My Luoc was also bombed every three or four days and repeatedly hit with napalm. The peasants took to farming at night to avoid the attacks, but still they remained in their hamlet.

One market day in May 1966, local children ran through My Luoc, shouting out a warning: Americans were in the area—they had captured a guerrilla, but he had escaped. Not long after, U.S. troops came charging into the market. "They just said 'VC, VC,'" recalled Le Thi Chung. Pham Thi Cuc, whose house was steps away, remembered it too. "They opened fire on the local civilians. They were only older women and children," she said. Frightened, Chung fled and hid in some nearby bushes. She couldn't see what was unfolding, but she heard gunshots, explosions, and bursts of automatic fire.

With the Americans on a rampage, a number of villagers raced for Cuc's bomb shelter, the best-built in the area. Le Thi Xuan headed there with her two sons in tow and took cover. Cuc, carrying two children, also dashed for her own shelter, but a bullet struck her leg, another one grazed her head, and she fell by the entrance. An American approached her. "I thought he was reaching for a bandage for my wound," she recalled. "But he threw a grenade into the bunker." The blast killed Xuan's older son and wounded her five-year-old boy.[24]

All the young men in the village had fled before the Americans arrived. When Le Thuan, one of the local guerrillas, returned, he found his home burned and his five-year-old daughter dying of a gunshot wound.[25] Chung emerged from her hiding spot after the Americans were gone and saw her friends and neighbors scattered around the market, some injured, others dead. "A total of sixteen people were killed," she recalled. "One family lost five people." And that wasn't the end of it for My Luoc. A monument erected in the village also memorializes two later mass killings by U.S. and South Vietnamese troops, which took the lives of another seventeen residents.[26]

In June 1966, just a few weeks after the market day massacre in My Luoc, an elderly man named Tran Lanh was walking to the refugee camp at Ai My when marines shot and killed him along with several other civilians. The next day, Lanh's son Tran Cau, a high school student, received permission from the local district chief to travel along with three men to retrieve his father's body. On the instructions of the official, who had cleared the plan with a local U.S. Marine commander, the men wore white clothes, carried a white flag with a red cross, and brought a letter of introduction written in English. Nevertheless, marines seized and blindfolded the four Vietnamese, tore up their letter and the flag, and marched them a long distance away. Eventually, the Americans removed their blindfolds and told them to go. When the Vietnamese had walked about 130 feet, however, the marines opened fire on them, killing Cau and one of his companions and wounding another.[27]

Around that same time, Philip Caputo's marines found themselves near the hamlet of Giao Tri (2), not far from Giao Tri (3), the hamlet that they had destroyed earlier. His platoon had suffered heavy losses from mines and booby traps, and Caputo sent his men on a revenge patrol into the village, ostensibly to capture two suspected guerrillas who had been sighted there. "If they give you any problems, kill 'em," he told his men. Caputo didn't have the authority to order such a mission, but he said, "Don't sweat that. All the higher-ups want is bodies." "I knew he was going to kill those men on the slightest pretext," Caputo later wrote of the patrol's leader. The patrol entered the hamlet and quickly went to work, beating a woman and killing two unarmed young men—who turned out to be innocent civilians. Caputo was court-martialed for murder, but the charges against him were eventually dropped, and he received only a letter of reprimand.[28]

Revenge missions were not an uncommon occurrence. On August 27, 1966, a marine platoon commander went looking for volunteers for a four-man "hunter-killer" team that was officially tasked with killing armed VC—or, according to court-martial documents, "anyone found outside at night." Lance Corporal Frank Schultz, however, saw the assignment as a means to avenge fellow marines killed in combat. He eagerly put himself forward, saying that he "knew the area and could get a VC." After the team set an ambush near Khai Dong hamlet in the early morning hours, Schultz, according to a fellow marine, announced that he would bust into one of the nearby hootches, grab a "gook," and kill him. Schultz later testified that he saw a light flickering in a home.

I wanted to get to that house. I had to kill a VC for those guys, I just had to kill one . . . I went to the house and there was a man in there . . . I pulled him out in front of the house and he was pulling out his ID card and was showing it to me but this didn't matter to me because I had seen many VC before that I'd killed with ID cards on them identical to that. I ... shoved him down the trail ... I brought my rifle to my shoulder and shot him.

There is no evidence that the man killed by Schultz, virtually at random, was even a sympathizer of the NLF, let alone a guerrilla.[29]

Vietnamese sources estimated that by August 1966, the marines in Quang Nam had killed more than 4,600 civilians and wounded more than 5,200, the overwhelming majority of them women and children.[30] The situation had spun so far out of control that a few months later, Lieutenant General Lewis Walt, the commander of III Marine Amphibious Force, sent a secret communiqué to two top generals, noting, "I am greatly disturbed, as I am sure you are, by the number of serious incidents involving allegations of felonies by Marines against Vietnamese civilians."[31] But despite Walt's concern the carnage continued.

———

The next year only brought more death and destruction to Quang Nam. On January 31, 1967, marines received fire near the hamlet of Thuy Bo. Captain Edward Banks, the senior company commander, called in air and artillery strikes in response, and the following day assaulted the hamlet, only to find that the revolutionary forces had already withdrawn. "During the next two days," according to a Marine Corps history, "local Vietnamese peasants brought in 22 dead and 18 wounded villagers," victims of the American air strikes, artillery, and small-arms fire. After an investigation, the Marine Corps deemed the civilian casualties in the hamlet to be "a regrettable corollary" to the battle. The marines also claimed an enemy body count of 101 at a cost of just six American lives—a remarkably high ratio, which suggests that some of those officially recorded as "enemy" dead may have been unarmed civilians.[32] Banks later admitted: "You never knew who was the enemy and who was a friend ... Some of them were Viet Cong ... They all looked alike."[33]

Jack Hill, one of the marines under Banks's command, remembered being pinned outside the village for many hours under intense enemy fire. When resistance faded, Hill said, "We was the first team in, we unloaded several rounds. We dropped a couple of grenades in the hootches to get the people out . . . I mean we didn't speak perfect Vietnamese so in order to get them out of there you either cranked off a couple of rounds or you dropped your M-26 grenade down there and they get the message and they come on out of there."[34]

Le Thi Ton, a resident of Thuy Bo, remembered the events this way.

When [the Americans] came to my house, there were ten family members inside, including my 14-year-old son. Four or five soldiers came right over . . . They just turned around and threw a grenade into the house. Nine or ten people were blown to pieces. I was the only one who . . . survived. My son and everyone else just fell dead. I was wounded and extremely frightened and crawled quickly into a corner of the house. Although the grenade had already exploded, the soldiers fired their guns at the people to make sure that nobody would survive.

Another villager, Nguyen Bay, recalled: "They came and asked us about the Vietcong. There were only women and children around then and we didn't know where the VC were. But they shot at us anyway." According to Thuong Thi Mai, "After they killed the people, they burned down all the houses . . . Even dead children were burned."[35] In all, survivor Nguyen Huu recalled, more than 140 people were killed in the hamlet.[36]

Looking back, Hill explained to an interviewer: "You got an angry 18-year-old kid behind the gun and he's just seen his buddy gettin' killed. And he's not gonna have no remorse for who's on the receiving end of that 60 caliber machine gun." Hill didn't dispute the Vietnamese version of events, pointing out that there "wasn't nothing unusual about burning them hootches down and digging them Vietnamese people out of them holes and scattering animals, pigs and chickens around." "I didn't shoot any old ladies and kids," he continued. "I know half the guys in my squad didn't shoot no old ladies and kids." When it came to the other half, he offered only this: "I can't account for how they acted."[37]

Not all the violence against civilians in Quang Nam happened in the anger-laden, adrenaline-fueled aftermath of a firefight, though. When W. D. Ehrhart began his tour in early 1967, he was struck by the sight of his fellow marines wantonly abusing civilian detainees at the marines' compound. Most of these detainees were elderly men and women or young women with children. They had been bound, hand and foot, with wire and brought in on top of armored vehicles that stood some eight feet off the ground. As Ehrhart recalled, "The Marines . . . began pitching and kicking people over the sides onto the sand in a quick succession of thuds, groans, sharp screams, snapping of breaking bones, and soft crying."[38]

Not long afterward, Ehrhart went into the field for the first time on a "County Fair" mission—an operation in which a village was cordoned off and searched in tandem with some type of marine-run "civic action" event, such as a meal or a musical performance. The idea was to find draft dodgers and NLF sympathizers while winning hearts and minds. But the marines whom Ehrhart saw indulged instead in what, by then, were typical tactics: forcing civilians from their houses, confiscating their rice, killing their animals, grenading bomb shelters, and destroying houses. "You goddamn gook motherfucker!" Ehrhart remembered one marine bellowing as he kicked an old man in the ribs. He saw another torture an elderly civilian during a field interrogation.[39]

Ehrhart himself was hardly guilt-free. "Over a relatively short period of time, you begin to treat all of the Vietnamese as though they are the enemy. If you can't tell, you shoot first, ask questions later," he told an interviewer.[40] On one occasion, he saw a figure in "black pajamas" running along a paddy dike, muttered "Dung Lai" (halt), and fired off a kill shot. The victim turned out to be a fifty- to sixty-year-old unarmed woman, who was called in as a dead VC. And American artillery, of course, did not discriminate by gender either. On a later patrol through a small hamlet decimated by U.S. shelling, Ehrhart recalled, "there was no one around but a middle-aged woman sitting amid the rubble in a dark pool of coagulated blood. She was holding a small child who had only one leg and half a head, and she had a tremendous gaping chest wound that had ripped open both of her breasts."[41]

Marine John Merson, who served in Quang Nam around the same time, had similar memories. One night in April 1967, his unit sprang an ambush on sampans traveling on a river in Dai Loc District, killing about twenty civilians—all of whom turned out to be women, children, and old men.[42] That same month, a U.S. patrol happened upon twenty-four fishermen, mostly old men, from Ha My hamlet as they were preparing to head out to sea in the early morning hours. The Americans herded them together and opened fire, killing all but one. Nguyen Hieu, a local resident, saw the scene just afterward—heads and chests ripped open by the bullets, bodies torn apart. His fifty-one-year-old father was among the victims. "It was so terrible," he told me decades later. "There were men lying all around."[43]

Marine Ed Austin recorded the results of another April 1967 operation in Quang Nam in his diary. "We got one VC with a weapon at 7:00. At 7:30 we went through a ville. The guys killed two men— murdered them—and two water buffalo calves, all just for kicks. They also made a girl undress and stood there laughing at her standing there nude." A week later he wrote, in a letter to his parents: "There are more civilians killed here per day than VC either by accident or on purpose and that's just plain murder. I'm not surprised that there are more VC. We make more VC than we kill by the way these people are treated. I won't go into detail but some of the things that take place would make you ashamed of good old America."[44]

"Just plain murder" is an apt description of what went on throughout the province. The little cluster of homes known as Que Chau (4), for instance, suffered trauma after trauma throughout the conflict. One day in April 1967, Le Thi Dang told me, U.S. troops killed three elderly women in a bunker. That same day, her father, too old and frail to run for shelter, was shot inside his house, which was then set on fire.[45]

On June 4, 1967, American troops entered the hamlet of Phu Nhuan (2), whose inhabitants had already been repeatedly shelled and harassed by U.S. patrols—the soldiers sometimes forcing the civilians to stand around them as human shields, or to walk ahead of them on trails in case the paths were booby-trapped.[46] This time, Nguyen Hoc, a farmer in his forties, fled to a neighboring subhamlet when the Americans arrived, but his mother was among the women, children, and few men who stayed behind. When Hoc returned, he found scores of people killed, houses and bodies burned, and animal carcasses scattered everywhere. His mother was dead; she had been roped to an armored vehicle and dragged around the hamlet.[47]

Thai Thi Ly, another farmer in Phu Nhuan (2), was working in the fields when the Americans came. She rushed to her mother-in-law's home to find her daughter, and then hid as the Americans opened fire on villagers in their homes. Ly survived, but a shrapnel wound to the head robbed her of sight in one eye.[48] In all, fifty-two villagers were killed and thirteen wounded. Most of the dead were children, elderly men, and women, including an expectant mother, the cousin of the guerrilla Ho Ngoc Phung.[49] "When I came home," he told me years later, "I found them. Her belly had been split open and you could see the baby."[50] A few days after the massacre, American troops returned and opened fire on a group of survivors, killing four or five more women and children and wounding fourteen others.[51]

The following month, U.S. troops arrived in Phi Phu, an NLF-governed hamlet where farming families had grown vegetables and raised silkworms before American bombing and shelling and home burnings threw life into chaos. An NLF document mentions an "extremely savage massacre of women and children" in which thirty-two villagers were killed.[52] About forty years later, I spoke with three village elders in Phi Phu: Truong Thi Hong, a sleepy-eyed woman; her husband, Tran Ba, an intense seventy-six-year-old who had served as a local guerrilla; and tiny, wizened Tran Thi Nhut, who had worked as a liaison for the NLF during the war. They described how the Americans had forced about twenty non-combatants into a trench that the guerrillas had dug. The soldiers opened fire and then blew up the trench, burying the bodies. Elsewhere in the hamlet, others were killed in smaller groups.

Nhut and Ba were hiding in bunkers during the massacre and escaped the slaughter. When Nhut emerged, she found her seventy-year-old mother and twelve-year-old son dead and her home burned. Hong, who had been outside the village during the killing, returned to find that her house, too, had been burned to the ground. Inside it were the corpses of three old men who had been shot.[53]

After telling me their stories, the village elders led me through a quiet garden to a secluded area that was neither cultivated nor manicured, but lushly verdant and dotted with small palms. Tucked away there stood a tiny, unassuming gray stone monument with red script, offering a spare account of the massacre.[54] Later, another villager brought me a list of the names of the dead: Ngo Thi Sau, Cao Muoi, Cao Thi Thong, Tran Cong Chau Em, Nguyen Thi Nhi, Cao Thi Tu, Le Thi Chuyen, Dang Thi Doi, Ngo Thi Chiec, Tran Thi Song, Nguyen Thi Mot, Nguyen Thi Hai, Nguyen Thi Ba, Nguyen Thi Bon, Ho Thi Tho, Vo Thi Hoan, Pham Thi Sau, Dinh Van Xuan, Dinh Van Ba, Tran Cong Viet, Nguyen Thi Nham, Ngo Quang Duong, Duong Thi Hien, Pham Thi Kha, Huynh Van Binh, Huynh Thi Bay, Huynh Thi Ty, Le Van Van, Le Thi Trinh, Le Thi Duong, and Le Vo Danh and her unborn child.[55]

Along with such mass killings, American troops in Quang Nam were also carrying out a continuous string of atrocities against individual Vietnamese who were unlucky enough to fall into their hands. In October 1967, for example, following a firefight in the countryside, members of Company B, 1st Battalion, 35th Infantry, stumbled upon an unarmed young boy. "Somebody caught him up on a hill and they brought him down and the Lieutenant asked who wanted to kill him, who wanted to shoot him," medic Jamie Henry later told army investigators. A radioman and another medic volunteered for the job. The radioman, Henry said, "kicked the boy in the stomach and the medic took him around behind a rock and I heard one magazine go off complete on automatic." The child was called in as an enemy KIA.

A few days after this incident, members of that same unit brutalized an elderly man to the point of collapse and then threw him off a cliff without even knowing whether he was dead or alive. A couple days after that, they used an unarmed man for target practice. In a sworn statement to army criminal investigators, unit member Andrew Akers said: "Frank [Pollard] put his weapon to his side like John Wayne and let it go at the man. [John] Perry was also firing his .45 caliber weapon at the man." Jamie Henry also saw the man, telling army investigators, "He had been shot quite a few times and as I walked through they were shooting him with a .45 caliber pistol." And less than two weeks later, members of Company B reportedly killed five unarmed women, whom Lieutenant Glenn Eisenhour reported to higher command as five enemy kills.[56] Questioned later by army investigators, unit members rattled off a litany of other brutal acts committed by the company: an unarmed woman in her sixties executed on an officer's orders; an unarmed elderly man killed in cold blood; a living woman who had an ear cut off while her baby was thrown to the ground and stomped on; a man purposely crushed to death by an armored vehicle; bunkers grenaded with civilians inside.[57]

One of their sister units, Company A, was in the meantime cutting its own brutal path through the province. Around November 10, medic Nolan Jones witnessed four or five members of Alpha Company sexually assault a Vietnamese girl.[58] It was only one of many atrocities he would see committed by the unit, ranging from assault to rape to murder. "I saw guys just shoot people for nothing. They'd see an old person walking down the trail and shoot," he later said.[59] His fellow troops, he explained, "abused the people, shot people, they burned their villages up, threw their food away, shot up their animals, and I mean this happened regularly, this didn't happen just one or two times."[60]

The marines continued their efforts, too. Even the official command chronology of the 1st Battalion, 5th Marines, indicates the heavy toll on civilians. On November 12, for example, a member of Company C "accidentally" fired an M-79 round that wounded a young girl. On the twenty-first, a patrol from D Company gunned down an apparently unarmed woman because she ran from them. On the twenty-seventh, in response to twenty to thirty rounds of small-arms fire, members of Company C called in an artillery mission that killed four civilians but no guerrillas. On the thirtieth, a "60mm mortar H&I round" fired by members of Company C left three civilians dead and seven wounded.[61] And so it went.

As the killings spread through the province, the number of people forced from their homes rose. "American soldiers burned down everything I had," explained a seventy-five-year-old man at Cam Chau refugee camp, just outside the town of Hoi An, in 1967. "My house, my haystack, my garden, 46 coconut trees, I miss my home very much, especially because I'm a farmer and there's no land to farm around here."[62] By the fall of 1967, Quang Nam had more than 100,000 people crammed into government camps, plus several thousand in camps in the city of Da Nang, and about 80,000 in slums, shantytowns, and other informal settlements.[63] Less than a year later, the official numbers topped 238,000, the most of any province in South Vietnam.[64]

Early 1968 brought the Tet Offensive and the allied response, which quickly turned into an orgy of massacres. On February 7, 1968, with Da Nang and Hoi An still under pressure from Vietnamese revolutionary forces, General Westmoreland flew to Quang Nam for a "head knocking" session with top army and Marine Corps commanders in the area. He was forceful. "Get troops between the enemy and Da Nang Air Base . . . get at it; we've got to take some risks," he barked.[65] That same day, Company B of the 1st Battalion, 35th Infantry—the unit that had thrown an old man off a cliff the previous fall—fought a difficult battle out in the countryside beyond Hoi An, losing five men.

The next morning, the men of Company B headed for a small, nameless hamlet with a new mission. "The order of the day," infantryman Gregory Newman told army investigators, "was to search and destroy and kill anything in the village that moved."[66] Unit member Alexander Freeman recalled similar instructions: "We were told that we were going on a search and destroy mission," and that the commanding officer "did not want to see anything walking when he came through."[67] Jose Victor Davila-Falu later told army investigators that the unit had received orders from higher headquarters to "kill everything that breathed."[68]

"When we went into the village, there were no enemy there, just villagers," unit member Robert Miller told me years later. "We went in to fight, but there was no enemy there."[69] While some in the unit busied themselves killing livestock, others singled out a teenage girl and dragged her into a home. Miller saw the girl naked inside the hootch with a gun to her head, and Staff Sergeant Wilson Bullock remembered her screams.

A short distance away, the medic Jamie Henry sat down to rest in a Vietnamese home, where he was joined by a radioman. On the radio, he heard 3rd Platoon leader Lieutenant Johnny Mack Carter report to Captain Donald Reh that he had rounded up nineteen civilians. Carter wanted to know what should be done with them. As Henry later told an army investigator: "The Captain asked him if he remembered the Op Order [Operation Order] that had come down from higher that morning which was to kill anything that moves. The Captain repeated the order. He said that higher said to kill anything that moves."

Hoping to intervene, Henry headed for Reh's position. As he neared it, though, Henry saw members of the unit drag the naked teenager out of the house and throw her into the throng of civilians, who were squatting together in a group.[70] Then, he said, four or five men around the civilians "opened fire and shot them. There was a lot of flesh and blood going around because the velocity of an M-16 at that close range does a lot of damage."[71] It was all just another day in the life for Company B, albeit a particularly gory one. By the end of his tour, Henry said he knew of "at least 50 civilians executed by our company and with as little provocation as on [the day of that massacre], not in the heat of battle or from air or artillery strikes—deliberate murder."[72]

The actions of Company B were hardly an anomaly. Heonik Kwon, an expert on war crimes in the region, notes that "at least six large-scale killings" by allied forces took place there during the first three months of 1968. In fact, his research shows that during this period, district communist cells reported nineteen separate mass killings in Quang Nam to the provincial authority.[73]

One of these occurred just four days after the Company B massacre, when South Korean troops received isolated sniper fire near the hamlet of Phong Nhut (2). In response, they launched a ground assault on the nearby village of Phong Nhi, many of whose residents had relatives in the South Vietnamese forces. When U.S. Marines and South Vietnamese troops followed on the heels of the Koreans, they walked into a horror show. One marine took photos of the aftermath: clumps of corpses, burned houses, a woman—still alive—whose left breast had been hacked off, a ditch filled with the bodies of women and children. "Those villagers," he recalled, "were all shot at close range or stabbed with bayonets."[74]

Tran Thi Duoc, a sixteen-year-old who survived the massacre, recounted how the Koreans had gathered the villagers and then gunned them down en masse. "I was too scared at the shooting site," she said, "and tried to stay still like I was dead. But one Korean soldier saw me, and I joined my two hands in front of my breast, knelt before him and begged for my life, but he shot at me." The shot blew off several fingers on Duoc's hands, and she lost consciousness. When she awoke, she found that her two brothers and both of her parents had been killed, and her three-month-old sister had been stabbed with a knife or bayonet. In all, about eighty civilians perished in the bloodbath and another fifteen were wounded.[75]

One U.S. Marine stationed near Phong Nhi wrote, "Even *we* felt it was above & beyond acceptable bounds."[76] But given the brutality exhibited by Americans throughout Quang Nam, what the Koreans had done was barely out of the ordinary. And, in any case, the actions of the Koreans were hardly separable from those of the U.S. forces, since South Korean troops essentially functioned as American mercenaries. In its quest to "internationalize" the war, the Johnson administration provided funds to modernize the Korean military, helped cover expenses such as training, equipment, and the transport costs for bringing the Korean contingent to Vietnam, and paid a significant part of their salaries while they served there.[77]

On February 25, 1968, Korean troops entered Ha My—the hamlet where an American patrol had killed twenty-three fishermen the previous year—and herded residents into several locations. Some villagers were expecting food and candies to be handed out, but what came next was a slaughter that went on for two hours, leaving 135 people dead—almost all of them women, teenage girls, elderly men, toddlers, and infants. Only three of those slain were military-aged men. Later in the day, bulldozers arrived to scrape the entire area flat.[78]

————

Two provinces southward, in Quang Ngai, Americans were carrying out a similarly bloody campaign. They regarded most of the province as hostile, and hostile was how they acted in return. But "friendly" enclaves weren't necessarily spared.[79] In July 1965, for example, after the revolutionary forces overran a government outpost in the majority Catholic village of Ba Gia, U.S. and South Vietnamese commanders decided, in the words of one U.S. officer, to "unload on the whole area." Ba Gia was blasted by bombs, rockets, and cannon fire for three straight days. By the time U.S. and South Vietnamese ground troops entered the village—now a nightmare landscape of shattered stucco and torn-apart bamboo homes—the guerrillas had long since withdrawn. A reporter watched as four local residents carrying a pallet with a wounded man "stared hatefully at American advisors accompanying the Vietnamese marines." When asked about the number of innocents killed, the villagers bitterly replied: "many." Afterward, a U.S. officer prophetically remarked, "There will be many more civilians killed that way as time goes on."[80]

The following month, U.S. Marines conducted a search-and-destroy operation in and around heavily populated villages on the Van Tuong Peninsula, which resulted in 688 enemy troops reportedly killed but only 109 weapons captured.[81] During the mission, the entire village of Van Tuong (4) was obliterated, and numerous civilians were wounded. Indeed, according to a battalion commander, multiple villages "were severely damaged or destroyed by napalm or naval gunfire," even though "the military necessity of doing so was dubious."[82] Another officer, though, saw no problem with the way that the operation had been carried out. In his after-action report, he recommended that in the future "all hostile villages . . . Should be

Prep'ed [with heavy ordnance] regardless of civilian casualties prior to jumping off."[83]

Just as in Quang Nam, the devastating artillery attacks and aerial bombings pounding Quang Ngai took place alongside incidents of breathtaking brutality from American ground troops. One such horrifying event was vividly reconstructed from military records a few years later by Normand Poirier, a reporter for *Esquire*. A detailed magazine write-up of an atrocity case of this kind was unusual during the war, but the suffering chronicled in the article was all too typical.

On September 23, 1966, Poirier related, a unit of marines descended on Xuan Ngoc hamlet and began their rampage by breaking into the house of sixty-one-year-old Nguyen Luu, a rice farmer and carpenter. They punched, kicked, and slashed the unarmed man, while a marine yelled "veee-ceee" at him. The intruders tore up his civilian ID card and wrecked his home. As Luu's young nieces screamed in terror, his nearly seventy-year-old wife was manhandled and his sister mercilessly kicked.

Soon after, the door to Nguyen Truc's home burst open. His wife bolted for their five children, but the marines grabbed her and shoved her out the door. The thirty-eight-year-old rice farmer was then beaten until he could no longer stand. Next, two marines grabbed him by the legs and held him upside down while another delivered a devastating kick to his face. Shrieks and sobs filled the air.

The screams reached the home of sixteen-year-old Nguyen Thi Mai, who took shelter in the cellar with her mother and aunt. As the three cowered in the basement, the marines peered in and motioned for them to come out. The two older women obeyed, but Mai froze in fear. A hand reached in, grabbed her leg, and yanked her out. The marines tore up the women's civilian ID cards. Then one of the Americans grabbed Mai around the neck and clapped a hand over her mouth. Two others grabbed her legs, threw her to the ground, and roughly tore off her pants.

Busting into five or six more homes in similar fashion, the marines terrorized the hamlet without finding any weapons or contraband, or even a single piece of information about the enemy. Then they smashed into the home of eighteen-year-old Bui Thi Huong and her twenty-year-old husband, Dao Quang Thinh, a farmer too ill to serve in the army. Their three-year-old son also lived in the hut, as did Thinh's mother, his sister, and her five-year-old daughter. The marines accused Thinh of being a VC and beat him nearly unconscious, then propped him up against the front of his home next to his terrified sister and mother and the two young children.

Huong was dragged to the side of the house. A marine held his hand over her mouth; others pinned her arms and legs to the ground. They tore off her pants, ripped open her shirt, and groped her. Then the gang rape began. First one marine. Then another. Five in all. Huong's sobs elicited more screams of protest from her husband, so the marines began beating him again, after which a burst of gunfire silenced him. Her mother-in-law's sobs ended after another staccato burst, and her sister-in-law's after a third. Soon Huong could no longer hear the children. Then came a crack and a blinding flash, followed by searing pain that brought her to the ground.

The marines exploded a grenade to make the scene "look good," then radioed in their results: three dead VC. But back at the command post, they told their lieutenant that the shootings had not taken place at the prearranged ambush site and that some civilians were accidentally killed. The officer had the men bring him to the hamlet and saw the carnage for himself.

Though he was shocked by the killings, the lieutenant formulated a plan to cover up the crimes. Thinh's body was dragged to the originally planned ambush site, half a mile away, and the marines faked a firefight there. They also doctored up the massacre site in Xuan Ngoc. When they lifted the naked, blood-streaked body of Thinh's five-year-old niece, the child cried out. Somehow the girl had survived the shooting, but Private First Class John Potter saw to it that this time she wouldn't live. He told the other marines to count, and kept time "mashing up and down with his rifle," according to a fellow unit member. Another recalled, "I said one . . . two . . . three . . . And he was hitting the baby with the [rifle] butt!"

The marines did not notice that Bui Thi Huong was also still alive, though unconscious from a gunshot wound. When she awoke hours later, in severe pain and soaked in blood, a neighbor helped get her to a U.S. Marine base for treatment. There, Huong informed a Vietnamese interpreter about her rape and the massacre of her family. He, in turn, relayed the information to a sympathetic American doctor, who verified that she had been sexually assaulted, then went to the battalion commander and reported the crimes. If Huong hadn't survived the massacre, remained unconscious during the marines' return, been brought to the base, and spoken to a courageous interpreter who found an American officer who intervened on her behalf, it is likely that—as with so many other massacres—the events at Xuan Ngoc would never have come to light. Even with her testimony and a subsequent official investigation, three of the nine Americans involved in the massacre were found not guilty, and four others received only short jail terms.[84]

Less than a month after the rape and slaughter at Xuan Ngoc, on October 19, 1966, U.S. and Korean troops arrived in Dien Nien hamlet. Some of the locals fled in fear, but many stayed to protect their homes and belongings. The allied forces searched the homes and herded local people at gunpoint into a large group, where they sat in the sun, in a state of extreme fear, well into the afternoon. At about 3 PM, the first shots rang out, ripping into the civilians. Some bolted for their lives but were gunned down in nearby partially flooded rice paddies; the boots of pursuing soldiers pressed the faces of the wounded into the water, drowning them. Many other villagers simply froze and were torn apart by gunfire. Several bodies fell on top of Vi Thi Ngoi, and the tiny woman lay still, feigning death amid the blood and gore. After the troops left the hamlet, Ngoi stood up and saw that the area was filled with corpses; among those who did not run away, she was one of only two survivors.[85] A monument in Dien Nien lists 112 civilians killed in the massacre.[86]

A similarly horrific scene played out in nearby Phuoc Binh after South Korean troops arrived there on November 9, 1966. The younger men of the hamlet, who were regularly targeted by allied military forces, fled to a nearby South Vietnamese army base, leaving only women, children, and old men behind. The Koreans "killed our livestock for food without asking or paying for it," recalled one female resident, but otherwise the situation was calm for two days. Then, on the third day, the soldiers began rousting the people from their homes and calling them "VC." The woman grabbed her children and fled. When local men returned to Phuoc Binh a week or so later, they found only bodies. The villagers had been shot in front of their homes or killed by grenades inside their houses, and the hamlet had been burned.[87] A monument to the massacre in Phuoc Binh lists the names of sixty-eight victims, most of them women and children.[88]

Yet another massacre took place on December 6, 1966, when Korean forces killed two hundred people in An Phuoc hamlet.[89] Overall, South Korean troops reportedly committed no fewer than fourteen massacres in Quang Ngai in 1966.[90] Kim Ki-tae, a Korean officer, offered a matter-of-fact description of one of these bloodbaths: "We'd pushed 29 unarmed youths aged between 20–35 years into a bombing pit and shot them all to death."[91]

For Vietnamese villagers, perhaps the most unnerving thing about American and Korean patrols was the unpredictability of the soldiers' behavior. In Nhon Hoa hamlet, a villager named Phan Van Nam explained to me that sometimes U.S. troops handed out candies. Sometimes they shot at people. Sometimes they passed through a village hardly touching a thing. Sometimes they burned all the homes. "We didn't understand the reasons why they acted in the way they did," he told me.[92] Nam and other villagers described how on March 22, 1967, Nhon Hoa was visited by Korean troops and a couple of Americans. It was anyone's guess what the outcome would be when they collected a group of villagers together—until the soldiers opened fire. Eighty-six of the eighty-eight people there were killed, including forty-five children, thirty women, and eleven elderly men. Only two old women survived. That same day, another eighteen people were killed at a separate site nearby.[93]

Throughout this time, heavy aerial bombardment and artillery strikes continued to pound Quang Ngai as well. In the spring of 1967, elements of the 25th Infantry Division engaged in "a series of fierce battles . . . utilizing helicopter assaults to surround a fortified village and then employing artillery and air strikes to destroy the enemy in his fortifications." In just three months, from May through July 1967, the division fired over 42,000 artillery rounds into the province's Duc Pho and Mo Duc districts. Supporting units fired yet more artillery rounds, which, army documents boasted, "added great depth and power to the H&I program of the brigade."[94]

A high-ranking officer told the *New Yorker* correspondent Jonathan Schell that while 20,000 villagers had moved to refugee camps, an estimated 52,000 of them were still living in areas of Duc Pho targeted by harassment and interdiction fire.[95] In nearby Mo Duc, when Schell asked a pilot about the people who had lived in the district's bombed-out areas, he was told that there was no need to worry about them: "All the personnel that were down there were pretty much V.C."[96] An official 25th Infantry Division report similarly insisted that 80 percent of the people of Duc Pho were "communists or communist sympathizers."[97]

Such attitudes help explain the string of atrocities reportedly committed in the Duc Pho/Mo Duc border region in the spring of 1967 by Charlie Company, 2nd Battalion, 35th Infantry, under the command of Captain James Lanning. These included the killing of civilians and unarmed prisoners, as well as mutilation of corpses and burning of villages and crops. At least some of the acts were allegedly carried out on orders from higher commanders.[98]

In May 1967, according to sworn testimony given to an army criminal investigator, Lanning, while leading troops, ordered the execution of a wounded detainee. Radioman James Stockdale remembered the incident as a straightforward command from Lanning: "Get rid of him." At that point, another officer helped put the wounded prisoner in a boat, pushed it into a flooded rice paddy, riddled the man with bullets, and then tossed a grenade into the boat.[99]

According to Paul Halverson, a soldier and military combat correspondent who accompanied the unit, such "outright cold-blooded killings" of prisoners and civilians occurred repeatedly. Sometimes one or two people were gunned down, sometimes more than ten at a time.[100] On one occasion, Halverson saw the soldiers cover a wounded woman with a straw mat and set her on fire. This deliberate killing of noncombatants, he said, was "cold-blooded murder."[101] When asked about the total number killed by the unit, Halverson stated, "The entire time I was over there—just by Charlie Company—I'd say it would be in the hundreds."[102]

According to army documents, Halverson saw Lieutenant Gary Meyers gun down an "elderly VN [Vietnamese] man who had surrendered and was unarmed."[103] In Halverson's words, "He looked like he was in his 80s. He came up with his hands in prayer fashion. He was bowing." But Meyers, Halverson recalled, commanded, "Shoot him." When Halverson wouldn't do it, Meyers "raised his rifle up, took aim and shot him in the side of the head."[104]

Unit member Richard Porte likewise remembered noncombatants killed for expediency's sake as an alternative to taking prisoners or detaining people. "It was easier to dispose of them," he said. "It happened all the time."[105] Meanwhile, another unit member, Sergeant Lonnie Gentry, recalled that it was commonplace for the soldiers to fire on anyone who ran—including, on one occasion, a boy about eight years old.[106]

Of course, the practice of shooting children and other noncombatants just because they ran was by no means confined to Lanning's company. After returning to the United States, David Bressem, who had been a helicopter copilot with B Troop, 1st Squadron, 9th Cavalry Regiment, told army investigators about seeing the results of one such incident near Duc Pho. One day in the summer of 1967, Bressem said, he noticed from his helicopter three or four bodies lying in a field, "among them a dead Vietnamese boy of about ten years, who still held the halter of a cow in his hands." Radio conversations then informed him that there was "a body count of 33 people" in the field altogether, "of which a third were military age males, and the rest were women and children." They had been spotted taking "evasive action"—that is, trying to run across the open stretch of land—and that had justified the deaths of all of them, male and female, young and old.

This was not an isolated occurrence. In public testimony a year later, Bressem testified about one particularly egregious incident.

> We flew over a large rice paddy and there were some people working in the rice paddy, maybe a dozen or fifteen individuals, and we passed a couple of times low over their heads and they didn't take any action, they were obviously nervous, but they didn't try to hide or anything. So we then hovered a few feet off the ground among them with the two helicopters, turned on the police sirens and when they heard the police sirens, they started to disperse and we opened up on them and just shot them all down.[107]

Even flimsier pretexts for killing were often employed by other troops. At around the same time as Bressem's helicopter missions, the "Tiger Force"—a forty-five-man reconnaissance platoon of the 1st Battalion, 327th Infantry, 101st Airborne Division—was carrying out just such a string of wanton atrocities. In one typical incident, which took place near Duc Pho in early May 1967, Tiger Force members took a prisoner, tortured him, forced him to run, and then gunned him down. The next month, in the same area, another prisoner was bound, tortured, and killed; a Tiger Force trooper executed a teenage boy and cut off his ears; and another reportedly killed a prisoner by slitting his throat. In the Song Ve Valley, the Tiger Force soldiers killed an elderly villager and planted a grenade on his body.

As the months wore on, the platoon's murders mounted. On July 28, Tiger Force troops opened fire on a group of unarmed elderly farmers, killing four of them. Separately, that same day, they executed two elderly blind men.[108]

Toward the end of the summer of 1967, Jonathan Schell flew over the ravaged Song Ve Valley in a forward air controller's plane. Defoliants had killed the vegetation and nearly every home had been destroyed. The 101st Airborne Division was to blame, said the pilot. When Schell asked an army information officer about what he had seen, he was told that U.S. troops "didn't destroy that valley." Questioned further, the officer clarified his statement. There had been "no *plan* of destroying the valley," he explained, but after VC were spotted there, "we inserted two battalions back into the valley, and then it got destroyed in the process of denying it to the enemy."[109]

Villagers who survived the American assault lost not only their homes but also their rice and cattle. Jammed into a refugee camp, one woman lamented, "They bring us here and spill us onto this dry land; they give us some rice and some corn, but not enough for us and our children. Now our children are dying; soon they will all be dead. We are thrown here and left to die. And when we die, there is no one to provide funeral clothes or coffins for our burial and we are buried like dogs." Some of the refugees soon began sneaking back to the Song Ve Valley to brave life in a free-fire zone.[110]

The dangers of trying to live in Song Ve and the surrounding area were enormous—a point made vividly clear in August 1967 by the *Screaming Eagle* military newspaper, which proudly noted that the 2nd Battalion, 320th Artillery, had recently fired its 250,000th artillery round from a mountaintop overlooking the valley. The bombardment left the region's rice paddies pockmarked with craters, while homes all around were burned and battered.[111]

Schell tallied up the effect of American tactics on Quang Ngai and its people. "From the air," he wrote,

> the roofs of houses that were still standing appeared as dark-brown squares; the ashes of houses that had been recently burned appeared as gray squares; and the rain-washed clay foundations of houses that had been destroyed more than a month or so earlier appeared as red or yellow squares. When houses had been burned by troops on the ground, their walls—of clay-and-bamboo or stone—were usually still standing, but the walls of houses that had been bombed or bulldozed were flattened, or strewn over the rice fields. The pattern of destruction was roughly the same throughout the densely populated area of fields and villages lying between the mountains and the sea.[112]

Using such aerial surveillance, military maps, and interviews with U.S. ground commanders, Schell was able to compile comprehensive statistics about the level of destruction.[113] In Quang Ngai's Binh Son District, for example, he found that aside from a belt of untouched houses along a main road, 70–80 percent of all homes had been wiped out all the way to the sea. In neighboring Son Tinh District, some areas had suffered even more.[114] He made the obvious point, although it was a truth seldom expressed at the time: the war in Quang Ngai, as in many well-populated areas of Vietnam, was a battle less against enemy forces than against the South Vietnamese people.[115] Even a conservative formula developed by a

Defense Department analyst put the number of civilian casualties in the province each year at 33,000. Other sources put the figure at 50,000.[116]

A secret inquiry into Schell's findings, commissioned by Ambassador Ellsworth Bunker and conducted with General Westmoreland's consent, would confirm the carnage—but the inquiry would never be made public. "Mr. Schell's estimates are substantially correct," the report admitted, though it claimed that there were "some very important political and military reasons for the scope of destruction in this area." Those reasons all boiled down to the fact that the majority of the people of Quang Ngai supported the National Liberation Front, not the South Vietnamese government.[117]

Meanwhile, American troops in Quang Ngai came and went; the Tiger Force, for instance, moved by the late summer of 1967 into neighboring Quang Tin Province, where it would continue its string of atrocities.[118] But no matter which particular units were operating in Quang Ngai, the brutality against civilians never abated. In a series of letters home to his parents in late 1967 and early 1968, Specialist Leslie Lantos lamented the way that the men of Alpha Company, 2nd Battalion, 35th Infantry, mistreated the people of Duc Pho District. "I have always been disgusted with many things that take place out in the field, such as rape and degrading & humiliating old villagers," he wrote in one note. And in another letter, Lantos admitted that the unit's actions did not stop short of murder. "I've seen innocent people killed simply because someone wanted to kill 'a gook,'" he wrote.[119]

Lantos's company was hardly alone. On the evening of September 4, 1967, for example, members of the Company C, 1st Battalion, 35th Infantry, under the direction of Platoon Sergeant Otis Redmond and led by Lieutenant Donald Cinnamond, found themselves traveling along the shore of An Khe Lake near the hamlet of Dien Truong (8). The soldiers had spent the afternoon in the hamlet conducting a civic action program, during which they'd shared a hot meal with the villagers and passed out candies and soaps to local children. Now, they were moving from the village to a nighttime defensive position.

As the soldiers proceeded along the lake, they spotted two boys from Dien Truong in a sampan; the youngsters had been sent fishing by their father as the GIs left. The troops were directed to fire over the children's heads in an effort to force them to return to shore. Sergeant Redmond, however, took aim and shot directly at one of the boys, wounding him. The second boy rushed the boat toward the shore, but as he reached the shallows Redmond shot again, killing the wounded youngster and then his brother. The two boys were called in as enemy KIAs.[120]

A few months later, another innocent fisherman in the province was similarly killed by U.S. forces. As Sergeant Michel Pagano related to an army investigator, in December 1967 or January 1968 he'd watched an infantryman take aim at an old man fishing in a lake near the village of Sa Huyhn. The soldier told Pagano that a captain at the nearby base had seen the fisherman through binoculars and said, "Get him." "With his M-16 on automatic," recalled Pagano, the soldier "fired an entire clip of ammunition at the old man. The man fell out of his boat into the water." The captain at the base, Pagano told investigators, was Ernest Medina—the commander of Charlie Company, 1st Battalion, 20th Infantry.

The shooting witnessed by Pagano was not an isolated incident for Medina's Charlie Company. In January 1968, a patrol by members of the company spotted two Vietnamese fishermen in boats in the same lake. Lieutenant Michael Low, the officer in charge, apparently radioed in to ask for instructions. Medina's response was terse: "You know what to do with them." One of the fisherman, an army investigation concluded, was shot and killed instantly. The other was wounded and swam to the shore, where he was finished off by a soldier. Both, according to testimony, were unarmed civilians.[121]

A month or so later, according to witnesses, members of Low's unit were sent into a village with a mandate for murder.[122] In a sworn

statement to investigators, unit member Thomas Kinch described
how the mission unfolded.

> Low told us that when we got to the village we were to shoot every-
> one including women, children, and old men. After we were on the
> patrol . . . he changed the order to kill only young men. When we
> arrived at the village . . . I walked around the corner of a hut and
> came upon a man repairing a fishing net. I told this man in Viet-
> namese to get out of there. He just looked at me and smiled . . . I
> then heard Low on the other side of the hut, so I called to LT Low
> and told him that I had a young gook. Low replied "you haven't
> killed him yet," that's when I pulled the trigger and shot the man . . .
> he fell backwards off the stool he was sitting on and layed on the
> ground moaning . . . I looked at the man I had shot and then walked
> away.[123]

Another unit member then killed the wounded man on Low's
orders. The body was mutilated by a medic and called in as an enemy
killed in action.[124]

As the days went on, the situation in Charlie Company continued
to degenerate. As one soldier put it, "First you'd stop the people,
question them, and let them go. Second, you'd stop the people, beat
up an old man, and let them go. Third, you'd stop the people, beat up
an old man and then shoot him. Fourth, you go in and wipe out a
village."[125] On March 14, 1968, after a booby trap killed one soldier
and severely wounded two others, members of the unit went on a
rampage through several hamlets. They beat up a villager on a bicycle, assaulted children, and set upon an unarmed woman. "They shot
and wounded her," one GI wrote in a letter home to his father later
that day. "Then they kicked her to death and emptied their magazines in her head."[126] Two days later, the men of Charlie Company
carried out the massacre at My Lai.

While members of Charlie Company were herding terrified villagers into the infamous drainage ditch, the men of Bravo Company, 4th Battalion, 3rd Infantry, were sent to the nearby coastal hamlet of My Khe (4). Like the soldiers who entered My Lai, Company B encountered no enemy forces as they approached. In fact, peering through heavy brush and trees, the Americans saw only civilians—mostly women, children, and old men—going about their household chores. Nevertheless, Lieutenant Thomas Willingham had his two machine gunners pour preparatory fire into the enclave.[127] When the machine guns stopped, the Americans entered the hamlet.

As Willingham's radioman, Mario Fernandez was in a position to see everything his commander did. According to army documents, Fernandez said that the point team—the first men into the hamlet—indiscriminately sprayed the area with rifle fire. Then the rest of the unit entered the village and Willingham gave orders to destroy it.[128] Infantryman Homer Hall said that they moved through the village grenading bunkers without checking to see if civilians were sheltering inside. "They just threw it in there without calling them out," agreed unit member Jimmie Jenkins. According to Fernandez, when Vietnamese did come out from the bunkers, they were shot. "Some guys picked out a woman and two childs, two kids," Jenkins recalled. "They squatted down and I watched two guys cut them down." Other villagers were gunned down while attempting to run to safety.[129] As one soldier put it, "It was like being in a shooting gallery."[130]

Infantryman Donald Hooton, according to an army report, "killed an unidentified Vietnamese boy by shooting him in the head with, presumably, a .45 caliber pistol."[131] One witness from the unit later told Seymour Hersh what he saw that day. "I remember that the baby was about [10 feet away] and he fired at it with a .45. He missed. We all laughed. He got up three or four feet closer and missed again. We laughed. Then he got right up on top of him and plugged him." By this time, said one unit member, "the word was out. You know, like you more or less can do anything you like."[132] An American who kept count said that 155 people died at My Khe, and an official U.S. Army investigation found "no reliable evidence to support the claim that the persons killed were in fact VC."[133]

Ron Ridenhour, who later exposed the My Lai massacre based on accounts he collected from other soldiers, witnessed his share of atrocities firsthand while serving as a helicopter door gunner in Quang Ngai. On his first combat mission, Ridenhour saw the other door gunner on his chopper, who had been instructed to fire in front of a fleeing and apparently unarmed Vietnamese, accidentally shoot the man instead. The pilot got on the radio and called an officer on the ground to check out the wounded man. "The officer gets there, runs up to him," Ridenhour recalled, "stops, leans down, looks at him, stands up, pulls out his .45, cocks it, BOOM! He shoots the guy in the head."

At least six or seven times in his four-month span with the helicopter company, which lasted through April 1968, Ridenhour saw similar scenes unfold below his hovering aircraft. "We'd say, OK, here's someone who is looking suspicious or whatever. And some infantrymen would walk up to him and just shoot him. I mean, no provocation . . . I'm talking about murder."[134] Over the course of those four months, Ridenhour's unit killed about 36 guerrillas. In the eight months prior, another unit had worked over the same area and claimed 700 to 800 kills. "What that said to me," Ridenhour recalled, "since we were out doing the same thing, exactly the same thing in exactly the same area, was that they were just out there killing a lot of people. They were being a lot less discriminating than we were about who we were engaging."[135]

What Ron Ridenhour witnessed from his helicopter and Jonathan Schell observed from a military plane; what army medic Jamie Henry and marine lieutenant Philip Caputo saw on their patrols; what villagers like Bui Thi Huong and Vi Thi Ngoi lived through in their hamlets—that is the essence of what we should think of when we say "the Vietnam War." While we have only fragmentary evidence about the full extent of civilian suffering in South Vietnam, enough similar accounts exist so that roughly the same story could have been told in a chapter about Binh Dinh Province in the mid-1960s, Kien Hoa Province in the late 1960s, or Quang Tri Province in the early 1970s, among others. The incidents in this chapter were unbearably commonplace throughout the conflict and are unusual only in that they were reported in some form or recounted by witnesses instead of vanishing entirely from the historical record.

5

UNBOUNDED MISERY

The Vietnamese who lived in the remote countryside—what Americans called "the boonies"—suffered the most during the war, with thousands of civilians slain by ground troops and many more killed by bombing raids and artillery barrages. But even away from the secluded villages and isolated hamlets, far removed from the threat of ambushes and booby traps that constantly put soldiers on edge, U.S. troops still inflicted near-constant suffering on large segments of the population. The "mere-gook" mentality meant that throughout South Vietnam, the attitude of American forces was characterized by an utter indifference to Vietnamese lives—and, quite often, by shocking levels of cruelty.

The refugees who fled the increasingly inhospitable countryside and flooded into South Vietnam's urban areas were among those for whom the war made everyday life a misery. In cities like Saigon, Da Nang, and Qui Nhon, refugee ghettos housed huge numbers of Vietnamese in hovels made of garbage.[1] One U.S. officer recalled a typical city slum constructed of American refuse: "Discarded soft drink and beer cases and pallets were salvaged and reappeared as the walls of shacks, giving only the barest protection from the weather. Scraps of sheet metal became roofs. Worn tires became playpens. Used aircraft fuel tanks became water tanks."[2] Such squalid shantytowns, lacking even basic sanitation or reliable water supplies, sprang up on the outskirts of almost every major city, provincial capital, and district capital.[3]

In 1962, Saigon had a population of 1.4 million. After the heavy bombardment of rural areas began, the capital city swelled to 4 million (in a country that had only about 19 million people altogether)—the highest population density of any city in the world, twice that of Tokyo, its nearest rival.[4] At a Senate subcommittee hearing dealing with the plight of Vietnamese refugees, Dr. Herbert Needleman, the head of a charity devoted to child war victims, painted a striking picture.

> Saigon itself is becoming a garbage heap rising out of a cloud of smog. We lived in a Vietnamese home on a small, urban street. In the morning on the way to breakfast, we would encounter the bodies of rats run over by motorcycles at night. One sees garbage piles 8 feet tall by 20 feet square with children picking through them. Homeless children, sometimes completely nude, walk the streets and sleep in doorways.[5]

According to the South Vietnamese government, Saigon officially had no refugees. In reality, the city was overflowing with them.[6] By 1971, three-quarters of all urban residents in South Vietnam had, tellingly, been born elsewhere. And whereas city dwellers had once accounted for only 10 to 15 percent of South Vietnam's population, that proportion swelled to 36 percent by 1968, and 43 percent by 1974.[7]

Some Americans were untroubled by the situation in Saigon. In a 1968 *Foreign Affairs* article, the Harvard political scientist Samuel Huntington suggested that the United States "may well have stumbled upon the answer to 'wars of national liberation'" through what he called "forced draft urbanization and modernization."[8] It was a concept he had worked out the year before in a secret study he wrote for the State Department.[9] Huntington proposed that the "urban slum, which seems so horrible to middle-class Americans, often becomes for the poor peasant a gateway to a new and better way of life." In the cities, he claimed, unemployment was low, and some peasants earned five times as much as they had in their villages.[10] In other words, as Huntington saw it, bombing the Vietnamese out of the countryside and into the slums represented a marked step up for them.

Those who really examined the refugee ghettos, however, found a far grimmer reality. As the reporter Frances FitzGerald noted:

> Americans do not normally walk through the slums. Not the real slums . . . Hidden within a tangle of canals, between main streets fronted with respectable houses, these slums are difficult to find, but are more revealing specimens for their isolation. Gigantic sewers, lakes full of stagnant filth, above which thatched huts rise on stilts, crammed together but connected by only a thin strip of rotting board.[11]

By 1966 Saigon's infant mortality rate had reached a staggering 36.2 percent, higher than anywhere else in the country.[12] In the following years, the situation only worsened. Thanks to a nearly thousandfold increase in motorized traffic, the capital became ever more congested, while piles of rotting garbage lay uncollected beneath a pall of smog.[13] Not surprisingly, the urban areas saw a spike in the incidence of endemic diseases, such as cholera, dysentery, tuberculosis, typhoid, smallpox, and even bubonic plague.[14]

The landless, jobless refugees struggled desperately to keep their families fed and sheltered. Runaway inflation put even the most basic necessities out of reach: as the United States inundated the country with aid money, corruption flourished, consumer prices skyrocketed up to 900 percent between 1964 and 1972, and the cost of rice, the primary Vietnamese staple, rose more than 1,000 percent.[15] Perhaps the clearest indication of the ruin brought about by the American

War was the number of poor men and women who volunteered to collect Saigon's garbage. "They wanted to be in the bottom of the garbage truck," recalled a MACV spokesman after the war. "Here they could sort out and save the edibles in a clean white cloth and let it drip until they got off duty."[16]

Women and children got the worst of it. By the war's end, as many as 500,000 women in Vietnam had turned to prostitution.[17] Even those who did not strictly turn to sex work often found that servicing the American war machine offered the only employment available. Many young women became "bar girls," putting on miniskirts and makeup to coo at GIs and entreat the Americans to buy them an overpriced nonalcoholic drink called "Saigon tea"—the profits from which they split with the bar owners. Some got jobs as "hootch maids," cleaning up after GIs and doing their laundry; others worked on American bases, filling sandbags or serving food in mess halls; and some sold sodas to troops in the field or dealt drugs to the soldiers, often disguising them as cigarettes.

Refugee children, too, had to earn money to help feed their families. Many turned into beggars, pickpockets, or thieves. Others became house servants, shoeshine boys, trash pickers, or pimps for their mothers and sisters. Alongside them, bands of street urchins thronged the cities. By 1972, it is estimated that there were at least 100,000 children in South Vietnam separated from their parents.[18] Frances FitzGerald vividly described the street gangs, made up of war orphans and army deserters, which lived by their own Hobbesian codes: "They roam like wolf packs, never sleeping in the same place twice, scavenging or stealing what they need to live on."[19]

For the refugees, all of this further devastated the traditional patterns of rural life, which emphasized filial piety and respect for elders.[20] And the squalid, overcrowded cities offered little to look forward to. Tellingly, when students at a Saigon teachers' college were asked on an English exam to name fifteen occupations, almost none listed jobs like doctor, engineer, or even the one they were theoretically studying for—teacher. Instead, they cataloged the kind of work that the American War had made ubiquitous: shoeshine boy, laundry maid, car washer, and the ever-present bar girl.[21]

To the region surrounding Saigon, such as the province of Hau Nghia just to the west of the capital, the American War brought another set of everyday miseries. Unlike the populous northern coastal provinces of Quang Nam and Quang Ngai, the tiny, inland Hau Nghia wasn't overwhelmed by the Americans' so-called big unit war. The vital roadways that crisscrossed the province, however—including a stretch of Route 1, the national highway, as it wound its way from Saigon to the Cambodian border—gave it great strategic importance.[22]

While securing the main roadways in the area, U.S. troops took time out to shoot at birds and grave sites, scaring the Vietnamese working in nearby rice paddies. Tanks rumbled through fields and orchards, destroying the meager sources of sustenance. One villager complained, "When the rice was nearly ripe and secondary crops were in the 'time of gold,' they were all damaged by tanks . . . Anything they can reach they run over."[23]

In October 1967, residents of Hau Nghia's Bau Tre hamlet—a government-sanctioned New Life settlement where refugees were supposedly safe from the ravages of the countryside—showed a Civil Operations and Revolutionary Development Support (CORDS) team various orchards and gardens that had been completely destroyed by American tanks. The villagers also suffered when nighttime patrols by U.S. armored vehicles, known as "Roadrunner" operations, were fired on by guerrillas. Predictably, the Americans replied with indiscriminate fire, damaging homes and driving a large segment of the population from the hamlet.[24]

Continual complaints from villagers even prompted the South Vietnamese chief of the province, Lieutenant Colonel Ma Sanh Nhon, to request an end to the Roadrunner missions, but they continued.[25]

Two Vietnamese women struggle to salvage items from their home in Quang Tin Province after it was set on fire by members of the U.S. Army's 1st Squadron, 1st Cavalry, and allied South Vietnamese militia.

The smoldering shell of a home burned by American and South Vietnamese troops in Quang Tin Province.

One of the lime gatherers in Binh Long Province killed in August 1970 by soldiers from the 25th Infantry Division.

Pham Thi Luyen standing at the graves of her parents, who were both killed by U.S. Marines during the 1967 massacre in Trieu Ai village.

U.S. Marines blow up "bunkers and tunnels used by the Viet Cong" in a Viet-namese village. Frequently, such "bunkers" were nothing more than bomb shelters dug by villagers for protection from U.S. bombing and shelling.

Bui Xich (*above*) lost two sons when artillery shelling collapsed his family's bomb shelter in Thanh Son hamlet, Binh Dinh Province. Luong Dai (*below*), also of Thanh Son hamlet, lost seven family members in a similar bunker collapse.

Pham Thi Hien's home in Thanh Son hamlet was destroyed at least five times during the war, as Americans tried to drive the villagers into a "concentration area." When Hien persisted in staying in her ancestral hamlet, she was detained by American and South Vietnamese soldiers, who accused her of supporting local guerrillas. She was beaten and subjected to water torture.

The Saigon fire department had the job of collecting the dead from the streets during the 1968 Tet Offensive. They had just placed this young girl, killed by U.S. helicopter fire, in the back of their truck when her distraught brother found her.

Nguyen Thi Lam was working in a rice paddy in the Mekong Delta in 1968 when a helicopter swooped in and began firing on the farmers. Her sister-in-law was killed on the spot, and Lam lost a leg in the attack.

A soldier from the 9th Infantry Division walks past a "Viet Cong base camp" going up in flames in the Mekong Delta. All types of buildings in the Vietnamese countryside were seen as military targets by U.S. forces, including homes and schools.

A U.S. airstrike unleashes napalm in an area south of Saigon.

After one sniping incident prompted a U.S. counterattack that injured several civilians and destroyed many homes in Bau Tre, an American adviser also questioned the army's response. A spokesman for the 25th Infantry Division countered by blaming local civilians for the episode. If they wanted to avoid future attacks, he said, they had to tell Americans whenever the Viet Cong were present in the hamlet.

On February 28, 1968, Bau Tre villagers did just that—and paid a heavy price. Arriving to oust the guerrillas, troops from the 25th Division promptly lost an armored personnel carrier to enemy fire. In response, the remaining APCs took up positions along one side of the hamlet and called in helicopter gunships. By the time the helicopters arrived, the guerrillas had, of course, withdrawn, but the choppers began strafing Bau Tre anyway, and the armored personnel carriers also opened fire. In the end, no dead guerrillas were found in the hamlet. At least twenty-two civilians were killed or wounded, however, and fifty-eight houses were destroyed.[26]

Similar incidents took place throughout Hau Nghia. In July 1968, Cu Chi District adviser Major Donald Pearce wrote an angry memo complaining that a string of disproportionate responses to small-scale enemy actions had caused civilian casualties and extensive property damage. "To return a few AK47 rounds with the main gun on an M48 tank and thus destroy homes and kill sleeping civilians is wrong and is a problem," he wrote. "Any Vietnamese were assumed to be VC and treated as such," Pearce recalled after the war. "Troops would always report that they found enemy bunkers, even though we kept telling them that every house had a bunker for protection from our fire . . . Once I sifted through remains of some houses destroyed in a village on Highway 1 toward Trang Bang. I found a grandmother and four children suffocated from flames."[27]

In a September 1968 memo, Major General Ellis Williamson, the commander of the 25th Infantry Division, similarly rebuked his troops for their indiscriminate use of small arms and explosives, which had "resulted in death or injury to both Vietnamese nationals and the farm animals upon which they depend for a livelihood." "In this," he wrote, "I do not refer to artillery accidents or incidents, but senseless acts which are perpetrated for a number of reasons such as 'scaring' people or 'test-firing' weapons." But though Williamson decried the random firing as "senseless," the habit did not spring up out of nowhere. Rather, it came from a deep-rooted lack of concern about Vietnamese civilian lives—a carelessness exemplified by Williamson's own signature policy of unleashing 1,000 rounds of artillery against the countryside in return for every single round received from the enemy. Williamson himself admitted the "inclination of many of us to look on the Vietnamese as inferior people, thus generating attitudes of disdain, lack of respect and even contempt for their customs and traditions."[28]

Not long after Williamson's pronouncements, troops from the division's 2nd Battalion, 12th Infantry, began preparing to take control of An Thinh, a village about thirty-five miles west of Saigon that had been under NLF control for years.[29] According to Charles Benoit, an American adviser in the area, "someone at the 25th Division had decided that this 'red' hamlet was too close" to Trang Bang, the district capital, "and therefore had to be pacified." This would involve opening the road through the village to military traffic, which could then use it as an alternative to Route 1. As a start, the Americans demolished a nearby bridge and installed a sturdier model that could support armored vehicles. In the process, they destroyed a home, damaged a few others, and injured at least one man, while an eleven-year-old girl was killed by a "stray bullet."[30] It was a harbinger of things to come.

Soon, U.S. troops moved into An Thinh without making the slightest preparations to provide food or shelter for its 5,000 residents. The only discernible plan was destruction. Each morning, during the first week of the operation, ten armored personnel carriers rolled into the village, shooting up homes and nearby tree lines, as the Americans began clearing 150- to 200-yard-wide corridors on each side of the road to provide security from enemy ambush.

Joining refugees from other battered villages in the area, An Thinh residents waited each day in nearby Trang Bang until the Americans pulled out at around 4 PM. Every evening they returned to what remained of their homes to gather a few belongings or harvest some vegetables, leaving again before dark, when harassment-and-interdiction artillery fire began raining down.[31] Helicopters patrolling the area for snipers scared villagers away from rice paddies that were ready for harvest.[32] Ground troops also destroyed bamboo storage bins filled with the families' remaining supplies of rice, regarding these as "Viet Cong caches."[33] One reporter recalled watching as a woman "returned to find her house a smoking pile of rubble, which an army bulldozer had gratuitously spread around."[34] Benoit, the American adviser, wrote: "They knew their houses and belongings were burning down one by one and that their rice was ready to be harvested. They knew that each afternoon upon their return they simply found more destruction."[35]

As the process continued, U.S. troops became increasingly angry about intermittent sniper fire and mines placed by guerrillas overnight.[36] A captain in charge of one unit proclaimed "that his mission was to open this road and that he had CG [commanding general] clearance to level this village if he met with any resistance at all." The officer claimed that he was attempting to limit damage to civilian property, Benoit noted, but "he seemed pretty sure despite his restraint that this village was not going to last much longer."[37]

During the second week of the operation, the Americans beat back an attack by the revolutionary forces and then called in B-52 strikes on the surrounding rice paddies. Inside the village, yet more houses were damaged by tank rounds, and others were destroyed during what was called "recon-by-fire"—essentially, shooting into random areas to see if anyone fired back.[38] Rome plows then finished the job, scraping away the remnants of homes, gardens, wells, and fruit trees.[39] "We're gonna make damned sure Charlie knows we're here to stay," announced one soldier.[40] "I looked at the ruined, shot-up houses, thinking of war movies taken in Germany," Benoit recalled. "There was little difference."[41]

Soon after, Colonel Nhon arrived with a propaganda and entertainment troupe. The team had been assigned to entertain the villagers and welcome them into the Saigon government's control, while Nhon was to spend the night in An Thinh to prove that it was "pacified." No locals could be found for an audience, however, and the plans were shelved until the next morning, when villagers were rounded up from the surrounding area and herded into a cow paddock.

A reporter in attendance recalled, "The people sat stony-faced and silent in the morning sun and listened to Colonel Nhon tell them that if they did not cooperate [with the Saigon government] he would send the Americans back on more operations."[42] Benoit, who was also there, described an old man standing up after Nhon opened the floor to the villagers. "Tears were visible in his eyes as he explained to the province chief that his house had burned along with all his belongings. He asked if this was how the Americans helped the Vietnamese people."[43] Many others who had the same experience began to sob, too. In the midst of it all, Nhon asked the elderly man whether he supported the VC. When the old farmer said he that would follow whichever side controlled the village, since he had no other choice and simply wanted peace, the province chief replied, "No one remains in the middle in this struggle; if you are not with our side, then you must be with them."[44] The old man was promptly arrested by the national police as a VC sympathizer.[45]

Nhon stridently denounced the VC, telling his audience that the revolutionaries had brought about the destruction of the village. Then he waded into the crowd, asking them to air their grievances. Villagers again complained to Nhon about their homes being burned and bulldozed. They were even more vociferous about the senseless destruction carried out by the Americans: cupboards smashed by hand, smoke grenades thrown into wells, fruit trees needlessly knocked down, and troops defecating in the remaining homes.[46] Nhon became enraged. "Shitting in the houses!" he shouted at Colonel Carl Bernard, the U.S. senior provincial adviser for Hau Nghia, who was also in attendance. "You hear what American soldiers do? What the hell!" Bernard walked over to the 25th Division company commander and asked if it was true. "Sir, I don't know anything about An Thinh, I'm new here," the captain replied. "When I arrived it looked to me like a bomb had hit this place and these were just a bunch of abandoned houses."[47]

As the entourage of officials moved through the village, Bernard lectured the company commander on the basics of winning hearts and minds. "It does no good to shoot up all the houses like this," he admonished. "We were only reconning by fire," the puzzled young officer replied; "this is a free fire zone, isn't it?" Bernard exploded: "My good man, *no* this is *not* a free fire zone; this is a village, and those people back there used to live in this village." The group continued on, stopping at the charred remains of a home. Just then, leaflets began to flutter down from the sky, directing villagers to inform against the Viet Cong.[48]

Within a few weeks, the dozens of damaged houses in An Thinh had multiplied to several hundred, thanks to new U.S. troops who favored calling in withering artillery barrages at any sign of trouble.[49] And nearby areas were suffering, too. In a hamlet not far from An Thinh, Benoit visited a store whose glass display cases had been shattered by rock-throwing American troops as they sped by in multi-truck convoys. After repairing the cases several times, the mother and daughter running the store had given up. "I asked her if she reported these incidents to anyone," Benoit wrote. "She asked to whom. She had not, because she didn't know what good it could possibly do." Benoit also soon learned that a young girl from the same hamlet had been killed when a tank accidentally blasted a temple there.[50]

In November 1969, almost a year after the An Thinh operation began, Benoit returned to find the village in complete shambles and the road in ruins, having "been destroyed by the tanks and APC's, which had provided security to the bulldozers pacifying the area." In a then-classified RAND report, he mused:

> It was ironic for me to reflect that, at the time, the rationale had been to open this road to military traffic, thereby pacifying the hamlets . . . now the irony was complete. The very road that had offered the justification for the military aspects of the operation had been destroyed by the means we had chosen to implement the operation! The road was now impassable to any kind of vehicle, military or civilian.[51]

As Benoit wandered through the remains of An Thinh—now a "ghost town in the full sense of the word"—he encountered a pitiful band of stragglers. Anyone with money, they told him, had left the village. Only the poor remained, and even they sent their children to Trang Bang each night for security. Benoit saw a woman he knew standing in what had been her home before a bulldozer had knocked it down. "She was busy sprinkling DDT among the remaining beams to kill termites," he wrote, and waiting for compensation that he told her might never come. He also recalled finding "an old peasant living alone in a small straw hut, [who] explained he had no place to go. He could still fend for himself and didn't want to be a burden on his children." The man told Benoit that "he would like to move somewhere else where it was safer but only had land here which he could farm. Elsewhere he would starve or become a burden."[52]

In his RAND report, Benoit summed up the situation.

> Traffic along Route 1 was about the same as I had known it six months before, both in terms of quantity and manner. Military convoys were just as frequent, speeding just as recklessly as before.

A stop by the CORDS office had produced the same long lists of traffic accidents involving both property loss and serious injury or death to Vietnamese civilians. Claims were piling up. It appeared that claims against the U.S. Government took as long as ever to be processed. One of the problems seemed to be that the claims office in Saigon simply mailed information via Vietnamese mail to the claimants. When after an appropriate time no reply was received, the claim was accordingly canceled. Unfortunately, the Vietnamese mail service only with great difficulty ever reaches an individual at the hamlet level. Many houses are unnumbered, in which case the letter remains unclaimed at the village or hamlet office.[53]

Some compensation payments did get made. From mid-September 1968 through January 1969, 583 families in Hau Nghia Province received compensation from Saigon authorities or the U.S. military for deaths, injuries, or damages.[54] But such payments hardly demonstrated any remorse or second thoughts by the Americans about their tactics. As specialist Michael Erard, who served with the 173rd Airborne Brigade, explained, "We would pay them what they called a 'solacium payment.' Now the solacium payment was a condolence type payment . . . It in no way implied or implicated us as the perpetrators of this. So we would pay them a certain amount of money for people lost."[55]

In 1968, the going rate for adult lives was thirty-three dollars, while children merited just half that.[56] In one instance, after two members of Huynh Van Thanh's family were crushed to death by cargo dropped from a U.S. helicopter, the American military paid him about sixty dollars and gave him some surplus food, a bottle of liquid soap, two coloring books, and a box of crayons.[57] Other payments for U.S. misdeeds were made by the Saigon government. After the killing of twenty-three fishermen by American troops in Quang Nam Province in 1967, for example, South Vietnamese authorities gave each of the families who had lost a relative 110 kilograms of rice.[58] Most often, however, victims and survivors received no aid at all. Few rural Vietnamese had any idea how to lodge a formal complaint, apply for compensation, or even contact the American officials in the first place.

By failing to accept responsibility for deaths and attempting to buy off Vietnamese grief over dead children for absurdly low amounts—about what a radio cost in America at the time—the United States explicitly commodified and devalued Vietnamese life.[59] As James William Gibson put it, the solacium system was "the most perverse exercise of turning people's lives and deaths into ledger entries."[60]

The "long lists of traffic accidents" that Benoit wrote about often stemmed from utter recklessness. "We had this idea that we were king of the fucking hill," remembered veteran (and later novelist) Larry Heinemann. "We ran people off the road . . . We felt invincible."[61] Marine James Kelly recalled a member of his convoy crushing a three-wheeled scooter loaded with animals and personal belongings and then driving off in his armored vehicle. "We didn't stop after the so-called *wreck*," he wrote in his memoir. When word of the incident reached his commander, he wrote, "we came up with some half-assed, lame-brained excuse." Although Kelly knew perfectly well that they were guilty of leaving the scene of a crash, he summed up the basic American response succinctly: "We didn't give a damn."[62]

Running down civilians with jeeps, trucks, tanks, and other armored vehicles was a commonplace occurrence.[63] For instance, after Robert Boheman of the army's 255th Transportation Detachment ran over and killed two Vietnamese sleeping by the side of the road, he struck and injured three others who were waving their arms to get him to stop.[64] On July 7, 1968, after hitting a parked car with his jeep, John Gamble of the army's 11th Supply Company fled the scene, speeding through Saigon's streets before plowing into a Vietnamese man and his two children on a motorbike. According to court-martial documents, "the motorbicycle was dragged some 92 feet before the mangled dead bodies of the victims came to rest at various distances from the Vietnamese vehicle."[65] And on Christmas Day 1969, Robert Fleenor of the 57th Aviation Company "borrowed" a five-ton tow truck and went for a joyride through Kontum Province. He struck and injured an eight-year-old boy, killed an eight-year-old girl, and then killed a fifty-three-year-old man in three separate hit-and-run incidents on a single stretch of road one-fifth of a mile long.[66]

Too often, the traffic "accidents" seemed anything but accidental. A navy corpsman remembered one this way: "An old woman was walking along the road right outside our battalion area and she was run down by a truck. And they brought her in and she died . . . The road wasn't crowded. I don't know if the truck driver, you know, meant to run her down, but there was never an investigation launched. He had no remorse about it at all. It was just another gook who got in the way."[67] An American medic who saw the carnage from another incident, which left two boys dead, similarly suspected that it was a deliberate act.

> I found out they'd been hit by an American military truck and that there was this kind of game going on in which, supposedly, guys were driving through town gambling over who could hit a kid. They had some disgusting name for it, something like "gook hockey." I think they were driving deuce-and-a-halfs—big-ass trucks. The NCO who ordered me to clean the bodies could have cared less.[68]

The son of a South Vietnamese government official noted the Americans' sense of impunity: "You would see American GMC trucks go by and soldiers reaching down to whack a girl riding a bicycle. They would yank at her hat and she would get thrown and she would die. You would see Americans do this and feel like they can do anything in our country."[69] Often they could. Just as a soldier in the countryside could cut down anyone in black pajamas simply for running, so too an American driver could kill anyone on the road who happened to get in his way, and the bodies kept piling up.

Behind closed doors at top-level briefings, even MACV commander Creighton Abrams repeatedly complained about GIs who ran Vietnamese off the roads or threw beer cans at them.[70] But the behavior never stopped. Indeed, in addition to rocks, cans, and bottles, Americans regularly threw burning flares, tear gas canisters, and concussion grenades from passing convoys.[71] GIs also swung their rifles at passing Vietnamese and hurled metal C-ration cans at children begging by the roadside, injuring or even killing them.[72] Sometimes, soldiers in convoys also fired on roadside bystanders and passing vehicles, or shot up houses as a joke.[73]

On July 23, 1968, for example, artilleryman Lex Gilbert and his buddies began firing their weapons as they rode through the countryside in an army truck. Gilbert gestured toward a cluster of three homes, shouted "look at that roof!" and fired a burst from his M-60 machine gun at the middle house.[74] One of the bullets struck a sixteen-year-old Vietnamese girl in the head, killing her.[75] Similarly, on July 3, 1970, marine sergeant Joel McElhinney was riding in a truck, when a subordinate jokingly told him that he had "no balls." Laughing, McElhinney responded by firing three or four shots from his rifle, killing a woman walking by the side of the road.[76]

Homes, graves, and pagodas fell prey to the same sort of casual potshots and destructive impulses, fueled by a toxic mix of youth, testosterone, racism, anger, boredom, fear, alienation, anonymity, impunity, and excitement.[77] To some extent, the senseless destruction was the natural result of handing out weapons that packed tremendous firepower and could be fired from a great distance to young soldiers who were already at a great psychic distance from the very alien and confusing society they found themselves in. The M-79 grenade launcher, for example, allowed a soldier to kill from 430 yards away. This meant a GI could, say, target a water buffalo for kicks from the other side of a rice paddy and revel in the carnage from afar. Later in the war, even the standard M-16 rifle could be outfitted with a semiautomatic grenade launcher, a modification that, as military psychiatrist William Gault put it, made "every soldier a miniature artilleryman."[78]

Fancy new military technologies also encouraged GIs to fire their weapons for the simple thrill of it—what the historian Christian Appy calls the "hedonism of destruction . . . attested to by countless veterans."[79] Veteran William Broyles, for example, wrote of the intoxicating pleasure elicited by the destructive power of a "grunt's Excalibur"—the M-60 machine gun.[80] Aviator Randy Floyd, meanwhile, talked of the great "excitement" he felt as a bomber pilot, likening it to the exhilaration experienced by children shooting off firecrackers.[81] And it was not only the aviators or the machine gunners who could experience such childlike elation. The standard-issue M-16 carried by most infantrymen, after all, was not only potent—you could fire up to seven hundred rounds in a minute and tear off a limb at a hundred yards—but exceedingly compact and lightweight.[82] Indeed, the rifle resembled a child's plaything to such an extent that it came to be known as the "Mattel toy."[83]

Emboldened by the ease with which such lethal technology could be wielded, soldiers often shot first and asked questions later. One place where troops pulled the trigger with astounding ease was garbage dumps, which proliferated as the U.S. presence grew. Of all the sites of everyday atrocity, these might be the most revealing—encapsulating both the plight of vulnerable Vietnamese and the callous attitude of even those U.S. troops who were far removed from the stresses of combat.

Desperate Vietnamese often descended on the dumps near U.S. camps and outposts to forage through American trash for edible, salable, or useful items. Surprising numbers of them, mostly children, were shot there by rear-echelon guards operating under confusing orders or nonexistent rules of engagement.[84] Sometimes the official rationale was to protect U.S. property. Other times, the guards fired bullets or tear gas to "protect" children from possible dangers, like U.S. ordnance, that might find its way into the dumps. Often, no reason at all was offered beyond securing the heaps of trash.

In April 1969, for example, a soldier from the 82nd Airborne Division shot and killed a twelve-year-old boy to keep the child from rummaging in a base garbage dump in Hau Nghia Province.[85] The next month, at Landing Zone (LZ) Nancy in Quang Tri Province, members of the 1st Infantry Brigade, 5th Infantry Division—who regularly fired their M-16s and M-79s to scare off local kids—shot toward a group of ten to fifteen Vietnamese children scavenging in a dump, wounding a ten-year-old.[86] On July 22, 1970, sixteen-year-old Huynh Thi Tuoi ran after a cow that had bolted into the trash dump at LZ Snoopy in Quang Ngai Province. American troops at LZ Snoopy, like those at LZ Nancy, regularly fired live rounds over the heads of impoverished children in order to scare them away; that morning, however, a bullet slammed into Tuoi's skull, killing her.[87]

In 1971, Major Gordon Livingston, a West Point graduate who served as regimental surgeon with the 11th Armored Cavalry Regiment, testified before members of Congress about the ease with which Americans killed Vietnamese. "Above 90 percent of the Americans with whom I had contact in Vietnam," said Dr. Livingston, treated the Vietnamese as subhuman and with "nearly universal contempt."[88] To illustrate his point, Livingston told his listeners about a helicopter pilot who swooped down on two Vietnamese women riding bicycles and killed them with the helicopter skids. The pilot was temporarily grounded as the incident was being investigated, and Livingston spoke to him in his medical capacity. He found that the man felt no remorse about the killings and only regretted not receiving his pay during the investigation. According to Livingston, a board of inquiry eventually cleared the pilot of any wrongdoing and allowed him to resume flying.[89]

Among those whom Livingston counted in the 90 percent who regarded the Vietnamese as subhuman was his commander, General George S. Patton III. Son of the famed World War II general of the same name, the younger Patton was known for his bloodthirsty attitude and the macabre souvenirs that he kept, including a Vietnamese skull that sat on his desk. He even carried it around at his end-of-tour farewell party.[90] Of course, Patton was just one of many Americans who collected and displayed Vietnamese body parts. Given how contemptuously living Vietnamese were often treated by U.S. forces, it is not surprising that Vietnamese corpses were also often handled with little respect.

Some soldiers hacked the heads off Vietnamese to keep, trade, or exchange for prizes offered by commanders.[91] Many more cut off the ears of their victims, in the hopes that disfiguring the dead would frighten the enemy. Some of these trophies were presented to superiors as gifts or as proof to confirm a body count; others were retained by the "grunts" and worn on necklaces or otherwise displayed.[92] While ears were the most common souvenirs of this type, scalps, penises, noses, breasts, teeth, and fingers were also favored.[93]

"There was people in all the platoons with ears on cords," Jimmie Busby, a member of the 75th Rangers during 1970–71, told an army criminal investigator. Some would wear them, while others would sell the grisly trophies to air force personnel. "It was more or less an everyday occurrence that you might see someone with one."[94] Another member of the same unit, Tony Foster, told a CID agent: "I noticed numerous military personnel wearing or carrying various parts of the human anatomy. In detail I saw approximately 3–4 forefingers being carried in matchboxes; approximately 15–20 ears on rawhide-type cords being worn around different individuals' necks; and one penis which had been pickled and was being carried wrapped in gauze."[95]

Many soldiers mistreated corpses in other ways—dressing them up, clowning around with them, or mutilating them, often taking photos of their handiwork and filling scrapbooks with the results.[96] The correspondent Michael Herr recalled:

> There were hundreds of these albums in Vietnam, thousands, and they all seemed to contain the same pictures . . . the severed head shot, the head often resting on the chest of the dead man or being held up by a smiling Marine, or a lot of heads, arranged in a row, with a burning cigarette in each of the mouths, the eyes open . . . the VC suspect being dragged over the dust by a half-track or being hung by his heels in some jungle clearing; the very young dead . . . a picture of a Marine holding an ear or maybe two ears or, in the case of a guy I knew near Pleiku, a whole necklace made of ears . . . the dead Viet Cong girl with her pajamas stripped off and her legs raised stiffly in the air. . . . Half the combat troops in Vietnam had these things in their packs, snapshots were the least of what they took after a fight, at least the pictures didn't rot.[97]

Norman Ryman, of the 173rd Airborne Brigade, was one of these souvenir-collecting soldiers. After U.S. authorities discovered three human ears—along with an atrocity album—in a package he sent back to the United States, he explained that he was responsible for only two of the body parts. The other, he said, had been purchased from a soldier in the 101st Airborne Division, who "had a large jar of ears that he was selling."[98]

In addition to collecting souvenirs and gruesome photos, American troops mistreated corpses to send a message.[99] Troops in the field regularly carved their unit's initials or numbers into corpses, adorned bodies with their unit's patch, or left a "death card"— generally either an ace of spades or a custom-printed business card claiming credit for the kill.[100] Company A, 1st Battalion, 6th Infantry of the 198th Light Infantry Brigade, for example, left their victims with a customized ace of spades sporting the unit's formal designation, its nickname ("Gunfighters"), a skull and crossbones, and the phrase "dealers of death."[101] Helicopter pilots, such as Captain Lynn Carlson, occasionally dropped similar specially made calling cards from their gunships. One side of Carlson's card read: "Congratulations. You have been killed through courtesy of the 361st. Yours truly, Pink Panther 20." The other side proclaimed, "The Lord giveth and the 20mm [cannon] taketh away. Killing is our business and business is good."[102]

In a rather medieval display, some American troops hacked the heads off the dead and mounted them on pikes or poles to frighten guerrillas or local Vietnamese villagers.[103] Others, in a more modern variant of the same practice, lashed corpses to U.S. vehicles and drove through towns and villages to send a similar message.[104] And while South Vietnamese troops were often singled out in the press for making public displays of dead guerrillas, U.S. troops did much the same, sometimes even more spectacularly.[105] Alexander Haig—who went on to serve as a division brigade commander, vice chief of staff of the U.S. Army, and then President Nixon's chief of staff—recalled that in 1966, when he was the operations officer with the 1st Infantry Division, one tactic under discussion involved throwing bodies out of aircraft.

"I was there when some staffers recommended dropping dead North Vietnamese soldiers from helicopters . . . simply for the psychology of it," Haig remembered decades later. "I said 'If that happens I'm resigning right here and now.' And it didn't happen."[106] The historical record, though, contradicts Haig's last sentence. In November 1966, the *New York Times* reported that, following a particularly successful battle, an "elated" Lieutenant Colonel Jack Whitted of the 1st Infantry Division had the corpses of dead revolutionary troops loaded into a helicopter. "We're giving the bodies back to Victor Charles!" he shouted. "We'll dump the bodies in the next clearing."[107] The corpses were then hurled out.[108]

The disdainful attitude that led American troops to gleefully cut off ears and run down pedestrians by the roadside was even stronger when it came to a group that, for the young soldiers, was doubly "other": Vietnamese women. As a result, sexual violence and sexual exploitation became an omnipresent part of the American War.[109] With their husbands or fathers away at war or dead because of it, without other employment prospects and desperate to provide for their families, many women found that catering to the desires of U.S. soldiers was their only option.[110]

By 1966, as the feminist scholar Susan Brownmiller observed, the 1st Cavalry Division, the 1st Infantry Division, and the 4th Infantry Division had all already "established official military brothels within the perimeter of their basecamps."[111] At the 1st Infantry Division base at Lai Khe, refugee women—recruited by the South Vietnamese province chief and channeled into their jobs by the mayor of the town—worked in sixty curtained cubicles kept under military police guard.[112] Jim Soular of the 1st Cavalry Division recalled the setup at his unit's compound, known as Sin City.

> You had to go through a checkpoint gate, but once you were in there you could do anything. There were all kinds of prostitutes and booze. The [U.S.] army was definitely in control of this thing. The bars had little rooms in the back where you could go with the prostitutes. I know they were checked by the doctors once a week for venereal diseases.[113]

At Dong Tam, the 9th Infantry Division camp, the sign on a large building next to the headquarters read "Steam Bath and Massage." The troops knew it by a different name: "Steam 'n Cream." The building boasted approximately 140 cubicles filled with Vietnamese women and girls.[114] At another U.S. compound, the prices of sex acts were announced at an official briefing, and, for a time, "little tickets had been printed up . . . blue ones for blow jobs, and white ones for intercourse," recalled one patron to an army investigator. GIs paid a dollar or so for the former and around two for the latter.[115]

Everywhere, every kind of sex was for sale. "At the entrance to the MACV compound in Qui Nhon, a six-year-old girl is offering blow jobs," wrote one journalist sizing up the sex-work scene. "One night early on in my stay," he reported,

> I found myself with a thirteen-year-old girl on my lap *insisting* "we go make lub now" in the bordello her mother had thrown up opposite an American construction site. The bordello is made of sheets of aluminum somehow extricated from a factory just before attaining canhood. You can read the walls of the structure from a distance. They say "Schlitz, Schlitz," in rows and columns, over and over again.
>
> The girl wants $1.25. With some difficulty I refuse.[116]

Later in the war, even walking as far as the camp entrance would become unnecessary, as certain bases began allowing prostitutes directly into the barracks.[117]

"Hootch maids," who washed and ironed clothes and cleaned living quarters for U.S. servicemen, were also sometimes sexually exploited. As one maid put it, "American soldiers have much money and it seems that they are sexually hungry all the time. Our poor girls. With money and a little patience, the Americans can get them very easily."[118] And other women working on bases fell victim to sexual blackmail. One such case was revealed in an army investigation of Mickey Carcille, who ran a camp mess hall that employed Vietnamese women. By threatening to fire them if they did not comply, Carcille forced some of the women to pose for nude photographs and coerced others into having intercourse with him or performing other sex acts.[119]

In addition to sexual exploitation, sexual violence was an everyday feature of the American War—hardly surprising since, as

Christian Appy observed, "the model of male sexuality offered as a military ideal in boot camp was directly linked to violence."[120] From their earliest days in the military, men were bombarded with the language of sexism and misogyny. Male recruits who showed weakness or fatigue were labeled ladies, girls, pussies, or cunts.[121] In basic training, as army draftee Tim O'Brien later wrote in his autobiographical account of the Vietnam War, the message was: "Women are dinks. Women are villains. They are creatures akin to Communists and yellow-skinned people."[122]

While it's often assumed that all sexual assaults took place in the countryside, evidence suggests that men based in rear areas also had ample opportunity to abuse and rape women.[123] For example, on December 27, 1969, Refugio Longoria and James Peterson, who served in the 580th Telephone Operations Company, and one other soldier picked up a nineteen-year-old Vietnamese hootch maid hitching a ride home after a day of work on the gigantic base at Long Binh. They drove her to a secluded spot behind the recreation center and forced her into the back of the truck—holding her down, gagging, and blindfolding her. They then gang-raped her and dumped her on the side of the road. A doctor's examination shortly afterward recorded that "her hymen was recently torn. There was fresh blood in her vagina."[124]

On March 19, 1970, a GI at the base at Chu Lai, in Quang Tin Province, drove a jeep in circles while Private First Class Ernest Stepp manhandled and slapped a Vietnamese woman who had rebuffed his sexual advances. According to army documents, with the help of a fellow soldier Stepp tore off the woman's pants and assaulted her. The driver apparently slowed down the jeep to give the woman's attackers more time to carry out the assault, and offered his own advice to her: "If you don't fight so much it won't be so bad for you."[125]

Again and again, allegations of crimes against women surfaced at U.S. bases and in other rear echelon areas.[126] "Boy did I beat the shit out of a whore. It was really fun," one GI mused about his trip to the beach resort at Vung Tau.[127] The sheer physical size of American troops—on average five inches taller and forty-three pounds heavier than Vietnamese soldiers, and even more imposing in comparison to Vietnamese women—meant that their assaults often inflicted serious injuries.[128] Sometimes, Vietnamese women were simply murdered by angry GIs. One sex worker at a base in Kontum, known as "Linda" to the soldiers there, was gunned down after she laughed at a customer who, according to legal documents, "thought she was going to go out with another G.I."[129] On March 27, 1970, in Vung Tau, several Vietnamese prostitutes became embroiled in an argument with a soldier over payment. He assaulted a number of them and stabbed one to death.[130]

Most rapes and other crimes against Vietnamese women, however, did take place in the field—in hamlets and villages populated mainly by women and children when the Americans arrived. Rape was a way of asserting dominance, and sometimes a weapon of war, employed in field interrogations of women captives to gain information about enemy troops.[131] Aside from any such considerations, rural women were generally assumed by Americans to be secret saboteurs or the wives and girlfriends of Viet Cong guerrillas, and thus fair game.

The reports of sexual assault implicated units up and down the country. A veteran who served with 198th Light Infantry Brigade testified that he knew of ten to fifteen incidents, within a span of just six or seven months, in which soldiers from his unit raped young girls.[132] A soldier who served with the 25th Infantry Division admitted that, in his unit, rape was virtually standard operating procedure.[133]

One member of the Americal Division remembered fellow soldiers on patrol through a village suddenly singling out a girl to be raped. "All three grunts grabbed the gook chick and began dragging her into the hootch. I didn't know what to do," he recalled. "As a result of this one experience I learned to recognize the sounds of rape at a great distance . . . Over the next two months I would hear this sound on the average of once every third day."[134]

In November 1966, soldiers from the 1st Cavalry Division brazenly kidnapped a young Vietnamese woman named Phan Thi Mao to use as a sexual slave. One unit member testified that, prior to the mission, his patrol leader had explicitly stated, "We would get the woman for the purpose of boom boom, or sexual intercourse, and at the end of five days we would kill her."[135] The sergeant was true to his word. The woman was kidnapped, raped by four of the patrol members in turn, and murdered the following day.[136]

Gang rapes were a horrifyingly common occurrence. One army report detailed the allegations of a Vietnamese woman who said that she was detained by troops from the 173rd Airborne Brigade and then raped by approximately ten soldiers.[137] In another incident, eleven members of one squad from the 23rd Infantry Division raped a Vietnamese girl. As word spread, another squad traveled to the scene to join in.[138] In a third incident, an American GI recalled seeing a Vietnamese woman who was hardly able to walk after she had been gang-raped by thirteen soldiers.[139] And on Christmas Day 1969, an army criminal investigation revealed, four warrant officers in a helicopter noticed several Vietnamese women in a rice paddy, landed, kidnapped one of them, and committed "lewd and lascivious acts" against her.[140]

The traumatic nature of such sexual assaults remains vivid even when they are couched in the formal, bureaucratic language of military records. Court-martial documents indicate, for instance, that after he led his patrol into one village, marine lance corporal Hugh Quigley personally detained a young Vietnamese woman—because "her age, between 20 and 25, suggested that she was a Vietcong." The documents tell the story.

> After burning one hut and the killing of various animals, the accused with members of the patrol entered a hut where the alleged victim was. The accused, seeing the victim, grabbed for her breast and at the same time attempted to unbutton her blouse. As the victim held her child between the accused and herself, she pulled away.

At this time, the accused pulled out his knife and threatened to cut the victim's throat. The baby was taken from the victim and then the accused took the victim by the shoulders, laid her on the floor and then pulled her blouse above her breast and lowered her pants below her knees. The accused then knelt by the head of the victim, took his penis out of his pants and made the victim commit forced oral copulation on him. After a few minutes of this act the accused then proceeded to have non-consensual intercourse with her . . . The same witnesses who saw the accused commit these alleged acts will testify that the victim was scared and trembling.[141]

Quigley was found guilty of having committed forcible sodomy and rape.[142]

Some commanders, like an army colonel who investigated allegations of rape in an infantry battalion, nevertheless sought to cast Vietnamese women as willing participants. Writing about the heavily populated coastal regions of I and II Corps, he conjectured that in those areas "the number of young women far exceeds the number of military age males," so the local women undoubtedly welcomed the attentions of American troops as a means to "satisfy needs long denied." Assuming that all Vietnamese women longed for intercourse with armed foreigners marching through their villages, the colonel blithely concluded, "The circumstances are such that rape in contacts between soldiers . . . and village women is unlikely."[143]

The colonel's theory about universally willing partners becomes even more preposterous when we consider the shockingly violent and sadistic nature of some of the sexual assaults. One marine remembered finding a Vietnamese woman who had been shot and wounded. Severely injured, she begged for water. Instead, her clothes were ripped off. She was stabbed in both breasts, then forced into a spread-eagle position, after which the handle of an entrenching tool—essentially a short-handled shovel—was thrust into her vagina.[144] Other women were violated with objects ranging from soda bottles to rifles.[145]

At My Lai, a number of soldiers became "double veterans," as the GIs referred to men who raped and then murdered women. As the writers Michael Bilton and Kevin Sim reported, "Many women [at My Lai] were raped and sodomized, mutilated, and had their vaginas ripped open with knives or bayonets. One woman was killed when the muzzle of a rifle barrel was inserted into her vagina and the trigger was pulled."[146] In one sexual assault, three men held a teenage girl to the ground and violated her. Afterward, the girl was shot in the head and killed.[147]

As the record of the war indicates in copious fashion, however, such crimes were hardly confined to My Lai. A marine who had served in Quang Tin Province, for example, testified that a nine-man squad entered a village ostensibly to capture "a Viet Cong whore." The men located a woman, then serially raped her. The last one of them shot her through the head.[148]

Once some American soldiers had vulnerable women or girls at their mercy, there was no apparent limit to their brutality. In June 1968, an elderly Vietnamese man with no known connection to the revolutionary forces and two teenage girls alleged to be enemy nurses were detained by members of the 198th Light Infantry Brigade and taken to an American base for questioning. During their interrogation, the two girls, seventeen and fourteen years old, had their blouses torn open. They were viciously beaten with sticks, punched, slapped, kneed, and told that they would be murdered the next day. Then they were led to an area where U.S. troops were stationed for the night, and rumors of impending rape spread among the GIs.[149]

A sergeant began what would be a night of sexual sadism by raping the seventeen-year-old. At nearly the same time, a corporal raped the fourteen-year-old. Minutes later, the younger child was forced, at knifepoint, to perform oral sex on another soldier. This was followed by an attempted rape of the fourteen-year-old by still another soldier, who eventually forced her to perform fellatio on him. Yet another soldier followed and forced the child to perform oral sex on him as well. Witnesses later said that she was seen being abused by at least two more GIs after this, and was heard crying throughout the night.[150]

Meanwhile, two other soldiers may have had forcible intercourse with the older Vietnamese girl. Afterward, the sergeant who first raped her violated her for a second time. Then she was raped by the corporal who had first assaulted the younger girl. In the morning the seventeen-year-old was seen covered in blood and in a state of shock, while the younger teen was being raped again by another corporal. By this time, a witness said, she was "unconscious, with her legs in the air over the guy's shoulders." The corporal who had first raped her said that while her new attacker whooped and laughed through-out the assault, the child was "limp as a wet rag." It was, he testified, "more like torture than sex." In all, the sergeant who began the series of rapes said, each girl was violated some ten to twenty times.[151]

Later that day, in an area crowded with soldiers, the elderly man was given a rifle and, at gunpoint, ordered to kill the younger girl. He fired but succeeded only in blowing away part of the girl's chin and neck. She was then executed by an American. The older girl was left alive, though only barely so, and later disappeared.[152]

Over the course of the war, tens if not hundreds of thousands of Vietnamese were detained, like these unfortunate teenagers, by U.S. and South Vietnamese forces. For some it was only a minor inconve-nience: they were held for a few hours, questioned, and then released. Some were forced to spend a day baking in the sun, often with a bur-lap sack over their heads, but still escaped relatively unscathed. For many other Vietnamese, though, being detained would quickly turn into a nightmare ordeal.

Slaps, punches, kicks, sexual assaults, electric shocks, and the "water-rag" treatment—known today as waterboarding—were just a few of the abuses that American and South Vietnamese soldiers inflicted on their prisoners.[153] Bounced from one facility to another, from an American military base to a joint American–South Vietnamese interrogation center to a prisoner-of-war camp and back again, some detainees endured round after round of mistreatment. Others were sent to jails or prisons, sometimes languishing there for years without a trial or even an official charge against them. Some of the unluckiest would be dispatched to prison-island hellholes like Con Son and Phu Quoc, overcrowded complexes where abuse and neglect were the norm. And with the American and allied forces placing little value on prisoners' lives, outright murder was no anomaly.[154]

As with other crimes in Vietnam, the documentary record of detainee torture is sparse but exceptionally suggestive. For example, the files of the Vietnam War Crimes Working Group—the secret Pentagon task force set up to monitor war crimes in the wake of the My Lai massacre—describe 141 substantiated instances in which U.S. soldiers tortured civilian detainees or enemy prisoners of war with fists, sticks, bats, water, or electric shock. But this is the merest tip of the iceberg: most of these cases came from just one investigation of the 172nd Military Intelligence Detatchment, a single unit of fifty to a hundred men, one of many such American units in Vietnam. Vietnamese and American accounts of the war indicate that torture was also routine in Vietnam's massive incarceration archipelago, which officially included four national prisons (sometimes referred to as "rehabilitation centers"), thirty-seven provincial prisons, and more than five hundred assorted jails and detention centers built by the U.S. and the Saigon government.[155] And at the hundreds of U.S. and South Vietnamese military bases with short-term detention facilities, abuse was reportedly no less a matter of de facto policy.

The Americans and their allies were not the only side in the conflict to mistreat captives. Despite denials by former officials of the North Vietnamese regime, torture was certainly employed by Hanoi against U.S. prisoners of war.[156] However, the Vietnamese revolutionary forces only ever held about eight hundred Americans. By contrast, U.S. and South Vietnamese military and civil authorities arrested or imprisoned as many as several hundred thousand civilians and members of the revolutionary forces over the course of the war.[157] Many were detained because they were suspected of political crimes, revolutionary sympathies, or simply of holding views at odds with the South Vietnamese government. Others were picked up thanks to personal or political grudges, or sometimes for no discernible reason at all.

The everyday brutality of the Saigon government was a matter of public knowledge from the early years of the war.[158] In 1965, Neil Sheehan, writing in the *New York Times*, and William Tuohy, in the *New York Times Magazine*, painted vivid portraits of standard operating procedures in Southeast Asia. Vietnamese military, police, and paramilitary forces, wrote Sheehan, "frequently shoot Vietcong captives out of hand, beat or brutally torture them." He cataloged common methods, mentioning electrical shock, the dragging of prisoners behind vehicles, and water torture.[159] Tuohy offered an even grimmer picture.

> Anyone who has spent much time with Government units in the field has seen the heads of prisoners held under water and bayonet blades pressed against their throats . . . In more extreme cases victims have had bamboo slivers run under their fingernails or wires from a field telephone connected to arms, nipples or testicles. Another rumored technique is known as "the long step." The idea is to take several prisoners up in a helicopter and toss one out to loosen the tongues of the others.[160]

Tuohy and other reporters attributed the worst such abuses to Vietnamese allies, asserting that only a "few" American military personnel would sanction such brutal, "Vietnamese" methods.[161] One American intelligence officer, Captain Ted Shipman, an adviser to Vietnamese interrogators, echoed this sentiment to another reporter.

> You see, they *do* have some—well, methods and practices that *we* are not accustomed to, that we wouldn't use if we were doing it, but the thing you've got to understand is that this is an Asian country, and their first impulse is force. . . . Only the fear of force gets results. It's the Asian mind. It's completely different from what we know as the Western mind . . . Look—they're a thousand years behind us in this place, and we're trying to educate them up to our level.[162]

Education was, indeed, on the docket, just not in the ways Shipman suggested. For over a decade, going back to 1950, the Central Intelligence Agency had worked on perfecting a range of torture techniques that included electric shock and ruthless psychological abuse. The research culminated in a secret 1963 CIA-produced handbook known as the "Kubark Counterintelligence Interrogation" manual, and from 1962 to 1974 the CIA worked through the U.S. Agency for International Development (better known as USAID) to teach its interrogation techniques to security agents around the world, including many Vietnamese.[163] Some, such as policeman Le Van An, even trained in the United States. The thesis that An wrote at the Washington, D.C.–based International Police Academy is instructive. "Despite the fact that brutal interrogation is strongly criticized by moralists," he proclaimed, "its importance must not be denied if we want to have order and security in daily life."[164]

The CIA also set about modernizing and expanding the South Vietnamese intelligence infrastructure, conducting hands-on training for Vietnamese counterparts at Saigon's National Interrogation Center. By the end of 1965, South Vietnam had an interrogation center in every province, where electrical torture, beatings, and rape were commonplace. By 1971 the CIA techniques had been taught to 85,000 South Vietnamese government agents.[165]

Before he deployed to Vietnam in 1964, Green Beret Master Sergeant Donald Duncan was taught brutal interrogation procedures by American instructors with a wink and a nod. "When we asked directly if we were being told to use these methods the answer was, 'We can't tell you that. The Mothers of America wouldn't approve.'"[166] But there was little doubt about the instructors' intent. "Your job is to teach the various methods of interrogation to your counterpart," he was told. "If the prisoner is not disposed to talk voluntarily, it is hardly the time or place to be concerned with the Geneva Conventions."[167] Executing prisoners was also addressed, Duncan recalled. "We were continuously told 'You don't have to kill them yourself— let your indigenous counterpart do that.'"

In Vietnam, Duncan saw such practices in action. Time after time, he wrote, Americans stood by or even deliberately transferred prisoners to South Vietnamese forces for "'interrogation' and the atrocities which ensued." On one occasion, a commander told Duncan that he had almost ordered him, over the radio, to execute four prisoners. When Duncan said that he wouldn't have done it, the commander replied, "Oh, you wouldn't have had to do it; all you had to do was give them over to the Vietnamese."[168]

Those in the field weren't the only ones who knew what was going on. Even top Washington officials couldn't remain blind to it. The International Committee of the Red Cross repeatedly notified the U.S. government that it was violating the 1949 Geneva Conventions by ignoring its responsibility to ensure that prisoners handed over to South Vietnamese authorities received humane treatment. On August 10, 1965, Secretary of State Dean Rusk finally agreed that the United States would apply all provisions of the Geneva Conventions in Vietnam.[169] A year later, however, W. Averell Harriman, the ambassador-at-large for Southeast Asian affairs and the diplomat in charge of all prisoner-of-war matters, sent a secret telegram to Deputy Ambassador to South Vietnam William Porter suggesting that compliance was still not forthcoming. Despite a public declaration from the United States military that it was "observing both the letter and spirit of the Geneva Conventions in Vietnam," Harriman expressed concern that the United States had been "violating [the] Convention and will continue to violate it."[170]

As General Westmoreland noted, "Transferring the prisoners to the South Vietnamese did nothing to lessen American responsibility for those that American troops had captured."[171] Nevertheless, the State Department continued to release fact sheets to the press touting Saigon's "humanitarian treatment" of prisoners and the "dignity and respect" accorded to those locked away.[172]

What really went on in Saigon's detention facilities was recounted by a former prisoner. "I was then five months pregnant," she told an interviewer. "I was taken to the special police station and tortured for one month, six days. During that time I suffered the water torture, I was beaten, they applied electrodes to my nipples and genitals, and so I almost miscarried. I was angry and cursed them to their faces, and this led to more beatings."[173]

No one was safe from the brutality. An ailing eighty-six-year-old grandmother was among those battered by her captors. "I get sick often, why put me in jail? I am old, and haven't committed any crime, but the Special Forces soldiers beat me up mercilessly," she complained.[174] And after allied bombing destroyed his home and identification papers, a veteran of the South Vietnamese army was captured by U.S. troops. "Two Americans with two interpreters questioned me twice," he recalled. "I was beaten twice, too. Both the Americans and Vietnamese beat me."[175]

Nguyen Thi Sau was arrested in 1968 by South Vietnam's "security police" and taken in for questioning. She recounted her ordeal a few years later.

After I was arrested I was beaten so badly, even now I sometimes have headaches, and nosebleeds and ear bleeds. In those days, all we were getting to eat was rotten fish, so we asked for some vegetables. But when we complained, we were beaten and chained and lime powder was thrown on us and they poured water on us and we had nowhere to run . . . we could do nothing but stand where we were and get the water and the lime all over us. Some of us lost our teeth and our hair. And when the lime got wet, it just boiled, bubbling all over us. Our hair fell out and our skin became covered with sores. They said that if we were innocent, they would beat us until we were guilty. And if we were guilty they would beat us until we repent.[176]

Another detainee also vividly described her mistreatment at the hands of American and South Vietnamese interrogators. "They tried to force me to confess that I was involved with the Vietcong. I refused to make such a statement and so they stuck needles under the tips of my ten fingernails saying that if I did not write down what they wanted, and admit to being Vietcong, then they would continue the torture," she recalled. When she didn't comply, she recounted, "They tied my nipples to electric wires, then gave me electric shocks, knocking me to the floor every time they did so. They said if they did not get the necessary information they would continue with the torture. Two American advisers were always standing on either side of me."[177] And yet another young woman recalled that wires were applied "to one of my nipples and vagina" and that she was shocked to the point of fainting. The torture was repeated until she suffered convulsions.[178]

Such stories proliferated throughout the country. In 1968 and 1969, the International Committee of the Red Cross toured sixty U.S.-administered detention facilities where captives were interrogated before being turned over to South Vietnamese authorities. They found evidence of abuse—including beatings, burnings, and electrical torture of prisoners of war and civilian detainees alike—in every one of those camps.[179] As a result of repeated electrical torture, many victims experienced violent seizures and other chronic debilitating effects, such as headaches, ear bleeds, and dizziness.[180]

Prisoner abuse by both Saigon's forces and the Americans was as varied as it was brutal. Some captives were confined to tiny barbed-wire "cow cages" and sometimes jabbed with sharpened bamboo sticks while inside them. Others were subjected to stress positions that caused both physical agony and psychological torment. Some were locked in stifling rooms or sweltering metal shipping containers. Many were left to dehydrate in the unrelenting sun or purposely confined with prisoners suffering from contagious diseases.

Some detainees were placed in large drums filled with water; the containers were then struck with great force, which caused internal injuries but left no physical scars. Many others were subjected to various forms of water torture, including being forced to ingest unsafe amounts of water or noxious concoctions, a method sometimes called "taking the submarine." Some were suspended by ropes for hours on end or hung upside down and beaten, a practice called "the plane ride." Others were chained with their hands over their heads, arms fully extended, so that their feet could barely touch the ground—a version of an age-old torture called the strappado. Untold numbers were subjected to electric shocks from crank-operated field telephones, battery-powered devices, or even cattle prods. Still others had the soles of their feet beaten. Some had their fingernails torn out or pins or bamboo slivers stuck beneath them, or their fingertips crushed, or whole fingers cut off. Others were cut, suffocated, burned by cigarettes, or beaten with truncheons, clubs, sticks, bamboo flails, baseball bats, and other objects. Many were threatened with death or even subjected to mock executions.[181]

Daily torture was just part of a larger system of mass detention in prisons designed to break the spirit. Some of the most unfortunate detainees ended up in South Vietnam's infamous Con Son Prison, known for its tiny "tiger cages." It was a complex of seven camps on a small island off the southern coast, housing up to 10,000 prisoners. Most of the inmates were there for political offenses, and many were sentenced at kangaroo court–style proceedings or held without any trial at all.[182] For years, despite official denials, stories of heinous acts and deplorable conditions had filtered out of that Vietnamese version of Devil's Island.[183] In the summer of 1970, the American aid-worker-turned-journalist Don Luce finally arranged to give visiting U.S. congressmen Augustus Hawkins of California and William Anderson of Tennessee, who were part of a bipartisan House congressional committee touring Vietnam, a firsthand look.

American and South Vietnamese officials had long claimed that the notorious tiger cages were a thing of the past, but Luce managed to steer the congressmen away from their tour guide and into an off-limits area. There, they found a series of windowless stone cells roughly five feet wide and nine feet long, each of which housed three to five Vietnamese.[184] Through the bars that served as the cells' ceilings, the Americans looked down to see men shackled to the floor—either handcuffed to a bar or in leg irons. A bucket of lime powder sat above each cell. The lime was ostensibly for cleaning purposes, but the prisoners told another story: they said that the caustic substance was regularly thrown down as a punishment, choking and burning them. After an initial reluctance, the detainees spoke freely of their thirst, hunger, and the beatings they endured. One yelled out that he had been shackled for months on end. Another described how sand and rocks were mixed in with their meager meals of rice. A Buddhist monk said he had been imprisoned for more than three years, ever since he had publicly called for an end to the war.[185]

Hearing high-pitched screaming, the Americans ran to another area and found more cages. Each held five women, ranging in age from fifteen to seventy years old. Some pleaded for water. Others lay motionless on the floor. Most were covered in sores.[186] When the congressional delegation emerged from the secret area, their American minder was livid that they had gone there, and admonished them for the affront to the South Vietnamese prison chief. "You have no right to interfere with Vietnamese affairs . . . You are guests of Colonel [Nguyen Van] Ve. You aren't supposed to go poking your nose into doors that aren't your business."[187] Congressman Hawkins countered that since 90 percent of the Saigon government's budget came from the United States, it was definitely his business. Colonel Ve shot back, "These are very bad people . . . They will not salute the flag. They will not even salute the American flag."[188]

Hawkins and Anderson wrote a detailed report about the horrific conditions that they discovered at Con Son, but the full twelve-member congressional committee suppressed almost all of it and included only a brief paragraph about the prison in the official seventy-page account of their tour of Vietnam. According to Anderson, "Some of the committee members had serious reservations" about publicizing conditions in the prison.[189] Anderson himself was not so reticent. "It was the most shocking treatment of human beings I have ever seen," the decorated navy combat veteran bluntly told the *Washington Post*. He said the prisoners were rail thin and sickness was rampant. He had talked with a teenage girl who spoke some English and learned that she had been arrested during a political demonstration some seven months before. For two months, she had not had a bath. "She looked pitiful," Anderson said.[190]

Press accounts like this forced the Saigon government to announce that it was doing away with the notorious tiger cages. The South Vietnamese officials initially wanted to make the prisoners build their own replacement isolation cells, labeling this a "self-help" project, but after the prisoners refused the Americans took over.[191] A consortium of four U.S. construction firms—including Brown & Root, later a part of Halliburton and now KBR—eventually received a contract from the U.S. Navy, paid for through the U.S. Food for Peace program, to build new cells for Con Son. They turned out to be two square feet *smaller* than the old tiger cages.[192]

Despite all the publicity about the appalling conditions at Con Son, little changed. During inspections several months after Hawkins and Anderson visited the prison, U.S. advisers and medical personnel observed 1,500 prisoners still chained up. Of the 110 detainees that they examined, all but one showed signs of lower limb paraly-sis.[193] A few years later, when some of the tiger-cage prisoners were released, *Time* magazine described their ghastly state: "It is not really proper to call them men any more. 'Shapes' is a better word—grotesque sculptures of scarred flesh and gnarled limbs . . . They do not stand up. Years of being shackled in the tiger cages have forced them into a permanent pretzel-like crouch. They move like crabs, skittering across the floor on buttocks and palms."[194]

Con Son was not the only prison hellhole that Americans helped to build. In the late 1960s, to relieve rampant overcrowding in POW camps, the Americans and South Vietnamese conceived of a new prison camp to be built on Phu Quoc, a southern island near Cam-bodia.[195] Once it was up and running, however, Phu Quoc became just one more black site in the Vietnamese gulag. In May 1971, a Red Cross delegation visited the prison, prompting a high-level, back-channel U.S. memo, which noted that their observers found "the camp had not improved since [a] Feb 71 visit and that mistreatment of PW [prisoners of war] was very bad."[196] The Red Cross noted that many prisoners were assaulted and subjected to collective punish-ments. Some had had their toenails torn out. The delegation also found that some detainees may have been beaten to death.[197]

In 2008, I spoke with a former Phu Quoc prisoner, a farmer who said that he had never served with the guerrillas but was arrested anyway. After being tortured by his South Korean captors, he was hauled off to a South Vietnamese jail and then finally sent on to Phu Quoc. He was held there for years with neither a hearing nor a trial, and was regularly tortured by government agents. During the day, he said, the prisoners at Phu Quoc were left outside to bake in the sun. At night, when the temperature dropped, many were crammed into overcrowded cells and repeatedly doused with cold water.[198] According to another prisoner, after one detainee died during a tor-ture session, the other inmates went on a hunger strike; in response, the guards shot and killed around forty of the captives.[199]

Huynh Thi Hai told me that in 1968, American "commandos"—in all likelihood members of the elite Navy SEALs—arrived by boat in her Mekong Delta village. They killed three of her sons and took away another, a twenty-year-old who (unlike his elder brother) was not a guerrilla. He eventually ended up in Phu Quoc. When he was released five years later, his mother and sisters said he was a shell of the young man he had been. Prematurely aged and absentminded, with his hearing damaged by torture, he never fully recovered.[200]

On a day-to-day basis, places like Phu Quoc, Con Son, and the provincial interrogation centers were run by South Vietnamese authorities, which allowed Americans to maintain a certain distance from the brutal abuse of prisoners there—even if that abuse was meted out with American acquiescence, if not outright approval, and included techniques that had been taught by American instructors. But throughout the war, American forces also took an active, personal role in torturing detainees.

In January 1969, for example, Lieutenant William Bishop and his team of SEALs and Vietnamese interrogators kidnapped Tran Cong Dai, a South Vietnamese school principal. Dai was a member of the Viet Cong Infrastructure, according to a Vietnamese informant—who had been told this by another informant, who had heard it from a third informant, who, in turn, had heard it "from someone else." "In essence," an inquiry by military investigators concluded, "the source of the information is unknown." This fourth-hand hearsay, however, was enough for Bishop's team to wreck Dai's home, lock him in a metal shipping container, and later subject him to a beating. After that, according to a summary of Dai's testimony, "an American . . . came over and tied his hands and a plastic bag was put over his head. He soon passed out and came to on the ground. [Dai] then stated that he started to fight when the plastic bag was put over his head again and he lost consciousness a second time." Dai was held captive in U.S. and then South Vietnamese facilities for approximately ten days before being released "for lack of evidence."[201]

U.S. interrogators in particular seem to have employed torture as a matter of routine. Though most of the evidence is anecdotal, surviving military records do offer one detailed criminal investigation of the torture conducted by the 172nd Military Intelligence (MI) detachment. The inquiry resulted from the allegations of Lieutenant Colonel Anthony Herbert, a battalion commander with the 173rd Airborne Brigade, and the case file paints a stunning picture of everyday atrocities.

In late February or early March 1969, Herbert saw David Carmon, Thomas Hoar, and Nguyen Trong Khan, three members of the 172nd MI, interrogating a civilian detainee in a sugarcane field in Binh Dinh Province. The Vietnamese detainee was pinned to the ground, with a member of the 172nd MI sitting on his chest. "As I approached," said Herbert, "they were asking questions and pouring water over the rag forcing the Vietnamese to in-take water via his nose and mouth causing him to gag."[202]

Not long after this incident, Herbert told criminal investigators, he had walked in on the torture of a young Vietnamese woman at the 172nd MI's base camp facility. After repeatedly hearing a female voice crying out "me baby-son"—meaning that she was a child—he had entered the room and found an American captain and a sergeant alongside a Vietnamese interrogator.[203] "The girl was sitting with some wire leads going from her hands to a field telephone," Herbert said. When she gave an answer the interrogators disliked, the sergeant slapped her and then the captain nodded to the Vietnamese man, who cranked the telephone. This was "the first time I realized they were actually using the electricity," Herbert recalled. "The girl was shivering and shaking and began to scream, 'me baby-son' again." Herbert said that he reported the incident to his superior,

Colonel J. Ross Franklin, but was told that since the Vietnamese interrogator was the one who actually cranked the telephone, the situation was of no concern.[204]

That same month, a soldier told Herbert about a torture session in progress. Herbert again strode into the MI compound, where he found two interrogation sessions going on simultaneously in separate metal shipping containers. In each, a teenage girl was being beaten by South Vietnamese interrogators with a piece of bamboo that had been fashioned into a scourge. "They were lovely girls who were giving the wrong answers," Herbert wrote in his memoir. "The first wrong answer brought the flail on the hand. The next one brought the flail smack across the face. Then across the breast, taking off skin, nipples—and the screams were hideous."

Herbert told an army investigator that he had reported this incident to Colonel Franklin as well. Franklin had replied, though, that if no Americans actually struck the girls it was "none of our business." Herbert was dissatisfied with the answer. Noting that Americans were present in the area where the torture was occurring, Herbert said, "I then told him that since this was happening in an American compound it was our business and that if we condoned such, I felt we too were responsible."[205]

When the army finally did launch an investigation into the 172nd MI several years later, it found evidence of abuse exceeding anything Herbert had seen. The inquiry indicated that for at least twenty straight months, from March 1968 to October 1969, prisoners and civilian detainees were consistently "subjected to cruelty and maltreatment," with much of it carried out by American MI troops. Indeed, it appeared that the American interrogators considered torture to be a routine part of their work.

A report by army criminal investigators concluded that the unit's executive officer, Captain Norman Bowers, had witnessed some of the torture firsthand. Years later, though, Bowers told me that he had never seen or approved any abuse of prisoners, despite the testimony of subordinates to the contrary. Bowers's superior, Colonel J. Ross Franklin, the deputy commander of the 173rd Airborne Brigade, also claimed to know nothing about torture in the unit. Like Bowers, he maintained that he had never noticed the anguished cries of prisoners echoing through the compound. Housed in an officers' quarters with an air conditioner running, he explained, "I really wouldn't hear much of anything, other than friendly 'arty' [artillery] shooting once in a while."[206]

Unit member Robert Stemme, on the other hand, said that he couldn't miss the round-the-clock evidence of torture. "My bed was maybe 30 feet from where all this stuff was going on. So I could hear this . . . all night long," he told me. "It was pretty standard practice that people got slapped around or hit with things, or guns pointed at them, or whatever. Field telephones—all those things—were tools of the trade."[207] For army criminal investigators, Stemme identified thirteen fellow unit members and military policemen he had personally witnessed torturing detainees. He testified that Bowers had overseen the abuse and then helped cover it up.[208]

When additional unit members were questioned, a sordid saga emerged. One of the military policemen, William O'Sullivan, admitted to abusing prisoners in various ways, including the use of water torture. He described his method as follows: "I then had [the South Vietnamese interrogator Le Van] Hiep hold the girl . . . I then took, what I believe was a tee-shirt, probably my own tee-shirt and placed it over her nose and mouth, holding it in place with my hand, and poured water on the rag. This caused the person to lose breath and ingest some water."[209]

The interrogator David Carmon—the man Herbert had seen carrying out water torture in the sugarcane field—similarly confessed to using water torture, as well as to administering electrical shocks to detainees from a field telephone while Bowers watched. He also said that he had seen unit member David Smith striking prisoners and had witnessed Franciszek Pyclik employ water torture and electric shocks. Additionally, Carmon described for the investigators an interrogation that he had carried out with Paul Giaccaglia and Le Van Hiep in the fall of 1968. According to a CID summary, Carmon and another member of the MI team had "slapped the Vietnamese and poured water on his face from a five gallon can." The man then passed out "and was carried to the confinement cage where he was later found dead."[210]

Other unit members told similar stories. Giaccaglia testified that he and Carmon had subjected detainees to electrical shocks and that he had witnessed David Smith strike a detainee with a wooden board. Mistreatment of detainees, Robert Honore assured the investigators, was "common procedure." Larry Smith admitted to striking a detainee. Thomas Hoar confessed that he abused prisoners with electric shocks. Nguyen Hoat, a Vietnamese unit member, offered evidence that he, Carmon, Hiep, Honore, and James Cochran had used electrical torture, while Robert Newman and Eberhard Gaspar had also mistreated prisoners. Do Van Dinh testified to Honore's use of electrical torture on detainees and offered corroboration that Carmon and Hiep had abused a prisoner who later died. Pham Cong Khanh admitted that he had beaten detainees and had witnessed Carmon use electrical torture. Hiep told investigators that he had struck detainees. Unit members Fred Pampuch, Arthur Sunderbruch, James Chestnut, and Gerald Ney all confirmed that detainees had been maltreated. Captain Daniel Rodgers admitted that he had witnessed Carmon use water torture.[211]

Stacy Peterson, another unit member, recalled Paul Smilko and Hiep interrogating the wife of a suspected NLF supporter. "The woman was lying on a table with a towel over her face and water was being poured on the towel . . . This procedure went on for about 15 minutes."[212] Military policeman Willard McFalls told CID that he had observed prisoners being beaten by guards and had witnessed Hiep, Trubby May, Thomas Hoar, and Larry Tackett utilize a variety of harsh methods.[213] May, in turn, said that he, Hoar, Tackett,

O'Sullivan, Peterson, Carl Hubbard, Frederick Brown, Bob Parker, David Smith, and Larry Smith had abused prisoners with electrical torture and water torture. Tackett said that he had seen Carmon and Pyclik beat prisoners many times, had watched Pyclik threaten prisoners with a bayonet, and had witnessed David Smith beat captives on multiple occasions, including breaking a board over a prisoner's back.[214] Brown told investigators that he, Tackett, Carmon, and Robert Carey had employed water torture and administered electrical shocks to prisoners with the knowledge and consent of Bowers, and that Bowers had personally subjected noncombatants to electrical torture. And so it went.[215]

The detailed interviews conducted by the army indicated that formal charges were warranted against at least twenty-two interrogators. By the time of the belated investigation, most of them had left military service, and the army made it a practice not to pursue legal proceedings against discharged individuals. Still, that left three active duty U.S. personnel—Franciszek Pyclik, Eberhard Gaspar, and Norman Bowers—facing the possibility of court-martial. Yet their respective commanders refused to take any legal action against them.[216]

Years later I tracked down David Carmon and asked him about carrying out torture. He was unrepentant. "I am not ashamed of anything I did," he said, adding that if faced with a similar situation he would do it again. He also emphasized that I shouldn't be so naive as to believe that the 172nd MI was exceptional. "These methods were used by all units," he told me.[217] In 1971, it was revealed that an official army investigation of "Torture of Prisoners of War by U.S. Officers" had come to much the same conclusion, noting that violations of the Geneva Conventions were "widespread" and that torture by U.S. troops was "standard practice."[218]

The brutality regularly exhibited by interrogators behind closed doors at U.S. bases was also frequent among troops in the field. American soldiers in the countryside regularly beat, slapped, punched, and kicked civilian detainees and captured prisoners.[219] Sometimes, the abuse seemed to fall into the realm of outright sadism. Abraham Cooke, a veteran of multiple tours in Vietnam, told CID agents about watching an artilleryman "in a camp somewhere in the Thuy Hoa area cut off about four fingers of a prisoner. I think he was trying to interrogate the man and used a machete on his hand. One of the members of my unit saw this act, took his M-16 and shot the prisoner."[220]

Cooke interpreted the shooting as a mercy killing, an extreme response to a shocking act of torture. In fact, however, executing prisoners or putting them in situations where they might perish was hardly uncommon. Detained civilians and captured guerrillas were often used as human mine detectors and regularly died in the process.[221] In many units, prisoners were also killed under the guise of having been shot while attempting to escape, in order to increase the body count.[222] These acts were often far from subtle, but few were investigated.[223]

The wink-wink attitude that American and allied forces had toward executing prisoners is exemplified by a confidential 1968 communiqué from a U.S. adviser to a high-level American official. The adviser described a conversation with Lieutenant General Pham Xuan Chieu, who had been South Vietnam's director of police before attending the U.S. Command and General Staff College and becoming secretary general of the country's National Leadership Council. "Chieu said he himself had killed many communists," the adviser noted, detailing Chieu's method.

> If a prisoner didn't talk, he asked a special squad to escort the prisoner to an open field, to let the prisoner make an attempt to escape and then to shoot him. A report was then prepared stating that while being taken from A to B, the prisoner had attempted to escape, refused to stop after three warning shots, and was then killed. A notation was entered on the record that the corporal in charge had

been reprimanded for inattention to duty . . . "Some of my corpo-
rals had stacks this thick of such reprimands. Whenever we had
visits from some Human Rights Commission, we merely showed
them these records and were covered perfectly," Chieu said with a
delighted grin.[224]

As Chieu's account makes clear, murdering prisoners was often
a premeditated act, not merely something that occurred in the "heat
of battle" or the "fog of war."

A high-profile incident from 1969 underscores the deliberate way
that detainee killings could be carried out. In June of that year, two
Green Berets sat down with Colonel Robert Rheault to discuss the
fate of Thai Khac Chuyen, an intelligence operative they had come to
suspect was a Viet Cong double agent. They had lured Chuyen into a
trap, kidnapped him, interrogated him for days, had a Special Forces
doctor drug him with sodium pentothal (a supposed truth serum),
and subjected him to relentless polygraph examinations. Failing to
break him, they had consulted with the CIA about how to proceed.
One of the agency's officers, Clement Enking, reportedly told them
that the CIA could not officially sanction murder, but that killing
Chuyen "might be the only way out."[225]

Rheault told the men to "make up a plan."[226] After constructing
an elaborate ruse to cover their tracks, the Green Berets drugged
Chuyen, taped his mouth shut, and tied his wrists behind his back.
Then they wrapped him in a poncho and took him by boat into the
South China Sea. Out in the ocean, they attached chains and two tire
rims to the poncho, shot Chuyen in the head with a .22-caliber pistol, and dumped his corpse into the water.[227]

From premeditated execution of prisoners, it was only a small
step to systematic targeted killings—that is, assassinations of specific
individuals without any attempt to capture them alive or any thought
of a legal trial. The CIA organized, coordinated, and paid for several
such projects. In the words of one CIA analyst, these efforts were

designed to use "techniques of terror—assassination, abuses, kid-nappings, and intimidation—against the Viet Cong leadership." The principal "counterterror" effort of this kind was the Phoenix pro-gram, which employed elite U.S. troops as well as South Vietnamese and other hired guns to "neutralize" members of the "Viet Cong infra-structure," as the Americans called civilians working for the NLF.[228]

The task sounded straightforward, but the results were muddled and murderous. In 1969, the program reported 19,534 enemy "neu-tralizations," including 4,832 people killed. But only 150 of those "neutralized" were classified as senior NLF cadres. If the thousands liquidated were not the revolution's top civilian officials, then who were they? Tellingly, when Robert Komer, the head of the civilian side of the U.S. war effort, asked his friend Colonel Robert Gard to be the military deputy to the Phoenix program, Gard flatly refused. "I didn't know a lot about it except that it was an assassination pro-gram, subject to killing innocents," he told me years later. Similarly, Lieutenant Colonel William Corson called the operation "a bounty program" with little regard for guilt or innocence.[229]

It didn't take long for word to spread that Phoenix was a corrupt, informant-driven enterprise in which a significant number of non-combatants, some completely innocent, were captured, interrogated, or assassinated—that is, kidnapped, tortured, and killed—merely to meet quotas, win bounties, or settle grudges.[230] The Distinguished Service Cross recipient Vincent Okamoto, who worked in the Phoe-nix program, categorized it as "uncontrolled violence" that some-times degenerated into nothing more than "wholesale killing."[231] Even William Colby, the program's director, conceded that there were some "illegal killings," while Pentagon documents, distributed at the highest levels of the government, admitted that some Saigon officials were "using the program against personal enemies."[232]

In testimony before the House Operations Subcommittee in 1971, Colby, who was by then the U.S. pacification chief in Vietnam, dis-closed that the Phoenix program had by then killed at least 20,587 people.[233] Before the same subcommittee and in other public testimony, the military intelligence veteran K. Barton Osborn described the blank check given to Phoenix operatives to torture and murder with impunity. The examples he offered included the case of a detainee killed by having a dowel driven into his ear with a mallet, and the more general use of field telephones to shock noncombatants "into submission."[234]

Phoenix was a program run amok, but it was also the logical result of a military campaign driven by the body count and run under the precept of the mere-gook rule. For the Vietnamese, the American War was an endless gauntlet of potential calamities. Killed for the sake of a bounty or shot in a garbage dump, forced into prostitution or gang-raped by GIs, run down for sport on a roadway or locked away in a jail to be tortured without the benefit of a trial—the range of disasters was nearly endless.

While no exact figures are available, there can be little question that such events occurred in shocking numbers. They were the very essence of the war: crimes that went on all the time, all over South Vietnam, for years and years. When you consider this, along with the tallies of dead, wounded, and displaced, the scale of the suffering becomes almost unimaginable—almost as unimaginable as the fact that somehow, in the United States, all that suffering was more or less ignored as it happened, and then written out of history even more thoroughly in the decades since.

6

THE BUMMER, THE "GOOK-HUNTING" GENERAL, AND THE BUTCHER OF THE DELTA

The pervasiveness of brutality during the Vietnam War went hand in hand with a culture of defensiveness, denial, and, ultimately, impunity. Paper over any problems, conceal faults, bury bad news as much as possible; such was the standard operating procedure for commanders throughout the Vietnam years. Young officers looking to move up the chain of command knew that the appearance of battlefield success was the main thing that mattered, and that their superiors looked askance on anyone rocking the boat. So even when detailed, reliable atrocity allegations came from soldiers within the army's own ranks, the military often tamped down the reports, suppressed investigation findings, or dragged out the cases for as long as possible. And if any perpetrators were charged, they could frequently count on military juries or friends in high places to let them off with very little punishment—or with none at all.

Take Sergeant Roy Bumgarner of the army's 1st Cavalry Division and then 173rd Airborne Brigade in Binh Dinh Province, a soldier who reportedly amassed an astonishing personal body count of more than 1,500 enemy KIAs, sometimes logging more kills with his six-man "wildcat" team than the rest of his 500-man battalion combined.[1] In March 1968, Private Arthur Williams, a sniper on Bumgarner's scout team, told military authorities that on "at least four occasions" he had witnessed Bumgarner kill unarmed Vietnamese civilians—men doing nothing more than working in rice paddies or walking near their villages. In one incident, Williams told a lieutenant colonel from the inspector general's office, the team had crept up on two men working in a rice paddy. As Bumgarner took careful aim, one of the farmers spotted him and threw up his hands in surrender, but the sergeant shot him in the shoulder anyway. Both men then began shouting in Vietnamese, which Williams took to be panicked pleas for the Americans to hold their fire; neither one of them ran. Nevertheless, as the second man moved to help support his injured friend, Bumgarner unleashed a steady stream of shots, killing them both.

Williams also related a separate incident in which Bumgarner killed a young boy. And he mentioned that Bumgarner regularly planted "chicom"—Chinese communist—grenades on the bodies so that they could be called in as enemy dead.[2] "I've got nothing against Sgt Baumgardner [sic] except this mad urge to kill," Williams told the lieutenant colonel. "I don't want him to get in trouble but I can't know of what is happening and say nothing. More people will be killed."[3]

Williams's effort was for naught. "The Bummer," as he was known to his fellow troops, was a popular and well-regarded soldier's soldier; even Williams called him a "good man." He had the support of the other members of his team and, especially, of his superiors. Williams was painted as a malcontent, and his allegations were left to twist in the wind. Bumgarner continued leading "wildcat" teams on missions in the countryside, and Williams's prediction soon came true.[4]

On the morning of February 25, 1969, forty-one-year-old Nguyen Dinh set off after breakfast to irrigate the fields in his hamlet. The paddies were dry, and the villagers depended on him. His wife, Phan Thi Dan, handed him her wedding ring for safekeeping. The couple had sold a pig to pay for it, and she didn't want to lose it in the pond where she was going to collect shrimp to feed to their ducks. Later that morning, Dan heard "the rattling sounds of bullets, then one big explosion—boom." Not long after, a friend ran up to Dan, shouting that the Americans had shot her husband. Stunned, Dan stood frozen for a moment, then dropped her nets and started running toward the noise.

At the same time, Huynh Thi Nay was also running down a footpath toward the paddies. She had just come back from the market when a neighbor told her that U.S. soldiers had detained two duck herders and an irrigation worker. Nay raced to the place where she knew her teenage son Pham Tho was tending the family's ducks. "When I reached there," she remembered, "I found a pair of bamboo cages . . . with a flock of ducklings on one side. I called out 'Tho, Tho,' about three times, but no one replied." She sped on, reaching a jackfruit tree, where she spotted her son's duck-herding pole on the ground and his conical hat perched on a branch. Then she saw the bodies: her son and two others, riddled with bullets, laid out like the spokes of a wheel with their feet pointed outward. "It became as dark as night. I couldn't stop crying," Nay later recalled. "I was running back to the hamlet, crying all the way. My eyes were so full of tears, I couldn't see my way."[5]

Dan got a closer look at the grisly scene. The three victims were "badly mutilated," she said. The bodies had "no heads . . . spinal marrow and brains were splattered everywhere." The pain and rage she felt would stay with her throughout her life. "When I get flashbacks, that fit of fury still arises in me" was how she put it when I talked to her in 2006, almost four decades after the killings.[6]

It was Roy Bumgarner who had marched Nguyen Dinh, Pham Tho, and an even younger boy named Nguyen Kich to that secluded spot next to a jackfruit tree. When questioned later, Bumgarner told a tale of a typical combat operation: his six-man team had spotted three Vietnamese men and killed them when they bolted. Upon inspection, he said, the team found a number of weapons nearby. The three Vietnamese were then added to the body count. But what really happened, other unit members would later say, was cold-blooded murder: unarmed, defenseless civilians shot, their heads blown off with a grenade, and weapons planted to make them appear to be enemy combatants.[7]

An investigation followed, and another soldier from Bumgarner's team, twenty-year-old Specialist James Rodarte, admitted that the Vietnamese were unarmed and not running. They had been seated on the ground, he told investigators, when Bumgarner gave an order to fire. According to Rodarte, Bumgarner's M-16 tore the men to pieces, and the victims were already dead when, on Bumgarner's orders, he exploded a grenade near their heads. The sergeant then produced enemy weapons, which had been captured in an earlier engagement and smuggled back into the field, and briefed Rodarte on the cover story they were to use.[8]

Peter Berenbak was a young Civil Affairs officer serving on the same base as Bumgarner and his team when the murders occurred. That February day, one of his subordinates knocked on his door and told him that something had happened in the nearby friendly hamlet of Hoi Duc. He might want to investigate, the man suggested. When Berenbak drove up in his jeep, the bodies had already been carried in from the field and were spread out on a poncho liner beneath the "New Life Hamlet" sign. An old man on the scene was insisting Americans had gunned down the three, but Berenbak couldn't believe it. "Americans don't do things like this," he remembered telling himself.[9]

As the inquiry moved forward, allegations arose about Bumgarner's history of similar killings. "I've heard of Bumgarner doing it before—planting weapons on bodies when there is doubt as to their military status," Charles Boss, one of the members of the wildcat team, told an army criminal investigator. "Only a couple weeks ago I heard that Bumgarner had killed a Vietnamese girl and two younger kids (boys), who didn't have any weapons." Another unit member said that, while previously serving with a different squad, he'd also heard about Bumgarner planting grenades to cover up crimes. Berenbak would hear the same buzz. A friend in brigade intelligence told him that Bumgarner had been investigated for similar crimes on three previous occasions, once for killing children.[10]

Rodarte, for his part, told investigators that Bumgarner had advised him not to worry. "He said don't make a statement, that we had everybody on our side and we could get out of it." When the investigators spoke to him, the young soldier was wearing a souvenir from the patrol: Phan Thi Dan's wedding ring.[11]

In short order, Rodarte and Bumgarner were charged with premeditated murder and court-martialed. At Bumgarner's trial, superior officers and fellow sergeants lined up to praise the thirty-eight-year-old sergeant as a model combat leader, noting his long record of military service. Before joining the army in 1958, Bumgarner had been a marine for a decade. When he arrived in Vietnam in 1965 to serve with the army's 1st Cavalry Division, that was actually the fourth time that "The Bummer" had been deployed in Asia, having previously served with the marines in the late 1940s during the Chinese Civil War, in the 1950s during the suppression of the Huk rebellion in the Philippines, and through two tours of duty in Korea.[12] Bumgarner himself took the stand to testify about the medals he had earned, ranging from a Silver Star—the third-highest military decoration awarded for valor in combat—to a medal he had recently received for disregarding his personal safety in an attempt to save the lives of fellow soldiers.[13]

What did not come out at the trial was just how troubled Bumgarner's military career had been. Marine Corps records indicate that Bumgarner had been court-martialed, busted down in rank, and served a number of brief periods of confinement in the United States, the Philippines, and Japan. Then, in 1961, after joining the army, Bumgarner had pleaded guilty to assault and disorderly conduct and sentenced to another three months' confinement. But rather than hear about this checkered disciplinary record—or the various allegations of previous killings of noncombatants in Vietnam—the court-martial jury listened instead to witnesses like Lieutenant Colonel John Nicholson, a West Point grad who had been Bumgarner's battalion commander during parts of 1968–69. According to Nicholson, the sergeant was "tops" as a noncommissioned officer and an incredibly talented troop leader. He testified that the work of Bumgarner and his team was "outstanding."[14]

Rodarte was acquitted at his own court-martial and tried to avoid testifying at Bumgarner's trial. When he was finally compelled to do so, the story he told was markedly different from the one he had given the criminal investigators. He had previously said that the Vietnamese victims were unresisting, that the killing was wrong, that Bumgarner was "out of his mind," and that he had feared that the old soldier might assault him. At Bumgarner's trial, though, Rodarte's testimony was confused and confusing, and he now insisted that he'd believed the unit was taking enemy fire when the Vietnamese were killed.[15]

Berenbak, the Civil Affairs lieutenant, had the opportunity to attend the last day of court-martial proceedings. During the lunch break, he was shocked to see Rodarte and Nicholson sitting together with Bumgarner in the mess hall and laughing it up. When Berenbak reported the gathering to the prosecutor, that officer "just shook his head" and told him that "Bumgarner was probably going to get off because of 'the M.G.R.—the Mere Gook Rule.'"

In the end, Bumgarner was in fact convicted, but only of unpremeditated murder. He never spent a single day in prison for his crimes. Instead, for the deaths of three innocent Vietnamese civilians, he was sentenced only to be reduced in rank and fined ninety-seven dollars a month for twenty-four months. On appeal, that, in turn, was reduced to six months. The sentence pushed Berenbak over the edge. "At that point I gave up in disgust," he told me decades later, "because he had basically gotten away with murder."[16]

But while Bumgarner's cold-blooded killings shook Berenbak to his core, they left the army unfazed. On March 31, 1972, Berenbak—safely home from the war—opened the day's *New York Times* to see a familiar face smiling back at him. There was Roy Bumgarner in jungle fatigues with a beret on his head, illustrating an article on Americans for whom Vietnam had become a second home. Berenbak was particularly incensed by the fact that Bumgarner was photographed with his arm around a young Vietnamese boy, just like one of those he had been convicted of killing. "I've stayed because I like my work," Bumgarner said in the article, explaining that he had done everything in his power to remain in Vietnam.[17]

It turned out that after his 1969 court-martial, Bumgarner never even left the field. Busted down to private, he continued serving in Vietnam and reenlisted in the army in February 1970 with a request to remain in-country. The army obliged. Before the end of the year he was a sergeant again and would continue to request service in Vietnam even as troop levels fell. By the time his face graced the pages of the *Times*, he was one of only 5,000 U.S. infantrymen left in the country.[18]

After reading the story, Berenbak fired off a letter to the editor of the *Times* in which he unabashedly called Bumgarner a "murderer." He related the basics of the Bumgarner case and the allegations he had heard that, three times previously, the old soldier had been linked to the "murder of innocent civilians." It was pointless, Berenbak wrote, to lament the failure of military justice, but "discovering that he is still in Vietnam and then presented to your readers as a lovable fighting man—that disturbs me . . . I cannot help but wonder if in the last three years he might not have been under investigation again."

The *Times* told Berenbak that they were passing along his letter to the foreign desk. That was the last he heard from the newspaper. He also forwarded his missive to his congressional representative, Peter Frelinghuysen, with a cover note. "Isn't there something that can be done?" the young veteran asked. The congressman, in turn, sent on the note to the army and received a response a few weeks later from Colonel Murray Williams. Bumgarner's "reenlistment was authorized," wrote Williams, noting that a court-martial conviction did not bar an individual from service, that the army had a great need for infantrymen in Vietnam at the time, and that Bumgarner had "volunteered for such a vacancy." As Williams saw it, "SGT Bumgarner, although convicted by a court-martial, for which he paid a debt, is contributing positively in his chosen profession."[19]

The story of Roy Bumgarner, convicted of murdering three innocents and alleged to have killed many more on his way to that vaunted 1,500-plus body count, says much about the American way of war. While the sergeant was certainly atypical, spending the better part of seven years in Vietnam when most men served just a single twelve- or thirteen-month tour, what's most notable is that his peers did not consider his actions beyond the pale.[20] Indeed, many of the men with whom he served regarded him as something of a super-soldier, lauding him for his courage, combat prowess, and his care for his young troops. The former drill instructor had an enormous impact on the teenagers and twenty-somethings he led, teaching them how to survive in combat and thrive as soldiers.[21] When asked about the operation in which he killed Pham Tho, Nguyen Kich, and Nguyen Dinh, Bumgarner told the court that he was actually breaking in a new team and regarded the experience as a lesson in war fighting. "It would be a hunter-killer mission," he explained during his trial, "but also it would be a training mission."[22]

For years, Bumgarner was able to flout the U.S. military's official rules of engagement and violate the laws of war without ever paying a significant price. Just how many civilians died at Bumgarner's hand will never be known, but we do know this: He killed innocent people simply because they were Vietnamese and then labeled them as enemy dead. He mutilated bodies and planted weapons on those he murdered to conceal his crimes. He instructed subordinates to take part in his misdeeds and then help cover them up. And he trained countless impressionable young men in his methods. The military knew all of this and still welcomed his continued service. Roy Bumgarner could have been stopped, but instead the military was his enabler.

While Bumgarner was building up his body count in Binh Dinh, Colonel John Donaldson—a former Olympian with movie-star looks and an advanced degree in international affairs—was embarking on his own killing spree in neighboring Quang Ngai Province. A graduate of West Point, Donaldson had followed in the family footsteps: his older brother, his father, an uncle (a World War I air ace), both of his grandfathers (one of whom won the Medal of Honor during the Civil War), and one great-grandfather had also all graduated from the prestigious military academy.[23] He arrived in Vietnam in September 1968 and took command of the Americal Division's 11th Infantry Brigade the following month, eager to make his mark.

It was soon an open secret among the troops that Donaldson and other commanders were killing civilians. One officer remembered that Donaldson and the chief intelligence officer "had the reputation of being gook hunters. The way I heard it the pair flew around in the colonel's chopper with a crate of grenades, 'frags' they were called, and popped them in the rice fields over the 'dinks' who would attempt to run for cover when the chopper swooped down to chase them."[24] Another Americal officer recalled that Donaldson was "obsessed with having a good kill ratio and a good body count. . . . He was just a dink hunter."[25]

On January 2, 1969, helicopter pilot Walter Seger of the 174th Aviation Company, fed up with what he was seeing, formally reported that Donaldson had intentionally killed a Vietnamese civilian from his helicopter. It was a serious charge, but for years nothing came of it. The reason for the lack of follow-up became clear only some time later, when evidence surfaced that Seger's commanding officer was

r, was also implicated in killing civilians from the unit's heli-
s.[33]

this time, Donaldson was racking up medals at a pace that
ave rivaled even his rising body count. During his six months
mand of the 11th Brigade, the colonel was awarded two Dis-
shed Flying Crosses, two Silver Stars, a Bronze Star, twenty Air
s, a Soldier's Medal, and a Combat Infantryman's badge—
one medal per week. He was also rapidly moving up the mili-
od chain. In March 1969, Donaldson became the chief of staff
entire American Division, and in September he was made
nt division commander and promoted to the rank of one-star
l. When his Vietnam tour ended in March 1970—by which
he had picked up nine more Air Medals and two Legions of
—Donaldson returned to the Pentagon to serve as a top strat-
anner under the Joint Chiefs of Staff.[34]

naldson's meteoric rise was checked only in the summer of
when he became entangled in the army's belated inquiry into
y Lai massacre. Although the mass killing itself had occurred
rch 1968, half a year before Donaldson arrived in Vietnam, he
le a subject of interest to investigators because a key report
that bloody day had vanished from the American Division
uarters while Donaldson was serving as the division's chief of
Ultimately, Donaldson was identified as the only person to
equisitioned the documents before they disappeared from a
secure safe—but the investigation was unable to prove that he
estroyed the files, so no action was taken against him.[35]

more serious consequence of the My Lai inquiry, as far as
ldson was concerned, was the attention it brought to the sub-
Vietnam war crimes in general. One of the soldiers called in
estioning about the massacre mentioned that some senior offi-
d engaged in "gook-hunting" from helicopters above Quang
6 With the army already taking considerable heat over the My
assacre, Walter Seger's nearly two-year-old allegations came to

"aware of Seger's allegations at the time o

"influenced Seger and others, including a

Brigade and military police personnel, not

As with the army's decision to disregard

Bumgarner, this cover-up would soon have

the first few weeks of January 1969, Donal

reportedly targeted and killed an unarmed

colonel announced that they would report

On January 25, 1969, another unarmed Vi

Donaldson's orders about ten miles northw

according to multiple witnesses. As helicopte

remembered it, "There was a Vietnamese

hootch about ten feet. General Donaldson sai

aircraft commander remembered it too. "Fir

Donaldson say before the man was raked wit

helicopter commander stated that between

March 1969, Donaldson killed seven to nine

from his chopper.[29]

Some of Donaldson's subordinates app

example. Grogan told army investigators that

Lieutenant Colonel William McCloskey—wh

mand of the 11th Brigade's 3rd Battalion, 1st I

two before—spotted a fifty-to-sixty-year-old m

ter. As Grogan recalled, the man was unarmed

ening moves. Nevertheless, McCloskey told Ri

helicopter's commander, "Okay Mr. C, grease h

remembered McCloskey saying "something t

him." The helicopter's crew chief then "fired a bu

gun fire, the rounds hit him and he fell off th

dead," Cichowski told an army investigator.[31]

was well outside its assigned area of operations,

the body count with fake coordinates.[32] Accord

Command Sergeant Major Arthur Carver, Donal

life, and an investigation ensued. Eventually, Army Criminal Investigation Command concluded that Donaldson, "on 13 separate occasions during the period October 1968 through March 1969 . . . while flying in a helicopter over Quang Ngai Province, fired at from the air and apparently killed or ordered the killing of, unarmed and unresisting Vietnamese persons."[37] Later, Donaldson would try to defend his behavior by saying that "in these hostile areas, when you spot a military-age male and you get shot at, you try to neutralize him."[38] In twelve of these thirteen documented instances, however, CID determined that there had been no ground fire received around the time of the killings.[39]

On May 10, 1971, *Time* magazine reported that an unnamed "brigadier general, who is currently serving a tour of duty in the Pentagon, has been accused by helicopter pilots and some of those who flew with him of murdering perhaps six Vietnamese . . . He has admitted to the killings in private, making a fine distinction between innocent civilians and possible Communists by saying he shot those who 'took evasive action' as his chopper whirred overhead."[40] The next month, the story, complete with Donaldson's name, was splashed across the front page of the nation's top newspapers; the general was officially charged with murdering six civilians and assaulting two others.[41] It was a historic moment. Not since 1901, when General Jacob Smith ordered his troops to turn a large swath of Samar Island in the Philippines into a "howling wilderness," had an American general been directly charged with committing war crimes.[42]

Donaldson was hardly resigned to a guilty verdict, however. Soon enough, according to Colonel Henry Tufts, the head of CID, "there were complaints and rumors that General Donaldson was moving around among the witnesses to our investigation, pressuring them to change their stories."[43] Others played their parts as well, including Donaldson's former subordinate Colin Powell, the future chairman of the Joint Chiefs of Staff and secretary of state. Powell, who had worked closely with Donaldson for eight months in Vietnam, filed an affidavit praising Donaldson as "an aggressive and courageous brigade commander" and defending his actions in Quang Ngai.[44] "The general technique used was to locate military-age males . . . from the air," Powell wrote. "If fire was received, fire was immediately returned by the helicopter in accordance with rules of engagement. If the individual attempted to evade without firing, it was up to the judgment of the senior occupant of the aircraft" whether to kill the person.[45]

On December 9, 1971, Donaldson's commanding general dismissed the charges against him, saying, "Evidence established that no offenses were committed by General Donaldson, then a colonel."[46] What that exculpatory evidence might have been, however, is a mystery. It did not make it into the army criminal investigations files, nor has it surfaced anywhere else.[47] Years later, an investigator who worked the case claimed that the army had Donaldson "dead to rights" until two key witnesses changed their testimony, apparently under pressure, and the case fell apart.[48] Donaldson would go unpunished.

As they made their murderous way through the Vietnamese countryside, Bumgarner and Donaldson personally added an untold number of innocents to the war's grim toll. But as horrific as Bumgarner's and Donaldson's actions were, their individual killing sprees pale in comparison with the industrial-scale slaughter that was set in motion around the same time by Julian Ewell, a battle-hardened World War II hero who had made colonel fast but then languished for years in desk jobs, including stints at the White House and the Pentagon. It was only in 1968 that Ewell, now a two-star general, finally got a field command in Vietnam, and he set out to make the most of the opportunity. Entrusted by the military with the crucial Mekong Delta region, and given carte blanche to do whatever he chose, the general would turn an already perilous situation for the

Vietnamese even worse and make the killing of civilians into standard operating procedure.

Spiderwebbed with canals and waterways, packed with groves of coconut palms, the Mekong Delta was South Vietnam's most fertile rice-producing region, and a noted revolutionary stronghold. Its inhabitants—some 5 to 6 million people packed into less than 15,000 square miles, almost eight times the population density of the United States at the time—had already suffered immensely from the American free-fire mentality.[49] In the spring of 1966, for example, in an area of the upper delta known as the Plain of Reeds, the pilot of an observation plane carrying the State Department official Daniel Ellsberg (who would become famous years later for leaking the Pentagon Papers to the *New York Times*) spotted two men running from a nearby boat. The pilot put the plane into a dive and attacked them. Ellsberg could plainly see that the men were unarmed, but the pilot repeatedly fired on them, claiming that they were "Viet Cong." Later, when Ellsberg asked him how he could tell, the pilot said that "there's nothing but VC in the Plain of Reeds." Other officials, though, told Ellsberg that there were almost 2,000 fishermen in the area, braving American attacks in order to feed their families.[50]

One army officer noted the reports of dozens of "Vietcong sampans" being sunk in the region and asked the obvious: "Don't they know the sampan is the bicycle of the Delta? . . . You cannot just go around sinking sampans in this country."[51] But such considerations did not stop the Americans. In a January 1967 incident, for instance, three U.S. helicopters strafed a fleet of two hundred sampans on the delta's Bassac River, killing thirty-one civilians and wounding another thirty-eight.[52]

American ground troops, too, sowed misery in the Mekong Delta throughout the late 1960s. In January 1967, 15,000 members of the 9th Infantry Division had deployed to the delta, and they left a wide swath of destruction in their wake.[53]

Lieutenant Joseph Callaway, for example, recalled the scene after one assault on a hamlet that happened to be near the area where his soldiers had received heavy enemy fire. After helicopter gunships "pulverized" the hamlet, the ground troops had moved in. "They had torched and killed everything the gunships had not destroyed," Callaway wrote in his memoir. "I sent my platoon on through and stood in the middle of the little hamlet with everything burning around me. There were no people here now. All the animals were dead—chickens, pigs, water buffalo, everything."[54] Over the course of his tour, Callaway said, "our most effective and often used means of communication eventually became violence."[55]

But all of this was merely a prelude to Ewell's arrival. Taking charge of the 9th Division in February 1968, right after the Tet Offensive, Ewell—together with his equally ambitious chief of staff, Colonel Ira Hunt—soon set about reshaping it into a force ready and willing to wage an unrestrained war on the delta's villages and deliver staggering body counts at all costs.[56] He restructured the "Old Reliables" to increase the number of infantrymen in the field, the number of helicopter gunships in the air, and the number of night operations for both.[57] According to Ronald Bartek, a fellow West Pointer who attended a briefing by Ewell, the general had a formula in mind for the conflict: "He wanted to begin killing '4,000 of these little bastards a month,' and then by the end of the following month wanted to kill 6,000," and so on from there.[58]

Ewell's outbursts at subordinates quickly became legendary, and no one could be in his presence for long without being exposed to his body-count fixation.[59] William Taylor, then a major assigned to division headquarters, recalled the general's typical threats to his field commanders: "What the fuck are you people doing down here, sitting on your ass? The rest of the brigades are coming up with a fine body count . . . If you can't get out there and beat 'em out of the bushes, then I'll relieve you and get somebody down here who will."[60] When I spoke with him decades later, Taylor assured me that during his service in the delta, the body count was "the most important measure of success ... and it came from the personal example of the 9th Division commander, General Julian Ewell. I saw it directly. Body count was everything." He then paused and, as if to make sure I couldn't possibly mistake his meaning, repeated, "To say that body count permeated everything in operations is not an exaggeration."[61]

A raft of witnesses told the same story. Battalion commander David Hackworth remembered Ewell screaming at subordinates, "Jack up that body count or you're gone, Colonel."[62] Lieutenant Colonel William Hauser similarly recalled that "very undue emphasis was placed upon body count ... commanders were under constant pressure to produce body count as a measure of their own effectiveness."[63] When Colonel John Hayes was queried on the same subject, he smiled, and, after a pregnant pause, he responded, "Considerable emphasis was placed on body count."[64] It didn't take long for Ewell to become known as "the Butcher of the Delta."[65]

Hunt, Ewell's chief of staff who also spent time as a brigade commander with the 9th Division, shared his boss's attitude wholeheartedly. His approach, he later said, was "pounding the shit out of the little VC bastards."[66] "I felt personally that we were pressured all the time," recalled James Musselman, the brigade operations officer under Hunt, when asked about the body count.[67] While navy admiral Robert Salzer wouldn't name names, he reported that one of the 9th Infantry Division's brigade commanders was "psychologically ... unbalanced. He was a super fanatic on body count. He would talk about nothing else during an operation ... you could almost see the saliva dripping out of the corners of his mouth."[68] Robert Gard, who would later succeed Hunt as the chief of staff, put it succinctly: "He went berserk."[69]

What Hackworth called the division's "shoot-first-ask-questions-later policy" yielded exactly the statistical dividends that the two commanders craved.[70] Before Ewell took over, the 9th Infantry Division had managed a ratio of about eight enemy dead for every American killed during large unit operations, which was slightly higher than the average of U.S. forces in Vietnam at the time.[71] But this wasn't enough for Ewell, who relentlessly pressed for more. As Hackworth later admitted, "A lot of innocent Vietnamese civilians got slaughtered because of the Ewell-Hunt drive to have the highest count in the land."[72] In March 1968, for example, U.S. helicopters strafed and sank four junks filled with civilians, one of countless such incidents on delta waterways. When an adviser complained and recommended halting the practice, he was overruled. Denying the river to guerrillas was judged more important than sparing civilian lives.[73]

By July, "elimination ratios" for Ewell's 9th Division were clocking in at nearly 14:1, and the general was just getting started.[74] That summer, planning began for a large-scale offensive to "maximize the opportunity presented during the dry season for ground, air-mobile, and water mobile operations," as an army overview put it. Dubbed "Speedy Express," the operation would run from December 1968 through May 1969, with 9th Division troops conducting missions across most of the delta provinces—most notably Kien Hoa and Dinh Tuong—in conjunction with other U.S. ground, air, and naval forces as well as South Vietnamese units.[75]

As the planning for Speedy Express progressed, politics intervened to give Ewell a mandate for even more military resources and an even freer hand in employing them. With the U.S. presidential election looming in the fall of 1968, Lyndon Johnson decided to jump-start stagnant peace talks with the North Vietnamese and the NLF in Paris. This immediately gave added importance to Speedy Express, as the Pentagon sought to bring the rice-rich region and its huge population under Saigon's control before any peace could break out. With the military eager for rapid results, Ewell became the wrong man in the wrong place at the wrong time for the Vietnamese of the Mekong Delta. The United States brought to bear every option in its arsenal: helicopter gunships firing off hundreds of rounds per minute, B-52s shaking the earth with their massive bomb loads, F-4

Phantoms dropping canisters of napalm by the ton, massive navy ships stationed off the coast that could hurl Volkswagen-sized shells at targets miles inland, Swift Boats patrolling the delta's waterways with machine guns, elite teams of Navy SEALs, large numbers of snipers, and, of course, regular infantry by the thousands.

"All of these efforts jelled in the winter and spring of 1968–1969, greatly increasing the combat power and flexibility of the division," Ewell and Hunt later wrote in their history of the 9th Division's operations in the delta.[76] The statistics bear this out. During the first month of Speedy Express, the 9th Infantry Division logged a 24:1 kill ratio. It would jump to an astounding 68:1 in March and an eye-popping 134:1 in April.[77] For the first quarter of 1969, the 9th Division had double the kill ratio of the next most prolific U.S. division. By April 1969, the Pentagon noted that of eight U.S. divisions then being tracked for statistical analysis, the 9th Infantry Division accounted for fully one-third of the enemy KIAs.[78]

Just as Ewell wanted, Vietnamese were dying all over the delta. They just weren't, in many cases, enemy troops. The guerrillas were well armed but incapable of going toe-to-toe with Ewell's war machine, so they generally avoided combat when faced with the full might of the Americans—breaking up into small units and either remaining constantly on the move or hunkering down in bunkers.[79] And while Ewell's heavy firepower certainly killed many guerrillas along with civilians, even in the face of the American onslaught it wasn't difficult for the revolutionary forces to replenish their ranks with new recruits and replacement troops. The army's own estimates showed that the number of enemy forces in the region never declined during Speedy Express and may even have increased slightly.[80]

For civilians in the Mekong Delta, meanwhile, Speedy Express made an already precarious existence more dangerous. Many villagers who lived through that period recall, in particular, the relentless threat posed by American helicopters. This recurring theme in their stories is hardly surprising; as Ewell himself noted after the war, shortly before Speedy Express began, "the Delta got a lot of extra choppers—air cav[alry] troops and assault helicopter companies."[81] From January through April of 1969 alone, the 9th Division's aviation battalion would fly a total of 4,338 gunship sorties. (In addition to the destruction inflicted by the 9th Division's own helicopters, the delta was pounded throughout this time by the newly arrived Cobra helicopter gunships of the Phantom III program, whose wholesale slaughter of civilians was so vividly described by senior adviser Louis Janowski as "nonselective terrorism.") These airborne attacks were key to Ewell's plans because, as he later wrote, "a cav troop worth its salt can get 50 to 100 kills a month."[82] But as another 9th Infantry Division veteran observed, "A Cobra gunship spitting out six hundred rounds a minute doesn't discern between chickens, kids and VC."[83]

December 1968, the first month of Speedy Express, also marked the introduction of "night search" hunter-killer missions. In these operations, spotters using starlight scopes—primitive night-vision devices—identified targets with a burst of tracer fire, which then signaled accompanying helicopter gunships to rake the area with machine guns. When top adviser John Paul Vann flew on some of these sorties, he found that troops using starlight scopes simply targeted any and all people, homes, and water buffalo they saw. Once anyone or anything had been spotted, the information was relayed to the flight commander and the helicopters would attack. No attempt was made, Vann said, to determine whether the people or structures were civilian, and large numbers of innocents were killed and wounded as a result.[84] Ewell admitted as much in a postwar interview, noting that, at night, "anybody that was out there was fair game." When "peasants" were killed during nighttime curfew, he said, that was just "tough luck."[85]

In a private letter to former Westmoreland deputy Robert Komer, Vann warned "the US is on very shaky ground on either the Phantom or other 'hunter-killer' airborne missions and literally hundreds of horrible examples have been documented by irate advisors, both military and civilian."[86] Among these appalled observers was Jeffrey Record, an assistant province adviser in the delta province of Bac Lieu. On one occasion, just after Speedy Express began, Record watched from a helicopter as Cobra gunships began strafing a herd of water buffalo and the six or seven children tending them. Within seconds, the tranquil paddy was transformed into a "bloody ooze littered with bits of mangled flesh," Record recounted. "The dead boys and the water buffalo were added to the official body count of the Viet Cong."[87]

When Record asked how the pilots could be certain of the status of people below, he was told that U.S. forces shot anyone who tried to run from a helicopter, because it was a sure sign that they were enemy fighters.[88] Janowski similarly heard from a number of helicopter crews and forward air control pilots, all of whom echoed this same notion. He told his superiors: "I know of no peasant in contested or VC controlled areas who is familiar with these ground rules. The only people who are sometimes familiar with these ground rules are the VC."[89] Despite this protest, the policy of shooting anyone who ran continued.

Other reasons given for killing Vietnamese during Speedy Express were often equally spurious. Shortly after he arrived at 9th Division headquarters, Major Taylor was up with Hunt in a helicopter flying over rice paddies not far from their base. Taylor recalled Hunt saying "something to the pilot and all of a sudden, the door gunner was firing a . . . machine gun out the door and I said 'what the hell is that?' He said, 'See those black pajamas down there in the rice paddies? They're Viet Cong. We just killed two of them.'" Later Taylor asked Hunt how he could tell Viet Cong from farmers, in the absence of ground fire or any visible weapons. "He said because they're wearing black pajamas. I said, 'Well Sir, I thought workers in the fields wore black pajamas.' He said, 'No, not around here. Black pajamas are Viet Cong.'"[90]

A villager from Dinh Tuong Province summed up the Vietnamese perception of American helicopters in the delta: "If a gunner saw
anyone, even a woman or a small child or a water buffalo, he blew
them apart."[91] And a reporter who found himself in a delta hamlet
as helicopters strafed it was left with the same impression. "They
seemed to fire whimsically and in passing even though they were not
being shot at from the ground nor could they identify the people as
NLF. They did it impulsively for fun, using farmers for targets as if in
a hunting mood."[92]

Trigger-happy Americans hovering in their gunships weren't the
only threat to Vietnamese civilians during Speedy Express. According to the military, almost 6,500 tactical air strikes were carried out
in support of the operation, dropping at least 5,078 tons of bombs
and 1,784 tons of napalm.[93] Air force captain Brian Willson, who
carried out bomb-damage assessments in free-fire zones throughout
the delta, saw the results firsthand. "It was the epitome of immoral-
ity," he later told an interviewer. "One of the times I counted bodies
after an air strike—which always ended with two napalm bombs
which would just fry everything that was left—I counted sixty-two
bodies. In my report I described them as so many women between
fifteen and twenty-five and so many children—usually in their mothers' arms or very close to them—and so many old people." When he
later read the official tally of dead, he found that it listed them as 130
VC killed.[94]

Ewell, for his part, claimed that the 9th Division stressed "discriminate and selective use of firepower," and that some portions of
their area of operations actually appeared "unharmed from the air."
Still, even he admitted that in "other areas, where this emphasis
wasn't applied or wasn't feasible, the countryside looked like the Verdun battlefields."[95]

In addition to the thousands of air strikes, the Mekong Delta was
pounded continuously by ground-based artillery. In just four months
during Speedy Express, from January through April 1969, the 9th

A U.S. marine burns a Vietnamese "hootch." The thatch-and-bamboo construction of most Vietnamese homes made them easy targets for American flamethrowers and Zippo lighters.

Vi Thi Ngoi was buried beneath the bodies of her neighbors in Dien Nien hamlet when U.S. and Korean forces herded local villagers together and then opened fire on the group. Ngoi survived by feigning death; a total of 112 civilians were killed in the 1966 massacre.

A boy killed by U.S. helicopter gunfire while on his way to church—a Catholic church whose members were supporters of the pro-American government in Saigon.

Nguyen Van Tuan was a schoolboy in the Mekong Delta when a napalm strike burned his face and left him permanently scarred.

A U.S. Marine Corps flame tank sets fire to a village in Binh Son District, Quang Ngai Province. Villages were often burned to drive civilians away from areas where the Vietnamese revolutionary forces enjoyed popular support.

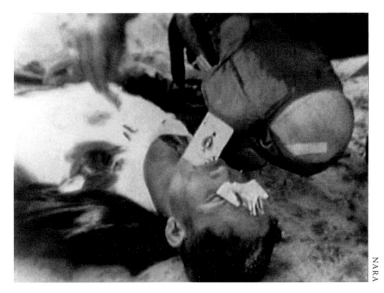

An ace of spades "death card" placed in the mouth of a Vietnamese corpse by members of the 25th Infantry Division in Quang Ngai Province.

A U.S. marine detains an elderly villager during an operation in Quang Nam Province.

Pham Thi Cuc (*above*) was wounded while trying to carry her children into a shelter during an American massacre in 1966 in the hamlet of My Luoc, Quang Nam Province. Le Thi Chung (*below*), who had hidden in some bushes, emerged to find that sixteen of her neighbors had been killed.

In February 1968, U.S.-allied South Korean troops slaughtered about eighty civilians in the village of Phong Nhi. American marines who followed on the heels of the Koreans noted that the villagers "were all shot at close range or stabbed with bayonets."

A disabled woman and a child watch as their village goes up in flames.

Tran Ba (*above*) and Tran Thi Nhut (*below*) hid in bunkers during the 1967 American massacre in the hamlet of Phi Phu, Quang Nam Province. More than thirty civilians were killed, including Nhut's seventy-year-old mother and her twelve-year-old son.

"On February 8, 1968, nineteen women and children were murdered in Vietnam by members of 3rd Platoon, B Company, 1st Battalion, 35th Infantry," Jamie Henry tells reporters at a press conference in February 1970. "I would like to emphasize that the murders of February 8, 1968, were not isolated incidents. . . . Incidents similar to those I have described occur on a daily basis and differ one from the other only in terms of numbers killed."

Division fired 311,083 artillery rounds into the delta countryside.[96] Robert Gard, who served under Ewell as an artillery commander, decried the division's "spray and slay" policies. "I tried very hard to stop the H&I fires, harassing and interdiction fires and to use fire support much more selectively," Gard told me.[97] Major Edwin Deagle, who served part of his tour as an aide to Ewell and Hunt, recalled "the tremendous amount of pressure that Ewell put on all of the combat unit operations, including artillery." This pressure, he said, "tended to create circumstances under which the number of civilian casualties would rise." Concerned specifically that Ewell's constant badgering had eroded most safeguards against firing near villages, he confronted his commander. "We'll end up killing a lot of civilians," he told Ewell.[98] Nevertheless, the bombardment continued.

Disregard for the Vietnamese meant that Americans shot early and often, no matter who might be trapped in the battle zone.[99] Deagle told me about one such incident. In the early days of Speedy Express, while serving as the executive officer of the 2nd Battalion, 60th Infantry, he was listening on the radio as one of his battalion's units stumbled into an ambush in a delta town. The company commander was almost instantly lost to enemy fire, leaving a junior officer in charge. Unable to outmaneuver the enemy forces and thoroughly confused, the lieutenant called in an air strike with imprecise instructions. The helicopter gunships, Deagle recalled, "fired a tremendous amount of 2.75[-inch rockets] into the town and that killed a total of about 145 family members or Vietnamese civilians."[100]

The carnage was evident even in official U.S. statistics, which, for instance, recorded that more than 13,000 civilians were wounded in IV Corps in just the first six months of 1969. This may even have been a significant undercount; one American general wrote that during Ewell's tenure the workload of provincial hospitals and foreign medical field teams was approximately "12,000 admissions monthly, 100,000 outpatient visits, and 1,000 major operations."[101] If just half of these were war victims, the total casualty count would be staggering.

An American medical team that went to the delta on a fact-finding mission during Speedy Express found that both Phong Dinh's five-hundred-bed provincial hospital at Can Tho and Dinh Tuong's provincial hospital at My Tho were "overflowing" with civilian war casualties. In both the Can Tho hospital and in Kien Phuong's Cao Lanh provincial hospital, the team noted, civilian war casualties accounted for up to 80 percent of all the patients.[102]

Despite its impressive kill ratios and incredibly high body counts, in August 1969 the 9th Infantry Division became the first U.S. division withdrawn from Vietnam. Some suspected that the slaughter of civilians was a reason; others saw the move only as part of the process of turning the fight over to the South Vietnamese. But whatever the motivation, the Pentagon clearly had not lost its confidence in Ewell. In the last months of Speedy Express, the hard-charging general was awarded a third star and promoted to command II Field Force, the largest U.S. combat command in the world at the time. And in the spring of 1970, he was tapped as the top U.S. military adviser for the Paris peace negotiations.

In May 1970, a few weeks before Ewell went off to Paris for the peace talks, a Vietnam veteran sat down to write a letter to General Westmoreland, now the army's chief of staff. The My Lai scandal had become front-page news in the United States just the previous fall, and the veteran had followed coverage of the massacre and allegations of other war crimes swirling around in the press. But he was writing to offer eyewitness testimony about an atrocity far larger and more damning than the death of five hundred civilians in a single village: the mass killing of civilians in the Mekong Delta during Speedy Express, month after month, hamlet after hamlet. The veteran detailed tactics, named names, and begged for the military to take action on its own. "I don't want to tell any Congressman for fear I will hurt the Army," he explained. The missive was anonymous; the veteran signed it, simply, "Concerned Sergeant."

The Concerned Sergeant letter was remarkable for the way it detailed a pattern of criminality far larger than any single incident. Referencing the murder of a detainee that had recently made headlines, he told Westmoreland: "My information about killing is worse than shooting prisoners one time, it is about nobody giving a damn about the Vietnamese." The Concerned Sergeant also pointed out that the body-count pressure he'd witnessed had come from the very top of the division. In the case of My Lai and in other incidents, he wrote, it always seemed to be enlisted men and low-level officers who ended up "getting in trouble," but the crimes originated with commanders. The veteran wanted to draw Westmoreland's attention not to a handful of massacres but to official command policies that had led to the killings of thousands of innocents.

> Sir, the 9th Division did nothing to prevent the killing, and by pushing the body [count] so hard, we were "told" to kill many times more Vietnamese than at My Lay, and very few per cents of them did we know were enemy . . .
>
> In case you don't think I mean *lots* of Vietnamese got killed this way, I can give you some idea how many. A battalion would kill maybe 15 to 20 a day. With 4 battalions in the Brigade that would be maybe 40 to 50 a day or 1200 to 1500 a month, easy. (One battalion claimed almost 1000 body counts one month!) If I am only 10% right, and believe me its lots more, then I am trying to tell you about 120–150 murders, or a My Lay each month for over a year.[103]

In this letter, and two others he sent the following year, the whistle-blower cataloged the various practices that resulted in mass civilian casualties, and explicitly branded David Hackworth and

Ira Hunt as war criminals. When Hunt was his brigade commander, the veteran wrote, the colonel was "always cussing and screaming over the radio from his [command-and-control helicopter] to the GIs or the gunships to shoot some Vietnamese he saw running when he didn't know if they had a weapon or was women or what."[104] As for Hackworth, who had been his battalion commander, the Concerned Sergeant cited his orders when it came to sampans: "I was a RTO [radio telephone operator] and I heard Col Hackworth talking to the gunship pilots, I guess. Anyway, he said there goes a boat. Then I didn't hear the pilots answer, but then Col Hackworth said I don't give a shit shoot them anyway women or not. He was very excited and angry and then he called the other company to ambush the boat."[105]

The veteran vividly described how the 9th Division's heavy firepower had wreaked havoc on populated areas. All it would take, he said, were a few shots from a village or a nearby tree line. "If anybody ever got sniper fire from a tree line we'd use gunships and artillery on the villages and go in later," the Concerned Sergeant wrote.[106] "And lots of times we'd be told to call for it even if we wasn't getting shot at. Then when we'd get in the village there would be women and kids crying and sometimes hurt or dead."[107] He found himself sympathizing with the civilians' plight because it was clear that they had no escape. "It was their farm land, and it looked like they didn't have any money to move," he recalled.[108] But the commanders had no such sympathy. The Concerned Sergeant recalled that when his unit's forward observer would say that regulations forbade firing on a village, the battalion commander would become enraged and declare "contact" with the enemy, which made it permissible to pour artillery fire into populated areas.[109]

The "number one killer" of civilians, the whistle-blower reported, was the unit's policy of shooting anyone who ran. "Run from the GIs, run from the gunships, run from the Loaches [LOHs, or light observation helicopters], the gunships and Loaches would hover

over a guy in the fields till he got scared and run and they'd zap him. GIs could see people in a field and start toward them and they'd run and get killed." Those slain were logged as guerrillas taking "evasive action"—a common euphemism that he'd personally heard more than a hundred times while serving as a radioman. Rarely, he said, were weapons found on these people.

Snipers, the veteran wrote, also regularly gunned down Vietnamese with no weapons and logged them as VC, while Hackworth made jokes about how there wouldn't be any farmers left in the delta thanks to the division's marksmen. And forcing civilians to travel ahead of patrols in order to trip any booby traps was yet another way in which innocents were killed. "None of us wanted to get blown away," the Concerned Sergeant wrote, but using civilians to set off mines was wrong. "They didn't want to get blown away either, but nobody cared about the Vietnamese. When a civilian hit a booby trap he'd most likely get called [in] as a body count too."

The letter also drew attention to the pitifully low number of weapons captured by the 9th Division, and pointed to this as evidence of Ewell's complicity in the slaughter of civilians.

> Compare them [body-count records] with the number of weapons we got. Not the caches, or the weapons we found after a big fight with the hard cores, but *a* dead VC with *a* weapon. The General just had to know about the wrong killings over the weapons. If we reported weapons we had to turn them in, so we would say that the weapons was destroyed by bullets or dropped in a canal or paddy. In the dry season, before the monsoons, there was places where lots of the canals was dry and *all* the paddies were. The General *must* have known this was made up.

According to the Concerned Sergeant, these killings all took place for one reason: "the General in charge and all the commanders, riding us all the time to get a big body count." Ultimately, he noted, "nobody ever gave direct orders to 'shoot civilians' that I know of, but the results didn't show any different than if . . . they had ordered it. The Vietnamese were dead, victims of the body count pressure and nobody cared enough to try to stop it."[110]

What Ewell, the infamous "Butcher of the Delta," had done during his time in Vietnam could not have been a great secret within the military. There was much gossip going around Vietnam that the 9th Division "didn't care what bodies" were included in the count, and even Ewell himself acknowledged that other commanders classed him in the company of "Attila the Hun."[111] Nevertheless, the whistle-blower's letter to Westmoreland created a buzz at the highest levels of the army. Within days, it was forwarded to R. Kenley Webster, the army's acting general counsel, who wrote a memo about the letter for Secretary of the Army Stanley Resor. Webster said that he was "impressed by its forcefulness" and "sincerity," and commissioned an anonymous internal report from a respected Vietnam veteran. This analysis endorsed the Concerned Sergeant's contention that obsession with body count likely led to civilian deaths. Webster sent the report to Resor, recommending that the secretary of the army confer with Westmoreland and Creighton Abrams—Westmoreland's successor as the commander of U.S. forces in Vietnam—about the allegations. According to army documents, Resor and Abrams did indeed discuss the matter that month, but no criminal investigation was launched.

In March 1971, having waited almost a year for the army to take action, the Concerned Sergeant wrote another letter, addressing it to Major General Orwin Talbott, who had made the decision to try Lieutenant William Calley for his crimes at My Lai. Then, in July, he sent a missive to the army's inspector general, Major General William Enemark, who had first assigned an investigator to Ron Ridenhour's letter.[112] In his letter to Enemark, the young whistle-blower expressed exasperation at having been ignored by Westmoreland and Talbott. "I am telling you to see if the Army will do anything about war crimes by high officers or just cover it up again," he wrote. If no action were taken, he threatened, he'd take his story to California congressman Ronald Dellums—who had spearheaded an ad hoc congressional panel looking into U.S. atrocities in Vietnam in the spring of 1971—or to the *New York Times*.[113]

The threats had some effect. In August 1971, well over a year after the Concerned Sergeant's first letter to Westmoreland, an army memo noted that the Criminal Investigation Division was ordered to identify the letter writer "to prevent his complaints [from] reaching Mr. Dellums." A few days later, Westmoreland's office directed criminal investigators to "assure him the Army is beginning investigation of his allegations." And in short order, CID reported that the division had "tentatively identified" the letter writer as George Lewis, a member of the 4th Battalion, 39th Infantry, of Ewell's 9th Division. He had served in Vietnam from June 14, 1968, to May 31, 1969, his tour concluding on the last day of Operation Speedy Express. CID said that it would seek an interview.[114]

On the same day as that CID report, however, a Westmoreland aide wrote a memo stating that the chief of staff had sought the advice of Thaddeus Beal, an army undersecretary and civilian lawyer. Beal counseled that since the Concerned Sergeant's letters were written anonymously, the army could legitimately discount them. The aide summarized Westmoreland's decision: "We have done as much as we can do on this case."[115] At a late September meeting between CID officials and top army brass, the barely begun investigation of the Concerned Sergeant's allegations was officially killed. Army records indicate that no one from the 9th Infantry Division was ever court-martialed for killing civilians during Speedy Express.[116]

The Concerned Sergeant's letters were eventually declassified, but never publicized, apparently lying all but forgotten until I uncovered them during my research in the National Archives. What, if anything, transpired between the army and George Lewis remains a mystery; he died in 2004, before I was able to locate him. Why the

Concerned Sergeant remained silent after threatening to bring his evidence to Dellums or the *New York Times* is likewise unknown.

Westmoreland's scuttling of the Speedy Express investigation spared the army from having to deal with another major atrocity scandal in the aftermath of My Lai and also served to shield his brethren from West Point. Westmoreland and Creighton Abrams were both proud members of the West Point class of 1936, while Ewell had graduated from the academy in 1939, and Ira Hunt in 1945. Many in the military spoke of a tacit "West Point Protective Association"—the WPPA—and the West Point clique assumed particular prominence during the Vietnam War. In 1968, twenty-two out of the twenty-four principal commanders and staff officers in the U.S. Army were all graduates of that prestigious military academy. Protecting West Pointers was thus essentially tantamount to protecting the military itself as an institution. Not surprisingly, quite a few West Point graduates implicated in war crimes saw the allegations against them conveniently disappear.[117]

Donaldson, West Point class of 1944, might also have been a beneficiary of the WPPA; Claire E. Hutchin, the commanding general who dismissed the murder charges against him based on mysterious "evidence" that appears nowhere in the files, was a West Pointer from the class of 1938. (Meanwhile, the disappearance of a vital report in the My Lai case while it was in Donaldson's custody was seen by some observers as intended to help protect yet other West Pointers in high-level posts within the division at the time of the massacre.)[118] And even though Bumgarner was not a West Point graduate, the WPPA's reach included him, too, since his crimes reflected directly on the West Pointers in the chain of command above him.

Bumgarner's shootings of civilians, Donaldson's "gook-hunting" missions, and Ewell's blood-soaked Speedy Express were emblematic of the entire American enterprise in Vietnam. If one man and his tiny team could claim more KIAs than an entire battalion without raising red flags among superiors; if a brigade commander could up the body count by picking off civilians from his helicopter with impunity; if a top general could institutionalize atrocities through the profligate use of heavy firepower in areas packed with civilians—then what could be expected down the line, especially among heavily armed young infantrymen operating in the field for weeks, angry, tired, and scared, often unable to locate the enemy and yet relentlessly pressed for kills? Indeed, in this atmosphere, it is remarkable that some U.S. soldiers did nevertheless blow the whistle on atrocities, lodging complaints and writing letters to commanders who bore a responsibility to investigate. But the rank-and-file troops who spoke out against murder were, for the most part, essentially powerless in the face of command-level cover-ups.

7

WHERE HAVE ALL THE WAR CRIMES GONE?

Throughout the early years of the Vietnam War, civilian suffering was everywhere and yet nowhere in the American media. News reports described thousands of incidents that violated the laws of war, but usually skipped blithely past the implications, neither labeling nor acknowledging the crimes.[1] And for every war crime that was mentioned in a newspaper or magazine, a mass of other evidence was covered up in the field or kept secret at higher command levels.

The secrecy went all the way up to the Pentagon. In 1967, for instance, after some newspaper reports about atrocities committed in Vietnam by members of the Special Forces, Defense Secretary Robert McNamara commissioned an inquiry to find out how well U.S. troops understood the Geneva Conventions. A team of agents headed by W. Donald Stewart, the chief of the Pentagon's Investigations Division for the Directorate of Inspection Services, compiled a 208-page report with shocking implications. More than 96 percent of the Marine Corps second lieutenants they surveyed, for example, indicated that they would resort to torture to obtain information. "I came back from South Vietnam thinking that things were out of control," Stewart recalled years later. But he knew that his findings "wouldn't have been good for the political image" of the military or the president, and the Pentagon certainly agreed. A high-ranking Defense Department official ordered the report to be placed in "review status," a form of bureaucratic limbo meant to kill it. Its findings were never made public.[2]

As time went on, though, some cover-ups began to crumble. In August 1969, after their elaborate scheme unraveled, seven members of the Special Forces were implicated in the torture and killing of the intelligence operative Thai Khac Chuyen. Whispers circulated about CIA involvement in the case, and the "Green Beret Affair" made the covers of *Time*, *Newsweek*, and *U.S. News and World Report*.[3] Soon, articles began to probe the Phoenix program, the agency's role in targeted killings, and, as the celebrated *Washington Post* reporter Ward Just put it, other "dirty business Americans have undertaken in this war."[4] This flurry of revelations would be short-lived, however; within a few weeks, under pressure from the CIA and the White House, Secretary of the Army Stanley Resor dismissed all charges against the Green Berets, foreclosing any possibility that further sordid details—including a dossier of CIA and Special Forces' assassinations put together by the defendants—might be entered into evidence in a courtroom.[5]

August 1969 also saw the publication of Normand Poirier's chilling *Esquire* article "An American Atrocity," which used military legal documents to reconstruct the 1966 rampage of U.S. Marines through the hamlet of Xuan Ngoc—including the gang-rape of eighteen-year-old Bui Thi Huong and the slaughter of her family. (The magazine sent proofs of the story to every major newspaper in the country, hoping to generate attention, but none showed the slightest interest.)[6] A few months later, in October 1969, the *New Yorker* published Daniel Lang's harrowing account of the 1966 kidnapping, gang-rape, and murder of Phan Thi Mao by an army patrol in II Corps. Lang's "Casualties of War," later adapted into a motion picture of the same name, not only revealed horrific crimes but also detailed the tremendous struggle of a lone whistle-blower—Sven

Eriksson—against a concerted cover-up by the four perpetrators and their superior officers. Eriksson survived a possible attempt on his life by one of the patrol members and steadfastly testified at multiple courts-martial as the proceedings stretched out over several years. He told Lang his story after becoming frustrated with the army's legalistic nitpicking and the light sentences ultimately given to the guilty men. Eriksson's account made it clear that such atrocities in Vietnam were commonplace. As Lang wrote: "Eriksson told me that it seemed clear to him in retrospect that he should have been prepared for Mao's death. It had been preceded by any number of similar occurrences. In one form or another, he said, they took place almost daily, but he was slow, or reluctant, to perceive that they were as much a part of the war as shells and targets were."[7]

The same month that "Casualties of War" was published, Arizona congressman Morris Udall sent Secretary of the Army Resor a statement written by a GI from the lone brigade of the 9th Infantry Division still remaining in Vietnam. "The affidavit is so specific and sincere that I feel it demands an investigation," the Arizona Democrat said in a cover note.[8] In his statement, the soldier described the capture, torture, and cold-blooded murder of a Vietnamese man—an increasingly familiar story by late 1969. This particular account was, however, unique in one way. It came from a dead man.

On September 12, 1969, twenty-one-year-old George Chunko had sent to his parents what he called "an actual account of an incident which occurred during a combat operation of which I personally witnessed."[9] Just days before, while on a "sweep-and-destroy" patrol, his unit had come upon a Vietnamese home. Inside it, Chunko wrote, they found a young Vietnamese woman, four young children, an elderly man, and a military-age male, later identified as Do Van Man. From the identification papers on the individuals, it appeared that Man may have been AWOL from the South Vietnamese army, and that the others present were his wife, his children, and his father-in-law.

Led by Lieutenant James Duffy, the unit was still under extreme pressure to produce a high body count, just as it had been in Ewell's days. The leader of the platoon, Chunko wrote, "fully aware of the young man's identity, seemingly ignored the knowledge . . . and proceeded to personally interrogate our 'prisoner.'"[10] In full view of his family, Man was stripped naked, "manhandled," and searched for "physical signs" that he was a member of the revolutionary forces. The platoon leader "found none, much to his dismay," added Chunko, "but nevertheless proceeded to treat (mistreat?) this individual as a captured enemy soldier."[11] Man was then taken outside and tied to a tree, as his wife fell to her knees, crying and begging for mercy. "It was obvious that our platoon leader took some sort of 'malicious' pleasure in humiliating her husband in her presence . . . In fact it appeared that her crying prodded him further in dehumanizing her husband. He conveyed to her that he would have her husband killed in the following morning."[12]

Later, Chunko watched as the prisoner was "ridiculed, slapped around and [had] mud rubbed into his face." When he asked his fellow unit members why they were torturing a man that no one believed was an actual VC, they said they were "just having a little fun." Repulsed, Chunko left the scene and began complaining about it to another soldier, but a platoon sergeant stepped in to shut him up.[13] Before the unit moved out the next morning, Chunko wrote, "the prisoner was taken into the nearby woodline by a few of us GI's. I distinctly heard 7 shots go off and saw the aforementioned GI's return from the woodline sans prisoner. The platoon leader, self appointed judge, jury and executioner had his breakfast content that he was doing a good job."[14] Man was called in as an enemy prisoner killed while trying to escape.

Only one day after Chunko wrote and signed his statement and mailed it off to his parents, he was killed as well. According to a confidential army communiqué, he was "hit by frags" during a nighttime "ambush patrol."[15] Chunko's parents, suspecting that their son had been murdered to cover up the crime, then forwarded his statement to Congressman Udall.[16]

In late November 1969, the army wrote back to Udall, informing him that it was investigating the killing of Do Van Man.[17] Lieutenant Duffy was court-martialed and, the following year, found guilty of premeditated murder—only to have the jury retract that verdict when they found out that it carried a mandatory life sentence.[18] Instead, the military court decided that the killing of Do Van Man would cost Duffy just six months in prison, with less than half his pay forfeited during that time. He wouldn't even have to leave the army.[19]

Military lawyers who observed the proceedings noted that the outcome appeared to be yet another example of the "mere-gook rule." Indeed, the only reason why Duffy wasn't acquitted altogether, some of them speculated, was that the army could no longer count on keeping the story entirely under wraps.[20] By the time of Duffy's trial, thanks to Ron Ridenhour and his persistent efforts to bring attention to the My Lai massacre, war crimes were finally front-page news.

Ridenhour had initially collected information about the 1968 massacre from various eyewitnesses while he was still serving in Vietnam. In April 1969, not long after returning to the United States, he sent registered letters to more than thirty military and civilian leaders in Washington, telling them that "something rather dark and bloody" had happened in the village. Ridenhour's letter, filled with names, locations, and descriptions of the mass killing, soon had Washington buzzing. Looking for a suitably low-level fall guy on whom to hang responsibility, the army settled on Lieutenant William "Rusty" Calley, who had commanded Charlie Company's 1st Platoon at My Lai and had no shortage of blood on his hands. (Conveniently enough, Calley was no West Pointer, but a product of the Officer Candidate School at Fort Benning, which churned out low-level commanders for Vietnam after just months of training; placing the blame entirely on him would avoid sullying the reputation of the army's academy-trained top ranks, thus protecting the public image of the army as a whole.) In September, Calley was charged with the murder of 109 "Oriental human beings" and quietly hidden away at Fort Benning.[21]

Trying to bring the massacre to wider attention, though, Ridenhour found the media still largely uninterested in exposing the truth about American activities in Vietnam. He shared his information with a reporter for the *Arizona Republic*, but an editor there refused to run the piece, which would have been the first article on My Lai to appear in the United States.[22] Through a literary agent, Ridenhour then offered his story to *Life*, *Look*, *Newsweek*, and *Harper's*; all of them passed. Only *Ramparts* showed interest, but Ridenhour was wary of the story being written off if it were published in a radical journal of the New Left.[23]

Like so many other atrocity accounts, the events at My Lai might have faded into oblivion. In the fall of 1969, though, the freelance journalist Seymour Hersh received a vague tip about an officer who had killed some seventy or eighty people. Hersh managed to find and interview Calley at Fort Benning, laying the foundation for a series of articles that would eventually win him a Pulitzer Prize. Despite the stunning quality of his reporting, *Life* and *Look* once again passed on the story.[24] Finding that newspapers were likewise uninterested, Hersh turned to Dispatch News Service, a little-known, left-leaning news agency, which finally got his story into the mainstream.[25]

On November 13, Hersh's article ran in thirty-five newspapers, including the *Chicago Sun-Times*, *St. Louis Post-Dispatch*, and *Milwaukee Journal*. Within a couple of weeks, the *Cleveland Plain Dealer* and *Life* had both published grisly photographs of the massacre taken by Ron Haeberle, including a heap of civilian bodies with children clearly among them. Adding fuel to the fire, Charlie Company's Paul Meadlo appeared in a CBS television interview with Mike Wallace, confessing his crimes.[26] He admitted that the troops had rounded up and shot hundreds of men, women, and children. "And babies?" Wallace asked repeatedly. "And babies," Meadlo replied.[27]

After many months of sitting on evidence of the My Lai slaughter, the army was visibly reeling. On November 21, 1969, Secretary of Defense Melvin Laird spoke privately to President Nixon's national security adviser, Henry Kissinger, about how—although he realized he couldn't—he'd "like to sweep the whole thing under the rug."[28] That same day, at Laird's urging, the White House communications director, Herbert Klein, warned Nixon's chief of staff, H. R. Haldeman, that the My Lai case could "develop into a major trial almost of the Nuremberg scope and could have a major effect on public opinion."[29] The Pentagon knew that it needed to contain the damage.

Within days, Westmoreland and Resor appointed Lieutenant General William Peers—a non–West Pointer who had commanded the 4th Infantry Division in Vietnam—to head an army inquiry into My Lai. The work was meant to give the appearance that the military was taking decisive action. Few people realized, though, that Peers's much-publicized inquiry was only supposed to explore the army's inadequate early investigations of the massacre at My Lai and the subsequent cover-up of the incident, not the killings themselves. The instructions from Westmoreland and Resor explicitly told Peers that "the scope of your investigation does not include . . . ongoing criminal investigations in progress."[30]

Peers, however, went beyond this limited mandate, and his panel's final report was far more frank than the army wished. As background to its investigation of the cover-up, the panel forthrightly stated that American soldiers had engaged in "widespread killing of Vietnamese inhabitants" in the area, and that these inhabitants were "comprised almost exclusively of old men, women, and children."[31]

The language of the inquiry's report left little doubt about what had occurred. It concluded that "the crimes visited on the inhabitants . . . included individual and group acts of murder, rape, sodomy, maiming, and assault on noncombatants," spoke of a "massacre" and "an almost total disregard for the lives and property of the civilian population," and concluded that the number of Vietnamese killed "may exceed 400."[32]

Moving on to the massacre's cover-up, the report then detailed a pattern of "deliberate suppression or withholding of information . . . at every command level from company to division."[33] Peers's panel particularly blamed Colonel Oran Henderson, the commander of the 11th Infantry Brigade, both for failing to stop the slaughter and for filing false reports about it afterward. Although Henderson had been hovering over the area in a command-and-control helicopter during the assault on My Lai—and also heard about the massacre in detail from several aviation unit personnel—he reported to his superiors that only about twenty civilians had died in the village, and that these had been accidentally killed by preparatory artillery or by cross fire between Americans and the Vietnamese revolutionary forces. (Henderson's superiors, the Peers report noted, then acted to conceal even those supposedly limited civilian deaths from higher headquarters.) When local Vietnamese accounts of the horrific massacre reached U.S. advisers in the area, Henderson was also instrumental in getting the army to disregard them as baseless propaganda.[34]

When Westmoreland and Resor saw a preliminary version of the report, the secretary of the army immediately summoned Peers. He didn't want to control the report, he stressed, but the message was clear: tone things down. At the press conference announcing the results of the inquiry, the Pentagon wouldn't even allow Peers to refer to the My Lai incident as a massacre. The version of the report released to the press in March 1970 was so heavily censored that it contained virtually no information about the massacre that hadn't already appeared in newspapers.[35] The actual findings of the Peers investigation were bottled up and kept secret for over four years, getting released only in late 1974, after the end of Richard Nixon's presidency.

The Pentagon was especially dismayed that Peers had chronicled not only the slaughter at My Lai by Charlie Company, 1st Battalion, 20th Infantry, but also the killings carried out on the same day in the nearby village of My Khe by the men of Bravo Company, 4th Battalion, 3rd Infantry. The whole Pentagon strategy centered on portraying My Lai as a one-off aberration, rather than part of a consistent pattern of criminality resulting from policies set at the top. Having two different massacres carried out within hours of each other by two entirely different army units in two separate villages was hardly compatible with that message. So when reporters asked about the events at My Khe, Peers sidestepped the questions, and Pentagon briefers simply lied, saying that that massacre had been perpetrated by South Vietnamese troops.[36] "Westmoreland covered his ass," Colonel Henry Tufts, the head of army criminal investigative command, would observe years later about the chief of staff's response to the My Lai affair. "He did what he had to do to sort of preserve the system."[37]

The heat generated by the coverage of the massacre got Nixon asking questions about other potential My Lais on the horizon. By the beginning of 1970, Westmoreland had assembled an unofficial task force from members of his staff to monitor allegations of war crimes and serve as an early-warning system for the Pentagon and the president. Over the next few years, the Vietnam War Crimes Working Group continuously kept an eye on the army's atrocity investigations and provided regular reports to the military brass and the White House. The group did not work to bring accused war criminals to justice or to prevent war crimes from occurring in the first place. Nor did it make public the constant stream of allegations flowing in from soldiers and veterans. As far as the War Crimes Working Group was concerned, these allegations were purely an image management problem, to be parried or buried as quickly as possible.

Over time, the group became a key part of the Pentagon's system for hiding the true nature of the war from the American public.[38]

The brass had good reason to be worried. As the 1970s began, the Pentagon's blanket denials about atrocities in Vietnam were definitely showing signs of fatigue. Seymour Hersh's My Lai exposé had changed things. Even if most atrocities were still buried with the bodies in rural hamlets that few Americans had ever heard of, more and more stories were finding their way to a reporter, past a Saigon bureau chief, over the wire to New York, and then into a newspaper or magazine. A decade into the war, and six years after Lyndon Johnson had flooded the country with combat troops, enough evidence had emerged to leave increasing numbers of Americans asking questions. What was really happening in Southeast Asia? What did it mean when reports described different units in different parts of the country at different times doing the same horrible things? Could there really be that many "bad apples" with the same inclinations? Or was something more sinister at work? Could America—the world's "good guys"—have implemented a system of destruction that turned rural zones into killing fields and made war crimes all but inevitable?

Indeed, for a brief moment in 1971, it looked as if the floodgates were about to burst. The coverage of atrocities was no longer confined to brief news articles without context. For years, the public had been seeing photos of dead and injured Vietnamese children in *Life* and other magazines, while the nightly news showed Vietnamese homes being consumed by flames.[39] Jonathan Schell's powerful inquiry into the utter devastation of Quang Ngai Province had come out in book form, as had Daniel Lang's account of the kidnapping, rape, and murder of Phan Thi Mao and Seymour Hersh's still incomparable account of the massacre at My Lai. Dozens of other books, such as the devastating volumes *In the Name of America* and *War Crimes and the American Conscience*, ate away at the notion that each atrocity brought to the attention of the American public was a singular incident.[40]

Denying the real American way of war in Vietnam, once a simple task for the U.S. military, was turning into a desperate scramble. Not long before, any mention of American criminality or the widespread nature of atrocities in Vietnam had been easily dismissed as leftist kookery or communist propaganda. But by 1971 years of revelations had opened a space for discussion. What had once been accepted only in antiwar circles was increasingly found credible in the mainstream. In 1970, Edward Herman's meaty little volume *Atrocities in Vietnam* had been published by tiny Pilgrim Press; but in 1971 it was the publishing giant Random House that put out *Crimes of War* by Richard Falk, Gabriel Kolko, and Robert Jay Lifton. Even if many Americans were still resistant, newspaper editors still wary, and television news executives eternally skittish, the accumulating evidence of a nightmare war in Vietnam was growing more difficult to ignore.

By early 1971, Telford Taylor, a retired army general who had served as chief counsel for the prosecution at the Nuremberg trials, was speaking out on ABC television's *Dick Cavett Show* and sparring in the pages of the *New York Times* with Secretary of the Army Stanley Resor and army general counsel Robert Jordan about the potential guilt of General Westmoreland himself. Resor and Jordan admitted that, in connection with My Lai, they had given thought to the Yamashita precedent: the case of a Japanese general who had been found guilty by an American military tribunal and executed in 1946 for failing to prevent atrocities by his troops, even though he had lost communication with the soldiers and had no direct control over them. Under the Yamashita standard, Taylor argued, war crimes committed by Americans in Vietnam—the widespread bombing and shelling of civilian hamlets in "free-fire" zones, the forced evacuations of peasants from their homes, and general failure to provide for the safety and care of civilians—could leave American commanders like Westmoreland in the dock.[41]

Apparently rattled, Westmoreland established a task force to examine the "Conduct of the War in Vietnam" (COWIN) and provide an insurance policy against Taylor and other critics. The group spent more than 5,000 man-hours putting together its whitewash of a report, which predictably concluded that war crimes allegations against the U.S. commander were "unfounded."[42] "While isolated criminal acts may have occurred during General Westmoreland's tenure in Vietnam," the report insisted, "they were neither widespread nor extensive enough to render him criminally responsible for their commission."[43]

In a brazen rewriting of history, the COWIN report attempted to distance Westmoreland from those policies most associated with his tenure in Vietnam: search-and-destroy operations, free-fire zones, and the "application of massive firepower." Instead, the report asserted that "General Westmoreland demanded strict adherence to the laws of war," and claimed that the rules of engagement he had put in place "established an elaborate system of checks and clearances with local officials to insure the safety of . . . civilians throughout the country."[44] The COWIN report even took specific aim at Jonathan Schell's coverage of the war, without ever mentioning the secret official inquiry—approved by Westmoreland himself—that had validated Schell's most crucial findings.[45]

Ultimately, the COWIN report wasn't made public, but its very existence testifies to the dramatically altered atmosphere in the country. It had been one thing for antiwar radicals to call the former top commander in Vietnam and now the army's chief of staff a war criminal, quite another for a retired American general who had prosecuted the top Nazis to say much the same. And Westmoreland was keenly aware of the hundreds of other atrocity allegations sitting in his office, as yet unknown to the public, many prematurely closed and buried with his help. Westmoreland was feeling the heat.

He was also watching his beloved army crumble around him. It may seem hard to believe now, but in 1971 the American military as an institution seemed to be on the verge of collapse. When Colonel Robert Heinl, a distinguished combat veteran as well as a military historian and analyst, examined its state in *Armed Forces Journal*, his evaluation was dire.

> The morale, discipline and battleworthiness of the U.S. Armed Forces are, with a few salient exceptions, lower and worse than at anytime in this century and possibly in the history of the United States. By every conceivable indicator, our army that now remains in Vietnam is in a state approaching collapse, with individual units avoiding or having refused combat, murdering their officers and noncommissioned officers, drug-ridden, and dispirited where not near-mutinous.

The state of revolt in the armed forces, Heinl concluded, was just shy of "the French Army's Nivelle mutinies of 1917 and the collapse of the Tsarist armies in 1916 and 1917."[46] A worse description was hardly possible.

The extreme levels of discontent meant that civilians and long-retired officers like Telford Taylor were not the only ones criticizing the army's conduct: active-duty soldiers and recently returned veterans were also speaking up against the military. By 1971, antiwar GIs were producing hundreds of underground newspapers that encouraged disobedience and rebellion.[47] In his article, Heinl counted no fewer than fourteen "GI dissent organizations (including two made up exclusively of officers)" that were operating more or less openly, plus "at least six antiwar veterans' groups which strive to influence GIs."

That April, in an unprecedented act, highly decorated veterans descended on Washington to return their medals and ribbons—honors that previous generations of American fighting men had always treasured. Gloria Emerson, who had covered the war as a correspondent for the *New York Times*, described the emotional scene.

They started to come on a Friday, an eccentric, a strange-looking army, wearing fatigues and field jackets, helmets and their old boonie hats, the same boots they had worn in Vietnam. Some brought bedrolls and all slept outdoors on a camping site on a small quadrangle on the Mall . . . All came with their discharge papers so their bitterest critics could not accuse them of being imposters, although some did anyway. There were a few men who did not have two legs, a few who could not rise from wheelchairs, but they were in good spirits and among their own.[48]

When the authorities erected a barricade to stop the protesters from reaching Congress, they simply reared back and hurled their Purple Hearts and Bronze Stars over the wood-and-wire wall onto the steps of the Capitol, in perhaps the single most iconic antiwar act in American history. A few dozen tried to get someone to arrest them as war criminals, but no one would. However, when 110 of the veterans sat down on the steps of the Supreme Court to protest its failure to rule on the constitutionality of the war, the police moved in. Without resistance, the men placed their hands on their heads, as prisoners were made to do in Vietnam, and were taken away.[49]

Young veterans were also coming forward by the hundreds to offer unambiguous testimony about the omnipresent atrocities in Vietnam, drawing crowds at public talks, antiwar rallies, and war crimes forums.[50] They were doing what no American fighting men had done for two hundred years: speaking out en masse against their own military. Describing the crimes committed in Vietnam in the name of America, they were, in effect, testifying against themselves. Their haunting accounts of assaults and rapes, torture and murder detailed not only what they had seen but, in many cases, what they had been ordered to do. "There was a lieutenant standing behind screaming at me to 'break' the man, 'break' being the military intelligence term to . . . get the information," former army interrogator Peter Martinsen told an assembled crowd in Washington.

And he was screaming to break him, and so I pushed [the prisoner] over backward and I almost broke his neck . . .

I finished that interrogation and I walked across our compound to another tent where interrogation was going on: a man of draftable age, no ID card. We were quite convinced he was a VC. And I proceeded to beat him with my fists. And you can beat a man senseless with your fists and not leave marks, except for a slight reddening of the skin perhaps. And this went on for some time . . . a lieutenant came in and he proceeded to beat the man to no effect, and then he wired electrical field-phone wires around the man's left wrist . . . and proceeded to "ring him up," as the term goes.

Now this didn't work . . . The lieutenant pulled down the man's trousers and proceeded to touch the electrical wires to the man's genitals and cranking the field telephone at the same time, giving him very painful shocks, all he got was a lot of "I don't know's" and some very violent screams.[51]

Vietnam Veterans Against the War, the largest and most significant of the antiwar veterans groups, boasted ten thousand members by the early 1970s, as ever more veterans felt the need to counter the official lies that they heard when they returned home.[52] Many had gone to Vietnam with their heads filled by visions of their fathers' war, as seen through the prism of the John Wayne movies of their childhoods.[53] The war they would fight, however, proved to be nothing like it had been on the silver screen. To drive home the realities of the war to ordinary Americans, some VVAW members stalked through small towns on mock search-and-destroy missions, wearing their old fatigues and carrying toy M-16 rifles. Sometimes they handed out a flyer.

A U.S. INFANTRY COMPANY JUST CAME THROUGH HERE!
IF YOU HAD BEEN VIETNAMESE—
We might have burned your house
We might have shot your dog

We might have shot you

We might have raped your wife and daughter

We might have turned you over to your government for torture

We might have taken souvenirs from your property

We might have shot things up a bit

We might have done ALL these things to you and your whole

TOWN!

If it doesn't bother you that American soldiers do these things every

day to the Vietnamese simply because they are "Gooks,"

Then picture YOURSELF as one of the silent VICTIMS.[54]

The VVAW membership ranks included Jamie Henry, the medic who had witnessed members of Company B, 1st Battalion, 35th Infantry, massacre a group of women and children in February 1968 during the Tet counteroffensive. Immediately after the massacre, Henry had made a vow to himself that he would expose the true nature of the war, but this proved to be an uphill battle. In Vietnam, when he'd spoken up about brutality, friends had warned him that if he said anything of the sort again he might get a bullet in the back during a firefight. After his return to the United States, Henry had gone right to the Judge Advocate's office at Fort Hood, Texas, but the army lawyer there also gave him a chilly reception. "The attorney for the Army told me that I should hold off on it until I was out of the service because . . . there are various ways of making people be quiet in the Army or doing things to make them disappear," Henry later recalled.[55] Even the radical magazine *Ramparts* had thought Henry's account too hot to handle. In late 1968, the magazine's military editor met with Henry and wrote up his story, but the article—which would have been the first American eyewitness account of a My Lai–style massacre to appear in print—was shelved.[56]

Only in the spring of 1970 did Henry's story finally make it into print, running in the debut issue of the short-lived muckraking magazine *Scanlan's Monthly*.[57] At a press conference, he told reporters that "incidents similar to those I have described occur on a daily basis and differ one from the other only in terms of numbers killed." The next day, a brief article about these remarks appeared in the *Los Angeles Times*, and army investigators finally met with Henry for an interview. But although they took a ten-page sworn statement from him, by this point Henry had little faith in military justice. "I never got the impression they were ever doing anything," he told me years later.[58]

Still, Henry did not give up. In January 1971, he joined more than one hundred other Vietnam veterans who testified in Detroit for a VVAW-organized event that they called the Winter Soldier Investigation.[59] (The name was taken from a pamphlet written by the revolutionary patriot Thomas Paine in 1776, which began: "These are the times that try men's souls. The summer soldier and the sunshine patriot will, in this crisis, shrink from the service of his country; but he that stands it now, deserves the love and thanks of man and woman.") Once again, Henry took the audience through his experience, in chilling detail.

We moved into a small hamlet, 19 women and children were rounded up as Viet Cong suspects [VCS] and the lieutenant that rounded them up called the captain on the radio and he asked what should be done with them.

The captain simply repeated the order that came down from the colonel that morning. The order that came down from the colonel that morning was to kill anything that moves . . . As I was walking over to him, I turned, and I looked in the area. I looked toward where the VCS were, supposed VCS, and two men were leading a young girl, approximately 19 years old, very pretty, out of a hootch. She had no clothes on so I assumed she had been raped, which was pretty SOP—and that's standard operating procedure for civilians—and she was thrown onto the pile of the 19 women and

children, and five men around the circle opened up on full automatic with their M-16s. And that was the end of that.

The Winter Soldier Investigation included testimonies from every
branch of the U.S. military and almost every major combat unit
from all periods of the war. By their very act of testifying, these veterans put the lie to any notion of bad apples and isolated incidents.
And many went beyond merely rattling off a list of individual atrocities. Instead, broadening their focus, the Winter Soldiers explicitly
pointed to superior officers and command policies as the ultimate
sources of the war crimes they had seen or committed. After describing several other killings of noncombatants that he had witnessed,
Henry told the audience: "I don't want to go into the details of these
executions because the executions are the direct result of a policy. It's
the policy that is important. The executions are secondary because
the executions are created by the policy that is, I believe, a conscious
policy within the military."[60]

As the year went on, the emphasis on command policies became
more and more a part of the public discourse. In March, the *New
York Times Book Review* splashed across its front page a seminal
essay by Neil Sheehan, an army veteran who had spent three years as
a combat correspondent in Southeast Asia. The essay's title alone was
explosive: "Should We Have War Crimes Trials?"[61] Sheehan's answer
was an unqualified yes. After cataloging thirty-three books detailing
various aspects of the U.S. way of war in Southeast Asia, Sheehan
wrote: "If you credit as factual only a fraction of the information
assembled here about what happened in Vietnam, and if you apply
the laws of war to American conduct there, then the leaders of the
United States for the past six years at least . . . may well be guilty of
war crimes." For the army's high command, Sheehan's essay represented everything they feared. In a report put together shortly after
the piece was published, one of the cadre of officers working out of

Westmoreland's office fretted about the effort to "propel the war crimes issue to the forefront of national attention and political debate."[62]

Sheehan's essay also inspired Daniel Ellsberg to leak to him Defense Secretary Robert McNamara's secret study of U.S. policy in Vietnam from the 1940s to 1968, which would soon become famous as the Pentagon Papers. (Ellsberg, who had helped to write the papers, no longer worked for the State Department, but he retained a high security clearance as a RAND Corporation employee and used it to copy the classified documents.) Outraged by the government's cover-up of the Green Beret affair, Ellsberg wanted, he later wrote, to expose "a system that lies automatically, at every level from bottom to top—from sergeant to commander in chief—to conceal murder."[63]

While the Pentagon Papers didn't deal with atrocities per se, the study contained candid analyses and secret documents outlining official lies that had kept the American public in the dark about the war through four presidential administrations. Chief among the revelations was the fact that, despite high-minded public rhetoric, U.S. war managers had little if any concern for the Vietnamese people, regarding South Vietnam as nothing more than a strategic site in the Cold War power struggle. Sheehan's first articles about the secret study ran in the *New York Times* in June 1971, and the airing of decades' worth of deceptions—along with the government's strenuous efforts to prevent newspapers from publishing more of the material—added to the growing public perception that the Pentagon could not be trusted.[64]

More and more, the tide of public opinion was turning against the ongoing conflict. Just a week after the Pentagon Papers began to be made public, the International Commission of Enquiry into United States Crimes in Indochina brought together scholars, journalists, and other experts on the war in Oslo, Norway. Several American veterans testified, including a bomber pilot, an artillery forward observer, an infantryman, and an interrogator; they were joined, in an almost unprecedented move, by Vietnamese survivors, who offered eyewitness accounts of the war from the civilian side.[65] The commission's conclusion was stark and damning. The numerous witnesses, it said,

> together have given a remarkably consistent overall picture of the U.S. warfare in Indochina. We have listened to U.S. soldiers, formerly attached to different branches of the military in Indochina, revealing what they did to the local population—acts often influenced by racial bias acquired during the course of their upbringing and military training. We have listened to statements from victims— from men and women and children—about what they have experienced of torture, imprisonment, attacks from the air or deportation. Whole villages and vast areas of their country have been destroyed. In addition to all this, we have received information from medical doctors, scientists and journalists concerning what they have seen. It all adds up to the same picture . . .

> The Commission is convinced that the crimes committed in Indochina are not only the results of actions of individual soldiers and officers. Clearly, these crimes are the results of the long-term policy of the United States in Southeast Asia, and the main burden of responsibility must lie with those who have been making this policy.[66]

Top Washington officials, however, were not about to go down without a fight. With long experience at covering up war crimes, they knew just how to evade the burden of responsibility that the Oslo commission so unambiguously placed on them. Drag out all investigations as long as possible, intimidate witnesses, obstruct courts-martial, and hope that the public would eventually lose interest; throughout the early 1970s, this would be the military's steadfast approach.

My Lai was a perfect case study. Aside from Lieutenant Calley, the initial CID investigation of the massacre had involved forty-four former members of Charlie Company as well as two other officers. Of them, the army decided to charge thirty with major crimes, but later quietly dropped the charges against seventeen former servicemen, leaving only the thirteen men who were still on active duty. By April 1971, the Pentagon was saying that an exhaustive study had determined that discharged soldiers could not be tried.[67] This was a lie: behind the scenes, in a written opinion from December 1969, the army's general counsel, Robert Jordan, had made it clear that military commissions or tribunals could be used to try ex-soldiers.[68] The only difficulty was that such military commissions would have required an order from the White House. "We would have needed the President's support to proceed," Jordan explained years later, and "the President of United States didn't support prosecution of Vietnam war crimes."[69]

Not that such prosecutions would necessarily have made much difference. In late 1970, when proceedings began against the active-duty men, case after case had quickly evaporated, as powerful generals dismissed charges and military juries let perpetrators off the hook. Sergeant Charles Hutto, one of the first men to be tried, was acquitted at his court-martial even though he himself had described the events at My Lai as "murder" to an army investigator, adding: "I wasn't happy about shooting all the people anyway. I didn't agree with all the killing, but we were doing it because we had been told."[70] Eventually, Calley would be the only person convicted in connection with the massacre—as if the deaths of more than five hundred civilians, carried out by dozens of men at the behest of higher command, were his fault alone.

The story was much the same when it came to the cover-up of the My Lai massacre. The Peers panel had named twenty-eight officers, including two generals, as being involved in the cover-up. (Four of them were already deceased by the time of the report.) The colonel tapped by Westmoreland to draft charges, however, chose to pursue legal action against just eleven of the officers that the Peers panel had named. When members of the panel tried to charge four additional officers, Secretary of the Army Resor personally stepped in to shield one of those men. A total of just fourteen officers thus ultimately had to face charges relating to the cover-up. Twelve of them saw their cases dismissed before trial; the other two, including Colonel Henderson, were acquitted.[71]

Meanwhile, the My Khe massacre that the Peers panel had also detailed in its report was effectively buried by the military. All the evidence amassed about it was classified as top secret and hidden away in Pentagon files, and the case was left to die in conspiratorial silence.[72]

And with the combined efforts of CID and the War Crimes Working Group, the military set about burying other cases as well. Army agents intimidated potential witnesses and whistle-blowers, plied them with alcohol during interviews, entreated them to lie, and carried out overt surveillance meant to bully them into silence. Some government agents showed up at workplaces to demonstrate their power to jeopardize jobs. Others attempted to bully friends and relatives, or tried to get them to undermine a veteran's credibility.[73] As official investigations of war crimes cases dragged out for years, passing from one agent to another, sent up the chain of command and kicked back down for reinvestigation, they were often strung out until most suspects were considered beyond the reach of military justice.[74]

Steven Chucala, legal adviser to CID chief Henry Tufts, later tried to excuse the routine mismanagement of war crimes allegations, saying that the CID was overworked and understaffed. He also admitted that the entire army investigative and judicial system was aligned against the process. Agents were blasé about investigations, while generals running stateside bases were reluctant to press charges. Even when court-martial proceedings did get launched, prosecutors had little inclination to perform their best, and military juries were unlikely to convict. "Everybody wanted Vietnam to go away," Chucala recalled.[75]

In the spring of 1971, Secretary of Defense Melvin Laird ordered the army's Criminal Investigation Division to be brought under tighter Pentagon control. In theory, this measure was supposed to lead to greater accountability and oversight. In practice, it allowed key Defense Department officials to take an even more active role in suppressing war crimes cases.[76] Investigations could now be quashed at the highest levels—and evidence suggests that, indeed, they were.

One Tiger Force officer, for example, recalled that during the army's investigation of his unit's war crimes, he was personally summoned to the Pentagon to attend a meeting with a major general at his side. According to the officer, an official showed them a legal brief that said the case had been closed. That brief, the officer explained, essentially said: "Yep, there's wrongdoing there, and we know about it. But basically it's not . . . in the best interest of this, that, and the other to try to pursue this." What Tiger Force troopers had done in Quang Ngai and Quang Tin, the officer said years later, was "kept awful quiet. This was a hot potato. See, this was after [the My Lai scandal], and the Army certainly didn't want to go through the publicity thing" again.[77]

Or take the case of Robert Miller, a soldier from Jamie Henry's unit who provided a sworn eyewitness statement to army criminal investigators corroborating Henry's allegations about the massacre in Quang Nam. As the investigation proceeded, Miller was visited by a colonel who claimed to know their former company commander from the Pentagon. "The colonel was there to find out if I was going to go public," Miller later recalled. When the colonel got belligerent and insulted him, Miller threw him out of his home. Still, the visit had its effect. When CID agents returned, Miller clammed up and refused to tell them anything more.[78]

High-level intervention was even more striking when it came to the investigation of atrocities reported by Lieutenant Colonel

Anthony Herbert. The allegations included Herbert's descriptions of torture at the 172nd Military Intelligence Detachment compound, as well as other horrific stories—such as his account of an incident in which South Vietnamese forces looted and burned a village, beat civilians, and murdered several detainees, all in the presence of a U.S. military adviser.[79] In late 1970, General Westmoreland sent out a memo directing that a special team be put together to deal with Herbert's charges. "I will be kept informed of progress made," he decreed.[80] As a result, CID created a "Herbert Task Force," headed by Major Carl Hensley, to conduct an unusually comprehensive investigation.[81]

The army's inquiry quickly bore out Herbert's atrocity claims. At that point, Hensley's wife, Dolores, recalled, "Carl withdrew into a shell, stopped eating, did not talk to the children and did not or would not talk to me." Soon after, he went to a doctor for "his nerves" and began taking medication and seeing a military psychiatrist. He talked in "abstract terms about problems on the job," the psychiatrist, Major William Legat, subsequently said in a sworn statement.[82] Hensley "couldn't discuss his job," Legat told me years later. "My impression was that it was because there was something big he was keeping secret."[83]

In his memoir, Herbert recalled that Hensley phoned him in early April 1971 to say "the crimes had occurred the way [Herbert] said they had." The major promised to talk to CID chief Henry Tufts and "get some results."[84] At home, however, Hensley became ever more despondent. "He kept saying that he had suppressed information and could get four to ten years at Leavenworth for what he knew," his wife later told army investigators. "I asked what did he know and he kept saying, 'Enough, enough, it goes all the way up to the highest.'" Then, she added, "He went into a deeper state of depression and kept saying the only way out was to shoot himself." On April 15, after their children had left for school, Hensley asked his wife to take their baby downstairs so he could take a nap. She did but then slipped off her shoes and crept back up the stairs, where she "found him standing in the bedroom with a shotgun. I screamed 'Carl give me the god-damned gun!' He pulled the trigger."[85]

Hensley's daughter Karla, who was thirteen at the time, came home from school to see a swarm of army agents at her house, rummaging through her father's belongings and confiscating papers. "They pulled the trash cans. They left nothing behind," she recalled years later. A neighbor of the Hensleys had a similar recollection: "The military came in and swept the house clean . . . Every piece of paper they turned over . . . They went through the trash . . . They went through their books. They searched through everything."[86]

The very next day—despite the fact that Hensley left no known suicide note, no interviews had been conducted with his family, and no investigation of the death had been carried out—a Pentagon spokesman announced that CID chief Henry Tufts had already "fully explored" the circumstances of Hensley's death and could find "absolutely no connection" between it and the Herbert investigation.[87] (In late 1971, the assistant to the army's general counsel would write privately to CID legal adviser Chucala, informing him that such assertions had been inaccurate and that there was, indeed, evidence to substantiate a connection.)[88] When CID did finally conduct an inquiry into Hensley's death, they made sure to interview Dr. Legat; as he later recalled, "They were concerned about some war crimes incidents in Vietnam." But the army's files mention nothing on the subject, and the entire investigation of the suicide seemingly ignored the question of what information Hensley might have suppressed.[89]

In the end, the army admitted nothing. Herbert would retire from the military in 1972, but criminal investigators would continue to work his case—mainly by going through his memoir and looking for ways to attack him.[90] By 1973 they had compiled a fifty-three-page catalog of alleged discrepancies in Herbert's public accounts of his time in the military. "This package . . . provides sufficient material to impeach this man's credibility; should this need arise, I volunteer for the task," Tufts wrote in a letter to Creighton Abrams, who had by then succeeded Westmoreland as army chief of staff.[91] The scores of atrocities that the army uncovered as a result of Herbert's charges would remain secret for decades.

With the My Lai trials fizzling out, and the army efficiently bottling up hundreds of other atrocity allegations, including the Tiger Force killings, the issue of war crimes gradually began to fade from public consciousness. The memorable testimonies offered by veterans at the Winter Soldier Investigation were, ultimately, just personal stories. Without some official confirmation from formal investigations and military trials, it was all too easy for skeptics to dismiss them as politically motivated exaggerations, mere antiwar agitprop.

At the same time, Nixon was steadily rebranding the conflict. A policy of "Vietnamization"—handing the ground war over to South Vietnamese forces and drawing down U.S. troops—had begun in the waning days of the Johnson administration, and by mid-1971 it increasingly pushed the war off the newspaper front pages. Fewer American combat troops and fewer American deaths, plus a war fatigue that struck newsrooms and living rooms alike, increasingly reduced the ongoing conflict to a secondary issue. "Once we've broken the war in Vietnam," Henry Kissinger, Nixon's national security adviser, told the president, "no one will give a damn about war crimes."[92]

What's more, the exposure of My Lai paradoxically worked against bringing other war crimes to public attention. Atypically large as far as massacres by ground troops were concerned, My Lai dwarfed other mass killings, making many of the atrocity allegations that surfaced later seem small and less newsworthy by comparison. It was almost as if America's leading media outlets had gone straight from ignoring atrocities to treating them as old news, with just a brief flurry of interest in between. Only something "bigger" than My Lai, in scale and scope, might then have galvanized national attention. Westmoreland knew of at least one such potentially game-changing revelation: Operation Speedy Express, which had unleashed nonstop death for half a year across thousands of square miles densely crowded with civilians. But with the army having quickly killed any investigation into the Concerned Sergeant's letters—and with the anonymous letter writer himself falling silent after his first few messages—it appeared that the details of this operation would, like so many other atrocities, forever remain a secret from the general public.

Unlike the hundreds of atrocity reports and allegations that were neatly buried in Westmoreland's office by the War Crimes Working Group, however, Speedy Express did not simply disappear. Back in February 1968, the same month that Julian Ewell had taken command of the 9th Infantry Division in the Mekong Delta, another American had arrived in Vietnam for his first "tour": *Newsweek* reporter Kevin Buckley, a Yale graduate who quickly became a press corps mainstay. By 1971 Buckley was serving as *Newsweek*'s Saigon bureau chief, and his hires included a young Vietnamese-speaking former aid worker named Alexander Shimkin. And Shimkin, it turned out, was more than a little obsessive.

The son of a retired military intelligence officer turned college professor, Shimkin had spent his spare time when he was growing up filling notebook after notebook with the order of battle for the armies of World War I: unit identifications, command structure, troop strength, and so on. Years later, he had his family send those notebooks to him in Vietnam, to keep himself busy at night. He liked to amass knowledge, to absorb it, to roll it around in his mind and figure out what it all meant.

So it was hardly surprising that when Shimkin arrived at *Newsweek*, he made a beeline for the archive of yellowing papers that the U.S. military had long been handing out to reporters. The only surprising thing was that the magazine had bothered to hold on to these souvenirs from the "Five O'Clock Follies," the military's much-disparaged nightly press briefing, which had America on the verge of victory every day for years. The hard-copy documents accompanying these briefings, though, were in fact often packed with potentially useful data. But most reporters didn't bother to crunch the numbers, perhaps because at this late date in the war they considered any official military pronouncements to be little more than the stuff of late-show punch lines.

Shimkin, however, took to the papers as if they contained the secrets of the Somme and Verdun. He digested the contents and typed up copious notes. Somewhere along the line something clicked. All those lopsided "battles" in which sampans were sent to the bottom of the Mekong's murky depths without a single injury to an American; all those enemy forces wiped out with only a weapon or two to show for it—the accumulated stories felt somehow wrong. And when Shimkin looked at the overall numbers, he knew they *were* wrong. Something dark had taken place in the delta: a mega–My Lai, a massacre that had gone on not for an afternoon but for a full six months.

Neither Shimkin nor Buckley knew about the Concerned Sergeant letters. But when Shimkin took his preliminary findings to his bureau chief, Buckley knew that they had something big. Almost four years covering Vietnam had opened Buckley's eyes to the war's brutal reality. He had seen the Americans respond to the May 1968 "mini-Tet" by utterly destroying District 8, Saigon's gleaming model of urban renewal. He had taken note of cheerleading "kill boards" toting up the dead at base camps and bloodthirsty slogans emblazoned on helicopters. When Shimkin brought him the results of his document dig, Buckley immediately sensed that the story was worth pursuing in a major way.[93]

In the course of their investigation, Buckley and Shimkin found that the 9th Infantry Division had reported killing 10,899 enemy troops during Speedy Express, even though it recovered only 748 weapons.[94] By comparison, South Vietnamese forces fighting along-side the 9th Division—long disparaged for their lack of combat prowess—had captured more than ten times as many weapons.[95] For some weeks in March and April 1969, the 9th Division's kills-to-weapons ratios were simply ridiculous. During the week of April 19, for instance, 699 guerrillas had been added to the division's body count (at the cost of a single American life), but only nine weapons were captured.[96]

Over the second half of 1971, the two reporters mined almost every source available to them to learn more about the operation. They spoke to American military officers, 9th Infantry Division veterans, and American advisers who had worked in the delta. They traveled—on foot, by jeep, in boats, and even by raft—into the areas hit hardest by Speedy Express to interview South Vietnamese officials and the villagers filtering back to their ruined hamlets. They surveyed vast areas of destruction—gunfire-pocked buildings, house-less bunkers, cratered rice fields, endless groves of decapitated coconut trees. All the evidence pointed to utterly unrestrained violence on a grand scale.

Analyzing medical records in the Ben Tre provincial hospital in Kien Hoa, which served one tiny area of the delta, Buckley and Shimkin found that during Speedy Express it had treated 1,430 civilians who had been wounded by U.S. firepower—adding up to more than 200 civilian casualties for every month of the operation around Ben Tre alone. And this calculation was certainly an undercount of the true toll. "Many of the people who were wounded in Kien Hoa never got to any hospital because they died on the way," one U.S. official told Buckley. "Many others were treated at home, or in hospitals run by the VC or in small dispensaries operated by the [South Vietnamese army]. The people who got to Ben Tre were lucky and lived nearby."[97]

Overall, an American official with long experience in the delta told Buckley that as many as 5,000 of the people killed by Speedy

Express were noncombatants. The detailed investigation conducted by Buckley and Shimkin themselves arrived at estimates of the same magnitude.[98]

In late November 1971, Buckley sent a letter to MACV, drawing their attention to the lopsided kills-to-weapons ratio. "Research in the area by *Newsweek* indicates that a considerable proportion of those people killed [during Speedy Express] were non-combatant civilians," Buckley wrote.[99] The colonel who headed the MACV information branch soon replied, confirming the ratio and many of the details that the *Newsweek* reporters were uncovering, such as the high percentage of casualties inflicted at night and by helicopters. He insisted, however, that Buckley's claim about civilian casualties could not be substantiated. Instead, the military contended that many of the dead were simply *unarmed* guerrillas. What's more, Buckley's request to interview MACV commander Creighton Abrams was rejected. The MACV spokesman stated that Abrams (who in fact had been briefed on the Concerned Sergeant's allegations by the secretary of the army the year before) had "no additional information on the operation."[100]

Another prominent official trying to steer clear of Buckley's way at this time was John Paul Vann, who had witnessed the fallout of Speedy Express firsthand. According to David Farnham, Vann's deputy, Vann told him that he was ducking Buckley's questions about the operation because the subject was "so sensitive." Unwittingly echoing the Concerned Sergeant's letter, Vann said that Speedy Express had been, in effect, "many My Lais."[101]

Vann had good reason to keep quiet. Though at one point an outspoken critic of U.S. military strategy, he had always been committed to winning the war, and by 1971 he had talked top officials into believing that he was the man to accomplish the task. Now the third-highest-ranking American serving in Vietnam—and the first civilian in U.S. history to be placed in command of U.S. military forces in wartime—he wasn't about to let the American effort be destroyed by scandal.[102] While in Washington for the Christmas holiday, he and Farnham met with Westmoreland and army vice chief of staff Bruce Palmer Jr. to discuss the implications of Buckley's forthcoming story.[103]

At the meeting, Vann told Westmoreland and Palmer that Ewell's 9th Division had wantonly killed civilians to boost its body count and further the general's career, and singled out nighttime helicopter gunship missions as the worst of the division's tactics. According to Farnham, Westmoreland put on a "masterful job of acting," claiming repeatedly that he had never before heard such allegations. When Vann mentioned the upcoming *Newsweek* exposé, Westmoreland directed his aide and Farnham to leave the room. He said that he, Palmer, and Vann needed to discuss "a very sensitive subject," and he didn't want the aides to hear the discussion lest they be compelled to testify about it at a later date.[104]

Buckley knew that he had the military running scared. He told his editors in New York that, according to a military insider, "both MACV and the Pentagon are extremely worried about our research into Speedy." Another official told Buckley that the military had long waited for this particular shoe to drop. As he put it, "MACV was afraid they had a PR disaster on their hands with that division and were surprised when it didn't happen."[105]

Now, several years after Ewell's reign of terror had ended, the PR disaster was finally upon them. Buckley and Shimkin filed a nearly 5,000-word exposé on the horrors of the operation, plus a powerful sidebar filled with eyewitness testimony from Vietnamese survivors. The results were damning. The piece exposed wanton killing on a massive scale and appeared to conclusively answer the questions the reporters asked in the story's lead: "Was the My Lai massacre an isolated incident? Or were civilian casualties a constant, accepted and indeed inevitable result when American combat units with enormous firepower fought in populated areas? Was My Lai only a particularly gruesome application of a policy which in fact killed many more civilians than were killed in that small village?"[106] It was the stuff of Pulitzer Prizes and congressional hearings. For *Newsweek*, it was a potential blockbuster; for the military, a surefire nightmare.

On January 17, Buckley cabled the first draft to New York. But instead of rushing the story into print, *Newsweek*'s editors pushed back. They claimed that articles about civilians killed by "indiscriminate" fire were nothing new, objected to Buckley's linking of My Lai and Speedy Express, and requested that the article be radically shortened. They wanted Buckley to focus on a single war crime, not the overarching American way of war.[107]

In private cables to New York, Buckley responded by pointing out that the magazine's editors were urging him to cut exactly what terrified the military. "They do not fear revelation of more specific atrocities as much as they fear a report which will . . . focus on the inevitability of casualties as a result of command policy." A My Lai–style exposé would simply be laid at the feet of some lieutenant or captain, Buckley explained, whereas the story that he and Shimkin wrote

> points the finger at the top echelon instead of the bottom. Indeed, it is not charges of indiscriminate use of firepower which they fear. Instead, it is charges of quite discriminating use—as a matter of policy in populated areas . . . it is to say that day in and day out that division killed noncombatants with firepower that was anything but indiscriminate. The application of firepower was based on the judgment that anybody who ran was an enemy and indeed, that anyone who lived in the area could be killed.[108]

Still, Shimkin headed back to the delta for further reporting, where he turned up yet more corroborating Vietnamese witnesses, and Buckley then reworked the article, striving to get it into print before his scheduled departure from Indochina in early 1972. At the opening of the new draft, Buckley wrote: "Four years here have convinced me that terrible crimes have been committed in Vietnam. Specifically, thousands upon thousands of unarmed, noncombatant civilians have been killed by American firepower. They were not killed by accident. The American way of fighting this war made their deaths inevitable." He also presciently predicted that, with the Vietnamization of the conflict, "there may never be an accounting for these crimes."[109]

With the New York editors still dragging their feet and the article in limbo, Buckley handed over the reins of the Saigon bureau and took a long vacation. When he returned to New York in the spring of 1972, he again pushed for the article's publication, finally asking for the right to freelance it elsewhere. *Newsweek*'s editors refused, fearing they might be seen as fainthearted for not publishing the exposé themselves. "At last I got a reason out of the editor Kermit Lansner," Buckley told an interviewer some years later. "He told me that it would be a gratuitous attack on the [Nixon] administration at this point to do another story on civilian deaths after the press had given the army and Washington such a hard time over My Lai."

Buckley and Shimkin's piece, whittled down to 1,800 words, finally appeared in the June 19, 1972, issue of *Newsweek*, which hit the newsstands around June 12. Billed as Buckley's Vietnam farewell piece, it was bylined only to him and was irreparably compromised by editing that excised much of Buckley and Shimkin's reporting. Many key facts, eyewitness interviews, and even any mention of Julian Ewell's name were all left on the cutting room floor. In its eviscerated state, the article attracted only a slight ripple of interest. The story of Speedy Express, which should have been even more explosive than Seymour Hersh's exposé on My Lai, quickly faded away.[110]

Had Buckley and Shimkin's investigation been published in full form in January or February 1972, it might have proven to be the crest of the wave of interest in war crimes allegations, resulting in irresistible public pressure for high-level inquiries. Had the army been called to account, had Westmoreland's cover-up unraveled under the glare of hearings, had the suppressed allegations of the Concerned Sergeant been brought to light and linked to reports from the whistle-blowing advisers in the Mekong Delta as well as to the testimony of veterans at the Winter Soldier Investigation, and had other veterans been emboldened to step forward, Speedy Express might have transformed the country's understanding of the entire conflict. With the military already buckling under the weight of internal dissent, it might have blown the lid off the entire American project in Vietnam and called the American way of war into serious question.

Of course, none of those might-have-beens ever happened.

On June 15, 1972, a *Newsweek* reporter in Washington asked if either the Pentagon or MACV were "conducting any investigation of the reports that the 9th Infantry Division killed about 5,000 civilians in 'Operation Speedy Express' in the Mekong Delta?" The Defense Department simply answered "no": a response as unambiguous as it was untrue. An internal *Newsweek* cable from Nick Proffitt, Buckley's successor as Saigon bureau chief, noted that a "high MACV source says Army launched a probe into Newsweek Speedy Express story with purpose of compiling a rebuttal. So far, investigation has come to the conclusion that story was right on target and indeed most of those killed during operation were civilians."[111]

In fact, on the day the *Newsweek* article appeared in the United States, a cable had shot from the Pentagon to Saigon about the piece, and by the morning of June 14 the chief of the MACV inspector general's investigative division was already working on an analysis of the article and of Speedy Express. A week and a half later, he presented his findings, including a startling admission.

While there appears to be no means of determining the precise number of civilian casualties incurred by US forces during Operation Speedy Express, it would appear that the extent of these casualties was in fact substantial, and that a fairly solid case can be constructed to show that civilian casualties may have amounted to several thousand (between 5,000 and 7,000).[112]

The inspector general's report called Buckley's article "irresponsible" and attempted, at every turn, to minimize American culpability. Nevertheless, its conclusions were stunning. Not only did the report paint the *Newsweek* figure of 5,000 noncombatant deaths as a low-end estimate, which meant that noncombatants were likely the majority of those killed by U.S. forces during Speedy Express, but it also validated Buckley's contention that civilian deaths were "a constant, accepted and indeed inevitable result" of Ewell's operation. Moreover, the secret report acknowledged that commanders had initiated the atrocities with eyes wide open: "The U.S. command, in its extensive experience with large scale combat operations in Southeast Asia, appreciated the inevitability of significant civilian casualties in the conduct of large operations in densely populated areas such as the Delta."[113]

The inspector general's findings were the ultimate smoking gun. But they, too, were expertly suppressed. The information would be kept secret not only from Buckley—and, as a result, the American people—but from lawmakers as well. In a letter to Buckley that fall, Senator J. William Fulbright, chair of the Senate Foreign Relations Committee, lamented the "difficulties" encountered by the committee when it tried to get any answers from the military. "I would like to pursue the matter," Fulbright assured Buckley, but he seemed resigned to being stonewalled: "I am very doubtful that anything can be done to fix responsibility for possible atrocities committed in connection with Operation Speedy Express." And when the Iowa senator and army veteran Harold Hughes directly questioned Pentagon officials about Speedy Express, they had a ready answer. In a September 1972 letter, Deputy Assistant Secretary of Defense Dennis Doolin explained to Hughes that MACV was unable to substantiate Buckley's estimate of civilian victims and had told him so while the article was being prepared. "No information developed by any source since that time has been able to substantiate it as well," Doolin now wrote. "Nevertheless, you may rest assured that the Departments of Defense and the Army will continue to investigate specific allegations of war crimes as they are reported."[114]

John Paul Vann died in a noncombat-related helicopter crash in Vietnam days before Buckley and Shimkin's article was published in *Newsweek*. About a month later, Shimkin was killed while on assignment in Quang Tri Province. Buckley took a year's sabbatical and eventually left *Newsweek*. The Concerned Sergeant stayed silent, and his letters remained buried in the army's secret archives, as did the army investigation that validated his allegations and Buckley and Shimkin's findings. With them all went the last, best chance for the truth about the war to finally emerge.

In 1973, Ewell and Hunt were commissioned by the army to document their methods for use by future commanders. The book they produced, titled *Sharpening the Combat Edge*, whitewashed the history of their time in the Mekong Delta, failed to even mention Speedy Express by name, and completely ignored the allegations against them save for a few dismissive lines. "The 9th Infantry Division and II Field Force, Vietnam have been criticized on the grounds that 'their obsession with body count' was either basically wrong or else led to undesirable practices," Ewell and Hunt wrote. "The basic inference that they were 'obsessed with body count' is not true." Instead, they claimed, their methods had ended up "'unbrutalizing' the war."[115] A few decades later, Hunt would write a history of the 9th Infantry Division in Vietnam that, not surprisingly, also almost totally ignored allegations about the mass killing of civilians.[116]

To say that the military's top-level cover-ups and *Newsweek*'s partial suppression of its own investigation were effective would be an understatement. There have been more than 30,000 nonfiction books published on the Vietnam War since the conflict began, but only a

tiny fraction focus on American atrocities.[117] Of these, nearly all the
ones written since 1975 concentrate exclusively on the My Lai massacre, or narrowly investigate a particular subject. And while some
of the texts on atrocities written during the war cast a wider net, they
were necessarily anecdotal, fragmentary, and speculative, lacking
official documentary evidence and a comprehensive picture of the
war's entire duration across the various regions of the country. Only
by combining veterans' testimonies, contemporaneous press coverage, Vietnamese eyewitness accounts, long-classified official studies,
and the military's own formal investigations into the many hundreds
of atrocity cases that it knew about can one begin to grasp what the
Vietnam War really entailed.

After the war, most scholars wrote off the accounts of widespread
war crimes that recur throughout Vietnamese revolutionary publications and American antiwar literature as merely so much propaganda. Few academic historians even thought to cite such sources,
and almost none did so extensively. Meanwhile, My Lai came to
stand for—and thus blot out—all other American atrocities. Vietnam
War bookshelves are now filled with big-picture histories, sober studies of diplomacy and military tactics, and combat memoirs told from
the soldiers' perspective. Buried in forgotten U.S. government archives,
locked away in the memories of atrocity survivors, the real American
war in Vietnam has all but vanished from public consciousness.[118]

WANDERING GHOSTS

On a sunny July afternoon in 2010, I stood amid a solemn crowd of people gathered in the intense California heat. Some of them were dressed in suits and ties, others in casual attire; a few had come in military uniforms. There were some somber words, a three-volley salute. And then Jamie Henry's coffin was lowered into the ground.

I came back to the same spot early the next day, alone now, contemplating the freshly turned mound of earth in the crisp morning stillness, and my thoughts ran back to the first time I had met Henry in person, almost five years before. We had arranged a visit at his home, a cozy house with a white post-and-rail fence around it, nestled in the foothills of the Sierra Nevadas. Arriving, I knew that I'd found the right place: Henry had hung a fluorescent pink ribbon from a tree in his front yard to catch my eye, and it had done the trick. But when he opened the door to me, I was shocked. I had expected him to be much larger. Larger than life, actually.

That's what happens, I suppose, when you live with an oversized idea of someone for years before meeting him. The idea of a rare man with the courage to step forward, ignore threats, and put names to murderers; the courage to stand up for women and children gunned down in a hamlet halfway across the planet, a distant place to which

no Americans had ever given a thought unless they'd walked through
it with weapon in hand.

Unconsciously, I guess I'd assumed that one had to be physically
imposing to exhibit that type of bravery. But Henry wasn't much
taller than me—and I'm no giant. He was leaner than I expected,
too. His hair had gone white at the temples. His face was weathered
and well lined. He had what you might call a rugged look, a mountain-
man appearance but without the bulk or the beard, and with icy blue
eyes that were more kindly than steely. He sat me down at his dining
room table, and we began to look over the phonebook-sized stacks of
documents I had brought—several reams of photocopied army files.
These were the records of the three-and-a-half-year inquiry that
army investigators had conducted into Henry's atrocity allegations,
following up on his sworn statement about a string of brutalities that
had culminated in the massacre of some nineteen innocent civilians
six weeks before My Lai.

I knew Henry's case by heart by this point, but he himself had
had no idea that these files existed until I'd called him up out of the
blue. Now he saw that dozens of other soldiers from his company,
fellow witnesses to the killings, had talked to army investigators as
the Vietnam War wound down. Veteran after veteran had told the
investigators the same basic story: nineteen or so women and children rounded up and held under guard while an American officer
went looking for volunteers to carry out a superior's orders to "kill
anything that moves."

The army had never bothered to tell Henry—let alone the American people—that it had established that what he'd said was true. Nor
had it taken any action. Not one man was ever jailed, disciplined, or
even charged with any crime in connection with the massacre. The
entire investigation, so seemingly thorough and meticulous, had
been carried out for no discernible reason at all.

Henry and I talked for most of that day. We spoke about his
memories of the massacre and the other atrocities he'd witnessed,

about the threats he'd endured from fellow soldiers when he spoke out against their brutality, about his efforts to force the army to investigate and his long struggle to get the American public to listen. He seemed calm enough throughout the conversation. Only later would he tell me that after I finally left he had stayed in his chair for an hour, shaking uncontrollably.[1]

Jamie Henry was not the only person I met while writing this book whose memories of the war proved too vivid, too excruciating, even several decades after the events. There were so many others. I will never forget, for instance, my interview with Ho Thi A, the survivor of the 1970 massacre in the tiny rural hamlet of Le Bac (2). In measured tones, she described for me how, as a young girl, she'd taken cover in a bunker with her grandmother and an elderly neighbor, scrambling out just as a group of marines arrived—and how one of the Americans had then leveled his rifle and shot the two old women dead while she watched. She told me her story calmly, collectedly. It was only after I moved on to more general questions about the hamlet that she suddenly broke down, sobbing convulsively. There was nothing I could do to comfort her. For ten, fifteen, twenty minutes and more, despite all her efforts to restrain herself, the flood of tears kept pouring out.[2]

In Vietnam, where the "lives" of the deceased are believed to be inextricably intertwined with those of the living, it is thought that those who die a "bad death" may be forced to suffer as "wandering ghosts," trapped in a limbo between our world and the land of the dead. In this shadow land, they forever reexperience the violence that ended their lives, unable to attain peace until the living truly acknowledge them and the fate they suffered.[3] The idea of such wandering ghosts is an unfamiliar one for most Americans, but we should not be too quick to dismiss it. The crimes committed in America's name in Vietnam were our "bad death," and they have never been adequately faced. As a result, they continue to haunt our society in profound and complex ways.

Despite the decades that have passed, despite the presidents who have attempted to rebrand the war or dispatch it to the dustbin of history, Americans are still in the thrall of a conflict that refuses to pass quietly into the night. Never having come to grips with what our country actually did during the war, we see its ghost arise anew with every successive military intervention. Was Iraq the new Vietnam? Or was that Afghanistan? Do we see "light at the end of the tunnel"? Are we winning "hearts and minds"? Is "counterinsurgency" working? Are we applying "the lessons of Vietnam"? What are those lessons, anyway?

The true history of Vietnamese civilian suffering does not fit comfortably into America's preferred postwar narrative—the tale of a conflict nobly fought by responsible commanders and good American boys, who should not be tainted by the occasional mistakes of a few "bad apples" in their midst. Still, this is hardly an excuse for averting our eyes from the truth. For more than a decade I have combed through whatever files I managed to locate, searched out the witnesses who remained, and listened as best I could. What I've ended up with can offer, I hope, at least a glimpse of the real war: the one that so many would like to forget, and so many others refuse to remember.

NOTES

INTRODUCTION: AN OPERATION, NOT AN ABERRATION

1. Charles R. McDuff, letter to Richard M. Nixon, Public Correspondence—White House, M–Z, War Crimes and Other Topics, 1971, Record Group 319, Records of the Army Staff, Office of the Deputy Chief of Staff for Personnel (ODSPER), Records of the Vietnam War Crimes Working Group, Vietnam War Crimes Working Group Central File, National Archives and Records Administration (hereafter cited as NARA), College Park, Maryland, Box 5.
2. Franklin M. Davis, letter to Charles R. McDuff, in ibid.
3. Michael Bilton and Kevin Sim, *Four Hours in My Lai* (New York: Penguin, 1993), 381, 97–99; Michal Belknap, *The Vietnam War on Trial* (Lawrence: University Press of Kansas, 2002), 171.
4. Seymour Hersh, *Cover-Up* (New York: Random House, 1972), 3–4; Bilton and Sim, *Four Hours in My Lai*, 111–14, 117, 128–34, 216; Seymour Hersh *My Lai 4* (New York: Vintage 1970), 57.
5. Many detailed works on the My Lai massacre exist. Among the best are Bilton and Sim, *Four Hours in My Lai*, and Hersh, *My Lai 4*. For a unique and often-ignored account of child victims of My Lai, see Betty Lifton and Thomas Fox, *Children of Vietnam* (New York: Atheneum, 1972), 100–109.
6. Hersh, *Cover-Up*, 27, 165–66.
7. Committee to Denounce the War Crimes of the U.S. Imperialists and Their Henchmen in South Vietnam, *Crimes Perpetrated by the US Imperialists and Henchmen against South Viet Nam Women and Children* (Saigon: Giai Phong, 1968), 25; "The American Devils Devulge Their True Form," attached to Oran K. Henderson, "Report of Investigation (April 24, 1968), 224-04 ROI Concerning Atrocities Committed by Members of C Co. 1/20th Inf, TF Barker, Americal Divison, NARA. Henderson, "Report of Investigation (April 24, 1968)"; William M. Hammond, *Public Affairs: The Military and the Media, 1968-1973* (Washington, D.C.: Center of Military History, 1996), 223–24.

Bilton and Sim, *Four Hours in My Lai*, 215–20, 305–6; Joseph Goldstein, Burke Marshall, and Jack Schwartz, *The My Lai Massacre and Its Cover-Up: Beyond the Reach of Law? The Peers Commission Report with a Supplement and Introductory Essay on the Limits of Law* (New York: Free Press, 1976), 34–37; Jonathan Unger, "Electric Message," *Far Eastern Economic Review* (July 3, 1971), 6–7.

8. "Pentagon Says Viet Killings Exaggerated," *Washington Post*, November 17, 1969; Philip Knightly, *The First Casualty: From Crimea to Vietnam; The War Correspondent as Hero, Propagandist and Myth Maker* (New York: Harcourt Brace Jovanovich, 1975), 392; Tom Engelhardt, *The End of Victory Culture: Cold War America and the Disillusioning of a Generation* (New York: Basic Books, 1995), 219; Bilton and Sim, *Four Hours in My Lai*, 253–64.

9. Goldstein, Marshall, and Schwartz, *The My Lai Massacre and Its Cover-Up*, 3, 317–45; Bilton and Sim, *Four Hours in My Lai*, 307.

10. Bilton and Sim, *Four Hours in My Lai*, 307, 322–23, 337; "Calley, William Lawes," in *The Encyclopedia of the Vietnam War*, ed. Spencer Tucker (New York: Oxford University Press, 2000), 53.

11. David L. Anderson, ed., *Facing My Lai: Moving Beyond the Massacre* (Lawrence: University Press of Kansas, 1998), 56.

12. Nick Turse and Deborah Nelson, "Civilian Killings Went Unpunished," *Los Angeles Times*, August 6, 2006.

13. Ibid.; John Prados, *Vietnam: The History of an Unwinnable War, 1945–1975* (Lawrence: University Press of Kansas, 2009), 10; Noam Chomsky, *Necessary Illusions: Thought Control in Democratic Societies* (Boston: South End Press, 1989), 158–60; Neil Sheehan, "Should We Have War Crimes Trials?" *New York Times Book Review*, March 28, 1971; Knightly, *The First Casualty*, 434–35; Seymour Melman et al., *In the Name of America: The Conduct of the War in Vietnam by the Armed Forces of the United States as Shown by Published Reports, Compared with the Laws of War Binding on the United States Government and on Its Citizens* (New York: Clergy and Laymen Concerned about Vietnam, 1968), 20–21.

14. For examples, see *U.S. Imperialists' "Burn All, Destroy All, Kill All" Policy in South Vietnam* (Saigon: Giai Phong, 1967); Committee to Denounce the War Crimes of the U.S. Imperialists, *Crimes Perpetrated by the U.S. Imperialists*; Committee to Denounce the U.S.-Puppets' War Crimes in South Viet Nam on the U.S.-Puppets' Savage Acts Against Patriots Detained by Them, "Appendix: U.S.-Puppet Massacres of the Population in South Vietnam (From 1965 to 1969)"; *The American Crime of Genocide in South Viet Nam* (Saigon: Giai Phong, 1968); *A Crime Against the Vietnamese People, Against Peace and Humanity* (Hanoi: Democratic Republic of Vietnam, Commission for Investigation of the American Imperialists' War Crimes in Vietnam, 1966); Wholesale Massacres Perpetrated by U.S. Mercenary and

Puppet Troops in South Vietnam in the period between the Son My case (3/68) and the End of 1970; communiqué of the Committee to Denounce the U.S.-Puppets' War Crimes in South Viet Nam on their Crimes in 1969; Liberation Press Agency (in English), "Document Lists Allied 'Massacres' during Nixon's Tenure," January 8, 1972.

15. For examples of such books, see Edward S. Herman, *Atrocities in Vietnam: Myths and Realities* (Philadelphia: Pilgrim Press, 1970); Eric Norden, *America's Barbarities in Vietnam* (New Delhi: Mainstream Weekly, 1966); Labor Committee for Peace in Vietnam, *The Unspeakable War* (New York: Prometheus Paperbacks, 1966); Ralph Schoenman, *A Glimpse of American Crimes in Vietnam* (London: Goodwin Press, 1966); Bertrand Russell, *Appeal to the American Conscience* (London: International War Crimes Tribunal, 1966); Ronald Dellums, *The Dellums Committee Hearings on War Crimes in Vietnam: An Inquiry into Command Responsibility in Southeast Asia* (New York: Vintage Books, 1972); John Duffett, ed., *International War Crimes Tribunal, 1967: Stockholm, Sweden, and Roskilde, Denmark; Against the Crime of Silence; Proceedings* (New York: Simon and Schuster, 1970); Richard A. Falk, Gabriel Kolko, and Robert Jay Lifton, *Crimes of War: A Legal, Political-Documentary, and Psychological Inquiry into the Responsibility of Leaders, Citizens, and Soldiers for Criminal Acts in Wars* (New York: Random House, 1971); Indochina Peace Campaign, *Women Under Torture* (Santa Monica, Calif.: The Campaign, 1973); Erwin Knoll and Judith Nies McFadden, eds., *War Crimes and the American Conscience* (New York: Holt, Rinehart and Winston, 1970); James S. Kunen, *Standard Operating Procedure: Notes of a Draft-Age American* (New York: Avon, 1971); Melman, *In the Name of America*; Vietnam Veterans Against the War, eds., *The Winter Soldier Investigation: An Inquiry into American War Crimes* (Boston: Beacon Press, 1972); Sheehan, "Should We Have War Crimes Trials?"; Knightly, *The First Casualty*, 426–28, 434–39.

16. "Roots of a War (1945–1953)," from *Vietnam: A Television History*, PBS, 1983. For examples of revisionist works, see Guenter Lewy, *America in Vietnam* (New York: Oxford University Press, 1981); Harry G. Summers Jr., *On Strategy: A Critical Analysis of the Vietnam War* (Novato, Calif.: Presidio Press, 1982); Mark W. Woodruff, *Unheralded Victory: Who Won the Vietnam War?* (London: HarperCollins, 2000); B. G. Burkett and Glenna Whitley, *Stolen Valor: How the Vietnam Generation Was Robbed of Its Heroes and History* (Dallas, Tex.: Verity Press, 2000); and Lewis Sorely, *A Better War: The Unexamined Victories and Final Tragedy of America's Last Years in Vietnam* (New York: Harcourt, Brace, 1999).

17. For examples of evidence of war crimes that emerged in the twenty-first century, see Gregory L. Vistica, "What Happened in Thanh Phong," *New York Times Magazine*, April 29, 2001; Vistica, *The Education of Lieutenant Kerrey* (New York: St. Martin's Press, 2003); Michael D. Sallah and Mitch

Weiss, "Day 1: Rogue GIs Unleashed Wave of Terror in Central Highlands," *Toledo Blade*, October 22, 2003; Sallah and Weiss, "Day 2: Inquiry Ended Without Justice: Army Substantiated Numerous Charges—Then Dropped Case of Vietnam War Crimes," *Toledo Blade*, October 22, 2003; Sallah and Weiss, "Witness to Vietnam Atrocities Never Knew about Investigation," *Toledo Blade*, November 30, 2003; Nick Turse, "Kill Anything That Moves: U.S. War Crimes and Atrocities in Vietnam, 1965–1973," PhD diss., Columbia University, 2005; Heonik Kwon, *After the Massacre* (Los Angeles: University of California Press, 2006); Sallah and Weiss, *Tiger Force: A True Story of Men and War* (New York: Little, Brown, 2006); Turse and Nelson, "Civilian Killings Went Unpunished"; Deborah Nelson and Nick Turse, "A Tortured Past," *Los Angeles Times*, August 20, 2006; Nelson, *The War Behind Me* (New York: Basic Books, 2008); Heonik Kwon, "Anatomy of U.S. and South Korean Massacres in Vietnamese Year of the Monkey, 1968," *Japan Focus*, June 15, 2007; Nick Turse, "War Crimes Hunter: On the Trail of Atrocity in Vietnam," *In These Times*, July 28, 2008; Nick Turse, "'We Killed Her . . . That Will Be With Me the Rest of My Life': Lawrence Wilkerson's Lessons of War and Truth," TomDispatch.com, November 23, 2008, http://www.tomdispatch.com/post/175006; Nick Turse, "A My Lai a Month," *Nation*, December 1, 2008; Bernd Greiner, *War Without Fronts: The USA in Vietnam* (London: Bodley Head, 2009).

18. Martin J. Murray, "'White Gold' or 'White Blood'?: The Rubber Plantations of Colonial Indochina, 1910–40," in E. Valentine Daniel, Henry Bernstein, and Tom Brass, eds., *Plantations, Proletarians, and Peasants in Colonial Asia* (London: Frank Cass, 1992).

19. For a short synopsis of the many intricacies of the United States' Cold War rationale for the war, see Mark Bradley, *Vietnam at War* (New York: Oxford University Press, 2009), 52–56; Daniel Yergin, *Shattered Peace: The Origins of the Cold War and the National Security State* (Boston: Houghton Mifflin, 1977), 405–6; Christian Appy, *Working-Class War: American Combat Soldiers and Vietnam* (Chapel Hill: University of North Carolina Press, 1993), 148.

20. James W. Gibson, *The Perfect War: Technowar in Vietnam* (Boston: Atlantic Monthly Press, 2000), 81; Appy, *Working-Class War*, 17.

21. Quoted in Marilyn Young et al., *The Vietnam War: A History in Documents* (New York: Oxford University Press, 2002), 85.

22. Gibson, *The Perfect War*, 9, 81, 95.

23. Department of Defense/Defense Manpower Data Center, "Vietnam Conflict—Casualty Summary," May 16, 2008, http://siadapp.dmdc.osd.mil/personnel/CASUALTY/vietnam.pdf.

24. Larry Heinemann, *Black Virgin Mountain: A Return to Vietnam* (New York: Doubleday, 2005), 71fn; A. J. Langguth, *Our Vietnam: The War, 1954–1975* (New York: Simon and Schuster, 2002), 479–80.

25. William S. Turley, *The Second Indochina War: A Concise Political and Military History* (New York: Rowman and Littlefield, 2008), 170; William Thomas Allison, *The Tet Offensive: A Brief History with Documents* (London: Routledge, 2008), 20; Michael Lee Lanning and Dan Cragg, *Inside the VC and the NVA: The Real Story of North Vietnam's Armed Forces* (College Station: Texas A&M University Press, 2008), 46.

26. Figures on the number wounded refer to total incidence, not number of individuals. Department of Defense, "Vietnam Conflict—Casualty Summary"; Michael P. Kelley, *Where We Were in Vietnam: A Comprehensive Guide to the Firebases, Military Installations and Naval Vessels of the Vietnam War, 1945–1975* (Central Point, Ore.: Hellgate Press, 2002), B-19, B-20.

27. This study was flawed for several reasons, including a small sample size, underrepresentation of rural populations, and a failure to sample populations in high-mortality provinces such as Quang Ngai or Quang Nam. For more, see Ziad Obermeyer, Christopher Murray, and Emmanuela Gakidou, "Fifty Years of Violent War Deaths from Vietnam to Bosnia: Analysis of Data from the World Health Survey Programme," *British Medical Journal* 226 (2008), 1482–86; Charles Hirschman, Samuel Preston, and Vu Manh Loi, "Vietnamese Casualties During the American War: A New Estimate," *Population and Development Review* 21, no. 4 (December 1995), 793–97, 809.

28. Micheal Clodfelter, *Vietnam in Military Statistics: A History of the Indochina Wars, 1772–1991* (Jefferson, N.C.: McFarland, 1995), 257.

29. Christian Appy, *Patriots: The Vietnam War Remembered from All Sides* (New York: Viking, 2003), 164; Agence France Presse, "Hanoi Gives Official Count of 3 Million Dead in Vietnam War," April 4, 1995.

30. Clodfelter, *Vietnam in Military Statistics*, 257; Lewy, *America in Vietnam*, 451.

31. George Wilson, "U.S. Lacks Civilian Toll Study," *Washington Post*, April 6, 1971; Thomas Thayer, *War Without Fronts: The American Experience in Vietnam* (Boulder, Colo.: Westview Press, 1985), 125.

32. M. G. Wetherill, ASST DEPCORDS MACV, MAC 4032, "eyes only," to M. G. Freund, OJCS SACSA (March 30, 1969), Texas Tech; U.S. Department of State, "Civilian Casualties in Viet-Nam," Public Information Series, Bureau of Public Affairs (May 27, 1971), Vietnam Center and Archive, Texas Tech University (hereafter cited as Texas Tech).

33. Thayer says only that "the communists may have treated" some of the wounded. Thayer, *War Without Fronts*, 126–28; Appy, *Working-Class War*, 202; *Humanitarian Problems in South Vietnam and Cambodia: Two Years After the Cease-fire, A Study Mission Report Prepared for the Use of the Subcommittee to Investigate Problems Connected with Refugees and Escapees*, Senate Committee on the Judiciary (January 27, 1975), 7.

34. Appy, *Working-Class War*, 202–3.

35. While Lewy did acknowledge that "in most cases villagers killed in

VC-dominated or contested areas were counted as enemy dead," he also failed to take this into account in his estimate. Lewy, *America in Vietnam*, 444–51.

36. Gerald Hickey, *Shattered World: Adaptation and Survival Among Vietnam's Highland Peoples During the Vietnam War* (Philadelphia: University of Pennsylvania Press, 1993), xxxi; Hirschman, Preston, and Loi, "Vietnamese Casualties During the American War"; Thayer, *War Without Fronts*, 125; Derek Summerfield, "Raising the Dead: War, Reparation, and the Politics of Memory," *BMJ* 311 (August 19, 1995), 495–97; Robert McNamara, "The Post–Cold War World; Implications for Military Expenditure in Developing Countries," in *Proceedings of the World Bank Annual Conference on Development Economics, 1991* (Washington, D.C.: International Bank for Reconstruction and Development, 1991), 97; Agence France Presse, "Hanoi Gives Official Count of 3 Million Dead."

37. Obermeyer, Murray, and Gakidou, "Fifty Years of Violent War Deaths."

38. This is especially true given issues of underreporting of casualties and the limitations of multiyear demographic modeling (the study of changes in the size and composition of populations over time). Issues include, for example, the particular wartime potential for entire Vietnamese families to be wiped out at once, such as in bomb shelter collapses. Richard Garfield, "Measuring Deaths from Conflict," *BMJ* 336 (June 28, 2008), 1446–47.

39. Obermeyer, Murray, and Gakidou, "Fifty Years of Violent War Deaths"; Agence France Presse, "Hanoi Gives Official Count of 3 Million Dead"; "War Killed 3m Says Hanoi," *Financial Times* [London], April 5, 1995; Appy, *Patriots*, 164; Spencer Tucker, "Casualties," in Tucker, ed., *The Encyclopedia of the Vietnam War*, 64.

40. Gloria Emerson, *Winners and Losers: Battles, Gains, Losses and Ruins from a Long War* (New York: Random House, 1976), 357; *Problems of War Victims in Indochina*, Hearings of the Subcommittee on Refugees and Escapees, Senate Committee on the Judiciary, part 1: *Vietnam* (May 8, 1972), 51; and *Viet Nam: Destruction [and] War Damage* (Hanoi: Foreign Languages, 1977), 24.

41. Lewy, *America in Vietnam*, 443–44; Vietnam National Defense Ministry, *History of the United Resistance against Invasion of the United States of America (1954–1975)*, vol. 8: *A Final Triumph* [Lị sử kháng chiến chống Mỹ cứu nước (1954–1975), tập 8: Toàn thả] (National Politics Publishing House [Nha xuat ban Chinh Tri Quoc Gia], 2008). *Civilian Casualty, Social Welfare and Refugee Problems in South Vietnam*, part 1, Hearings before the Subcommittee on Refugees and Escapees, Senate Judiciary Committee (June 24–25, 1969), 71. See also "Civilian Casualties Are Said to Be High," *New York Times*, July 16, 1967; Agence France Presse, "Hanoi Gives Official Count of 3 Million Dead."

42. Lewy, *America in Vietnam*, 452; Hearings before the Subcommittee

on Refugees and Escapees, Senate Judiciary Committee (June 24–25, 1969), 7.

43. "Parker Allegation File," War Crimes Allegations, Case Files, Record Group 319, Records of the Vietnam War Crimes Working Group, War Crimes Allegations, Case Studies, Box 6; "Ryman Incident," War Crimes Allegations, Case Summaries, Record Group 319, Records of the Vietnam War Crimes Working Group, War Crimes Allegations, Case Studies, Box 1.

44. "Szlosowski Incident," War Crimes Allegations, Case Summaries, Record Group 319, Records of the Vietnam War Crimes Working Group, War Crimes Allegations, Case Studies, Box 1. See also *United States v. Specialist Five (E-5) Victor G. Szlosowski,* RA 12704948, U.S. Army, 569th Military Intelligence Detachment, 196th Light Infantry Brigade (Separate), CM 417312, United States Army Board of Review, 39 C.M.R. 649, 1968 CMR LEXIS 321 (August 12, 1968); "Plantz Allegation" and "SP4 Miller Allegation," both in War Crimes Allegations, Case Summaries, Record Group 319, Records of the Army Staff, Office of the Deputy Chief of Staff for Personnel (ODSPER), Records of the Vietnam War Crimes Working Group, War Crimes Allegations, Case Studies, Box 1.

45. John M. Walton, "Summary of Investigation, Company A, 2nd Battalion, 60th Infantry, 1st Infantry Division" (Aug. 27–31, 1970).

46. John Johns, interview with Nick Turse and Deborah Nelson, 2006; Turse and Nelson, "Civilian Killings Went Unpunished"; Gary D. Solis, *Son Thang: An American War Crime* (New York: Bantam Books, 1998), 211; Solis, "Military Justice, Civilian Clemency: The Sentences of Marine Corps War Crimes in South Vietnam," *Transnational Law and Contemporary Problems* 10, no. 1 (2000); Lewy, *America in Vietnam,* 324, 501 fn48; "Selected General Court Martial and Special Court Martial (BCD) Offenses Against Vietnamese," Convictions by General Court Martial for War Crimes, Record Group 319, Records of the Army Staff, Office of the Deputy Chief of Staff for Personnel (ODSPER), Records of the Vietnam War Crimes Working Group, Vietnam War Crimes Working Group Central File, Box 4; Judge Advocate General of the Navy, letter to Judge Advocate General of the Army (December 3, 1969), in Jack Taylor Collection, National Security Archive; George Lepre, *Fragging* (Lubbock: Texas Tech University Press, 2011), 209.

1: THE MASSACRE AT TRIEU AI

1. This is the date of the massacre according to the solar calendar. While Vietnamese villagers at the time generally used the lunar calendar, I use solar dates in this book when possible. The Americans knew the hamlet as Nai Cuu.

2. Do Hoa, interview with Nick Turse, January 18, 2008; sworn testimony of Wilson Dozier III, in Record of Trial of Rudolf O. Diener (March 18–20, 1968), 48; sworn testimony of Don Allen, in Record of Trial of Rudolf O. Diener, 336.

3. Sworn testimony of Olaf Skibsrud, in Record of Trial of Rudolf O. Diener, 207.

4. Sworn testimony of Eddie Kelly, in ibid., 107.

5. Sworn testimony of Edward Johnson, in ibid., 6.

6. For a sanitized, army-approved look at Vietnam-era basic training, see the film *The Men from the Boys: The First Eight Weeks*, Department of the Army, Office of the Chief of Information (n.d.). For more, see Myra MacPherson, *Long Time Passing: Vietnam and the Haunted Generation*, new edition (Bloomington: Indiana University Press, 2001), 69; Christian Appy, *Working-Class War: American Combat Soldiers and Vietnam* (Chapel Hill: University of North Carolina Press, 1993), 86–90; James R. Ebert, *A Life in a Year: The American Infantryman in Vietnam* (New York: Ballantine Books, 1993), 32.

7. For more on basic training, see Donald Duncan, *The New Legions* (New York: Random House, 1967), 98–99; Gary Bray, *After My Lai* (Norman: University of Oklahoma Press, 2010), 15–18; Ron Kovic, *Born on the Fourth of July* (New York: Akashic Books, 2005), 84–99; Joanna Bourke, *An Intimate History of Killing: Face to Face Killing in the Twentieth Century* (New York: Basic Books, 1999), 67.

8. For more, see Phil Ball, *Ghosts and Shadows* (Jefferson, N.C.: McFarland, 1998), 9; Appy, *Working-Class War*, 89–90.

9. For examples, see Dave Grossman, *On Killing: The Psychological Cost of Learning to Kill in War and Society* (New York: Little, Brown, 1996), 251–52; Appy, *Working-Class War*, 95; Bourke, *An Intimate History of Killing*, 69; Robert J. Lifton, *Home from the War; Vietnam Veterans: Neither Victims Nor Executioners* (New York: Simon and Schuster, 1973), 42–43; MacPherson, *Long Time Passing*, 312, 334.

10. For more, see John Sack, "M," *Esquire*, October 1966. Quoted in Appy, *Working-Class War*, 95.

11. Statement of William Patterson (April 6, 1971), "Patterson Allegation," War Crimes Allegations, Case Files, NARA.

12. Dan Barnes, interview with Nick Turse, January 16, 2009.

13. For more on the Americans' use of slurs in regard to the Vietnamese, see Christian Appy, *Patriots: The Vietnam War Remembered from All Sides* (New York: Viking, 2003), 355–56, 482; Jack Shulimson et al., *U.S. Marines in Vietnam: The Defining Year, 1968* (Washington, D.C.: History and Museums Division, 1997), 616fn; MacPherson, *Long Time Passing*, 16; Michael Bilton and Kevin Sim, *Four Hours in My Lai* (New York: Penguin, 1993), 21; Harry Maurer, *Strange Ground* (New York: Henry Holt, 1989), 154; Daniel Lang, *Casualties of War* (New York: Pocket Books, 1989), 19; R. W. Apple,

"G.I.'s Vocabulary in Vietnam Is Beaucoup Exotic," *New York Times*, November 3, 1965; James Olson and Randy Roberts, *My Lai: A Brief History with Documents* (New York: Bedford Books, 1998), 8; Donald Duncan, "The Whole Thing Was a Lie!" *Ramparts*, February 1966, 16.

14. For more, see James S. Kunen, *Standard Operating Procedure: Notes of a Draft-Age American* (New York: Avon, 1971), 39; Wallace Terry, *Bloods: An Oral History of the Vietnam War* (New York: Ballantine Books, 1984), 90.

15. For more on initial experiences, see Frederick Downs, *The Killing Zone* (New York: Norton, 1978), 18.

16. For more, see Appy, *Working-Class War*, 130–37; Eric Bergerud, *The Dynamics of Defeat: The Vietnam War in Hau Nghia Province* (Boulder, Colo.: Westview Press, 1991), 119. For more manifestations of this larger concept, see Phil Ball, *Ghosts and Shadows* (Jefferson, N.C.: McFarland, 1998), 8; "Caution About Kids," *Army Digest*, September 1967, 19.

17. Lifton, *Home from the War*, 195–96; *The United States Army in South Vietnam*, Troop Topics DA Pam 360 234 (Washington, D.C.: Government Printing Office, September 1968), 10.

18. Barnes, interview.

19. Duncan, *The New Legions*, 169.

20. Barnes, interview.

21. James Henry, interview with Nick Turse and Deborah Nelson, October 1, 2005.

22. Guenter Lewy, *America in Vietnam* (New York: Oxford University Press, 1981), 366.

23. Quoted in Bourke, *An Intimate History of Killing*, 177. For more, see John Merson, *War Lessons: How I Fought to Be a Hero and Learned That War Was Terror* (Berkeley, Calif.: North Atlantic Books, 2008), 41; Lifton, *Home from the War*, 42.

24. One chaplain who taught such courses noted that recruits were told to obey even unjust orders and raise issues only later. When he taught a refresher class to soldiers in Vietnam and posed the question of the outright murder of civilians on command, he found that even at a chaplain's class there were still soldiers who told him they would "obey the order no matter what." Record of Trial of James Rodarte, Nha Trang, Vietnam (May 14–19, 1969), 9; Appy, *Working-Class War*, 92–93.

25. Appy, *Working-Class War*, 106–7.

26. Lieutenant General Bruce Palmer, the deputy commander of U.S. forces in Vietnam, would later note that "instruction in the Geneva Conventions has tended to be abstract and academic, rather than concrete and practical." Hays Parks, "Crimes in Hostilities," *Marine Corps Gazette*, August 1976, 20; Bernd Greiner, *War Without Fronts: The USA in Vietnam* (London: Bodley Head, 2009), 93; Bernard Fall, "Vietnam Blitz: A Report on an Impersonal War," *New Republic*, October 9, 1965, 19.

27. Jack B. Matthews, "Training in the Geneva Conventions Pertaining to Prisoners of War" (July 25, 1967), in Training in the Geneva Conventions Pertaining to Prisoners of War—Defense Exhibits AAA and NNN (Folder 168 [b]), Record Group 319, Records of the Army Staff, Office of the Chief of Military History, Records Relating to the Courts Martial of 1st LT W. Calley, CAPT V. Hartman, 1LT R. Lee, and CAPT O'Conner, Box 18.

28. The Directorate for Inspection Services team that carried out the survey noted that they were "pleased with the caliber of instruction being presented at the Infantry Center." "Resume of Report on Inspection of Geneva Convention and Handling of POW at Fort Benning," in Training in the Geneva Conventions Pertaining to Prisoners of War (see preceding note).

29. Greiner, War Without Fronts, 101.

30. Terence Smith, "Troops Warned on War Conduct," New York Times, December 7, 1969.

31. William Greider, "Teaching of War Law Revitalized by Army," Washington Post, February 14, 1971.

32. Joseph Goldstein, Burke Marshall, and Jack Schwartz, The My Lai Massacre and Its Cover-Up: Beyond the Reach of Law? The Peers Commission Report with a Supplement and Introductory Essay on the Limits of Law (New York: Free Press, 1976), 315.

33. Sworn testimony of Wilson Dozier III, in Record of Trial of Rudolf O. Diener, 51; sworn testimony of Robert Labicki, in Record of Trial of Rudolf O. Diener, 266; Pham Thi Luyen, interview with Nick Turse, January 18, 2008; Hoa, interview; Nguyen Van Phuoc, interview with Nick Turse, January 18, 2008.

34. A. A. Berman, Investigating Officers Reports; cases of Captain Maynard, Second Lieutenant Bailey, and Lance Corporal Diener (January 5, 1968), in United States v. Rudolf O. Diener (March 18–20, 1968), 2; Hoa, interview; Phuoc, interview.

35. Sworn testimony of Ronald Toon, in Record of Trial of Rudolf O. Diener, 154–55; sworn testimony of Wilson Dozier III, in Record of Trial of Rudolf O. Diener, 40; sworn testimony of Robert Labicki, in Record of Trial of Rudolf O. Diener, 254; Record of Trial of Rudolf O. Diener, 4.

36. Sworn testimony of Ronald Toon, in Record of Trial of Rudolf O. Diener, 155–57.

37. Luyen, interview.

38. Sworn testimony of Lester Beard, in Record of Trial of Rudolf O. Diener, (1968), 380.

39. Sworn testimony of Don Allen, in ibid., 344.

40. Sworn testimony of Edward Johnson, in ibid., 7–10, and sworn testimony of Wilson Dozier III, in ibid., 39–45.

41. Sworn testimony of Wilson Dozier III, in ibid., 43, 45, 39–40.

42. Sworn testimony of Terry Spann, in ibid., 88, and John Bailey, statement to William Gilfillan, in ibid., enclosure 6.
43. Sworn testimony of William Steen, in ibid., 132.
44. Sworn testimony of Don Allen, in ibid., 348; sworn testimony of William Steen, in ibid., 132; sworn testimony of Clifford Bijou, in ibid., 72–73; sworn testimony of Richard Hamming, in ibid., 118–19; sworn testimony of James Anderson, in ibid., 61–62.
45. Phuoc, interview.
46. Ibid.
47. Luyen, interview; Phuoc, interview.
48. There was, apparently, a cluster of bunkers, but exactly who was in each bunker is unclear. In the end, it seems that all survivors were called up and gathered before being pushed to the nearby river. Luyen, interview.
49. Philip D. Beidler, *Late Thoughts on an Old War: The Legacy of Vietnam* (Athens: University of Georgia Press, 2004), 32; Philip Caputo, *A Rumor of War* (New York: Henry Holt, 1996), 140.
50. Sworn testimony of Wilson Dozier III, in Record of Trial of Rudolf O. Diener, 45.
51. Luyen, interview.
52. Ibid.
53. Sworn testimony of James Anderson and sworn testimony of Eddie Kelly Jr., both in Record of Trial of Rudolf O. Diener; Phuoc, interview.
54. Spann later claimed that he wasn't sure whether Bailey's shots actually hit Tuyen, and said that they couldn't find the body. Sworn testimony of Terry Spann, in Record of Trial of Rudolf O. Diener, 91–92.
55. Luyen, interview; Phuoc, interview; sworn testimony of William Steen, in Record of Trial of Rudolf O. Diener, 136.
56. Sworn testimony of Wilson Dozier III, in Record of Trial of Rudolf O. Diener, 40, 42.
57. Sworn testimony of Edward Johnson, in ibid., 10–11.
58. Ibid., 11–12; sworn testimony of Wilson Dozier III, in Record of Trial of Rudolf O. Diener, 40; sworn testimony of James Anderson, in Record of Trial of Rudolf O. Diener, 62.
59. Sworn testimony of Clifford Bijou, in Record of Trial of Rudolf O. Diener, (1968), 74.
60. Sworn testimony of Eddie Kelly Jr., in ibid., 110; sworn testimony of James Anderson, in ibid., 64; sworn testimony of Wilson Dozier III, in ibid., 40–44; John Bailey, statement to William Gilfillan, in ibid., enclosure 6; sworn testimony of William Steen, in ibid., 134.
61. Nguyen Van Phuoc believed that the people were shot inside the bunker, but evidence suggests they were shot aboveground and their bodies were thrown back inside. Phuoc, interview.
62. Luyen, interview; Phuoc, interview; Hoa, interview.

63. Hoa, interview.

64. Luyen, interview.

65. Gary Kulik, *War Stories* (Dulles, Va.: Potomac Books, 2009), 210–44; Berman, Investigating Officers Reports; cases of Captain Maynard, Second Lieutenant Bailey, and Lance Corporal Diener, 2.

66. The historian Gary Kulik published an account of this massacre, in which he endeavored to answer the question "What Happened in Quang Tri?" but did not seek out Vietnamese witnesses. Kulik, *War Stories*, 203–44.

67. For more, see Record of Trial of Rudolf O. Diener.

68. Neil Sheehan, review of *Conversations with Americans*, by Mark Lane, *New York Times Book Review*, December, 27 1970; 1/1st Marines, Command Chronology for the Period October 1, 1967, to October 31, 1967.

69. Arnold Dibble, "Bombing Perils Saigon's Bid to Win Delta Loyalty," *Chicago Tribune*, March 10, 1968; Don Oberdorfer, *Tet: The Turning Point in the Vietnam War* (New York: Da Capo, 1985), 151; George O'Connor, Senior Officer Debriefing Report (February 25, 1968), 1; Victor Croziat, "Problems Relating to the Deployment of U.S. Ground Combat Forces to the Mekong Delta Area of South Vietnam," RAND Corporation (October 11, 1966), 10.

70. [Quang Nam] Province CORDS/PSOPS Advisor, "Quang Nam Province Briefing Paper" (Hoi-An, Quang Nam, December 1970), 2; GG III MAF [Lewis W. Walt] to CG FMFPAC [Victor Krulak], "Personal for LT Gen Krulak," November 25, 1965, Texas Tech; C. M. Plattner, "Marine Control of Air Tested in Combat," *Aviation Week and Space Technology*, February 14, 1966, 93.

71. Harry Summers, *Vietnam War Almanac* (New York: Facts on File, 1985), 34–35; John Prados, *Vietnam: The History of an Unwinnable War, 1945–1975* (Lawrence: University Press of Kansas, 2009), 132.

72. U.S. Marines did undertake limited operations in the Mekong Delta and apparently killed civilians there as well. Tom Buckley, "Marines in Delta Continuing Sweep," *New York Times*, January 9, 1967. For more on USMC operations in the delta, see William Tuohy, "Mekong Invasion: Marine Task Force Assaults Delta," *Los Angeles Times*, January 7, 1967. For more on the power struggle, see Douglas Kinnard, *The War Managers* (New York: Da Capo, 1991), 61; Summers, *Vietnam War Almanac*, 40; Joseph W. Callaway Jr., *Mekong First Light* (New York: Ballantine Books, 2004), 105–6, 107–9, 126–27.

2: A SYSTEM OF SUFFERING

1. James W. Gibson, *The Perfect War: Technowar in Vietnam* (Boston: Atlantic Monthly Press, 2000), 14–27.

2. Ibid., 14; *Fog of War: Eleven Lessons from the Life of Robert S. McNamara*, director Errol Morris, Sony Pictures Classics, 2003.

3. Tom Engelhardt, *The End of Victory Culture: Cold War America and the Disillusioning of a Generation* (New York: Basic Books, 1995), 208.

4. Neil Sheehan, *A Bright and Shining Lie: John Paul Vann and America in Vietnam* (New York: Vintage Books, 1988), 289.

5. Gibson, *The Perfect War*, 80; Christian Appy, *Working-Class War: American Combat Soldiers and Vietnam* (Chapel Hill: University of North Carolina Press), 156–57.

6. Westmoreland said in 1967 that the crossover point had finally been reached, but his claim rested on denying the very existence of hundreds of thousands of farmer-fighters in South Vietnam. Marilyn Young, *The Vietnam Wars, 1945–1990* (New York: Harper Perennial, 1991), 214–15.

7. Thomas Thayer, ed. [Assistant Secretary of Defense (Systems Analysis), Southeast Asia Division], *Southeast Asia Analysis Report/A Systems Analysis View of the War in Vietnam, 1965–1972* (Washington, D.C. [?]:Assistant Secretary of Defense [Systems Analysis], Southeast Asia Division, 1975), vol. 4 (*Allied Ground and Naval Operations*), vol. 9, (*Population Security*), and vol. 3 (*Viet Cong–North Vietnamese Operations*), 140; Gibson, *The Perfect War*, 80.

8. William C. Westmoreland, *A Soldier Reports* (Garden City, N.Y.: Doubleday, 1976), 273.

9. Scott Gartner and Marissa Meyers, "Body Counts and 'Success' in the Vietnam and Korean Wars," *Journal of Interdisciplinary History* 25, no. 3 (Winter 1995), 377–95.

10. Quoted in ibid., 380. Robert S. McNamara and Brian VanDeMark, *In Retrospect: The Tragedy and Lessons of Vietnam* (New York: Times Books, 1995), 238.

11. Gibson, *The Perfect War*, 112.

12. Ibid., 112–16; Appy, *Working-Class War*, 140.

13. Robert Peterson, *Rites of Passage* (New York: Ballantine Books, 1997), 316.

14. William Baker, interview with Nick Turse and Deborah Nelson, April 4, 2006.

15. For more, see Charles Gadd, *Line Doggie: Foot Soldier in Vietnam* (Novato, Calif.: Presidio, 1987), 161; Mark Jury, *The Vietnam Photo Book* (New York: Grossman, 1971), 42; Micheal Clodfelter, *Mad Minutes and Vietnam Months* (New York: Windsor, 1988), 237; Peterson, *Rites of Passage*, 316; Michael Sallah and Mitch Weiss, *Tiger Force: A True Story of Men and War* (New York: Little, Brown, 2006), 312.

16. Gary Nordstrom, interview with Nick Turse, 2008.

17. William J. Taylor Jr., interview with Neil Sheehan, November 11, 1975, Neil Sheehan Papers; Robert Gard, interview with Nick Turse and Deborah Nelson, 2006.

18. Quoted in Gibson, *The Perfect War*, 120.

19. For more on body-count incentives, see Christian Appy, *Patriots: The Vietnam War Remembered from All Sides* (New York: Viking, 2003), 301; "Infantry Unit Gave GIs Kill Rewards," *Los Angeles Times*, June 11, 1970;

Gloria Emerson, *Winners and Losers: Battles, Gains, Losses and Ruins from a Long War* (New York: Random House, 1976), 373, 65; Lewis Puller, *Fortunate Son* (New York: Grove Weidenfeld, 1991), 89; Michael Herr, *Dispatches* (New York: Alfred A. Knopf, 1977), 179; James Daley, *Black Prisoner of War: A Conscientious Objector's Vietnam Memoir* (Lawrence: University Press of Kansas, 2000), 52–53, 63–64; Scott Camil, "Undercover Agents' War on Vietnam Veterans," in Bud Schultz and Ruth Schultz, *It Did Happen Here: Recollections of Political Repression in America* (Berkeley: University of California Press, 1989), 320; Philip Caputo, *A Rumor of War* (New York: Henry Holt, 1996), 311.

20. Quoted in Appy, *Patriots*, 365.

21. Myra MacPherson, *Long Time Passing: Vietnam and the Haunted Generation*, new edition (Bloomington: Indiana University Press, 2001), 52.

22. Joel Yager, "Personal Violence in Infantry Combat," *Archives of General Psychiatry* 32 (February 1975), 258; Richard Fox, "Narcissistic Rage and the Problem of Combat Aggression," *Archives of General Psychiatry* 31 (December 1974), 808; Robert J. Lifton, *Home from the War; Vietnam Veterans: Neither Victims Nor Executioners* (New York: Simon and Schuster, 1973), 189, 394; Tony Perry, "For Marine Snipers, War Is Up Close and Personal: Teams Prove to Be a Major Weapon," *Los Angeles Times*, April 19, 2004; Anthony Herbert and James T. Wooten, *Soldier* (New York: Dell, 1973), 244–45; Ira Hunt, interview with Nick Turse and Deborah Nelson, January 26, 2006.

23. IG Investigation, 25th Infantry Division at request of James Utt, IG Investigation (May 12, 1969), NARA; Emerson, *Winners and Losers*, 65.

24. For more, see "Gimlet Scoreboard" in James P. Sterba, "Scraps of Paper from Vietnam," *New York Times Magazine*, October 18, 1970; *War-Related Civilian Problems in Indochina*, hearings of the Subcommittee on Refugees and Escapees, Senate Committee on the Judiciary, part 3: *Vietnam* (April 22, 1971), 28; 3rd Battalion, 3rd Marines, "Command Chronology" (April 7, 1966); Appy, *Working-Class War*, 144, 156; "Infantry Unit Gave GIs Kill Rewards," *Los Angeles Times*, June 11, 1970; Caputo, *A Rumor of War*, 168–69; 176th Assault Helicopter Company Unit History (Chu Lai, 1969); testimony of [?] Deloriea in Concerning Col. David Hackworth, vol. 2 of 8 vols., part 2 of 2 in Record Group 472, MACV, MACIG, Invest. Div., ROI, Box 120; Joe McGinniss, "Finds Marine Pacification Unit Kills Cong," *Chicago Tribune*, April 9, 1971; Ronald Dellums, *The Dellums Committee Hearings on War Crimes in Vietnam: An Inquiry into Command Responsibility in Southeast Asia* (New York: Vintage Books 1972), 187; Herbert and Wooten, *Soldier*, 427; Kenneth J. Campbell, *A Tale of Two Quagmires: Iraq, Vietnam and the Hard Lessons of War* (Boulder, Colo.: Paradigm, 2007), 28; Daniel Evans Jr. and Charles Sasser, *Doc: Platoon Medic* (New York: Pocket Books, 1998), 209; "What's in a Name: Aviation," *Army Digest*, September 1969, 65;

Charles Flood, *The War of the Innocents* (New York: McGraw-Hill, 1970), 88; Gary D. Solis, *Son Thang: An American War Crime* (New York: Bantam Books, 1998 [1997]), ix.

25. Testimony of [?] Deloriea in Concerning Col. David Hackworth.

26. For more, see "PLAF Repeated Attacks on a Series of Enemy Solid Bases," *South Viet Nam in Struggle*, January 1, 1969, 4; Cuu Long, "Impasse of Military Strategy in South Viet Nam," *South Viet Nam in Struggle*, February 1, 1969, 2–3; James Pickerell, *Vietnam in the Mud* (Indianapolis: Bobbs-Merrill, 1966), xiv; Eric Bergerud, *The Dynamics of Defeat: The Vietnam War in Hau Nghia Province* (Boulder, Colo.: Westview Press, 1991), 168; Guenter Lewy, *America in Vietnam* (New York: Oxford University Press, 1981), 81; Douglas Kinnard, *The War Managers* (New York: Da Capo, 1991), 75.

27. Quoted in Appy, *Patriots*, 365.

28. Robert Gray, sworn statement (January 20, 1970), in Military Police Report; Reports of Investigation, 1969–1972, Record Group 472, NARA; David Janca, sworn statement (February 3, 1970), in ibid.

29. Welkie Louie, sworn statement (January 13, 1970), in ibid.

30. Robert Wolz, sworn statement (February 3, 1970), in ibid.

31. David Janca, sworn statement (February 3, 1970), in ibid.

32. Kapranopoulous was tried and acquitted. Beard drowned during an operation the next month. Charges against Mattaliano were later dismissed. Statements of Ralph Loomis and Ariva Harris in "Kapranopoulous Incident," War Crimes Allegations, Case Files, Records of the Vietnam War Crimes Working Group, NARA.

33. The sentiments behind this dictum were voiced in the 1950s by a French lieutenant who said, "What is a Vietminh—A Viet Minh? He is a dead Vietnamese." They also harked back to the Philippines Insurrection and the American military axiom of "All Gugus look alike to me." Quoted in Gibson, *The Perfect War*, 63; Leon Wolff, *Little Brown Brother: America's Forgotten Bid for Empire Which Cost 250,000 Lives* (Philippines: Erehwon Press, 1971), 248, 252. For more, see Caputo, *A Rumor of War*, 72–74; Jonathan Schell, *The Real War: The Classic Reporting on the Vietnam War* (New York: Da Capo Press, 2000), 241; Bergerud, *The Dynamics of Defeat*, 168; Seymour Hersh, *My Lai 4* (New York: Vintage Books, 1970), 13; James S. Kunen, *Standard Operating Procedure: Notes of a Draft-Age American* (New York: Avon, 1971), 46, 52; Lifton, *Home from the War*, 33; *U.S. vs. Patrick Condron*, U.S. Court of Military Appeals, no. 20,414 (February 2, 1968); W. D. Ehrhart, *Vietnam-Perkasie: A Combat Marine's Memoir* (New York: Zebra Books, 1983), 240.

34. R. Kenly Webster, memorandum for Secretary [of the Army, Stanley] Resor (June 16, 1970), in "Concerned Sergeant Allegation," in War Crimes Allegations, Case Files, Record Group 319, Records of the Army Staff; Office of the Deputy Chief of Staff for Personnel (ODSPER), Records of the Vietnam War Crimes Working Group, War Crimes Allegations, Case Studies, Box 1.

35. Tab A, in ibid.

36. For more, see James R. Ebert, *A Life in a Year: The American Infantryman in Vietnam* (New York: Ballantine Books, 1993), 365; Joseph Goldstein, Burke Marshall, and Jack Schwartz, *The My Lai Massacre and Its Cover-Up: Beyond the Reach of Law? The Peers Commission Report with a Supplement and Introductory Essay on the Limits of Law* (New York: Free Press, 1976), 181; Normand Poirier, "An American Atrocity," *Esquire*, August 1969.

37. Seymour Hersh, *Cover-Up* (New York: Random House, 1972), 18–19.

38. "War Crimes Issues Communiqué," Liberation Press Agency, July 11, 1969; Pham Thi Nien, interview with Nick Turse, February 14, 2008; Pham Thi Tay, interview with Nick Turse, February 14, 2008; Dellums, *The Dellums Committee Hearings on War Crimes in Vietnam*, 190, 204; Notley Report of Investigation (November 11, 1971); Colonel Henry Tufts Archive, Labadie Collection, University of Michigan Special Collections Library, Ann Arbor.

39. For a thorough and detailed history of the Son Thang massacre, see Solis, *Son Thang*. For more, see Provisional Revolutionary Government of South Vietnam Information Bureau (Paris), "Wholesale Massacres Perpetrated by U.S. Mercenary and Puppet Troops in South Vietnam in the Period Between the Son My Case (3/68) and the End of 1970" (Paris: Committee to Denounce U.S. War Crimes in South Vietnam, 1970), and *United States v. Michael A. Schwarz*, Private (E-1), U.S. Marine Corps, NCM 71-0028, United States Navy Court of Military Review, 45 C.M.R. 852, 1971, CMR LEXIS 653 (October 29, 1971).

40. "Notley Allegation," War Crimes Allegations, Case Summaries, Record Group 319, Records of the Army Staff; Office of the Deputy Chief of Staff for Personnel (ODSPER), Records of the Vietnam War Crimes Working Group, War Crimes Allegations, Case Studies, Box 1.

41. Deborah Nelson and Nick Turse, "Lasting Pain, Minimal Punishment," *Los Angeles Times*, August 20, 2006; "Parker Allegation File," War Crimes Allegations, Case Files, Record Group 319, Records of the Army Staff, Office of the Deputy Chief of Staff for Personnel (ODSPER), Records of the Vietnam War Crimes Working Group, War Crimes Allegations, Case Studies, Box 6; Appy, *Working-Class War*, 202–3.

42. Quoted in W. D. Ehrhart, *Ordinary Lives: Platoon 1005 and the Vietnam War* (Philadelphia: Temple University Press, 1999), 268.

43. Jan Barry, ed., *Peace Is Our Profession* (Montclair, N.J.: East River Anthology, 1981), 22.

44. Quoted in Jeffrey Record, *The Wrong War: Why We Lost in Vietnam* (Annapolis: Naval Institute Press, 1998), viii.

45. Robert S. McNamara and Brian VanDeMark, *In Retrospect: The Tragedy and Lessons of Vietnam* (New York: Times Books, 1995), 269.

46. Jeffrey Kimball, *Nixon's Vietnam War* (Lawrence: University Press of Kan-

sas, 1998), 163; Robert Dallek, *Nixon and Kissinger: Partners in Power* (New York: HarperCollins, 2007), e-book (no page numbers).

47. Daniel Evans Jr. and Charles Sasser, *Doc: Platoon Medic* (New York: Pocket Books, 1998), 160. For more dark GI humor, see Appy, *Patriots*, 160; Gibson, *The Perfect War*, 142–43.

48. Herr, *Dispatches*, 59.

49. Hersh, *My Lai 4*, 11.

50. Evans and Sasser, *Doc*, 162.

51. Many alternative spelling of this slur were used, including "gugus" or "guggoes." For more, see David Roediger, *Towards the Abolition of Whiteness* (New York: Verso, 1994), 118; "American 'Devil Dogs' Maintain Order in Hayti," *Fort Wayne News Sentinel*, April 9, 1920; Herbert Seligman, "The Conquest of Haiti," *Nation*, July 10, 1920, 35; Solis, *Son Thang*, 115; Max Hastings, *The Korean War* (New York: Simon and Schuster, 1987), 287; "Korean Red Spots Own Force for G.I.s," *New York Times*, August 24, 1950; Rudy Tomedi, *No Bugles, No Drums: An Oral History of the Korean War* (New York: John Wiley, 1993), 80, 77; H. R. Kells, *Footsoldier in an Occupation Force: The Letters of Peter Lewis, 1898–1902* (Manila, Philippines: De La Salle University, 1999), 92, 115; Leon Wolff, *Little Brown Brother: America's Forgotten Bid for Empire Which Cost 250,000 Lives* (Philippines: Erehwon Press, 1971), 248; Gary R. Smith and Alan Maki, *Death in the Jungle* (New York: Ballantine Books, 1994), 151, 237; Ehrhart, *Vietnam-Perkasie*, 134, 157, 217; MacPherson, *Long Time Passing*, 16; Ben Sherman, *Medic* (New York: Ballantine Books, 2002), 113, 147; Herman Graham, *The Brothers' Vietnam War: Black Power, Manhood, and the Military Experience* (Gainesville: University of Florida Press, 2003), 56; Emerson, *Winners and Losers*, 121; William B. Gault, "Some Remarks on Slaughter," *American Journal of Psychiatry* 128, no. 4 (October 1971), 451–52; Clodfelter, *Mad Minutes and Vietnam Months*, 235, 274; Donald Duncan, *The New Legions* (New York: Random House, 1967), 155; Duncan, "The Whole Thing Was a Lie!" *Ramparts* 4, February 1966, 16; Kunen, *Standard Operating Procedure*, 33, 39.

52. For more, see Otto J. Lehrack, *No Shining Armor: Marines at War in Vietnam* (Lawrence: University Press of Kansas, 1992), 129, 149, 155, 185, 310, 340, 348; David Donovan [pseudonym], *Once a Warrior King* (New York: Ballantine Books, 1985), 260; Appy, *Patriots*, 355–56; Michael Lee Lanning and Dan Cragg, *Inside the VC and the NVA* (New York: Fawcett, 1992), 25; Robert Hemphill, *Platoon: Bravo Company* (New York: St. Martin's Press, 1998), 25, 69, 117; Robert Flynn, *A Personal War in Vietnam* (College Station, Tex.: Texas A&M, 1989), 58; Ehrhart, *Vietnam-Perkasie*, 43, 55, 91, 209, 262; John J. Cuthbertson, *Operation Tuscaloosa* (New York: Ivy Books, 1997), 24, 41, 217; Frederick Downs, *The Killing Zone* (New York: Norton, 1978), 18, 93, 113, 148–49, 216, 224–25; Michael Bilton and Kevin Sim, *Four Hours in My Lai* (New York: Penguin, 1993), 21.

53. Quoted in Lifton, *Home from the War*, 202.

54. Philip Knightly, *The First Casualty: From Crimea to Vietnam; The War Correspondent as Hero, Propagandist and Myth Maker* (New York: Harcourt Brace Jovanovich, 1975), 386.

55. Nick Turse and Deborah Nelson, "Civilian Killings Went Unpunished," *Los Angeles Times*, August 6, 2006; Appy, *Working-Class War*, 133–35, 294; Graham, *The Brothers' Vietnam War*, 61; Wallace Terry, *Bloods: An Oral History of the Vietnam War* (New York: Ballantine Books, 1984), 82; *U.S. vs. Gary J. Creek*, Company A, 3rd Battalion, 60th Infantry, 9th Division, CM 417555, U.S. Army Board of Review (August 27, 1968); "The 'Mere Gook Rule,'" *Newsweek*, April 13, 1970, 30; Deborah Nelson, *The War Behind Me* (New York: Basic Books, 2008); William Greider, "'Mere Gook Rule' Haunts Calley Trial," *Washington Post*, March 14, 1971.

56. For examples, see Herr, *Dispatches*, 178; Concerned Sergeant, letter to William Westmoreland (May 25, 1970), "copy reproduced on 27 August 1971," in "Concerned Sergeant Allegation," War Crimes Allegations, Case Files, War Crimes Working Group, Record Group 319, NARA; Julian Ewell and Ira A. Hunt, *Sharpening the Combat Edge: The Use of Analysis to Reinforce Military Judgment* (Washington, D.C.: Department of the Army, 1995), 222; Lifton, *Home from the War*, 202.

57. *Hearts and Minds*, director Peter Davis, producers Henry Lange and Bert Schneider, 112 minutes, BBS Productions/Rainbow Pictures Corporation, 1974.

58. See Lewis Sorley, ed., *Vietnam Chronicles: The Abrams Tapes, 1968–1972* (Lubbock: Texas Tech University Press, 2004), 316; Ellis W. Williamson, "Commander's Combat Note Number 4" (September 8, 1968), in "Case #69-109: Claim of Land Damage and Destruction of Gravesites in Tan Binh District, Gia Dinh," USARV IG Investigative Files (FY 69), Reports of Investigation Case Files, Inspector General Section, Headquarters, U.S. Army, Vietnam, Record Group 472, Box 17.

59. This is not to say that allied operations in Europe did not cause mass civilian casualties. For more, see William Hitchcock, *The Bitter Road to Freedom: The Human Cost of Allied Victory in World War II Europe* (New York: Free Press, 2009); Frances FitzGerald, *A Fire in the Lake* (Boston: Atlantic Monthly Press, 1972), 375.

60. For more on racism, see Ebert, *A Life in a Year*, 373; Mark Lane, *Conversations with Americans* (New York: Simon and Schuster, 1970), 179; Nicholas Warr, *Phase Line Green* (Annapolis: Naval Institute Press, 1997), 56.

61. Marilyn Young, *The Vietnam Wars, 1945–1990* (New York: Harper Perennial, 1991), 162; Gibson, *The Perfect War*, 102; Appy, *Working-Class War*, 153–55.

62. Kinnard, *The War Managers*, 69.

63. Herr, *Dispatches*, 61.

64. James Webb, *Fields of Fire* (Englewood Cliffs, N.J.: Prentice Hall, 1978), 130, quoted in Gibson, *The Perfect War*, 103.

65. Gibson, *The Perfect War*, 103–4; Appy, *Patriots*, xxiii.

66. "Type of Engagements in Combat Narratives," *The Pentagon Papers: The Senator Gravel Edition* (Boston: Beacon Press, 1971), vol. 4, 461–62.

67. Thayer, *Southeast Asia Analysis Report*, vol. 4, 7–9 [24–27—dual numbering system].

68. For more on Westmoreland and the "search-and-destroy strategy," see Kinnard, *The War Managers*, 39–41; Westmoreland, *A Soldier Reports*, 83.

69. For examples of massacres where troops recalled "search and destroy" as the order, see statement of Gregory Newman, September 21, 1972, in "Henry Allegation File [1 of 3]," War Crimes Allegations, Case Files, Record Group 319, Records of the Army Staff, Records of the Vietnam War Crimes Working Group, War Crimes Allegations, Case Studies, Case 32 (1), 1–2, 4–5; sworn testimony of Eddie Kelly Jr., Record of Trial of Rudolf O. Diener (March 18–20, 1968), 107; Bilton and Sim, *Four Hours in My Lai*, 99.

70. For more accounts of home and village burnings, see John Sack, "M," *Esquire*, October 1966; Ebert, *A Life in a Year*, 305; Peter Bourne, *Men, Stress, and Vietnam* (Boston: Little, Brown, 1970), 106–7; Frederick Downs, *The Killing Zone* (New York: Norton, 1978), 31.

71. For a similar assessment by a marine, see Scott Camil, Vietnam Veterans Project Interview, Oral History Research Office, Columbia University, 1979; testimony of Larry G. Holmes in *Report of the Department of the Army Review of the Preliminary Investigations into the My Lai Incident* (U), vol. 2, book 19, 2, 9–10.

72. For a prowar account of a search-and-destroy operation in which a civilian was killed, a detainee abused, animals were slain, bomb shelters grenaded, and civilians' possessions and homes burned by U.S. troops, see Gordon Baxter, *13/13 Vietnam Search and Destroy* (Cleveland, Ohio: World, 1967), 53–91, quoted in Appy, *Patriots*, 350.

73. See Neil Sheehan, "Should We Have War Crimes Trials?" *New York Times Book Review*, March 28, 1971; Telford Taylor, *Nuremberg and Vietnam: An American Tragedy* (Chicago: Quadrangle Books, 1970), 168.

74. For more, see Appy, *Working-Class War*, 195–99.

75. Quoted in W. Michael Reisman and Chris T. Antoniou, eds., *The Laws of War: A Comprehensive Collection of Primary Documents on International Laws Governing Armed Conflict* (New York: Vintage Books, 1994), 111–13.

76. Schell, *The Real War*, 68.

77. Edward Metzner, confidential memo, subject: gunship incident (September 23, 1970) in Vinh Binh—1970, in Record Group 472, MACV, MACIG, CORDS MR4, Office Dpty. CORDS, General Records, Box 20.

78. Lieutenant General Robert Cushman, SPECAT message for MGEN's Hochmuth, Anderson, Robertson, Knowles, and Brigadier General Herbold, CG III MAF 22093 6Z JUL 67, Texas Tech.

79. Some 61 percent said that the rules of engagement were "fairly well" adhered to. Kinnard, *The War Managers*, 54–55.

80. For more, see U.S. Army, *Final Report of the Research Project: Conduct of the War in Vietnam* (May 1971), 28–42; Appy, *Working-Class War*, 197–99.

81. Luong Thanh Cuong, interview with Nick Turse, February 21, 2008; Appy, *Working-Class War*, 199.

82. The combat correspondent Honda Katsuichi remarked on this behavior repeatedly. For more, see Katsuichi, "Villages in the Battlefield: The Vietnam War and the People," *Japan Quarterly* 15, no. 2 (April–June 1968), 164, 169; Herbert and Wooten, *Soldier*, 221.

83. "Case #69-65: Death of 7 Vietnamese Civilians (Woodcutters) by Aircraft Fire," USARV-IG Investigative Files, Record Group 472, USARV-IG Reports of Investigations, Box 14.

84. Ibid. Confusion exists in the records about whether seven of eight or eight of nine woodcutters were killed in the attack.

85. Ibid.

86. Robert E. Justice, "Report of Investigation—Surrounding the Death of Seven Woodcutters," in ibid.

87. Of course, in plenty of instances officers did resist the urge or were stopped. Peter Pace, who later became the chairman of the Joint Chiefs of Staff, recounts that when he was a young marine lieutenant in Vietnam, he was prevented from carrying out precisely such a scenario by a look from his platoon sergeant. For more, see Peter Pace, Commencement Address at the Citadel, May 6, 2006, http://www3.citadel.edu/pao/addresses/grad06_Gen PeterPace.html.

88. Quoted in Erwin Knoll and Judith Nies McFadden, eds., *War Crimes and the American Conscience* (New York: Holt, Rinehart and Winston, 1970), 66. *The Dellums Committee Hearings on War Crimes in Vietnam: An Inquiry into Command Responsibility in Southeast Asia* (New York: Vintage Books 1972), 168; testimony of Jimmie Jenkins in *Report of the Department of the Army Review of the Preliminary Investigations into the My Lai Incident* (U), vol. 2, book 19, 56; statement of 1LT Joseph G. Fay Jr. to Colonel Albert L. Hutson Jr., Colonel IG, "Case #68-15: Alleged War Crimes by Co. A 2d BN, 35th Inf, 3 Bde, 4th Inf Div toward POWs and Civilians," USARV IG Investigative Files (FY 70), Reports of Investigation Case Files, Inspector General Section, Headquarters, U.S. Army, Vietnam, Record Group 472, box 5; Michael D. Sallah and Mitch Weiss, "Day 1: Rogue GIs Unleashed Wave of Terror in Central Highlands," *Toledo Blade*, October 22 2003; "Haffey Incident," War Crimes Allegations, Case Summaries, Record Group 319, Records of the Army Staff; Office of the Deputy Chief of Staff for Personnel

(ODSPER), Records of the Vietnam War Crimes Working Group; War Crimes Allegations, Case Studies, Box 1; Robert Peterson, *Rites of Passage* (New York: Ballantine Books, 1997), 309–12; David W. P. Elliott, *The Vietnamese War: Revolution and Social Change in the Mekong Delta, 1930–1975*, vol. 2 (Armonk, N.Y.: M. E. Shape, 2003), 1159–60; David Hunt, *Vietnam's Southern Revolution: From Peasant Insurrection to Total War, 1959–1968* (Amherst: University of Massachusetts Press, 2009), 120, 162; Gloria Emerson, "Rehabilitation Is Rare for Vietnam's Many Wounded Civilians," *New York Times*, October 26, 1970; Concerned Sergeant, letter to William Westmoreland (May 25, 1970), "copy reproduced on 27 August 1971," in "Concerned Sergeant Allegation," War Crimes Allegations, Case Files, War Crimes Working Group, RG 319, NARA.

89. Louis F. Janowski, "End of Tour Report" (ca. 1970), Neil Sheehan Papers.

90. For examples, see John Merson, *War Lessons: How I Fought to Be a Hero and Learned That War Was Terror* (Berkeley, Calif.: North Atlantic Books, 2008), 21; Sallah and Weiss, *Tiger Force*, 301; Matthew Brennan, *Brennan's War: Vietnam, 1965–1969* (Novato, Calif.: Presidio, 1985), 79; "Patterson Allegation," War Crimes Allegations, Case Summaries, Record Group 319, Records of the Army Staff, Office of the Deputy Chief of Staff for Personnel (ODSPER); Records of the Vietnam War Crimes Working Group, War Crimes Allegations; Case Studies, Box 1; statement of Ronald H. Gibson, in "Hoag Allegation [part 1 of 4], Case 232 (1)," Army Staff, Deputy Chief of Staff, Vietnam War Crimes Working Group, War Crimes Allegations Files, Box 20, 2.

91. Statement of William Patterson in "Patterson Allegation."

92. Nguyen Thi Lam, interview with Nick Turse, January 8, 2008.

93. Norman E. Sakai, certificate of death for Nguyen Mai, in "Sou Allegation," Case Files, War Crimes Working Group, Record Group 319, NARA.

94. Robert Graham, "Vietnam: An Infantryman's View of Our Failure," *Military Affairs*, July 1984, 133.

95. Paul Cox, interview with Nick Turse, September 18, 2009.

96. Ibid. Cox originally remembered the massacre as occurring after April 1970, but acknowledged that he didn't write down dates, and his memory of the specific time frame—but not the events—was imperfect.

97. Ho Thi A, interview with Nick Turse, January 24, 2008.

98. Sallah and Weiss, *Tiger Force*, 291–92; Michael Sallah and Mitch Weiss, " 'Free-fire' Situation Set Stage for Abuses," *Toledo Blade*, October 21, 2003.

99. Cecil B. Currey, "Free Fire Zones," in Spencer Tucker, ed., *The Encyclopedia of the Vietnam War: A Political, Social and Military History* (New York: Oxford University Press, 1998), 140.

100. H. K. Eggleston, "Lessons Learned Number 20" (August 27, 1962), author's collection.

101. Westmoreland, *A Soldier Reports*, 40.

102. COMUSMACV, message to CINPAC, "Minimizing Non-Combatant Battle Casualties" (October 9, 1965), U.S. Army War College; Robert McNamara, "Memorandum for the President" (March 16, 1964), in *The Pentagon Papers*, vol. 3, 501; W. C. Westmoreland, "MACV Directive No. 525-3: Combat Operations: Minimizing Non-Combatant Battle Casualties" (September 7, 1965), U.S. Army War College.

103. COMUSMACV, message to CINPAC, "Minimizing Non-Combatant Battle Casualties" (October 9, 1965), U.S. Army War College.

104. For an example, see Headquarters, 3rd Brigade, 25th Infantry Division, "Operational Report and Lessons Learned, Period Ending 31 July 1967" (February 6, 1968).

105. One such leaflet read, in part: "Soon Naval gunfire is going to be conducted on your village to destroy . . . Vietcong supplies. We ask that you take cover as we do not wish to kill innocent people . . . And when you return to your village repel the Viet Cong so that the government will not have to fire on your village again." For more, see Appy, *Working-Class War*, 196–97; Gibson, *The Perfect War*, 283; Schell, *The Real War*, 204–13. Don Luce and John Sommer, *Vietnam: The Unheard Voices* (Ithaca: Cornell University Press, 1969), 170–71.

106. Free-fire zones also constituted an indiscriminate attack; there was no justification for claiming that issuing a warning to civilians eliminates the necessity of attacking only military targets. Prohibitions against indiscriminate attack were more explicitly defined in additional protocols to the Geneva Conventions that were added in 1977. For more, see Reisman and Antoniou, *The Laws of War*, 87–89. For a commonsense articulation of the legal issues surrounding free-fire zones, see Lewis M. Simons, "Free Fire Zones," in Roy Gutman, David Reiff, and Anthony Dworkin, eds., *Crimes of War 2.0: What the Public Should Know, Revised and Updated Edition* (New York: Norton, 2007), 189–90.

107. For more, see Betts and Denton, *An Evaluation of Chemical Crop Destruction*, 13–14; Kim Willenson et al., *The Bad War* (New York: Newsweek/Nal Books, 1987), 147.

108. Thayer, *Southeast Asia Analysis Report*, vol. 5 (*The Air War*), 30 [130—dual numbering system], and vol. 4, 207.

109. For more, see John Tirman, *The Deaths of Others* (New York: Oxford University Press, 2011), 162; File No. DT-114 (I), "Interviews Concerning the National Liberation Front of South Vietnam," RAND interviews (May 1966).

110. Nguyen Thi Lam interview; Pham Van Chap, interview with Nick Turse, January 8, 2008. For more on Nhi Binh, see Hunt, *Vietnam's Southern Revolution*, 120; David W. P. Elliott, *The Vietnamese War: Revolution and Social Change in the Mekong Delta, 1930–1975*, vol. 2 (Armonk, N.Y.: M. E.

Shape, 2003), 1159, 1164; David W. P. Elliott, *The Vietnamese War: Revolution and Social Change in the Mekong Delta, 1930-1975* [concise edition] (Armonk, N.Y.: M. E. Sharpe, 2007), 108, 289.

111. Le Thi Van, interview with Nick Turse, January 8, 2008.

112. John Dower, "An Aptitude for Being Unloved," in Omar Bartov et al., eds., *Crimes of War* (New York: New Press, 2002), 230.

113. Jack Langguth, "U.S. Decision to Bomb Inside South Vietnam Seen as Turning Point of War," *New York Times*, September 27, 1965.

114. Sheehan, "Should We Have War Crimes Trials?"

115. For more, see Gibson, *The Perfect War*, 225-31; Edward Doyle et al., *The Vietnam Experience: A Collision of Cultures* (Boston: Boston Publishing, 1984), 139; Louis Wiesner, *Victims and Survivors* (Westport, Conn.: Greenwood Press, 1988), 120, 122. Neil Sheehan heard a similar story the year before from a top U.S. general. Sheehan, "Should We Have War Crimes Trials?"; Tom Buckley, "Rural Vietnamese Swept Up by War into Refugee Camps," *New York Times*, October 28, 1967.

116. Quoted in Nguyen Cao Ky, *Twenty Years and Twenty Days* (New York: Stein and Day, 1976), 140-41. See also David Hunt, "Dirty Wars: Counterinsurgency in Vietnam and Today," *Politics and Society* 1, no. 38 (2010), 39.

117. For more, see FitzGerald, *A Fire in the Lake*, 344; Martha Duffy, "The Big Attrit," *Time*, August 28, 1972; Ngo Vinh Long, "Moving the People," in *Hearts and Minds* [book insert to *Hearts and Minds* movie]; text of secret cable from Robert Komer on South Vietnamese and U.S. preparedness to cope with and care for refugees and defectors from North Vietnam, issue date September 3, 1966, date declassified August 13, 1997, reproduced in Declassified Documents Reference System (Farmington Hills, Mich.: Gale, 2009); *The Pentagon Papers*, vol. 4, 441.

118. Elliott, *The Vietnamese War*, 336.

119. R. W. Apple, "Calley: The Real Guilt," *New Statesman* 81 (1971), 449.

120. For more, see Luce and Sommer, *Vietnam*, 148-149; Gibson, *The Perfect War*, 83.

121. Luce and Sommer, *Vietnam*, 148-49.

122. For more, see Louis Wiesner, *Victims and Survivors* (Wesport, Conn.: Greenwood Press, 1988), 38-41; Homer Bigart, "U.S. Helps Vietnam in Test of Strategy Against Guerrillas," *New York Times*, March 29, 1962.

123. "Officer Reports Burning of 13 Villages Last Month," *New York Times*, November 26, 1969.

124. Martin Teitel, "Again, the Suffering of Mylai," *New York Times*, June 7, 1972.

125. William Tuohy, "Shells Constant Peril in 'Leatherneck Square,'" *Los Angeles Times*, July 20, 1967.

126. Human Sciences Research, *A Study of Mass Population Displacement in the Republic of Viet-Nam, Part II: Case Studies of Refugee Resettlement* (McLean, Va., 1969), 7–43.

127. For more on the conditions of being resettled in Cam Lo, and Vietnamese reactions to the resettlement, see Ronald Spector, *After Tet: The Bloodiest Year in Vietnam* (New York: Free Press, 1993), 210; Willenson, et al., *The Bad War*, 111–12; Tom Buckley, "Rural Vietnamese Swept Up by War into Refugee Camps," *New York Times*, October 28, 1967.

128. Betty Lifton and Thomas Fox, *Children of Vietnam* (New York: Atheneum, 1972), 15–17.

129. Herbert Fronewys, "Trip Report," CORDS/Region I, Public Health Division (August 14, 1968), in Health and Sanitation, in Record Group 472, MACV, CORDS MR1, War Victims Division, General Records, Box 8.

130. Human Sciences Research, *A Study of Mass Population Displacement*, 53–73.

131. Ibid., 143–68.

132. This camp was not atypical. For more on life in the camps, see Lifton and Fox, *Children of Vietnam*, 17–21; William Pepper, "The Children of Vietnam," *Ramparts*, January 1967, 59; Wiesner, *Victims and Survivors*, 91; FitzGerald, *A Fire in the Lake*, 428; Ehrhart, *Vietnam-Perkasie*, 80.

133. Health problems were not uncommon in the camps. That same year, a diarrhea and dysentery outbreak at a camp in Hau Nghia killed twenty-two people. Bui Thi Phuong Lan, "When the Forest Became the Enemy and the Legacy of American Herbicidal Warfare in Vietnam," PhD diss., Harvard University, 2003, 146; Buckley, "Rural Vietnamese Swept Up by War into Refugee Camps," quoted in Sheehan, "Should We Have War Crimes Trials?"

134. Schell, *The Real War*, 247.

135. For an example, see Regional Refugee Officer, Refugees Report for May 1967 (June 5, 1967), in Monthly Regional Reports, 1966–1967, in Record Group 472, MACV, CORDS MR1, War Victims Division, Box 22, NARA. Gibson, *The Perfect War*, 233; Charles Smith, *U.S. Marines in Vietnam: High Mobility and Standdown, 1969* (Washington, D.C.: USMC History and Museums Division, 1988), 283.

136. E. A. Vastyan, "Civilian War Casualties and Medical Care in South Vietnam," *Annals of Internal Medicine* 74, no. 4 (April 1971), 616, 619.

137. For more on the "civilian half," see Bergerud, *The Dynamics of Defeat*, 141–55; Mark Jury, *The Vietnam Photo Book* (New York: Grossman, 1971), 113–15; Richard Holdren, "Untitled Report on the Refugee Situation in I Corps, 1966–1968," in Civic Action Briefing and Background, in Record Group 472, MACV, CORDS, War Victims Division, Box 1; Schell, *The Real War*, 20.

138. Don Luce and John Sommer contend that in 1965 and early 1966 people

were fleeing "the Viet Cong," but the reasons soon changed with "the massive allied offensives." For more, see Luce and Sommer, *Vietnam*, 174–75; Wiesner, *Victims and Survivors*, 59–60; Buckley, "Rural Vietnamese Swept Up by War into Refugee Camps."

139. Gary D. Murfin/Human Science Research, "Field Research Memorandum No. 7: The Refugee Situation in Kien-Giang Province" (June 30, 1968), 36.

140. Pacification Task Force/Pacific Technical Analysts, "Refugee Attitudes Toward Resettlement, Return to Village, Urban Migration and Occupational Change" (May 1970), 8.

141. "Bitter Fight for 'Little Hawaii': Marines Pursue Reds on An Hoa," *New York Times*, July 11, 1965.

142. 4th Marines, Command Diary for Period 1–31 July 1965 (August 7, 1965), 5.

143. Statement of Larry M. Farmer, June 29, 1972, in "Hoag Allegation [part 1 of 4], Case 232 (1)," Army Staff, Deputy Chief of Staff, Vietnam War Crimes Working Group, War Crimes Allegations Files, Box 20, 2.

144. Statements of Charles Downing, Davey Hoag, and Michael Garcia, "Hoag Allegation."

145. Pham Thi Hien, interview with Nick Turse, February 20, 2008.

146. A school in nearby Hoai An District was said to have been burned down almost thirty times by U.S. or RVN forces. "Classes Under the Bombing," *The Vietnam Courier*, issue 60 (1966). Luong Dai, interview with Nick Turse, February 20, 2008.

147. Luong Thi Oi, interview with Nick Turse, February 20, 2008; Bui Xich, interview with Nick Turse, February 20, 2008.

148. Dai, interview.

149. Ibid.; Xich, interview; Hien, interview; Oi, interview; Luong Hung, interview with Nick Turse, February 20, 2008; Duong Toan, interview with Nick Turse, February 20, 2008.

150. Dai, interview; Hien, interview.

151. Hien, interview.

152. For more on Masher/White Wing, see John Prados, *The Hidden History of the Vietnam War* (Chicago: Elephant Paperbacks, 1995), 111–20; Emerson, *Winners and Losers*, 84; Young, *The Vietnam Wars*, 163.

153. Some eighteen tons of white phosphorus may actually have been coded as "frag." Combat After Action Report, 1st Cavalry Division, Operation Masher, Operation White Wing (April 28, 1966), 6, Inclosure 16, np, Texas Tech.

154. Kuno Knoebl, *Victor Charlie* (New York: Frederick Praeger, 1967), 214.

155. David Sigler, *Vietnam Battle Chronology: U.S. Army and Marine Corps Combat Operations, 1965–1973* (Jefferson, N.C.: McFarland, 1992), 12; Combat After Action Report, Inclosure 12; FitzGerald, *A Fire in the Lake*, 304.

156. Neil Sheehan, "Vietnam Peasants Are Victims of War," *New York Times*, February 15, 1966.

157. Testimony of Frank Cota, Richard Clark, and David Vasquez, in Record of Trial of Walter Griffen, 1st Cavalry Division, APO San Francisco (July 25–26, 1967). In an unrelated incident, Sergeant Griffen was convicted of unpremeditated murder.

158. Brennan, *Brennan's War,* 15, 32.

159. MACCORDS, "The Refugee Problem," miscellaneous documents, My Lai/Peers Investigation, Jack Taylor Donation, Box 1, National Security Archive.

160. Luce and Sommer, *Vietnam,* 182.

161. Pacification Task Force/Pacific Technical Analysts, "Refugee Attitudes Toward Resettlement, Return to Village, Urban Migration and Occupational Change" (May 1970), 7–11.

162. Emerson, *Winners and Losers,* 84.

3: OVERKILL

1. Alan Moore, *Watchmen* (New York: DC Comics, 1995), 20.

2. Drones were used over North Vietnam. Michael Bibby, ed., *The Vietnam War and Postmodernity* (Amherst: University of Massachusetts Press, 1999), 190.

3. Stockholm International Peace Research Institute (SIPRI), *Anti-Personnel Weapons* (New York: Crane, Russak, 1978), 49.

4. Quoted in Eric Prokosch, *The Technology of Killing: A Military and Political History of Antipersonnel Weapons* (Atlantic Highlands, N.J.: Zed Books, 1995), 30.

5. Ibid., 81–114.

6. For more, see Gabriel Kolko, *Anatomy of a War: Vietnam, the United States and the Modern Historical Experience* (New York: Pantheon, 1985), 196; SIPRI, *Anti-Personnel Weapons,* 26; Jack Raymond, "Vietnam Gives U.S. 'War Laboratory,'" *New York Times,* May 3, 1965; William Beecher, "Unconventional Wars Spur U.S. to Develop Some Unusual Devices," *Wall Street Journal,* March 25, 1964; Larry Booda, "DOD, Industry Facing Vietnam Challenge," *Aviation Week and Space Technology,* April 13, 1964, 93.

7. James W. Gibson, *The Perfect War: Technowar in Vietnam* (Boston: Atlantic Monthly Press, 2000), 78.

8. William C. Westmoreland, *A Soldier Reports* (Garden City, N.Y.: Doubleday, 1976), 279–83.

9. Estimates of the true costs of the Vietnam War vary. For more, see Kolko, *Anatomy of a War,* 347; Gibson, *The Perfect War,* 9, 17; SIPRI, *Anti-Personnel Weapons,* 45.

10. Holly High et al., "Electronic Records of the Air War over Southeast Asia: A Database Analysis," draft 4.

11. For more, see Mark Bradley, *Vietnam at War* (New York: Oxford University Press, 2009), 128–31; Charles Kamps, "The JCS 94-Target List," *Aerospace Power Journal* (Spring 2001), 67–80; Mark Clodfelter, *The Limits of Air Power: The American Bombing of North Vietnam* (New York: Free Press, 1989), 117–46; Harrison E. Salisbury, *Behind the Lines: Hanoi, December 23, 1966–January 7, 1967* (New York: Harper and Row, 1967); Peter Weiss and Gunilla Palmstierna-Weiss, *'Limited Bombing' in Vietnam: Report on the Attacks Against the Democratic Republic of Vietnam by the U.S. Air Force and the Seventh Fleet, After the Declaration of 'Limited Bombing' by President Johnson on March 31, 1968* (London: Bertrand Russell Peace Foundation, 1969); Stephen E. Ambrose, "The Christmas Bombing", *MHQ: The Quarterly Journal of Military History* 4 (Winter 1992), 8–17; I. F. Stone, "Nixon's Blitzkrieg," *New York Review of Books*, January 25, 1973, 13–16; "Civilian Casualties Are Listed by Hanoi," *New York Times*, September 9, 1967; Wilfred Burchett, "Red Writers Say Haiphong Power Operating After Raid," *Washington Post*, April 26, 1967; Thomas Thayer, *War Without Fronts: The American Experience in Vietnam* (Boulder, Colo.: Westview Press, 1985), 80–81; Edward Miguel and Gérard Roland, "The Long Run Impact of Bombing Vietnam," National Bureau of Economic Research Working Paper (January 2006), 2–3. For the oft-ignored pilot's-eye view of a strike in North Vietnam, see John A. Parrish, *12, 20 & 5: A Doctor's Year in Vietnam* (New York: Dutton, 1972), 105–6.

12. The South Vietnamese air force reportedly contributed about 15,000 sorties of its own that year. Kuno Knoebl, *Victor Charlie* (New York: Frederick Praeger, 1967), 175. Jack Langguth, "U.S. Decision to Bomb Inside South Vietnam Seen as Turning Point of War," *New York Times*, September 27, 1965; Kenneth Sams, "The Air War in Vietnam," *Air Force*, December 1965, 72; Myron Allukian and Paul L. Atwood, "Public Health and the Vietnam War," in Barry S. Levy and Victor W. Sidel, eds., *War and Public Health*, (Washington, D.C.: American Public Health Association, 2000), 217; Gibson, *The Perfect War*, 319.

13. Gibson, *The Perfect War*, 9.

14. Earl Tilford, "Air Power, Role in War," in Spencer Tucker, ed., *The Encyclopedia of the Vietnam War: A Political, Social and Military History* (New York: Oxford University Press, 1998), 7; Thayer, *War Without Fronts*, 80–81. For more, see Matthew Kocher et al., "Aerial Bombing and Counterinsurgency in the Vietnam War," *American Journal of Political Science* 55, no. 2 (2011), 5.

15. Kenneth Sams, "The Air War in Vietnam," *Air Force*, December 1965, 80, 83; Knoebl, *Victor Charlie*, 272.

16. "Bombs Kill 45 Villagers," *New York Times*, March 18, 1965.

17. "U.S. Jets Kill 15 Civilians, Wound 182; Plot to Sabotage Viet Election Reported," *Washington Post*, August 11, 1966. For a similar incident, see Tom Fox, "War Memories Haunt Still," *National Catholic Reporter*, April 28, 2000.

18. William Head, *War from Above the Clouds* (Maxwell Air Force Base, Ala.: Air University Press, July 2002), 40; Miguel and Roland, "The Long Run Impact of Bombing Vietnam," 2–3, 9, 9fn, 10.

19. A plan to remove all the population from Quang Tri to turn it into a "free killing zone" was floated but never fully implemented. Instead, the population lived under massive bombardment. A plan to clear the DMZ did get implemented. For more on the latter, see Richard Holdren, Untitled Report on the Refugee Situation in I Corps, 1966–1968, in Civic Action Briefing and Background, in Record Group 472, MACV, CORDS, War Victims Division, Box 1; John Randolph, "Saigon's New Plan: Civilian-Free Zone," *Washington Post*, April 13, 1967; Miguel and Roland, "The Long Run Impact of Bombing Vietnam," 2–3, 9, 9fn.

20. NLF/PRG sources put the casualty toll at more than one hundred dead and two hundred injured. Committee to Denounce the U.S.-Puppets' War Crimes in South Viet Nam on the U.S.-Puppets' Savage Acts Against Patriots Detained by Them, "Appendix: U.S.-Puppet Massacres of the Population in South Vietnam (From 1965 to 1969)," 1969. For more on air attacks in Quang Tri Province, see David Reed, *Up Front in Vietnam* (New York: Funk and Wagnalls, 1967), 140–41; "American Jets Bombed Village in South Vietnam, U.S. Reports," *New York Times*, March 6, 1967; Associated Press, "Civilian Dead Put at 95 in Raid in South Vietnam," *New York Times*, March 4, 1967; "Villagers Sift Debris of Homes, Others Still Hide in Fear," *Los Angeles Times*, March 5, 1967.

21. The strike on Lang Vei was deemed an "accident," as were scores of other deadly bombings. Miguel and Roland, "The Long Run Impact of Bombing Vietnam," 2.

22. Arthur Westing, "Sifting the Ashes of Quang Tri," *New York Times*, September 29, 1973.

23. Indeed, I personally saw unexploded ordnance in her village. Pham Thi Luyen, interview with Nick Turse, January 18, 2008.

24. Neil Sheehan, *A Bright and Shining Lie: John Paul Vann and America in Vietnam* (New York: Vintage Books, 1988), 618; Michael Gross, "An Analysis of Munitions Support to the U.S. Air Forces During the Vietnam War," thesis, Air Force Institute of Technology, September 1988, 88–89.

25. Many B-52 missions did strike inhabited areas. For more, see David W. P. Elliott, *The Vietnamese War: Revolution and Social Change in the Mekong Delta, 1930–1975*, vol. 2 (Armonk, N.Y.: M. E. Shape, 2003), 1162; Sheehan, *A Bright and Shining Lie*, 618; Christian Appy, *Working-Class War: Ameri-*

can Combat Soldiers and Vietnam (Chapel Hill: University of North Carolina Press, 1993), 254–55; Kolko, *Anatomy of a War,* 190; David Hunt, *Vietnam's Southern Revolution: From Peasant Insurrection to Total War* (Amherst: University of Massachusetts Press, 2008), 122; *War-Related Civilian Problems in Indochina,* Hearings of the Subcommittee on Refugees and Escapees, Senate Committee on the Judiciary, part 1: *Vietnam* (April 21, 1971), 154; Marilyn Young, *The Vietnam Wars, 1945–1990* (New York: Harper Perennial, 1991), 196; John Pilger, *The Last Day* (New York: Vintage Books, 1976), 42–44; Fox, "War Memories Haunt Still"; Betty Lifton and Thomas Fox, *Children of Vietnam* (New York: Atheneum, 1972), 95.

26. Jacques Leslie, "Quang Tri Refugees Had Lost Hope, Expected to Die Soon," *Los Angeles Times,* July 24, 1972.

27. Ibid. For more on experiencing a B-52 strike, see Ronald Spector, *After Tet: The Bloodiest Year in Vietnam* (New York: Free Press, 1993), 286; *War-Related Civilian Problems in Indochina,* part 1, 154; Kevin Buckley, "Pacification's Deadly Price," *Newsweek,* June 19, 1972, 42; David Chanoff and Doan Van Toai, *Portrait of the Enemy* (New York: Random House, 1986), 109–10, 166.

28. Only 6 percent of B-52 sorties in Southeast Asia from 1965 to 1972 targeted North Vietnam, 27 percent for Laos, and 12 percent for Cambodia. Head, *War from Above the Clouds,* 95; Thayer, *War Without Fronts,* 83; Allen Hassan and David Drum, *Failure to Atone: The True Story of a Jungle Surgeon in Vietnam* (Sacramento, Calif.: Failure to Atone Press, 2006), 54; "Dinh Tuong: Hell in a Small Place," *Time,* September 11, 1972; William Head, "Arc Light," in Tucker, *The Encyclopedia of the Vietnam War,* 21.

29. Sheehan, *A Bright and Shining Lie,* 618.

30. Micheal Clodfelter, *Vietnam in Military Statistics: A History of the Indochina Wars, 1772–1991* (Jefferson, N.C.: McFarland, 1995), 236. The Stockholm International Peace Research Institute estimated the amount of napalm expended in Indochina to be 388,091 tons; see Stockholm International Peace Research Institute (SIPRI), *Incendiary Weapons* (Cambridge, Mass.: MIT Press, 1975), 50, 96.

31. SIPRI, *Incendiary Weapons,* 154.

32. Mitchell K. Hall, "Napalm," in Tucker, *The Encyclopedia of the Vietnam War,* 282–83; Christian Appy, *Patriots: The Vietnam War Remembered from All Sides* (New York: Viking, 2003), 173, 242; Sheehan, *A Bright and Shining Lie,* 533.

33. Appy, *Patriots,* 242.

34. Nguyen Van Tuan, interview with Nick Turse, January 11, 2008.

35. Quoted in Richard Falk, "Introduction," in Frank Browning and Dorothy Forman, eds., *The Wasted Nations: Report of the International Commission*

of Enquiry into United States War Crimes in Indochina, June 20–25, 1971 (New York: Harper Colophon Books, 1972), xi.

36. SIPRI, *Incendiary Weapons*, 52–53; Leroy Thompson, *The U.S. Army in Vietnam* (New York: Sterling, 1990), 53–54.

37. Tran No, interview with Nick Turse, March 4, 2006.

38. Gloria Emerson, *Winners and Losers: Battles, Gains, Losses and Ruins from a Long War* (New York: Random House, 1976), 142; Prokosch, *The Technology of Killing*, 87.

39. Prokosch, *The Technology of Killing*, 84–85.

40. Robert Bunker, "Bombs, Dumb," in Tucker, *The Encyclopedia of the Vietnam War*, 44.

41. Prokosch, *The Technology of Killing*, 97, 100.

42. Nguyen Thi Chanh, interview with Nick Turse, January 11, 2008.

43. John T. Wheeler, "Bombs Kill Viet Village Innocents," *Washington Post*, July 19, 1965. For another example of a similar allied attack, see Louis Wiesner, *Victims and Survivors* (Westport, Conn.: Greenwood Press, 1988), 61.

44. Harry Rosenfeld, "U.S. Guns Knock Out Enemy—And Level a Refugee Hamlet," *Washington Post*, February 28, 1969.

45. "VC Invade Vote Areas and Kill 28," *Washington Post*, April 17, 1967; Tom Buckley, "U.S. Bomb Error, Second in 2 Days, Kills 14 Civilians," *New York Times*, April 17, 1967.

46. For examples of "accidents" and "errors" in air and artillery operations, see "Buddhist Monks Killed in Allied Bomb Error," *Los Angeles Times*, July 29, 1965; George Esper, "No Sanctuaries in S. Viet for Unarmed People," *Indiana Evening Gazette*, August 17, 1966; "Viet Officer Faces Trial in U.S. Bombing Error," *Los Angeles Times*, November 1, 1965; "G.I.'s Hunt Bodies of Vietnamese Killed When Plane Hit Hamlet," *New York Times*, December 26, 1966; "Bomb Hits Viet Village in Another Raid Error," *Los Angeles Times*, December 14, 1966; Robert Kaiser, "Help Never Comes to Bombed Village," *Washington Post*, January 11, 1970; "Allied Plane Kills 9 in a Bombing Error," *New York Times*, December 28, 1972; "2 on U.S. Cutter Killed in Jets' Attack Error," *Washington Post*, August 12, 1966; R. W. Apple, "2d Vietnam Town Bombed in Error," *New York Times*, November 9, 1965; John Maffre, "Plotting Error Blamed in Viet Village Bombing," *Washington Post*, November 1, 1965; "Marines Kill 271 N. Vietnamese Troops Near Buffer Zone," *Washington Post*, March 5, 1967; "Allies Press Attack on Hue Citadel," *Washington Post*, February 15, 1968; Charles Mohr, "Air Raid Fatal to 48 Laid to Saigon Error," *New York Times*, November 1, 1965; "The War: Escalation by Both U.S. and VC," *Los Angeles Times*, October 2, 1966; William Tuohy, "U.S. Taking Steps to Avoid Bombing Vietnam Civilians," *Los Angeles Times*, August 25, 1966.

47. Charles J. Boyle, *Absolution: Charlie Company, 3rd Battalion, 22nd Infantry* (Spotsylvania, Va.: Sergeant Kirkland's Press, 1999), 283–84; Robert

Rigg, "Killing or Murder?" *Military Review*, March 1971, 3. Rigg gives the date as February 13, 1968, and says that eighty people were killed. This village should not be confused with the village in Dinh Tuong Province of the same name. For more, see Robert Kaiser, "Help Never Comes to Bombed Village," *Washington Post*, January 11, 1970.

48. An NLF/PRG report put the total casualties at more than two hundred people. Committee to Denounce the U.S.-Puppets' War Crimes in South Viet Nam on the U.S.-Puppets' Savage Acts Against Patriots Detained by Them, "Appendix: U.S.-Puppet Massacres of the Population in South Vietnam (From 1965 to 1969)" (1969). Gene Roberts, "Doubt and Fear Fill Cairang, Hit in Error by U.S.," *New York Times*, August 20, 1968.

49. Quoted in Guenter Lewy, *America in Vietnam* (New York: Oxford University Press, 1981), 104.

50. Statement of Captain Thomas Pugh (October 17, 1972), in IG Investigation File 224-04, Allegations Made by Cecil Jimeson, IG Investigative Files, NARA.

51. For more on helicopter strikes, see "U.S. Copters Sank a Passenger Boat, South Vietnam Says," *New York Times*, January 13, 1966; James Trullinger, *Village at War* (Stanford, Calif.: Stanford University Press, 1994), 118.

52. Of these, 7,547,000 were combat assault sorties and 3,932,000 were gunship sorties. Simon Dunstan, *Vietnam Choppers: Helicopters in Battle, 1950–75* (New York: Osprey, 2003), 45; Stanley S. McGowen, "Helicopters, Employment of, in Vietnam," in Tucker, *The Encyclopedia of the Vietnam War*, 167–69; C. M. Plattner, "Marine Control of Air Tested in Combat," *Aviation Week and Space Technology*, February 14, 1966, 90; Shelby Stanton, *Vietnam Order of Battle* (New York: Galahad Books, 1987 [1981]), 287-91; Clodfelter, *Vietnam in Military Statistics*, 227.

53. Statement of Warrant Officer Cecil Jimeson (October 10, 1972) and statement of Warrant Officer Cecil Jimeson (October 9, 1972), both in IG Investigation File 224-04, Allegations Made by Cecil Jimeson, IG Investigative Files. NARA

54. Statement of Warrant Officer Thomas Equels (October 17, 1972), in ibid.

55. Statement of Warrant Officer Phillip Manual (October 17, 1972), in ibid.

56. Statement of Warrant Officer David Waldron (October 17, 1972), in ibid.

57. Thomas Bowen, Request for Phantom III and Target Description (February 6, 1970), in Record Group 472, MACV, MACIG, CORDS MR4, Office Deputy, CORDS, General Records, Box 20.

58. Thomas Le Vasseur, K-Bar incident of September 16, 1969 (October 10, 1969), in Bac Lieu—1969, and Philip Hamilton, memo to Col. Nguyen Van Ngou (June 18, 1969), in Record Group 472, MACV, MACIG, CORDS MR4, Office Deputy, CORDS, General Records, Box 12.

59. John Evans, "Civilian Casualties and Harrassment" (August 6, 1969) in Ba Xuyen—1969, in ibid.

60. Operational Report of the 307th Combat Aviation (Phantom) Battalion for Period Ending April 30, 1969, RCS, CSFOR-65 (RI) (U), 6, Operational Report of the 307th Combat Aviation (Phantom) Battalion for Period Ending July 31, 1969, RCS, CSFOR-65 (RI) (U), and Operational Report of the 307th Combat Aviation (Phantom) Battalion for Period Ending October 31, 1969.

61. Louis F. Janowski, "End of Tour Report" (ca. 1970), Neil Sheehan Papers.

62. Prokosch, *The Technology of Killing*, 61–63.

63. Robert H. Scales Jr., *Firepower in Limited War* (Washington, D.C.: NDU Press, 1990), 52.

64. Myron Allukian and Paul L. Atwood, "Public Health and the Vietnam War," in Barry S. Levy and Victor W. Sidel, eds., *War and Public Health* (Washington, D.C.: American Public Health Association, 2000), 217.

65. For more, see Andrew F. Krepinevich, *The Army and Vietnam* (Baltimore: Johns Hopkins University Press, 1986), 201.

66. For more, see Kolko, *Anatomy of a War*, 192; Thomas Thayer, ed. [Assistant Secretary of Defense (Systems Analysis), Southeast Asia Division], *Southeast Asia Analysis Report/A Systems Analysis View of the War in Vietnam, 1965–1972* (Washington, D.C. [?]:Assistant Secretary of Defense [Systems Analysis], Southeast Asia Division, 1975), vol. 4 (*Allied Ground and Naval Operations*), 207.

67. John M. Hawkins, "The Costs of Artillery: Eliminating Harassment and Interdiction Fire During the Vietnam War," *Journal of Military History* 70 (January 2006), 94–118.

68. For more, see Stuart A. Herrington, *Silence Was a Weapon: The Vietnamese War in the Villages* (Novato, Calif.: Presidio Press, 1982), 38–39; W. D. Ehrhart, *Vietnam-Perkasie: A Combat Marine's Memoir* (New York: Zebra Books, 1983), 79; William Beecher, "Questions on Songmy," *New York Times*, January 1, 1970; Clodfelter, *Vietnam in Military Statistics*, 232.

69. Quoted in Anthony Herbert and James T. Wooten, *Soldier* (New York: Dell, 1973), 225.

70. John Laurence, *The Cat from Hue: A Vietnam War Story* (New York: Public Affairs, 2002), 173.

71. For examples, see Herbert and Wooten, *Soldier*, 226; John Merson, *War Lessons: How I Fought to Be a Hero and Learned That War Was Terror* (Berkeley, Calif.: North Atlantic Books, 2008), 66–67; Hawkins, "The Costs of Artillery," 97.

72. CG III MAF [Robert Cushman], "Secret SPECAT Exclusive for MGENS Tompkins, Robertson, Koster and Anderson" (December 23, 1967), Texas Tech.

73. Douglas Kinnard, *The War Managers* (New York: Da Capo, 1991), 47.

74. Clodfelter, *Vietnam in Military Statistics*, 232.

75. Charles Benoit, "The Situation in Hau Nghia Province" (1968), 32–33. Folder

3, Box 49, Neil Sheehan Papers. For more on the prodigious use of H&I fire by the 25th Infantry Division, see Eric Bergerud, *The Dynamics of Defeat: The Vietnam War in Hau Nghia Province* (Boulder, Colo.: Westview Press, 1991), 135.

76. Jonathan Schell, *The Real War: The Classic Reporting on the Vietnam War* (New York: Da Capo Press, 2000), 68.

77. Krepinevich, *The Army and Vietnam*, 202.

78. For more, see Miguel and Roland, "The Long Run Impact of Bombing Vietnam," 2; SIPRI, *Anti-Personnel Weapons*, 26; Gibson, *The Perfect War*, 319; *Viet Nam: Destruction [and] War Damage* (Hanoi: Foreign Languages, 1977), 37; Arthur H. Westing and E. W. Pfeiffer, "The Cratering of Indochina," *Scientific American* 226, no. 5 (May 1972); Bernd Greiner, *War Without Fronts: The USA in Vietnam* (London: Bodley Head, 2009), 29.

79. Clodfelter, *Vietnam in Military Statistics*, 234.

80. Westing and Pfeiffer, "The Cratering of Indochina," 21, 24, 28.

81. Quoted in Edward Doyle et al., *The Vietnam Experience: A Collision of Cultures* (Boston: Boston Publishing, 1984), 113.

82. Westing and Pfeiffer, "The Cratering of Indochina," 25, 28.

83. Orville Schell, "Silent Vietnam," *Look*, April 6, 1971, 57–58; Arthur Westing, "Leveling the Jungle," *Environment* 13, no. 9 (November 1971), 6–10; Westing and Pfeiffer, "The Cratering of Indochina," 25, 27; Dr. Shutt and Wilson Adams, "Trip Report" (April 8, 1969), in Health and Sanitation, in Record Group 472, MACV, CORDS MR1, War Victims Division, General Records, Box 8.

84. *Viet Nam: Destruction [and] War Damage*, 26; Westing and Pfeiffer, "The Cratering of Indochina," 25, 27; Goro Nakamura, "Defoliation During the Vietnam War" in W. de Jong et al., eds., *Extreme Conflict and Tropical Forests* (Dordrecht, Netherlands: Springer, 2007), 153.

85. Jean Stellman et al., "The Extent and Patterns of Usage of Agent Orange and Other Herbicides in Vietnam," *Nature*, April 17, 2003, 685.

86. Hoang Ngoc Lung, "Strategy and Tactics," draft copy for final review, Indochina Refugee Authored Monograph Program, 109–10.

87. The jackfruit tree is sometimes referred to as *Artocarpus integrifolia*. Quoted in David Zierler, *The Invention of Ecocide* (Athens: University of Georgia Press, 2011), 131.

88. See Arthur Hadley, "The Soldiers: 'No One Cares Anymore,'" *Washington Post*, August 15, 1971; Richard Armstrong, "'Believe Me, He Can Kill You,'" *Saturday Evening Post*, March 25, 1967, 30–31.

89. The NLF estimated that 300,000 people per year were poisoned by chemical spraying, mainly herbicides. Over ten years, this yields an estimate of just 3 million. John Lewallen, *Ecology of Devastation: Indochina* (Baltimore, Penguin, 1971), 114; Richard Black, "Agent Orange Use 'Understated,'" *BBC*

News, http://news.bbc.co.uk/2/hi/americas/2954729.stm; Stellman, "The Extent and Patterns of Usage of Agent Orange," 685.

90. Commentators were already calling attention to the deleterious health effects of the defoliants in the 1960s. For more on defoliants, see William Pepper, "The Children of Vietnam," *Ramparts*, January 1967, 59; Bui Thi Phuong Lan, "When the Forest Became the Enemy and the Legacy of American Herbicidal Warfare in Vietnam," PhD diss., Harvard University, 2003, 224; Russell Betts and Frank Denton, *An Evaluation of Chemical Crop Destruction in Vietnam* (Santa Monica, Calif.: RAND/ARPA memorandum, October 1967), 16; Le Thi Nham Tuyet and Annika Johansson, "Impact of Chemical Warfare with Agent Orange on Women's Reproductive Lives in Vietnam: A Pilot Study," *Reproductive Health Matters* 9, no. 18 (November 2001), 156–64; Thayer, *Southeast Asia Analysis Report*, vol. 5 (*The Air War*), 172; Kolko, *Anatomy of a War*, 145; Elliott, *The Vietnamese War*, vol. 2, 1159; Hyoung-ah Kim et al., "Immunotoxicological Effects of Agent Orange Exposure on the Vietnam War Korean Veterans," *Industrial Health* 41 (2003), 158–66; Phan Thi Xinh et al., "Unique Secondary Chromosomal Abnormalities Are Frequently Found in the Chronic Phase of Chronic Myeloid Leukemia in Southern Vietnam," *Cancer Genetics and Cytogenetics* 168, no. 1 (2006), 59–68; Richard Stone, "Agent Orange's Bitter Harvest," *Science*, January 12, 2007, 177; Anh Ngo et al., "Association Between Agent Orange and Birth Defects: Systematic Review and Meta-Analysis," *International Journal of Epidemiology* 35, no. 5 (2006), 1220–30.

91. Stone, "Agent Orange's Bitter Harvest," 176–79; Ngo et al., "Association Between Agent Orange and Birth Defects, 1220–30.

92. One Vietnamese reported the impact on villagers near Ho Bo woods in Binh Duong Province: "They said . . . even under the French nothing so awful had ever occurred. They complained they weren't VC, so why had the Government destroyed their land and crops." Betts and Denton, *An Evaluation of Chemical Crop Destruction in Vietnam*, xii, 14–15, 17; Schell, "Silent Vietnam," 58.

93. As early as 1967, South Vietnam needed to import 750,000 tons of rice from abroad. Young, *The Vietnam Wars*, 177; Armstrong, "'Believe Me, He Can Kill You,'" 30; Schell, "Silent Vietnam," 58; Kolko, *Anatomy of a War*, 145; Bergerud, *The Dynamics of Defeat*, 71.

94. For more, see Young, *The Vietnam Wars*, 190–91; Thayer, *Southeast Asia Analysis Report*, vol. 5, 172.

95. Jan Barry, ed., *Peace Is Our Profession* (Montclair, N.J.: East River Anthology, 1981), 136.

96. Schell, "Silent Vietnam," 57.

97. The Department of Defense's ARPA also carried out experiments in an effort to create huge forest fires to burn down the jungles of Vietnam. In 1966, a private firm and the U.S. Department of Agriculture both undertook

studies on fires in tropical zones for the Department of Defense. And it didn't end there. Magnesium incendiary devices, dropped from B-52 bombers, were also pressed into service in an effort to create firestorms in Vietnamese forests. SIPRI, *Incendiary Weapons*, 58.

98. South Vietnam even became the proving grounds for a ninety-seven-ton behemoth known as the "transphibian tactical crusher"—a massive tree-crunching machine that a 1967 *Army Digest* article boasted "tramples and virtually chews up anything in its path." "Tree Eater Tested in Vietnam," *Army Digest*, December 1967, 16.

99. Westing, "Leveling the Jungle," 7; Duke Richard, "Rooting Out Charlie," *Army Digest*, November 1967, 56. Similarly, the 687th Engineer Company issued a press release when it cleared its 30,000th acre; it is quoted in James P. Sterba, "Scraps of Paper from Vietnam," *New York Times Magazine*, October 18, 1970.

100. Lan, "When the Forest Became the Enemy", 82–83; Westing, "Leveling the Jungle," 7.

101. Prokosch, *The Technology of Killing*, 73, fn13. For more, see Harry M. Rosenfield, "Hustling Colonel Helps Rebuild Hue," *Washington Post*, February 16, 1969; Edward Doyle et al., *The Vietnam Experience: A Collision of Cultures* (Boston: Boston Publishing, 1984), 141; Westing, "Leveling the Jungle."

102. Prokosch, *The Technology of Killing*, 73, fn13. For more, see Rosenfield, "Hustling Colonel Helps Rebuild Hue"; Doyle et al., *The Vietnam Experience*, 141; Westing, "Leveling the Jungle," 10.

103. For more on troops wielding Zippo lighters and village-burning operations, see Gibson, *The Perfect War*, 143–45; Sherry Buchanan, *Vietnam Zippos* (Chicago: University of Chicago Press, 2007); Tony Sargent, "United States Marine Corps Evacuate Citizens and Burn Village," CBS News, September 15, 1969; Elizabeth Farnsworth, "Years of Change," *PBS Newshour*, May 1, 2000, http://www.pbs.org/newshour/bb/asia/vietnam/vietnam_5-1.html;

104. George O'Connor, Senior Officer Debriefing Report, February 25, 1968, 6.

105. Gordon Baxter, *13/13 Vietnam Search and Destroy* (Cleveland, Ohio: World, 1967), 88.

106. James R. Ebert, *A Life in a Year: The American Infantryman in Vietnam* (Novato, Calif.: Presidio, 1993), 380, 389–92; Jamie Henry, interview with Nick Turse and Deborah Nelson, October 1, 2005.

107. Richard Brummett, letter to Melvin Laird (October 27, 1970), Record Group 319, NARA.

108. For examples of Vietnamese killed in cities by U.S. troops, see "U.S. Toll Called Lowest of Year," *Los Angeles Times*, July 8, 1970; "What's News—Business and Finance World-Wide," *Wall Street Journal*, December 9, 1970; "Viets Riot After GI Kills Youth," *Chicago Tribune*, December 9, 1970;

"Army Charges GI in Quinhon Killing," *Washington Post*, December 12, 1970; "1st Cavalry Beats Off New Red Assault; Reds Overrun Garrison; Americans Turn Back New Vietcong Assault," *Washington Post*, November 18, 1965; Hassan and Drum, *Failure to Atone*, 76.

109. "New U.S. Embassy Opens in Saigon," *New York Times*, September 29, 1967; Sheehan, *A Bright and Shining Lie*, 708; Don Oberdorfer, *Tet: The Turning Point in the Vietnam War* (New York: Da Capo, 1985), 3.

110. Hedrick Smith, "Westmoreland Says Ranks of Vietcong Thin Steadily," *New York Times*, November 22, 1967; Robert Young, "Bunker Tells LBJ of Progress in Viet," *Chicago Tribune*, November 14, 1967; Roy Reed, "Bunker Sees the President; Predicts Saigon Gain in '68," *New York Times*, November 14, 1967; Eric Wentworth, "Bunker Reports War Gain," *Washington Post*, November 14, 1967; Carroll Kilpatrick, "No Changes in Viet Policy Are Planned," *Washington Post*, November 16, 1967; Ernest Furgurson, "Westmoreland Predicts Vietnam 'Phase-Out' May Start in 1969," *Sun*, November 17, 1967; "Enemy Seen Weakened in Vietnam; Westmoreland Cites Progress," *Washington Post*, November 20, 1967; Sheehan, *A Bright and Shining Lie*, 698.

111. John Prados, *Vietnam: The History of an Unwinnable War, 1945–1975* (Lawrence: University Press of Kansas, 2009), 235–39; Sheehan, *A Bright and Shining Lie*, 718; Oberdorfer, *Tet*, 8–16, 31–35; David Zabecki, "Tet Offensive: The Saigon Circle," in *Vietnam War Encyclopedia*, ed. Spencer Tucker (New York: Oxford, 2000), 398; Sheehan, *A Bright and Shining Lie*, 710.

112. Oberdorfer, *Tet*, 34.

113. Prados, *Vietnam*, 239.

114. Quoted in Appy, *Patriots*, 93.

115. For more on devastation to other towns and cities during the Tet Offensive, see James Matthews, "A Combat Medic Remembers Tet," *Vietnam*, February 2007, 54, 58; Robert Hemphill. *Platoon: Bravo Company* (New York: St. Martin's Press, 1998), 192–97; Charles Benoit, "The Situation in Hau Nghia Province" (1968), 21, Folder 3, Box 49, Neil Sheehan Papers, Library of Congress, Washington, D.C.

116. Sheehan, *A Bright and Shining Lie*, 718.

117. Lewy, *America in Vietnam*, 127; Oberdorfer, *Tet*, 179. For photos of the devastation to the Cholon District of Saigon, see Dick Durrance, *Where War Lives* (New York: Hill and Wang, 1988), 128–29.

118. This was a summary of the testimony of a Vietnamese who worked for the Americans found in [redacted], confidential memo to General [Edward] Lansdale, "Subject: Talk with [redacted]" (February 9, 1968), Edward Lansdale Papers, National Security Archive. In his book *Tet: The Turning Point in the Vietnam War*, Don Oberdorfer recounts the same story with pseudonyms. Oberdorfer, *Tet*, 146–47.

119. Gibson, *The Perfect War*, 164; Sheehan, *A Bright and Shining Lie*, 719; Oberdorfer, *Tet*, 179.
120. As with U.S. war crimes and the massacre at My Lai, most discussions of crimes by the revolutionary forces have been reduced to accounts of the Hue massacre, but there was certainly no shortage of other atrocities committed by them—including kidnappings, attacks on civilians, village burnings, the destruction of refugee camps, and summary executions, among others. Most common among these were targeted—and sometimes quite gruesome—assassinations of South Vietnamese government officials, which were regularly carried out from 1959 onward. For an account from a "VC Assassin," see Chanoff and Toai, *Portrait of the Enemy*, 168–71. For more, see Bergerud, *The Dynamics of Defeat*, 67–68; Hunt, *Vietnam's Southern Revolution*, 51–55; Frances FitzGerald, *A Fire in the Lake* (Boston: Atlantic Monthly Press, 1972), 174; Regional Refugee Officer, Refugees Report for August 1966 (September 1, 1966), in Monthly Regional Reports, 1966–1967, in Record Group 472, MACV, CORDS MR1, War Victims Division, Box 1, NARA; Spot Report Civilian/Refugee Disaster files in War Victims—messages, 1969, in Record Group 472, MACV, CORDS MR1, War Victims Division, Box 12. For accounts of atrocities attributed to the revolutionary forces, see United States Mission in Vietnam, "Viet Cong Use of Terror: A Study" (Saigon, March 1967); Jay Mallin, *Terror in Vietnam* (Princeton, N.J.: Van Nostrand, 1966); Appy, *Patriots*, 66; "Rocket Attacks on Da Nang Kill 6," *Los Angeles Times*, April 17, 1969; "The War: Escalation by Both U.S. and VC," *Los Angeles Times*, October 2, 1966; Laurence Stern, "Shock Grips Red Massacre Village," *New York Times*, June 16, 1970; "U.S. Air Raids on North Heaviest in Five Months," *Washington Post*, April 5, 1967; "Enemy Shells Again Hammer Downtown Saigon, Airbase," *Hartford Courant*, June 12, 1968; "Allies Charge 42 Truce Violations: The War in Indochina," *Los Angeles Times*, May 9, 1971; Stewart Harris, "In Hue, Graves Disclose Executions by the Enemy," *New York Times*, March 28, 1968; Charles Mohr, "Vietnam Peasant, in the Middle, Protests Fire from Both Sides," *New York Times*, August 4, 1965; "10 Rockets Hit Saigon, Kill Six," *Washington Post*, June 21, 1968; Kate Webb, *On the Other Side* (New York: Quadrangle Books, 1972), 113–15; Nicholas Warr, *Phase Line Green* (Annapolis: Naval Institute Press, 1997), 135–36; Ronald Spector, *After Tet: The Bloodiest Year in Vietnam* (New York: Free Press, 1993), 206–7; Oriana Fallaci, *Nothing and So Be It* (Garden City, N.Y.: Doubleday, 1972), 263; "B-52s Bombard Enemy Routes Near Cambodia," *Washington Post*, September 25, 1968; Nguyen Cao Ky, *Twenty Years and Twenty Days* (New York: Stein and Day, 1976), 153; Stuart A. Herrington, *Silence Was a Weapon: The Vietnamese War in the Villages* (Novato, Calif.: Presidio Press, 1982), 64; Gene Roberts, "Village Endures Night of Terror," *New York Times*, February 1, 1968; Gary L. Telfer, Lane

Rogers, and V. Keith Fleming, *U.S. Marines in Vietnam: Fighting the North Vietnamese, 1967* (Washington, D.C.: USMC History and Museums Division, 1984), 174; Amnesty International, *Political Prisoners in South Vietnam* (London, 1973), 31; Greiner, *War Without Fronts*, 182–83; Trullinger, *Village at War*, 123; Louis Wiesner, *Victims and Survivors* (Westport, Conn.: Greenwood Press, 1988), 123, 161–62, 225–28; Graham M. Smith, "Communist Perpetrated Terror at the Village Level in South Vietnam," MA thesis, Creighton University, Omaha, 1975; Mission Council Memorandum No. 183 (April 10, 1967), LBJ Library; Robert S. Allen and Paul Scott, "U.S. Silence on Viet Atrocities Poses Puzzler as to Lodge's Stance," *Los Angeles Times*, May 26, 1964; "Quang Nam Province: The Fight Goes On," *Los Angeles Times*, June 19, 1970; Lewis Sorley, ed., *Vietnam Chronicles: The Abrams Tapes* (Lubbock: Texas Tech University Press, 2004), 135, 676; Chanoff and Toai, *Portrait of the Enemy*, 105–6; Armstrong, "'Believe Me, He Can Kill You,'" 72; Phil Ball, *Ghosts and Shadows* (Jefferson, N.C.: McFarland, 1998), 47; "[Memo] for the President from [Henry Cabot] Lodge" (April 19, 1967), LBJ Library; Edward Murphy, *Semper Fi: Vietnam* (New York: Ballantine Books, 1997), 116; Graham Cosmas and Terrence Murray, *U.S. Marines in Vietnam: Vietnamization and Redeployment, 1970–1971* (Washington, D.C.: USMC History and Museums Division, 1986), 218–19, 230; Oberdorfer, *Tet*, 130; Robert Flynn, *A Personal War in Vietnam* (College Station, Tex.: Texas A&M, 1989), 68; Beverley Deepe, "Atrocities Mount Day by Day in Viet- Nam," *Washington Post*, April 25, 1965.

121. Elsewhere during the offensive, the revolutionary forces exercised restraint to their detriment, according to some cadres, releasing many "cruel" South Vietnamese officials whom they had captured. Elliott, *The Vietnamese War* (concise edition), 319; Lewy, *America in Vietnam*, 274; Mark W. Woodruff, *Unheralded Victory: Who Won the Vietnam War?* (London: HarperCollins, 2000), 209.

122. These numbers have been disputed. One independent count put the number between 300 and 400. Another scholar estimated that as many as 5,700 were assassinated. For more, see D. Gareth Porter, "The United States Lied About North Vietnamese War Crimes During Tet," in Samuel Brenner, ed., *Vietnam War Crimes* (New York: Greenhaven Press, 2006), 112; Clodfelter, *Vietnam in Military Statistics*, 133; Laurence, *The Cat from Hue*, 83; Sheehan, *A Bright and Shining Lie*, 720; Douglas Valentine, *The Phoenix Program* (New York: Morrow, 1990), 179; Peter Braestrup, *Big Story*, vol. 1 (Boulder, Colo.: Westview Press, 1977), 282–85; David Zabecki, "Hue, Battle of," in Tucker, *The Encyclopedia of the Vietnam War*, 183; Young, *The Vietnam Wars*, 217–19.

123. Laurence, *The Cat from Hue*, 28.

124. Clodfelter, *Vietnam in Military Statistics*, 132–33. For more, see Philip J. Griffiths, *Vietnam Inc.* (New York: Phaidon Press, 2001), 128–35.

125. Quoted in Braestrup, *Big Story*, vol. 1, 277.

126. Ehrhart, *Vietnam-Perkasie*, 341.

127. Clodfelter, *Vietnam in Military Statistics*, 132–33; Zabecki, "Hue, Battle of (1968)" in Tucker, *Vietnam War Encyclopedia*, 183; Laurence, *The Cat from Hue*, 83; Young, *The Vietnam Wars*, 217; Warr, *Phase Line Green*, 124.

128. Quoted in Porter, "The United States Lied," 112.

129. Ernie Cheatham, interview with Neil Sheehan, July 18, 1977, Neil Sheehan Papers.

130. Eddie Adams, *Vietnam* (New York: Umbrage, 2008), 140–51.

131. "Goff Allegation," War Crimes Allegations, Case Summaries, Record Group 319, NARA. For more, see Young, *The Vietnam Wars*, 225; Bruce Franklin, *Vietnam and Other American Fantasies* (Amherst: University of Massachusetts Press, 2000), 14–21; Alyssa Adams, *Eddie Adams: Vietnam* (New York: Umbrage, 2008), 140–51; "U.S. Cautioning Saigon on Captives' Treatment," *New York Times*, February 5, 1968. A CID investigation failed to find evidence that seventeen or eighteen prisoners were killed.

132. South Vietnamese army troops then looted Hue. See FitzGerald, *A Fire in the Lake*, 397; Oberdorfer, *Tet*, 232–33. For more on post-Tet assassinations, see Seymour Hersh, *Cover-Up* (New York: Random House, 1972), 88.

133. "Peace Protection Committee Exposes U.S. Crimes," Liberation Radio (March 4, 1968), Texas Tech.

134. Sheehan, *A Bright and Shining Lie*, 719; Young, *The Vietnam Wars*, 220.

135. Lewy, *America in Vietnam*, 127.

136. Don Luce and John Sommer, *Vietnam: The Unheard Voices* (Ithaca: Cornell University Press, 1969), 257–58; Appy, *Patriots*, 295.

137. Appy, *Patriots*, 295. For more, see Griffiths, *Vietnam Inc.*, 136–43, 149; Greiner, *War Without Fronts*, 68.

138. Kevin Buckley, "'The Graham Greene Argument': A Vietnam Parallel that Escaped George W. Bush," *World Policy Review* 24, no. 3 (Fall 2007), 95.

139. Rufus Phillips, memorandum/report from Saigon, to Vice President Hubert Humphrey (June 1968), Edward Lansdale Papers, National Security Archive.

140. John Paul Vann, letter to Roger Darling, May 14, 1968, Neil Sheehan Papers.

141. For more, see Jeffrey Record, *The Wrong War: Why We Lost in Vietnam* (Annapolis: Naval Institute Press, 1998), 87–88. "John P. Roche urges WH to limit the use of air and artillery in the defense of Saigon." Miscellaneous. WHITE HOUSE. SECRET, issue date May 10, 1968, date declassified December 14, 1983, reproduced in Declassified Documents Reference System (Farmington Hills, Mich.: Gale, 2009).

142. Prados, *Vietnam*, 209; Earl Tilford, "Rolling Thunder, Operation," in Tucker, *The Encyclopedia of the Vietnam War*, 358–60.

143. Young, *The Vietnam Wars*, 271.

144. Ibid.

145. For more, see Jacques Leslie, *The Mark* (New York: Four Walls Eight Windows, 1995), 90–91; Leslie, "War Victim: Life Resumes Atop Rubble of Quang Tri," *Los Angeles Times*, July 10, 1973.

146. I visited the shells of these bombed-out buildings on January 17, 2008.

147. Arnold Isaacs, *Without Honor* (Baltimore: Johns Hopkins University Press, 1983), 26.

148. "Quang Tri Revolutionary Committee Scores U.S. 'Crimes,'" Liberation Press Agency (August 7, 1972); Leslie, "Quang Tri Refugees Had Lost Hope"; Leslie, *The Mark*, 91.

4: A LITANY OF ATROCITIES

1. Quoted in Marilyn Young, *The Vietnam Wars, 1945–1990* (New York: Harper Perennial, 1991), 165.

2. Carl Morris and F. J. West, *U.S. Fatalities During Vietnamization: Part II, Marine Fatalities in Quang Nam—A Method for Analysis* (Santa Monica, Calif.: Rand, 1970), 4.

3. Gary L. Telfer, Lane Rogers, and V. Keith Fleming, *U.S. Marines in Vietnam: Fighting the North Vietnamese, 1967* (Washington, D.C.: USMC History and Museums Division, 1984), 51.

4. Morris and West, *U.S. Fatalities During Vietnamization*, 10.

5. Ibid., 10–15, 29–39; Michael P. Kelley, *Where We Were in Vietnam: A Comprehensive Guide to the Firebases, Military Installations and Naval Vessels of the Vietnam War, 1945–1975* (Central Point, Ore.: Hellgate Press, 2002), B-19.

6. Philip Caputo, *A Rumor of War* (New York: Henry Holt, 1996), xiii, 87–89.

7. "The First Time He Killed a Man," *New York Post*, April 30, 1965.

8. Later in the tour, as further encouragement, another commander would promise Caputo's men extra beer in exchange for bodies. Caputo, *A Rumor of War*, 72, 74, 108–10, 118–19, 311.

9. Ibid., 74, 106–19, 311.

10. "Viet Bombs Kill 45 Villagers," *Chicago Tribune*, March 18, 1965; Committee to Denounce the War Crimes of the U.S. Imperialists and Their Henchmen in South Vietnam, *Crimes Perpetrated by the U.S. Imperialists and Henchmen Against South Viet Nam Women and Children* (South Viet Nam: Giai Phong, 1968), 21. A Reuters report referred to this village as Man Quang and noted a plane had been shot at from the village earlier in the day. This bombing may also be referenced by a villager who spoke of the village as Hoa Lang, in Martha Hess, *Then the Americans Came* (New York and London: Four Walls Eight Windows, 1993), 171.

11. Guenter Lewy, *America in Vietnam* (New York: Oxford University Press, 1981), 52.

12. Quoted in Young, *The Vietnam Wars*, 143.

13. For a full account, see Morley Safer, *Flashbacks: On Returning to Vietnam* (New York: Random House, 1990), 85–94; Safer, "The Burning of Cam Ne," *Reporting America at War* (PBS series), http://www.pbs.org/weta/reporting americaatwar/reporters/safer/camne.html, from Michelle Ferrari and James Tobin, eds., *Reporting America at War: An Oral History* (New York: Hyperion, 2003). Matches and Zippo cigarette lighters were also used against the village. The marines claimed a military victory against enemies in "fortified Vietcong bunkers," but there had been no battle, and the few bunkers were actually there because Cam Ne had been fortified as part of South Vietnam's Strategic Hamlet program; see Young, *The Vietnam Wars*, 144. For more on the marines' official account, see Peter Brush, "What Really Happened at Cam Ne?," History Net, http://www.historynet.com/ what-really-happened-at-cam-ne.htm. The marines also tried to downplay use of Zippos; see "Justify Viet Hut Burning," *Chicago Tribune*, August 6, 1965.

14. "Marines Raze 2 Viet Hamlets in Retaliation for Sniping," *Washington Post*, August 4, 1965; "Justify Viet Hut Burning," *Chicago Tribune*; Young, *The Vietnam Wars*, 144; Safer, *Flashbacks*, 92.

15. Quoted in Young, *The Vietnam Wars*, 143.

16. Ibid., 144.

17. For more examples of similar behavior, see Herbert L. Bergsma, *Chaplains with Marines in Vietnam* (Washington, D.C.: U.S. Marine Corps History and Museums Division, 1985), 42; "Fighter-Bomber Raids Take Toll of Viet Cong," *Los Angeles Times*, August 4, 1965; "A U.S. Marine Looks over His Shoulder at the Blazing Thatched Houses . . ." (AP photo), negative number 043892, August 6, 1965; Jonathan Larsen, "The Agony of Going Home," *Time*, May 10, 1971; Quang Nam Province Report (December 25, 1965), in I CTZ Province Reports, in Record Group 472, MACV, CORDS MR1, Plans Pro-grams and Reports Division, Monthly Province Reports, Box 1. The NLF source referred to the village as Chau Son. "The Thang Binh—Que Son Massacre," *South Vietnam in Struggle* (February 1, 1970), 3; "Civilians Killed by Marines," *New York Times*, August 3, 1965; James Pickerell, *Vietnam in the Mud* (Indianapolis: Bobbs-Merrill, 1966), 2.

18. Quang Nam Province Report (December 25, 1965).

19. "Marines' Jets in Error Hit Boats of South Vietnamese," *New York Times*, January 14, 1966.

20. Dao Van Cuc, interview with Nick Turse, January 21, 2008; Dao Van Suu, interview with Nick Turse. January 21, 2008.

21. Cuc, interview; Suu, interview. Shelling from artillery or offshore ships caused large numbers of casualties throughout the region, such as in the

coastal hamlet of Ha Binh (which may have been part of the Quang Tin Province during the war). Hoang Thi Kiem was among those injured there, suffering head wounds during one bombardment; her two young children were both killed in 1967 while racing to a bunker to take shelter from off-shore naval gunfire. Hoang Thi Kiem, interview with Nick Turse, January 25, 2008; Truong Cong Duc, interview with Nick Turse, January 25, 2008; Dinh Dau, interview with Nick Turse, January 25, 2008.

22. 3rd Battalion, 3rd Marines, Command Chronology (April 7, 1966), Texas Tech.

23. Otto J. Lehrack, *No Shining Armor: Marines at War in Vietnam* (Lawrence: University Press of Kansas, 1992), 74–80, 369.

24. Le Thi Chung, interview with Nick Turse, January 24, 2008; Vo Thi Hai, interview with Nick Turse, January 24, 2008; Pham Thi Cuc, interview with Nick Turse, January 24, 2008; Pham Thi Cuc, interviews with Nick Turse and Deborah Nelson, March 1, 2006, and March 3, 2006; Dao Sau, interview with Nick Turse and Deborah Nelson, March 1, 2006; Le Thi Xuan, interview with Nick Turse and Deborah Nelson, March 1, 2006.

25. Le Thuon, interview with Nick Turse and Deborah Nelson, March 1, 2006.

26. The monument reads, "Here, on the dates of 1 April 1967, 27 February 1969, and 10 January 1970, the 5th Regiment of the US Marines and the puppet troops launched mopping-up operations, massacred innocent civilians, causing the death of 33 persons and 16 [persons] injured." Most residents, however, said there was a mistake on the monument and that the primary massacre, which killed sixteen people, took place in 1966, not 1967. Chung, interview; Vo Thi Hai, interview with Nick Turse, January 24, 2008.

27. Report of Investigation Concerning the Alleged Killing or Wounding of Four Vietnamese Civilians by US Troops at Dai Loc, Quang Nam Province, June 1966, in Record Group 472, MACV, MACIG, Investigative Division, ROI, Box 43.

28. No one was ever convicted of any crime in connection with the murders. Caputo, *A Rumor of War*, 308, 316–36.

29. "Case of the Killer-Mission Corporal Who Killed a Vietnam Civilian," *El Paso Post*, March 6, 1967; "Court Upholds 25-Year Sentence for Marine in Vietnam Slaying," *Washington Post*, March 8, 1969; *United States v. Frank C. Schultz, Lance Corporal, U.S. Marine Corps,* appellant no. 21,055, United States Court of Military Appeals, 18 U.S.C.M.A. 133, 1969 CMA LEXIS 563, 39 C.M.R. 133 (March 7, 1969).

30. Committee to Denounce the War Crimes of the U.S. Imperialists, *Crimes Perpetrated by the U.S. Imperialists*, 26.

31. CG III MAF, secret message to CG First MARDIV, CG Third MARDIV (November 16, 1966).

32. Gary L. Telfer and Lane Rogers, *U.S. Marines in Vietnam: Fighting the North Vietnamese, 1967* (Washington, D.C.: USMC History and Museums Division, 1984), 51.

33. Edward Banks, interview in "America Takes Charge" from *Vietnam: A Television History*, PBS, 1983.

34. Jack Hill, interview in ibid.

35. Le Thi Ton, interview; Nguyen Bay, interview; and Thuong Thi Mai, interview; all in ibid.

36. Quoted in Hess, *Then the Americans Came*, 155. A monument in Thuy Bo honors 145 massacre victims. Heonik Kwon, *After the Massacre* (Los Angeles: University of California Press, 2006), 139. Nguyen Huu blamed the massacre on South Korean troops.

37. Jack Hill, interview in "America Takes Charge."

38. For more on 1/1st Marines operations, including the manhandling of civilians and ransacking of a hamlet outside Hoi An, see the photographer Robert Hodierne's series of Alpha Company, 1st Battalion, 1st Regiment, 1st Marine Division, taking part in Operation Lafayette in February 1967; photos accessible at http://vietnamphotography.com/imagesC.php?caption=Hoi %20An. W. D. Ehrhart, *Vietnam-Perkasie: A Combat Marine's Memoir* (New York: Zebra Books, 1983), 43, 47–48.

39. Ehrhart, *Vietnam-Perkasie*, 59-64.

40. W. D. Ehrhart, interview in "America Takes Charge."

41. Ehrhart, *Vietnam-Perkasie*, 130–31, 137–38, 166–67.

42. John Merson, *War Lessons: How I Fought to Be a Hero and Learned That War Was Terror* (Berkeley, Calif.: North Atlantic Books, 2008), 61–63.

43. Nguyen Hieu, interview with Nick Turse, January 23, 2008; Nguyen Coi, interview with Nick Turse, January 22, 2008.

44. Quoted in James R. Ebert, *A Life in a Year* (New York: Presidio, 1993), 392.

45. Le Thi Dang, interview with Nick Turse and Deborah Nelson, 2006; Nguyen Huu, interview with Nick Turse and Deborah Nelson, 2006.

46. Nguyen Hoc, interview with Nick Turse, February 12, 2008; Thai Thi Ly, interview with Nick Turse, February 12, 2008.

47. Hoc, interview.

48. Thai Thi Ly's legs were also badly scarred due to an artillery attack, and her arm was scarred for life in still another attack. Ly, interview; Hoc, interview.

49. Some locals say South Korean troops were involved. Massacre monument in Phu Nhuan hamlet (2), Duy Phu (sometimes referred to as Duy Hung, now known as Duy Tan), Duy Xuyen District. See also Deborah Nelson, *The War Behind Me* (New York: Basic Books, 2008), 130–31.

50. Ho Ngoc Phung, interview with Nick Turse and Deborah Nelson, 2006.

51. Hoc, interview; Ly, interview.

52. Committee to Denounce the War Crimes of the U.S. Imperialists, *Crimes Perpetrated by the U.S. Imperialists*, 23.

53. Truong Thi Hong, interview with Nick Turse, January 23, 2008.

54. Hong, interview; Tran Ba, interview with Nick Turse, January 23, 2008; Tran Thi Nhut, interview with Nick Turse, January 23, 2008.

55. The list is missing at least one name and perhaps several: while the NLF document says that the massacre killed thirty-two people, the inscription on the monument says that there were thirty-four people killed. List of massacre victims from Phi Phu hamlet provided to the author on January 23, 2008.

56. William Baker, interview with Nick Turse and Deborah Nelson, April 4, 2006; and the following material from "Henry Allegation," Case Files, War Crimes Working Group, Record Group 319, NARA: statement of James D. Henry, February 28, 1970; Jonathan P. Coulson, "CID Report of Investigation"; Coulson, "Summary Fact Sheet"; statement of Henry, February 28, 1970; statement of Andrew K. Akers, May 7, 1973; statement of Donald Richardson, February 9, 1973; Coulson, "CID Report of Investigation"; Coulson, "Summary Fact Sheet"; statement of Robert J. Lee, November 9, 1970; statements of Gregory Newman, September 21, 1972, and October 3, 1972. Baker disavowed any knowledge of atrocities by men in his unit. Some of these incidents may have taken place in neighboring Quang Tin Province.

57. Statements of Robert Miller, August 5, 1972; Lyle Fikan, December 19, 1972; Andrew K. Akers, May 7, 1973; and Wilson Bullock, November 16, 1972, all in "Henry Allegation"; Mark Lane, *Conversations with Americans* (New York: Simon and Schuster, 1970), 178; statements of Gregory Newman, September 21, 1972; Michael Rainey, December 6, 1972; Richard F. Avila, from the oral statement of Jose Victor Davila-Falu, February 13, 1973; Robert S. Seeley, from the oral statement of (?) Bennett, July 31, 1973; James Alexander, from the oral statement of Lawrence Edminister, February 7, 1973; Robert J. Lee, November 9, 1970; Andrew K. Akers, May 7, 1973; Gregory Newman, September 21, 1972, all in "Henry Allegation."

58. Statement of Nolan S. Jones, February 4, 1973, in "Henry Allegation."

59. Nolan Jones, interview with Deborah Nelson, November 9, 2005.

60. Nolan Jones, interview with Nick Turse, November 11, 2005.

61. Commanding Officer, 1/5th Marines, "Command Chronology for Period 1–30 November 1967" (December 1, 1967), 3/9, 3/13, 3/15, 3/17.

62. Tom Buckley, "Rural Vietnamese Swept Up by War into Refugee Camps," *New York Times*, October 28, 1967.

63. Regional Refugee Officer, Highlights in Refugee Activities for October 1967 (November 2, 1967), in Monthly Regional Reports, 1966–67, in Record Group 472, MACV, CORDS MR1, War Victims Division, Box 1, NARA; Frances FitzGerald, *A Fire in the Lake* (Boston: Atlantic Monthly Press, 1972), 345–48; Human Sciences Research, "A Study of Mass Population Displacement in the Republic of Viet-Nam, part 2: Case Studies of Refugee Resettlement" (McLean, Va., July 1969), 143.

64. MACCORDS, "The Refugee Problem," miscellaneous documents, My Lai/Peers Investigation, Jack Taylor Donation, Box 1, National Security Archive.

65. Phillip B. Davidson, *Vietnam at War: The History, 1946–1975* (Novato,

Calif.: Presidio Press, 1982), 493; Dan Oberdorfer, *Tet: The Turning Point in the Vietnam War* (New York: Da Capo Press, 1985), 189–90.

66. Statements of Gregory Newman, September 21, 1972, and Gregory Newman, October 3, 1972, in "Henry Allegation," 1–2 and 4–5, respectively.

67. Statement of Alexander Freeman, February 14, 1973, in ibid., 2.

68. Statement of Richard F. Avila, from the oral statement of Jose Victor Davila-Falu, February 13, 1973, in ibid., 1–2.

69. Robert Miller, interview with Nick Turse and Deborah Nelson, 2006.

70. Statement of James D. Henry, February 28, 1970, "Henry Allegation."

71. Ibid.

72. James Henry, as told to Donald Duncan, "The Men of Company 'B,'" *Scanlan's Monthly*, March 1970, 30.

73. Christos Frentzos, "From Seoul to Saigon: U.S.-Korean Relations and the Vietnam War," PhD diss., University of Houston, 2004, 267; Kwon, *After the Massacre*, 43–44.

74. Korean Actions (ROK Marines), in Record Group 472, MACV, MACIG, Investigative Division, ROI, Box 53.

75. Ibid.

76. Jack Shulimson et al., *U.S. Marines in Vietnam: The Defining Year, 1968* (Washington, D.C.: History and Museums Division, 1997), 614fn.

77. "Letters Raise Questions of U.S. Responsibility for Allied Atrocities," *New York Times*, February 13, 1972; Robert M. Blackburn, *Mercenaries and Lyndon Johnson's "More Flags": The Hiring of Korean, Filipino and Thai Soldiers in the Vietnam War* (Jefferson, N.C.: McFarland, 1994), 31–66.

78. Kwon, *After the Massacre*, 44–46; Ha My massacre monument, Thon Ha My Trung (formerly Xom Tay Ha My), Dien Duong village, Dien Ban District, Quang Nam Province.

79. In May 1965, for instance, U.S. jets pounded supposed "Vietcong soldiers" as they fled into the mountains, but it was found that 75 percent of those seeking treatment for napalm burns at a nearby Vietnamese hospital were "village women." Bernd Greiner, *War Without Fronts: The USA in Vietnam* (London: Bodley Head, 2009), 153; Jack Langguth, "Drive by Vietcong Wiping Out Gains of Saigon Troops," *New York Times*, June 6, 1965; testimony of Hoang Tan Hung, Reports Concerning Effects of U.S. Bombing—Delivered to the Tribunal [First Session], International War Crimes Tribunal, TAM 98, Box 3, Tamiment Library, New York University; *United States v. Marion McGhee,* record of trial (November 2–3, 1965), and *United States v Marion McGhee,* 2033210, Lance Corporal (E-3) U.S. Marine Corps, NCM 66-0484, United States Navy Board of Review, 36 C.M.R. 785, 1966 CMR LEXIS 151 (July 26, 1966).

80. John T. Wheeler, "Bombs Kill Viet Village Innocents," *Washington Post*, July 19, 1965; John Maffre, "War Is Dilemma for South Viet-Nam," *Washington Post*, July 22, 1965.

81. Lewy, *America in Vietnam* 54–55; Kenneth Sympson, *Images from the Otherland: Memoir of a United States Marine Corps Artillery Officer in Vietnam* (Jefferson, N.C.: McFarland, 1995), 17.

82. Quoted in Young, *The Vietnam Wars*, 161; Lewy, *America in Vietnam*, 55.

83. J. A. Doub, "Company 'K,' 3d Bn (Rein) 3d Marines After Action Report," no. 33 (August 23, 1965), Texas Tech.

84. GG III MAF [Lewis W. Walt] to COMUSMACV (November 17, 1966), Texas Tech; Normand Poirier, "An American Atrocity," *Esquire* (August 1969), 60–63, 132, 134; and *United States v. John D. Potter, Jr.*, 2128272, Private First Class, U.S. Marine Corps, NCM 67-1348, 39 C.M.R. 791, 1968 CMR LEXIS 366 (June 5, 1968). Potter was found guilty and sentenced to a dishonorable discharge and confinement at hard labor for life.

85. Le Cao Luu, interview with Nick Turse, February 16, 2008; Vi Thi Ngoi, interview with Nick Turse, February 16, 2008.

86. Luu, interview; Ngoi, interview; Dien Nien monument, Dien Nien hamlet, Tinh Son village, Son Tinh District, Quang Ngai Province. This massacre is also referenced in Frank Baldwin, Diane Jones, and Michael Jones, *America's Rented Troops: South Koreans in Vietnam* (Philadelphia: American Friends Service Committee, ca. 1974/1975), 43. Some details differ: the date of the massacre is given in that document as November 12, 1966, and the name of the village is listed as Son Loc. Air strikes and shelling also took a heavy toll on Dien Hien hamlet, as did assorted other attacks by U.S. forces. Le Cao Luu told me that his father, a fifty-four-year-old farmer, was shot to death by American troops while tending the family's cows in 1966.

87. Baldwin, Jones, and Jones, *America's Rented Troops*, 23.

88. Phuoc Binh monument, Phuoc Binh hamlet, Tinh Son village, Son Tinh District, Quang Ngai Province. This massacre is also referenced in "Atrocities in Vietnam," *Monthly Review*, January 1970, 35; Committee to Denounce the War Crimes of the U.S. Imperialists and Their Henchmen in South Vietnam, *Crimes Perpetrated by the U.S. Imperialists*, 24. Those sources list the death toll at fifty-four.

89. This massacre is also referenced in NLF documents, but the reported death toll is higher. Commission for the Denunciation of U.S. War Crimes in South Vietnam, "Crimes Perpetrated by the U.S. Imperialists," no. K7B; materials from the second Session of the International War Crimes Tribunal, TAM 98, Box 1, New York University; Baldwin, Jones, and Jones, *America's Rented Troops*, 24–25, 42.

90. Baldwin, Jones, and Jones, *America's Rented Troops*, 42–43.

91. "Retired ROK Colonel Says Unit Killed Vietnamese Civilians," *Yonhap*, April 19, 2000.

92. Phan Van Nam, interview with Nick Turse, February 18, 2008.

93. Phan Van Nam lost six relatives: his father, mother, older sister, younger brother, and two nieces. Phan Van Man lost seven: his father, mother, older

sister, uncle, two nieces, and one nephew. Phan Van Nam, interview with Nick Turse, February 18, 2008; Phan Van Man, interview with Nick Turse, February 18, 2008; Nguyen Huu Phuoc, interview with Nick Turse, February 18, 2008.

94. Jonathan Schell, *The Real War: The Classic Reporting on the Vietnam War* (New York: Da Capo Press, 2000), 219; Headquarters, 3rd Brigade, 25th Infantry Division, "Operational Report and Lessons Learned, Period Ending 31 July 1967," February 6, 1968.

95. Schell, *The Real War*, 214.

96. Ibid., 202.

97. Headquarters, 3rd Brigade, 25th Infantry Division, "Operational Report and Lessons Learned."

98. Jack Taylor, "Army Probers Pushing New Atrocity Quiz," *Oklahoman*, September 27, 1972; Headquarters, 3rd Brigade, 25th Infantry Division, "Operational Report and Lessons Learned."

99. "Halverson Allegations II," War Crimes Allegations, Case Summaries, War Crimes Working Group, Record Group 319, NARA. The investigation of Lanning lasted two years but charges were never filed. For more, see Jack Taylor, "Army Won't Charge Texan," *Oklahoman*, November 15, 1972.

100. Quoted in Taylor, "Army Probers Pushing New Atrocity Quiz."

101. "Past American Atrocities Are Coming to Light," *Fergus Falls* (Minn.) *Journal*, September 29, 1972.

102. Quoted in Taylor, "Army Probers Pushing New Atrocity Quiz."

103. Meyers's radioman said the officer had killed the unarmed man in a panic. Meyers was never charged with any crime. "Halverson Allegation I," War Crimes Allegations, Case Summaries, War Crimes Working Group, Record Group 319, NARA.

104. "Ex-GI Claims He Saw VCs Needlessly Slain," *Sheboygan Press*, September 29, 1972.

105. Quoted in Taylor, "Army Probers Pushing New Atrocity Quiz."

106. To judge by the available numbers, Lanning's company likely continued to kill civilians over the following months: an army study of the 2nd Battalion, 35th Infantry, from October 1967 to March 1968 found that Charlie Company had a "much higher kill rate" than the other four companies in the battalion. Albert L. Hutson, "Report of Investigation," "Case #68-15: Alleged War Crimes by Co. A 2d BN, 35th Inf, 3 Bde, 4th Inf Div toward POWs and Civilians," USARV IG Investigative Files (FY 70), Reports of Investigation Case Files; James Johnson, "Duncan Ex-GI Candid About War Role," *Oklahoman*, September 28, 1972.

107. "Bressum Allegation, Case 34," Army Staff, Deputy Chief of Staff, Vietnam War Crimes Working Group, War Crimes Allegations Files, Box 6; and Ronald Dellums, *The Dellums Committee Hearings on War Crimes in Vietnam: An Inquiry into Command Responsibility in Southeast Asia* (New

York: Vintage Books 1972), 282–94; Douglas Robinson, "Ex-Pilot Alleges Civilian Slayings," *New York Times*, April 7, 1970.

108. For a detailed account of the Tiger Force's crimes, see Michael Sallah and Mitch Weiss, *Tiger Force: A True Story of Men and War* (New York: Little, Brown, 2006); "Trail of Atrocities," *Toledo Blade*, http://www.toledo blade.com/assets/tigerforce/BigMap.pdf; Coy Allegation, "Information Paper, Coy Allegation (WCI—Tiger Force, 101st Abn Div" (August 1, 1974), Colonel Henry Tufts Archive, Labadie Collection, University of Michigan Special Collections Library, Ann Arbor.

109. Schell, *The Real War*, 244.

110. Earl Martin, *Reaching the Other Side: The Journal of an American Who Stayed to Witness Vietnam's Postwar Transition* (New York: Crown, 1978), 164–66.

111. Schell, *The Real War*, 221, 233–38.

112. Ibid., 199.

113. Erwin Knoll and Judith Nies McFadden, eds., *War Crimes and the American Conscience* (New York: Holt, Rinehart and Winston, 1970), 62–66; Neil Sheehan, *A Bright and Shining Lie: John Paul Vann and America in Vietnam* (New York: Vintage Books, 1988), 688. For more, see "The Military Half" in Schell, *The Real War*.

114. Schell, *The Real War*, 200.

115. Knoll and McFadden, *War Crimes and the American Conscience*, 64–66.

116. It was also estimated that by 1967, 3,500 to 4,000 untreated amputees were living in the province. Approximately 95 percent of them were thought to be rice farmers from the countryside. David Stickney, "Vietnamese Provincial Hospital in the War Zone," *Hospitals* 41 (October 1, 1967), 67–71; Sheehan, *A Bright and Shining Lie*, 687.

117. Westmoreland attempted to discredit Schell's reporting, even to the point of claiming that an area Schell said was ravaged was uninhabited. This was patently untrue. For more, see William Westmoreland, *A Soldier Reports* (New York: Dell, 1980), 377; Louis Wiesner, *Victims and Survivors* (Westport, Conn.: Greenwood Press, 1988), 388fn32. Quoted in Sheehan, *A Bright and Shining Lie*, 688–89.

118. Sallah and Weiss, *Tiger Force*, 134, 197–99, 209–12.

119. Lantos himself would be killed in action in April 1968. After Lantos's death, his father transcribed relevant portions of his son's letters in a note to army chief of staff General Harold Johnson. Francis L. Lantos, letter to Harold K. Johnson, April 28, 1968, "Case #68-15: Alleged War Crimes by Co. A 2d BN, 35th Inf, 3 Bde, 4th Inf Div toward POWs and Civilians," USARV IG Investigative Files (FY 70), Reports of Investigation Case Files, Inspector General Section, Headquarters, U.S. Army, Vietnam, Record Group 472, Box 5.

120. "Parker Allegation," War Crimes Allegations, Case Files, Record Group 319,

Records of the Army Staff, Office of the Deputy Chief of Staff for Personnel (ODSPER), Records of the Vietnam War Crimes Working Group; Case Studies, Box 6.

121. Statement of Thomas Pfeifer in "Fox Allegation," War Crimes Allegations, Case Summaries, Record Group 319, Records of the Army Staff, Office of the Deputy Chief of Staff for Personnel (ODSPER); Records of the Vietnam War Crimes Working Group, Case Studies, Box 1.

122. Statement of Randy Wininger in ibid. The War Crimes Working Group document refers to Kinch as John T. Kinch. His sworn statement reads Thomas John Kinch. For more, see William Greider, "Calley Defense: GIs Lulled by Orders to Kill All," *Washington Post*, December 17, 1970; "Fox Allegation," Box 1.

123. Statement of Thomas Kinch in "Fox Allegation."

124. Statement of Randy Wininger in ibid.

125. Robert M. Smith, "Months of Brutality Prior to Songmy Laid to G.I.'s," *New York Times*, April 12, 1970.

126. Seymour Hersh, *My Lai 4* (New York: Vintage Books, 1970), 37–38; Michael Bilton and Kevin Sim, *Four Hours in My Lai* (New York: Penguin, 1993), 92.

127. Seymour Hersh, *Cover-Up* (New York: Random House, 1972), 14.

128. Joseph Goldstein, Burke Marshall, and Jack Schwartz, *The My Lai Massacre and Its Cover-Up: Beyond the Reach of Law? The Peers Commission Report with a Supplement and Introductory Essay on the Limits of Law* (New York: Free Press, 1976), 171–74; summary of expected testimony (from members of Company B, 4th Battalion, 3rd Infantry, re: My Ke), author's collection.

129. Jenkins was also a radioman. Testimony of Jimmie Jenkins in *Report of the Department of the Army Review of the Preliminary Investigations into the My Lai Incident* (U), vol. 2, book 19, 58–59; summary of expected testimony (from members of Company B, 4th Battalion, 3rd Infantry, re: My Ke).

130. Quoted in Hersh, *Cover-Up*, 15–16.

131. Donald Ray Hooton, CID Report of Investigation (April 23, 1970).

132. Quoted in Hersh, *Cover-Up*, 15–16.

133. Officially, Company B claimed an enemy body count of 38 for the operation and stated, specifically, that none were women or children. Willingham would eventually be charged in the deaths of 20 civilians; these charges were later dropped. Vietnamese sources (Republic of Vietnam, NLF, and civilian) put the number between 80 and 97. Hersh, *Cover-Up*, 18–19; Goldstein, Marshall, and Schwartz, *The My Lai Massacre and Its Cover-Up*, 167, 174–75, 181; "Communiqué on Son My Massacre of the Committee to Denounce the War Crimes Committed by U.S. Imperialists and Their Henchmen in South Viet Nam," *South Vietnam in Struggle*, December 1, 1969.

134. "Vietnam Testimony: Two Veterans Recount Their Roles at My Lai," *Louisiana Endowment for the Humanities* (Winter 1995–96), 26–27.

135. David L. Anderson, ed., *Facing My Lai: Moving Beyond the Massacre* (Lawrence: University Press of Kansas, 1998), 35.

5: UNBOUNDED MISERY

1. For more, see Edward Doyle et al., *The Vietnam Experience: A Collision of Cultures* (Boston: Boston Publishing, 1984), 77–79; Don Luce and John Sommer, *Vietnam: The Unheard Voices* (Ithaca: Cornell University Press, 1969), 190; Christian Appy, *Working-Class War: American Combat Soldiers and Vietnam* (Chapel Hill: University of North Carolina Press, 1993), 289.

2. Quoted in Doyle et al., *The Vietnam Experience*, 79.

3. For more, see John Balaban, *Remembering Heaven's Face: A Story of Rescue in Wartime Vietnam* (Athens: University of Georgia Press, 2002), 55; Tom Buckley, "Rural Vietnamese Swept Up by War into Refugee Camps," *New York Times*, October 28, 1967.

4. Some sources put the population as low as 17 million. Neil Sheehan, *A Bright and Shining Lie: John Paul Vann and America in Vietnam* (New York: Vintage Books, 1988), 712. Luce and Sommer, *Vietnam*, 169.

5. *Civilian Casualty, Social Welfare and Refugee Problems in South Vietnam*, Hearings before the Subcommittee to Investigate Problems Connected with Refugees and Escapees, Senate Judiciary Committee (June 24–25, 1969).

6. Luce and Sommer, *Vietnam*, 169.

7. For example, the population of Qui Nhon reportedly swelled from 40,000 to 170,000, and that of Da Nang from 104,000 to 385,000. Louis Wiesner, *Victims and Survivors* (Westport, Conn.: Greenwood Press, 1988), 68; *Civilian Casualty, Social Welfare and Refugee Problems in South Vietnam*, part 1, 44; John Lewallen, *Ecology of Devastation: Indochina* (Baltimore: Penguin, 1971), 34; William Broyles, "The Road to Hill 10," *Atlantic*, April 1985; Sheehan, *A Bright and Shining Lie*, 712; Luce and Sommer, *Vietnam*, 169; *Viet Nam: Destruction [and] War Damage* (Hanoi: Foreign Languages, 1977), 25. For more, see Chester Cooper et al., *The American Experience with Pacification in Vietnam*, vol. 1 (Arlington, Va.: Institute for Defense Analyses, 1972), 49; Orville Schell, "Silent Vietnam," *Look*, April 6, 1971, 58; Gabriel Kolko, *Anatomy of a War: Vietnam, the United States and the Modern Historical Experience* (New York: Pantheon, 1985), 201–6.

8. Marilyn Young, *The Vietnam Wars, 1945–1990* (New York: Harper Perennial, 1991), 177; Samuel P. Huntington, "The Bases of Accommodation," in *The Vietnam War and International Law*, vol. 2, Richard Falk, ed. (Princeton, N.J.: Princeton University Press, 1969), 866.

9. Paper undertaken by Professor Samuel P. Huntington of Harvard University at the request of Policy Planning Council of DOS entitled "Political Stability and Security in South Vietnam." Miscellaneous. DEPARTMENT OF STATE, issue date December 1, 1967, date declassified September 17, 1990, reproduced in Declassified Documents Reference System (Farmington Hills, Mich.: Gale, 2009).

10. Huntington, "The Bases of Accommodation," 863.

11. Frances FitzGerald, "The Tragedy of Saigon," *Atlantic Monthly*, December 1966, 62.

12. Ibid., 64.

13. Schell, "Silent Vietnam," 58; Cooper et al., *The American Experience with Pacification in Vietnam*, vol. 1, 49; Peter Bourne, *Men, Stress, and Vietnam* (Boston: Little, Brown, 1970), 47–48.

14. For more on the plight of refugees, see Lewallen, *Ecology of Devastation*, 34; Sheehan, *A Bright and Shining Lie*, 687, 712; Wiesner, *Victims and Survivors*, 125; Luce and Sommer, *Vietnam*, 169–70; George Wilson, "A Setback for Pacification Program," *Washington Post*, April 3, 1972; Buckley, "Rural Vietnamese Swept Up by War into Refugee Camps"; Karen Peterson, "Saigon's Children of Sunshine or Shadows," *Chicago Tribune*, February 11, 1968; FitzGerald, "The Tragedy of Saigon," 64.

15. For more, see United States Congress, Senate Committee on the Judiciary, Hearings of the Subcommittee to Investigate Problems Connected with Refugees and Escapees, *War-Related Civilian Problems in Indochina*, part 1: *Vietnam* (April 21, 1971), 106; Mark Bradley, *Vietnam at War* (New York: Oxford University Press, 2009), 120–23, 170.

16. Quoted in James W. Gibson, *The Perfect War: Technowar in Vietnam* (Boston: Atlantic Monthly Press, 2000), 268.

17. By comparison, in 2011 Vietnam was considered to have a flourishing culture of prostitution, but with a population of more than 87 million—as opposed to the less than 20 million in South Vietnam during the war—the total number of prostitutes was estimated at 30,000–40,000. "Vietnam in Prostitution Crackdown," Agence France Presse, May 12, 2011. Saundra Pollack Sturdevant and Brenda Stoltzfus, *Let the Good Times Roll: Prostitution and the U.S. Military in Asia* (New York: New Press, 1992), 306; *Viet Nam: Destruction [and] War Damage*, 26–27; Myron Allukian and Paul L. Atwood, "Public Health and the Vietnam War," in Barry S. Levy and Victor W. Sidel, eds., *War and Public Health* (Washington, D.C.: American Public Health Association, 2000), 218; Ngo Vinh Long, "Moving the People," in *Hearts and Minds* (book insert to *Hearts and Minds*, director Peter Davis, producers Henry Lange and Bert Schneider, 112 minutes, BBS Productions/Rainbow Pictures Corporation, 1974); John Tirman, *The Deaths of Others* (New York: Oxford University Press, 2011), 160.

18. *War-Related Civilian Problems in Indochina,* part 3: *Vietnam* (April 22, 1971), 96; Phil Ball, *Ghosts and Shadows* (Jefferson, N.C.: McFarland, 1998), 20; Betty Lifton and Thomas Fox, *Children of Vietnam* (New York: Atheneum, 1972), 20, 23, 41–54; William Pepper, "The Children of Vietnam," *Ramparts,* January 1967, 60; Luce and Sommer, *Vietnam,* 187; Doyle et al., *The Vietnam Experience,* 86–87.

19. Frances FitzGerald, *Fire in the Lake* (Boston: Little, Brown, 1972), 431.

20. For more, see Kolko, *Anatomy of a War,* 204–5.

21. Appy, *Working-Class War,* 289.

22. Eric Bergerud, *The Dynamics of Defeat: The Vietnam War in Hau Ngia Province* (Boulder, Colo.: Westview Press, 1991), 1–6.

23. Wilbur Wilson, enclosure to memorandum for Commanding General II Field Force (November 30, 1967), 4–5.

24. Ibid., 5, 8.

25. For more on Nhon, see Bergerud, *The Dynamics of Defeat,* 274–75; Wilson, enclosure to memorandum for Commanding General II Field Force, 8.

26. Guenter Lewy, *America in Vietnam* (New York: Oxford University Press, 1981 [1978]), 72.

27. Quoted in Bergerud, *The Dynamics of Defeat,* 213–14.

28. Micheal Clodfelter, *Vietnam in Military Statistics: A History of the Indochina Wars, 1772–1991* (Jefferson, N.C.: McFarland, 1995), 232; Ellis W. Williamson, "Commander's Combat Note Number 4" (September 8, 1968), in "Case #69-109: Claim of Land Damage and Destruction of Gravesites in Tan Binh District, Gia Dinh," USARV IG Investigative Files (FY 69), Reports of Investigation Case Files, Inspector General Section, Headquarters, U.S. Army, Vietnam, Record Group 472, Box 17.

29. Len Ackland, "South Vietnam: Peace of Death," *Far Eastern Economic Review,* October 23, 1971, 22. Ackland refers to the village as An Thanh.

30. Roger Williams, "Pacification in Vietnam: The Destruction of An Thinh," *Ramparts,* May 1969, 22–23; Charles Benoit, "The Situation in Hau Nghia Province" (1968), 20, 15–16, Folder 3, Box 49, Neil Sheehan Papers.

31. Benoit, "The Situation in Hau Nghia Province," 25; Williams, "Pacification in Vietnam," 22–23. For more on suffering by others in the area, see Bergerud, *The Dynamics of Defeat,* 175–76, 233–34.

32. Benoit, "The Situation in Hau Nghia Province,"18–19.

33. Ackland, "South Vietnam: Peace of Death," 22.

34. Williams, "Pacification in Vietnam," 23.

35. Benoit, "The Situation in Hau Nghia Province," 19.

36. Williams, "Pacification in Vietnam," 23.

37. Benoit, "The Situation in Hau Nghia Province," 27.

38. Ibid., 19–26; Williams, "Pacification in Vietnam," 23.

39. Williams, "Pacification in Vietnam," 24.

40. Ibid., 23.

41. Benoit, "The Situation in Hau Nghia Province," 27.

42. Williams, "Pacification in Vietnam," 23–24.

43. Benoit, "The Situation in Hau Nghia Province," 44–45.

44. Williams, "Pacification in Vietnam," 24; Benoit, "The Situation in Hau Nghia Province," 25.

45. The man was released not long afterward. Benoit, "The Situation in Hau Nghia Province," 45, 47.

46. Williams, "Pacification in Vietnam," 24; Benoit, "The Situation in Hau Nghia Province," 45–48.

47. Williams, "Pacification in Vietnam," 24.

48. Ibid.

49. Benoit, "The Situation in Hau Nghia Province," 56.

50. Ibid., 31–32.

51. Charles Benoit, "Conversations with Rural Vietnamese," Rand document (April 1970), 18–19.

52. Ibid., 19–20.

53. Ibid., 4–5.

54. Bergerud, *The Dynamics of Defeat*, 234.

55. Generally, it is spelled "solatium." Vietnam Veterans Against the War, "Winter Soldier Investigation, Testimony Given in Detroit, Michigan, on January 31, 1971, February 1 and 2, 1971," *Congressional Record*, "Extensions and Remarks," April 7, 1971, 2825–2900, 2903–36, archived online at the Sixties Project, "Winter Soldier Investigation," http://lists.village.virginia.edu/sixties/HTML_docs/Resources/Primary/Winter_Soldier/WS_entry.html.

56. Thomas Thayer, *War Without Fronts: The American Experience in Vietnam* (Boulder, Colo.: Westview Press, 1985), 232. Adults wounded and hospitalized for at least seven days were eligible for about $15, as well. For more, see Gibson, *The Perfect War*, 310. Department of Defense estimates corroborate this, with reported payments ranging from $25.42 to $33.90. Foreign Affairs Division, Congressional Research Service, "Impact of the Vietnam War" (Washington, D.C.: Government Printing Office, 1971), 17. Seymour M. Hersh, *Cover-Up* (New York: Random House, 1972), 49.

57. OACSFOR-OT-RD-683335, Lessons Learned, Headquarters, 199th Infantry Brigade (SEP) (LT) (operational report for quarterly period ending July 31, 1968)/Adjutant General's Office (Army), Washington, D.C. (August 22, 1968), 21.

58. Nguyen Hieu, interview with Nick Turse, January 23, 2008.

59. The average cost of a table-model radio was $18.21. David Farber and Beth Bailey eds., *The Columbia Guide to America in the 1960s* (New York: Columbia University Press, 2001), 360.

60. Gibson, *The Perfect War*, 309–10. For more, see Thayer, *War Without Fronts*, 232.

61. Quoted in Christian Appy, *Patriots: The Vietnam War Remembered from All Sides* (New York: Viking, 2003), 244.

62. James Kelly, *Casting Alpha: Amtracs in Vietnam* (1st Books, 2002), 135–36.

63. For more, see "Case # 70-2: Death of Vietnamese Civilians on 3d, 2nd Destruction of Property," Reports of Investigation Case Files, Investigation and Complaint Division, Inspector General Section, NARA; Wilbur Wilson, enclosure to memorandum for Commanding General II Field Force, 3–4; *United States v. Private (E-2) Daniel H. McGhee, Jr.*, RA 13835167, U.S. Army, Headquarters and Headquarters Company, 196th Light Infantry Brigade (Separate), APO San Francisco 96256, CM 418055, United States Army Board of Review, 39 C.M.R. 663, 1968 CMR LEXIS 316 (August 21, 1968); Appy, *Patriots*, 444; Luce and Sommer, *Vietnam*, 190; John Sack, "M," *Esquire*, October 1966; Myra MacPherson, *Long Time Passing: Vietnam and the Haunted Generation*, new edition (Bloomington: Indiana University Press, 2001), 339; Benoit, "The Situation in Hau Nghia Province," 52; *United States v. Thomas White*, Record of Trial (August 24, 1970), Appelate Courts-Martial, SJA, RG 472, NARA; Lifton and Fox, *Children of Vietnam*, 80.

64. Boheman was sentenced to just eighteen months in prison. *United States v. Specialist Four (E-4) Robert Boheman*, RA 19833133, U.S. Army, 255th Transportation Detachment (ACFT REP), 222nd Aviation Battalion, APO San Francisco 96291, CM 417003, United States Army Board of Review, 39 C.M.R. 301, 1968 CMR LEXIS 437 (January 29, 1968); "Selected General Court Martial and Special Court Martial (BCD) Offenses Against Vietnamese," Central File, War Crimes Working Group, Record Group 319, NARA.

65. For the three deaths, Gamble was sentenced to confinement at hard labor for eight months, a forfeiture of seventy-three dollars in pay per month during those eight months, and reduction in grade. He never served a single day of his prison sentence. *United States v. Specialist Four John H. Gamble, Jr.*, US 63001956, U.S. Army, Eleventh Supply Company (Repair Parts) APO 96332, CM 419608, United States Army Board of Review, 40 C.M.R. 646, 1969 CMR LEXIS 798 (March 25, 1969); "Selected General Court Martial and Special Court Martial (BCD) Offenses Against Vietnamese."

66. *United States v. Specialist Four Robert B. Fleenor, Jr.*, U.S. Army, Fifty-Seventh Aviation Company (Assault Helicopter), APO San Francisco 96499, CM 423112, United States Army Court of Military Review, 42 C.M.R. 900, 1970 CMR LEXIS 671 (October 5, 1970).

67. Quoted in James S. Kunen, *Standard Operating Procedure: Notes of a Draft-Age American* (New York: Avon, 1971), 328.

68. Quoted in Appy, *Patriots*, 452.

69. Quoted in ibid., 297. For more on similar incidents, see James Trullinger, *Village at War* (Stanford: Stanford University Press, 1994), 117; Herman Graham, *The Brothers' Vietnam War: Black Power, Manhood, and the Military Experience* (Gainesville: University of Florida Press, 2003), 61.

70. Lewis Sorley, ed., *Vietnam Chronicles: The Abrams Tapes* (Lubbock: Texas Tech University Press, 2004), 285–86, 316. For more, see George O'Connor, Senior Officer Debriefing Report (February 25, 1968), 5.

71. "Case #72-56: Act Committed by 2d BN 5th Cav Along QL 1 on 29 Oct 71," USARV IG Investigative Files (FY 72), Reports of Investigation Case Files, Inspector General Section, Headquarters, U.S. Army, Vietnam, Record Group 472, Box 50; James R. Ebert, *A Life in a Year: The American Infantryman in Vietnam* (New York: Ballantine Books, 1993), 375, and Wilson, enclosure to memorandum for Commanding General II Field Force, 6.

72. "Case #72-56:Act Committed by 2d BN 5th Cav Along QL 1 on 29 Oct 71"; *United States, Appellee, v. Joe A. Attebury, Private First Class, U.S. Army, Appellant*, no. 21,896 United States Court of Military Appeals 18 U.S.C.M.A. 531, 1969 CMA LEXIS 744, 40 C.M.R. 243 (August 22, 1969); "Selected General Court Martial and Special Court Martial (BCD) Offenses Against Vietnamese"; "Schorr Allegation (VVAW-WSI)," War Crimes Allegations, Case Summaries, Record Group 319, Records of the Army Staff, Office of the Deputy Chief of Staff for Personnel (ODSPER), Records of the Vietnam War Crimes Working Group, War Crimes Allegations, Case Studies, Box 1; Vietnam Veterans Against the War, "Winter Soldier Investigation, Testimony Given in Detroit, Michigan, on January 31, 1971, February 1 and 2, 1971"; W. D. Ehrhart, *Vietnam-Perkasie: A Combat Marine's Memoir* (New York: Zebra Books, 1983), 272; Wilson, enclosure to memorandum for Commanding General II Field Force, 3; MacPherson, *Long Time Passing*, 207; Ebert, *A Life in a Year*, 375; Balaban, *Remembering Heaven's Face*, 60.

73. Kunen, *Standard Operating Procedure*, 51; "Brenman-Beitzel Allegation (VVAW)," War Crimes Allegations, Case Summaries, Record Group 319, Records of the Army Staff, Office of the Deputy Chief of Staff for Personnel (ODSPER), Records of the Vietnam War Crimes Working Group, War Crimes Allegations, Case Studies, Box 1; Wilson, enclosure to memorandum for Commanding General II Field Force, 6.

74. *United States v. Private First Class Lex G. Gilbert*, U.S. Army, Battery B, seventh Battalion, thirteenth Artillery, APO San Francisco 96368, CM 419632, United States Army Board of Review, 40 C.M.R. 596, 1969 CMR LEXIS 810 (March 3, 1969).

75. Gilbert served only nine months in confinement. "Gilbert Incident," War Crimes Allegations, Case Files, Record Group 319, Records of the Army Staff, Office of the Deputy Chief of Staff for Personnel (ODSPER), Records of the Vietnam War Crimes Working Group, War Crimes Allegations, Case Studies, Box 15; *United States v. Private First Class Lex G. Gilbert*.

76. *United States, Appellee v. Joel McElhinney, Sergeant, U.S. Marine Corps, Appellant*, no. 24,587, United States Court of Military Appeals., 21 U.S.C.M.A. 436, 1972 CMA LEXIS 722, 45 C.M.R. 210 (June 2, 1972).

77. For examples, see Ehrhart, *Vietnam-Perkasie*, 201–2; Patrol Report (no. 4 of August 16, 1965) (August 17, 1965), in 3/3d Marines, "Command Diary for the Period 1–31 August 1965" (September 3, 1965); Kelly, *Casting Alpha*, 47; Ehrhart, *Vietnam-Perkasie*, 64; Phil Ball, *Ghosts and Shadows* (Jefferson, N.C.: McFarland, 1998), 173; Robert Hemphill, *Platoon: Bravo Company* (New York: St. Martin's Press, 1998), 41; Young, *The Vietnam Wars*, 175; James H. Pickerell, *Vietnam in the Mud* (Indianapolis, Bobbs-Merrill, 1966), 25; Ronald Glaser, *365 Days* (New York: George Braziller, 1971), 103; MacPherson, *Long Time Passing*, 313; Ebert, *A Life in a Year*, 374; David Jones, Thoung Duc District Narrative Report for August 1968, Texas Tech; and "Case #69-109: Claim of Land Damage and Destruction of Gravesites in Tan Binh District, Gia Dinh."

78. Quoted in William B. Gault, "Some Remarks on Slaughter," *American Journal of Psychiatry* 128, no. 4 (October 1971), 453. Shelby Stanton, *Vietnam Order of Battle* (New York: Galahad Books, 1987 [1981]), 298–99; Ebert, *A Life in a Year*, 375.

79. Appy, *Working-Class War*, 262–64.

80. Quoted in Bourke, *An Intimate History of Killing*, 2.

81. Ibid., 137. Floyd's assessment and Appy's formulation follow that of the anthropologist Derek Freeman, who noted in 1964 that outward expressions of glee were common among those witnessing destruction or the infliction of pain. Quote from footage in *Hearts and Minds* movie.

82. Leroy Thompson, *The U.S. Army in Vietnam* (New York: Sterling, 1990), 47–48; Eric Prokosch, *The Technology of Killing: A Military and Political History of Antipersonnel Weapons* (Atlantic Highlands, N.J.: Zed Books, 1995), 60; Appy, *Working-Class War*, 263; Stanton, *Vietnam Order of Battle*, 299.

83. Appy, *Working-Class War*, 263; Jonathan Shay, *Achilles in Vietnam* (New York: Simon and Schuster, 1995), 17.

84. For pictures of U.S. dumps in South Vietnam, see Philip J. Griffiths, *Vietnam Inc.* (New York: Phaidon Press, 2001), 176–77. For more on children killed while scavenging or "stealing," accidental deaths, and U.S. mistreatment of Vietnamese in dumps, see John A. Parrish, *12, 20 & 5: A Doctor's Year in Vietnam* (New York: Dutton, 1972), 233, 240–41; National Military Command Center, "Memorandum for the Record: Accidental Killing of SVN Civilian" (December 8, 1970), Major General Walt, personal message for Major General Rosson (October 3, 1965), Texas Tech; Jonathan Neale, *A People's History of the Vietnam War* (New York: New Press, 2003), 117; MacPherson, *Long Time Passing*, 206.

85. "Case #69-107: Killing of a Vietnamese Boy by Mbrs of 1st Bn, 505th Inf, 3 Bde, 82d Abn Div," USARV IG Investigative Files (FY 69), Reports of Investigation Case Files, Inspector General Section, Headquarters, U.S. Army, Vietnam, Record Group 472, Box 17.

86. "Case # 69-51: Shooting of a Vietnamese Child Near LZ Nancy & Treatment of Civilians," in ibid.

87. "404-02 (70) General Court Martial File," Owens, J. H., NARA. For other types of mistreatment of Vietnamese in U.S. dumps, see David Bain, *After-Shocks: A Tale of Two Victims* (New York: Methuen, 1980), 70; "Franklin Allegation," War Crimes Allegations, Case Summaries, Record Group 319, Records of the Army Staff, Office of the Deputy Chief of Staff for Personnel (ODSPER), Records of the Vietnam War Crimes Working Group, War Crimes Allegations, Case Studies, Box 1.

88. "Statement of Dr. Gordon Livingston," in *The Dellums Committee Hearings on War Crimes in Vietnam: An Inquiry into Command Responsibility in Southeast Asia*, eds. Citizens Commission of Inquiry (New York: Vintage Books, 1972), 25.

89. For another similar helicopter case, see *United States v. Warrant Officer 1 Kenneth P. Cuthbertson*, U.S. Army, 282d Aviation Company (Assault Helicopter), 212th Combat Aviation Battalion, APO San Francisco 96349, CM 425290, United States Army Court of Military Review, 46 C.M.R. 977, 1972 CMR LEXIS 603 (December 22, 1972). "Statement of Dr. Gordon Livingston," 23, 25.

90. Some troops would boil off the flesh themselves. Jeff Stein, *A Murder in Wartime: The Untold Spy Story That Changed the Course of the Vietnam War* (New York: St. Martin's Press, 1992), 119; Philip Knightly, *The First Casualty: From Crimea to Iraq; The War Correspondent as Hero, Propagandist and Myth Maker* (Baltimore: Johns Hopkins University Press, 2004), 425.

91. For more, see Richard Armstrong, "'Believe Me, He Can Kill You,'" *Saturday Evening Post*, March 25, 1967; Malcolm Browne, "We're Turning into Animals," *True*, May 1966, 39, 74; Griffiths, *Vietnam Inc.*, 62; "Browne Allegation" and "Ashbaugh Incident," both in War Crimes Allegations, Case Summaries, Record Group 319, Records of the Army Staff, Office of the Deputy Chief of Staff for Personnel (ODSPER), Records of the Vietnam War Crimes Working Group, War Crimes Allegations, Case Studies, Box 1; Lewy, *America in Vietnam*, 329; "Esquire Magazine Allegation," War Crimes Allegations, Case Summaries, Record Group 319, Records of the Army Staff, Office of the Deputy Chief of Staff for Personnel (ODSPER), Records of the Vietnam War Crimes Working Group, War Crimes Allegations, Case Studies, Box 1; LTC Schopper, "Talking Paper: Allegations of War Crimes Other Than Son My" (April 11, 1971), Procedures and Responsibilities for Monitoring War Crimes Allegations, Record Group 319, Vietnam War Crimes Working Group Central File, Box 3; Bain, *After-Shocks*, 68; Charles Flood, *The War of the Innocents* (New York: McGraw-Hill, 1970), 101.

92. "Infantry Unit Gave GIs Kill Reward," *Los Angeles Times*, June 11, 1970; Ben Sherman, *Medic!* (New York: Ballantine Books, 2002), 162, 220; Ehrhart,

Vietnam-Perkasie, 112; Michael Clodfelter, *Mad Minutes and Vietnam Months* (New York: Windsor, 1988), 240; Ebert, *A Life in a Year*, 289–90; Bain, *After-Shocks*, 67; "Briese Allegation," War Crimes Allegations, Case Summaries, Record Group 319; "Zupho Incident," War Crimes Allegations, Case Summaries, Record Group 319; Lewy, *America in Vietnam*, 329; "Lawhon Incident," War Crimes Allegations, Case Summaries, Record Group 319; Appy, *Patriots*, 361; "Stephens Allegation (VVAW-WSI)," War Crimes Allegations, Case Summaries, Record Group 319; "Callander Incident," Army Staff, Deputy Chief of Staff, Vietnam War Crimes Working Group, War Crimes Allegations Files, Box 20; MacPherson, *Long Time Passing*, 80; Clodfelter, *Mad Minutes and Vietnam Months*, 235, 243–46; Ebert, *A Life in a Year*, 349.

93. Clodfelter, *Mad Minutes and Vietnam Months*, 235, 246; Michael Herr, *Dispatches* (New York: Alfred A. Knopf, 1977), 102; Bourke, *An Intimate History of Killing*, 30; Appy, *Patriots*, 159; Glaser, *365 Days*, 103; Michael Bilton and Kevin Sim, *Four Hours in My Lai* (New York: Penguin, 1993), 7; Ebert, *A Life in a Year*, 360–61. There was, of course, a long tradition of this behavior by whites in the American colonies and later by Americans in the United States. For more, see Thomas S. Abler, "Scalping, Torture, Cannibalism and Rape: An Ethnohistorical Analysis of Conflicting Cultural Values in War," *Anthropologica* 34 (1992), 8; James Axtell and William C. Sturtevant, "The Unkindest Cut, or Who Invented Scalping," *William and Mary Quarterly* series 3, 37, no. 3 (July 1980), 470.

94. Jimmie Busby, sworn statement to CID investigator, in "Callander Incident."

95. Tony L. Foster, sworn statement to CID investigators, in ibid.

96. For more, see Kunen, *Standard Operating Procedure*, 51; Douglas H. Hubbard, *Special Agent, Vietnam: Naval Intelligence* (Washington, D.C.: Potomac Books, 2006), 120–21; statement of Andrew K. Akers, May 7, 1973, in "Henry Allegation File [1 of 3]," War Crimes Allegations, Case Files, Record Group 319; Bourke, *An Intimate History of Killing*, 26; Gloria Emerson, *Winners and Losers: Battles, Gains, Losses and Ruins from a Long War* (New York: Random House, 1976), 373; MacPherson, *Long Time Passing*, 219. "Ryman Incident," War Crimes Allegations, Case Summaries, Record Group 319, case Studies, Box 1.

97. Herr, *Dispatches*, 198–99.

98. For more on Ryman, see MacPherson, *Long Time Passing*, 504–11. Norman Ryman, sworn statement to CID investigator, in "Ryman Incident." Army Staff, Deputy Chief of Staff, Vietnam War Crimes Working Group, War Crimes Allegations Files, NARA.

99. Kunen, *Standard Operating Procedure*, 51–52.

100. Ebert, *A Life in a Year*, 287–88, 358–59; Tom Engelhardt, *The End of Victory Culture: Cold War America and the Disillusioning of a Generation*

(New York: Basic Books, 1995), 219; Elaine Morgan, "Vietnam Vet Chron-
icles Experiences, Inspires Hope," *Tampa Tribune*, July 8, 2000; Ehrhart,
Vietnam-Perkasie, 165, 170; Kenneth J. Campbell, *A Tale of Two Quag-
mires: Iraq, Vietnam and the Hard Lessons of War* (Boulder, Colo.: Para-
digm, 2007), 28–29; Bain, *After-Shocks*, 68; John L. Plaster, *SOG: A Photo
History of the Secret Wars* (Boulder, Colo.: Paladin Press, 2000), 446;
Bourke, *An Intimate History of Killing*, 29; Graham, *The Brothers' Vietnam
War*, 57; Knightly, *The First Casualty*, 387; Kunen, *Standard Operating Pro-
cedure*, 50; "Boss Allegation," War Crimes Allegations, Case Summaries,
Record Group 319, Records of the Army Staff, Office of the Deputy Chief of
Staff for Personnel (ODSPER); testimony of Robert Wiktorski from Viet-
nam Veterans Against the War, "Winter Soldier Investigation, Testimony
Given in Detroit, Michigan, on January 31, 1971, February 1 and 2, 1971";
Flood, *The War of the Innocents*, 104; Griffiths, *Vietnam Inc.*, 61. For photos of various "death cards," see Mark Jury, *The Vietnam Photo Book* (New
York: Grossman, 1971), 21.
101. Jury, *The Vietnam Photo Book*, 21.
102. Quoted in Knightly, *The First Casualty*, 387.
103. Vietnam Veterans Against the War, eds., *The Winter Soldier Investigation:
An Inquiry into American War Crimes* (Boston: Beacon Press, 1972), 51.
104. Clifton D. Bryant, *Khaki-Collar Crime: Deviant Behavior in the Military
Context* (New York: Free Press, 1979), 302; "Case # 71-108, Alleged Mistreatment of Dead VC by Elements of Co C, 1st BN, 506th Inf.," Reports of
Investigation Case Files, Investigation and Complaint Division, Inspector
General Section, Headquarters, United States Army Vietnam, Record
Group 472; "Barbour-Droshagen-Morton Allegation (CCI)," War Crimes
Allegations, Case Summaries, Record Group 319, Records of the Army
Staff, Office of the Deputy Chief of Staff for Personnel (ODSPER), Records
of the Vietnam War Crimes Working Group; "Photo of the Year," *Wash-
ington Post*, December 17, 1966; "'Dusty Death' Brings Call for Apology;
God's Glory Held Reflected in Character Burden of Darkness Related by
Minister Message of Angels Held True Today," *Washington Post*, Decem-
ber 19, 1966; "APC Incident," War Crimes Allegations, Case Summaries,
Record Group 319.
105. Colonel Carl Bernard, memo to Lars Hydle, March 7, 1969, Neil Sheehan
Papers; Ball, *Ghosts and Shadows*, 171; David Chanoff and Doan Van Toai,
Portrait of the Enemy (New York: Random House, 1986), 166, 168; Stuart
A. Herrington, *Silence Was a Weapon: The Vietnamese War in the Villages*
(Novato, Calif.: Presidio Press, 1982), 92. For more, see Ebert, *A Life in a
Year*, 359.
106. Haig recalled that the original idea was to drop the corpses on North Viet-
namese troops, which would have been highly unlikely in practical terms.
Quoted in Appy, *Patriots*, 402.

107. Jonathan Randall, "G.I.'s Score Major Victory in Vietnam," *New York Times*, November 9, 1966.

108. "Whitted Incident," War Crimes Allegations, Case Summaries, Record Group 319, Records of the Army Staff, Office of the Deputy Chief of Staff for Personnel (ODSPER), Records of the Vietnam War Crimes Working Group, War Crimes Allegations, Case Studies, Box 1. For a similar incident, see Glaser, *365 Days*, 101.

109. Susan Jeffords, "Rape and the Winter Soldier," *Vietnam Generation* 5, nos. 1–4 (1994), 152–54. For more, see Susan Brownmiller's landmark work *Against Our Will: Men, Women and Rape* (New York: Bantam Books, 1981 [1975]). Other publications include Karen Stuhldreher, "State Rape: Representations of Rape in Viet Nam," *The Viet Nam Generation Big Book* 5, nos. 1–4 (March 1994), http://lists.village.virginia.edu/sixties/HTML_docs/Texts /Scholarly/Stuldreher_Rape.html; Jacqueline E. Lawson, "'She's a Pretty Woman . . . for a Gook': The Misogyny of the Vietnam War," in Philip K. Jason, ed., *Fourteen Landing Zones: Approaches to the Literature of the Vietnam War* (Iowa City: University of Iowa Press, 1991), 17.

110. Balaban, *Remembering Heaven's Face*, 155, 289–91; Appy, *Working-Class War*.

111. Brownmiller, *Against Our Will*, 94.

112. Sturdevant and Stoltzfus, *Let the Good Times Roll*, 306.

113. For more on "Sin City" see Matthew Brennan, *Brennan's War: Vietnam, 1965–1969* (Novato, Calif.: Presidio, 1985), 113, quoted in Appy, *Patriots*, 159.

114. Sherman, *Medic!*, 185–94.

115. At that compound, fellatio cost 500 piasters, and intercourse 1,000. The official exchange rate for most of the war was 84 piasters to the dollar, but in reality it was hundreds of piasters to the dollar on the black market. Gibson, *The Perfect War*, 244. Testimony of [?] Deloriea, in Concerning Colonel David Hackworth, vol. 2 of 8 vols., part 2 of 2, in Record Group 472, MACV, MACIG, Investigative Divison, ROI, Box 120.

116. Kunen, *Standard Operating Procedure*, 164–65.

117. Kolko, *Anatomy of a War*, 363; *United States v. Efra Moore*, Special Court Martial, Record of Trial, Record Group 472, NARA.

118. For more, see Alfred DeMailo, interview with Stephen Maxner (January 24, 27, 28, 2003), 104, the Vietnam Archive, Oral History Project, Texas Tech, quoted in Appy, *Working-Class War*, 290.

119. "Case #70-11: Unfair Punishment of SP6 Mickey Carcille, Art 15 Reduction," USARV IG Investigative Files (FY 70), Reports of Investigation Case Files, Inspector General Section, Headquarters, U.S. Army, Vietnam, Record Group 472, Box 20.

120. For more, see Sturdevant and Stoltzfus, *Let the Good Times Roll*, 325; Appy, *Working-Class War*, 102.

121. Robert J. Lifton, *Home from War: Vietnam Veterans; Neither Victims Nor Executioners* (New York: Simon and Schuster, 1973), 242–43; Lawson, "'She's a pretty woman . . . for a gook,'" 58; Appy, *Working-Class War*, 101.

122. Quoted in Appy, *Working-Class War*, 101–2; Sturdevant and Stoltzfus, *Let the Good Times Roll*, 325.

123. For example, when Susan Brownmiller comments on sexual assault during the Vietnam War in *Against Our Will*, her seminal history of rape, she posits that although the United States at one time had nearly 550,000 men in-country, most were not in the field in combat roles, and thus only a small minority had the opportunity to rape women at any given time. Brownmiller, *Against Our Will*, 99–100.

124. 404-02 (70) General Court Martial File, Longoria, R., and General Court Martial Files, Peterson, J., USARV Appelate Court Martial Record Group 472, NARA,

125. *United States v. Ernest H. Stepp,* Record Group 472, NARA.

126. For examples, see: 404–02 (73) GCM File Lovingwood, W. H., in USARV, Records of the Staff Judge Advocate. Record Group 472, NARA; "Szlosowski Incident," War Crimes Allegations, Case Summaries, Record Group 319, Records of the Army Staff, Office of the Deputy Chief of Staff for Personnel (ODSPER), Records of the Vietnam War Crimes Working Group, War Crimes Allegation, Case Studies, Box 1; *United States v. Specialist Five (E-5) Victor G. Szlosowski*, RA 12704948, U.S. Army, 569th Military Intelligence Detachment, 196th Light Infantry Brigade (Separate), CM 417312, United States Army Board of Review, 39 C.M.R. 649, 1968 CMR LEXIS 321 (August 12, 1968); "Alleged Rape and Other Matters in the 93d Evacuation Hospital," USARV IG Investigative Files (FY 69), Reports of Investigation Case Files, Inspector General Section, NARA; and 404-03 (73) Special Court Martial File, Craig, R. L. (*United States v. Robert Craig*), USARV, Records of the Staff Judge Advocate, NARA.

127. Jury, *The Vietnam Photo Book*, 117. For more, see "2 G.I.'s, AWOL for Weeks, Use PX and Walk Saigon's Streets," *New York Times*, February 9, 1966.

128. For more, see Robert M. White/U.S. Army Natick Labs, *Anthropometric Survey of the Armed Forces of the Republic of Vietnam* (Washington, D.C.: Advanced Research Projects Agency, 1964); Frank S. Besson Jr., "Keynote Address," *Annual Army Human Factors Research and Development Conference (14th)*, Office of the Chief of Research and Development (Army) ([Washington, D.C.: General Printing Office?], 1968), 13, figure 7.

129. "404-02 (70) General Court Martial File, McMahon, T," USARV Appelate Court Martial, Record Group 472, NARA.

130. The accused in this case was found not guilty of premeditated murder. "404-02 (70) General Court Martial File, Vung Tau Detachment," Record Group 472, NARA.

131. Bain, *After-Shocks*, 83.

132. Vietnam Veterans Against the War, *The Winter Soldier Investigation*, 46.

133. Wallace Terry, *Bloods: An Oral History of the Vietnam War* (New York: Ballantine Books, 1984), 82.

134. Tom Skeins, "Witness to Rape," in Victor Volkman, ed., *More Than a Memory: Reflections of Viet Nam* (Ann Arbor, Mich.: Modern History Press, 2009), 73–75.

135. Daniel Lang, *Casualties of War* (New York: Pocket Books, 1989), 26.

136. "Garcia Incident," War Crimes Allegations, Case Summaries, Record Group 319, Records of the Army Staff, Office of the Deputy Chief of Staff for Personnel (ODSPER), Records of the Vietnam War Crimes Working Group, War Crimes Allegations, Case Studies, Box 1. For more, see Lang, *Casualties of War*.

137. "Nguyen Thi Phai Allegation," War Crimes Allegations, Case Summaries, Record Group 319, Records of the Army Staff, Office of the Deputy Chief of Staff for Personnel (ODSPER), Records of the Vietnam War Crimes Working Group, War Crimes Allegations, Case Studies, Box 1.

138. Bilton and Sim, *Four Hours in My Lai*, 129.

139. Ibid., 82.

140. As might be expected, the victim told investigators that she had not been sexually assaulted. The perpetrators accepted nonjudicial punishments. "Brooks Allegation," War Crimes Allegations, Case Files, Record Group 319, Records of the Army Staff, Office of the Deputy Chief of Staff for Personnel (ODSPER), Records of the Vietnam War Crimes Working Group, War Crimes Allegations, Case Studies, Box 4.

141. Record of Trial of Hugh J. Quigley (October 28–November 6, 1970), 2–3, and Staff Judge Advocate, memorandum: Record for Trial, Case of Hugh J. Quigley (October 11, 1970), 2–3.

142. *United States v. Hugh Quigley, Jr.,* Lance Corporal (E-3), U.S. Marine Corps, NCM 710186, United States Navy Court of Military Review, 44 C.M.R. 718, 1971 CMR LEXIS 744 (July 29, 1971).

143. Albert L. Hutson Jr., "Report of Investigation Concerning Alleged War Crimes," "Case #68-15: Alleged War Crimes by Co. A 2d BN, 35th Inf, 3 Bde, 4th Inf Div toward POWs and Civilians," USARV IG Investigative Files (FY 70), Reports of Investigation Case Files, Inspector General Section, Headquarters, U.S. Army, Vietnam, Record Group 472, Box 5.

144. Vietnam Veterans Against the War, *The Winter Soldier Investigation*, 14.

145. Terri Nelson, *For Love of Country: Confronting Rape and Sexual Harassment in the U.S. Military* (Haworth Press, 2002), 35; Graham, *The Brothers' Vietnam War*, 57; Bilton and Sim, *Four Hours in My Lai*, 129.

146. Bilton and Sim, *Four Hours in My Lai*, 129. For more, see Lawson, " 'She's a Pretty Woman . . . for a Gook,' " 61–62.

147. Bilton and Sim, *Four Hours in My Lai*, 130.

148. Vietnam Veterans Against the War, *The Winter Soldier Investigation*, 29.

149. "Allegation 133," War Crimes Allegations, Case Summaries, Record Group 319, Records of the Army Staff, Office of the Deputy Chief of Staff for Personnel (ODSPER), Records of the Vietnam War Crimes Working Group, War Crimes Allegations, Case Studies, Box 13. Jack Crouchet, *Vietnam Stories: A Judge's Memoir* (Boulder: University of Colorado Press, 1997), 70–72.

150. "Allegation 133" and Crouchet, *Vietnam Stories*, 72–73.

151. Ibid., 72–75.

152. The officer who had originally given permission for the girls to be taken into the soldiers' area was alleged to have said, "If she's taken back to Military Intelligence . . . and she tells what happened . . . we'll all swing for it." No one did. Although court-martial proceedings were launched against numerous individuals, not a single soldier was separated from military service for taking part in the atrocities. Only one soldier was convicted of rape; he received a two-year sentence, and military documents suggest he may have served only seven months. "Potter Allegation"; Crouchet, *Vietnam Stories*, 78–82; and Brownmiller, *Against Our Will*, 107.

153. "Szlosowski Incident," War Crimes Allegations, Case Summaries, Record Group 319, Records of the Vietnam War Crimes Working Group, War Crimes Allegations, Case Studies, Box 1. See also *United States v. Specialist Five (E-5) Victor G. Szlosowski*, U.S. Army, 569th Military Intelligence Detachment, 196th Light Infantry Brigade (Separate), CM 417312, United States Army Board of Review, 39 C.M.R. 649, 1968 CMR LEXIS 321 (August 12, 1968).

154. Robert Scheer, "The Winner's War," *Ramparts*, December 1968, 27–28; classified/top secret memorandum from Cyrus Vance to Lyndon Johnson (March 3, 1967), available at NARA, Declassified Documents Reference System (Farmington Hills, Mich.: Gale, 2003); Neil Sheehan, "Vietnam: The Unofficial Brutality," *New York Times*, September 30, 1965; Alexander Casella, "The Politics of Prisoners of War," *New York Times Magazine*, May 28, 1972.

155. For more, see "Letter Charges Torture at Second Vietnamese Prison," *New York Times*, July 17, 1970; Amnesty International, *Political Prisoners in South Vietnam* (London, 1973), 6–8.

156. Abuse by U.S. forces was, in the estimation of General Harold Johnson, the army's chief of staff from 1964 to 1968, worse than what was meted out by the enemy. Bernd Greiner, *War Without Fronts: The USA in Vietnam* (London: Bodley Head, 2009), 79. For more, see Kim Willenson et al., *The Bad War* (New York: Newsweek/Nal Books, 1987), 224–34; David Lamb, *Vietnam, Now* (New York: Public Affairs, 2002), 186; Appy, *Patriots*, 482; Ngoc Bao, "American Prisoners Were Never Mistreated," in Samuel Brenner, ed., *Vietnam War Crimes* (New York: Greenhaven Press, 2006), 129–32;

"When John McCain Was My Captive," BBC News (June 23, 2008), http://news.bbc.co.uk/2/hi/asia-pacific/7459946.stm.

157. In 1972, Don Luce suggested that there were "*at least* 100,000 political prisoners of the Saigon regime in South Vietnam. Some estimates go as high as 400,000." That same year, Alexander Casella noted that Saigon admitted to holding 35,000 POWs and 31,000 prisoners in civilian jails, but also that "reputable" sources claimed 100,000–150,000 political prisoners, while the NLF placed the figure at 350,000. Amnesty International estimated 100,000 prisoners. The Buddhist Peace Delegation, the American Friends Service Committee, the South Vietnamese Committee on Prison Reform, and the Canadian Anglican Church all put the number at 200,000 or more. For more on South Vietnam prisoners, see: "U.S. Saigon Terror Policy and Prison Regime in South Viet Nam" (South Viet Nam Commission of Struggle for the Release of the Patriots and Peace-Lovers Still Detained by the Saigon Administration, May 1973) and "The Crimes Perpetrated by the Saigon Administration Against Detainees, Patriotic and Peace-Loving People and Against People Living in Areas Under Its Control in South Vietnam" (South Viet Nam: Giai Phong, 1973); Don Luce, "A Decade of Atrocity," in *The Wasted Nations: Report of the International Commission of Enquiry into United States Crimes in Indochina, June 20–25, 1971* (New York: Harper Colophon Books, 1972), 13, 19; Casella, "The Politics of Prisoners of War"; Indochina Peace Campaign, *Women Under Torture* (Santa Monica, Calif.: Indochina Peace Campaign, 1973), 3; Amnesty International, *Political Prisoners in South Vietnam*, i; Ngo Vinh Long, "Moving the People," in *Hearts and Minds* movie; Nelson Algren, "In the Eye of the Hurricane," *Los Angeles Times*, October 22, 1972; George McArthur, "S. Viet Prisoners—Torture Tales and Wild Claims," *Los Angeles Times*, July 21, 1973; Appy, *Patriots*, 221.

158. For examples, see Beverley Deepe, "Atrocities Mount Day by Day in Viet-Nam," *Washington Post*, April 25, 1965; Jack Langguth, "Brutality Is Rising on Both Sides in South Vietnam," *New York Times*, July 7, 1965; Akihiko Okamura, "Little War Far Away—and Very Ugly," *Life*, June 12, 1964; "Often Tortured," *Los Angeles Times*, August 28, 1965.

159. Sheehan, "Vietnam: The Unofficial Brutality."

160. William Tuohy, "War Is Hell and, by God, This Is One of the Prime Examples: A Big 'Dirty Little War,'" *New York Times Magazine*, November 28, 1965.

161. Ibid. For another example, see Herrington, *Silence Was a Weapon*, 74.

162. Jonathan Schell, *The Real War: The Classic Reporting on the Vietnam War* (New York: Da Capo Press, 2000), 112. Years later, in the 1970s, advisers were still advancing this argument. One of them explained, "Asians like to torture one another . . . Asians aren't my kind of people." Quoted in Indochina Peace Campaign, *Women Under Torture*, 19.

163. Alfred McCoy, *A Question of Torture: CIA Interrogation, From the Cold War to the War on Terror* (New York: Metropolitan Books, 2005), 5–8, 50, 60.

164. Quoted in ibid., 62.

165. McCoy, *A Question of Torture*, 60, 62–63.

166. Donald Duncan, "The Whole Thing Was a Lie!" *Ramparts*, February 1966, 14. For more, see Donald Duncan, *The New Legions* (New York: Random House, 1967), 156–59. For a similar experience, see Douglas Valentine, *The Phoenix Program* (New York: Morrow, 1990), 309.

167. Duncan, *The New Legions*, 159–60.

168. Duncan, "The Whole Thing Was a Lie!" 14, 21; Duncan, *The New Legions*, 165–70. Duncan wasn't the only Green Beret to complain about the practice. For another example, see "Brown Allegation," War Crimes Allegations, Case Summaries, Record Group 319, Records of the Army Staff, Office of the Deputy Chief of Staff for Personnel (ODSPER), Records of the Vietnam War Crimes Working Group, War Crimes Allegations; Case Studies, Box 1.

169. The South Vietnamese government made a similar announcement the next day. The Geneva Convention IV of 1949 holds that "persons protected by the convention are those who, at a given moment and in any manner whatsoever, find themselves, in case of conflict or occupation, in the hands of a Party to the conflict . . . of which they are not nationals." Quoted in W. Michael Reisman and Chris T. Antoniou, eds., *The Laws of War: A Comprehensive Collection of Primary Documents on International Laws Governing Armed Conflict* (New York: Vintage Books, 1994), 233. Charles Mohr, "Obey P.O.W. Code U.S. Soldiers Told: Mistreatment of Vietcong Is Called Criminal Offense," *New York Times*, December 1, 1965; Bernard Fall, "Vietnam Blitz: A Report on an Impersonal War," *New Republic*, October 9, 1965, 19; U.S. MACV, *Application of the Geneva Prisoner of War Convention in Vietnam* (Office of Information, October 1966), 2.

170. Classified/secret telegram from W. Averell Harriman to William Porter (August 24, 1966), available at LBJ Library, Declassified Documents Reference System; U.S. MACV, *Application of the Geneva Prisoner of War Convention in Vietnam*, 4; and William C. Westmoreland, *A Soldier Reports* (Garden City, N.Y.: Doubleday, 1976), 244–45.

171. Westmoreland, *A Soldier Reports*, 245. For more, see Casella, "The Politics of Prisoners of War"; Greiner, *War Without Fronts*, 76.

172. Office of Media Services, Bureau of Public Affairs, Department of State, Viet-Nam Information Notes: Prisoners of War, no. 9 (August 1967).

173. Interview with Hguyen [sic] Thi Thua, in Indochina Peace Campaign, *Women Under Torture*, 25.

174. File No. DT-264, "Interviews Concerning the National Liberation Front of South Vietnam," Rand interviews (October 1967).

175. File No. DT-270-III, "Interviews Concerning the National Liberation Front of South Vietnam," Rand interviews (November 1967).

176. Many prisoners, in fact, recalled being told that if they were innocent they would be beaten until they were guilty (or variations of the phrase). It was a common aphorism of their torturers. For more, see Sydney Schanberg, "Saigon Torture in Jails Reported," *New York Times*, August 12, 1972; Valentine, *The Phoenix Program*, 221; interview with Hguyen [sic] Thi Thua, in Indochina Peace Campaign, *Women Under Torture*, 28; Nguyen Thi Sau, in *Hearts and Minds* (book insert to *Hearts and Minds* movie).

177. Nguyen Thi Anh, in "America's Enemy," from *Vietnam: A Television History*, PBS, 1983. For more, see Jacques Leslie, *The Mark* (New York: Four Walls Eight Windows, 1995), 164–67.

178. Testimony of Tran Thi Van, quoted in "NLF Report on The Criminal Acts of Terror, Torture, Deportation and Inhuman Imprisonment Committed by the American Imperialists and Their Agents Against the Population of South Vietnam," No. K5B, materials from the second Session of the International War Crimes Tribunal, TAM 98, Box 1, New York University.

179. Greiner, *War Without Fronts*, 78.

180. For more, see Leslie, *The Mark*, 166–67, 174.

181. *Civilian Casualty, Social Welfare and Refugee Problems in South Vietnam*, part 1, 102–3; Kelly, *Casting Alpha*, 71; Valentine, *The Phoenix Program*; 310; Indochina Peace Campaign, *Women Under Torture*, 19; Schanberg, "Saigon Torture in Jails Reported"; "Letter Charges Torture at Second Vietnamese Prison," *New York Times*, July 17, 1970; George McArthur, "S. Viet Prisoners—Torture Tales and Wild Claims," *Los Angeles Times*, July 21, 1973; "Saigon Vows to Investigate Alleged Torture of Students," *New York Times*, April 22, 1970; John Duffett, ed., *International War Crimes Tribunal, 1967: Stockholm, Sweden, and Roskilde, Denmark; Against the Crime of Silence; Proceedings* (New York: Simon and Schuster, 1970 [1968]), 480; Luce and Sommer, *Vietnam*, 157; Jack Anderson, "Prisoners Tortured in S. Vietnam Jails," *Washington Post*, August 30, 1971; report by Pham Thi Yen, in testimony heard by the Second Session of the International War Crimes Tribunal; testimony of Nguyen Thi Tho, No. D6B, materials from the Second Session of the International War Crimes Tribunal; Amnesty International, *Political Prisoners in South Vietnam*, 23, 27–28.

182. The tiny sunken cells had originally been built by the French when the island was known as Poulo Condore. For more on Con Son and the tiger cages, see David Chanoff and Doan Van Toai, *Portrait of the Enemy* (New York: Random House, 1986), 99–100; Jacques Leslie, " 'Tiger Cage' Victims Cite S. Viet Torture," *Washington Post*, March 4, 1973; Thomas Foley, " 'Tiger Cages' for Viet Dissenters Described," *Los Angeles Times*, July 7, 1970; "The Cages of Con Son Island," *Time*, July 20, 1970; Sheehan, *A Bright and Shining Lie*, 158; Luce, "A Decade of Atrocity," 13–18.

183. For examples, see *Civilian Casualty, Social Welfare and Refugee Problems in South Vietnam*, part 1, 101–2; Committee to Denounce the War Crimes

of the U.S. Imperialists and Their Henchmen in South Vietnam, *Crimes Perpetrated by the U.S. Imperialists and Henchmen against South Viet Nam Women and Children* (Saigon: Giai Phong, 1968), 8–9.

184. Emerson, *Winners and Losers*, 343–44; "The Cages of Con Son Island," *Time*, July 20, 1970; Juan M. Vasquez, "House Unit's Report on Vietnam Termed 'Whitewash' by Aide," *New York Times*, July 8, 1970; Don Luce, "The Tiger Cages of Viet Nam," in Historians Against the War, eds., *Torture, American Style*, HAW Pamphlet 3 (2004), http://www.historians againstwar.org/resources/torture/luce.html.

185. Emerson, *Winners and Losers*, 344.

186. Ibid., 344–45.

187. Ibid., 345.

188. Ibid., 345–48; Vasquez, "House Unit's Report on Vietnam Termed 'Whitewash' by Aide"; Luce, "A Decade of Atrocity," 14; Luce, "The Tiger Cages of Viet Nam." For more on the horrors of the Tiger Cages, see Holmes Brown and Don Luce, *Hostages of War: Saigon's Political Prisoners* (Washington, D.C.: Indochina Mobile Education Project, 1973).

189. Vasquez, "House Unit's Report on Vietnam Termed 'Whitewash' by Aide."

190. George C. Wilson, "S. Viet Prison Found 'Shocking,'" *Washington Post*, July 7, 1970.

191. Luce, "A Decade of Atrocity," 14; Emerson, *Winners and Losers*, 348.

192. Notably, Halliburton later built "isolation cells" at the U.S. military base in Guantánamo Bay. Luce, "The Tiger Cages of Viet Nam"; Sheehan, *A Bright and Shining Lie*, 624; Luce, "A Decade of Atrocity," 14; Emerson, *Winners and Losers*, 348.

193. Greiner, *War Without Fronts*, 77.

194. Others were paralyzed. For more, see Leslie, *The Mark*, 171–73; Valentine, *The Phoenix Program*, 348–50; "The Other Prisoners," *Time*, March 19, 1973.

195. Mission Council Action Memorandum No. 181 (April 5, 1967), LBJ Library.

196. COMUSMACV TO CINPAC, "ICRC Visit to the CPWC, Phu Quoc Island" (May 24, 1971), NARA.

197. COMUSMACV TO CINPAC, "Conditions at Phu Quoc PW Camp" (June 11, 1971), NARA.

198. Nguyen Coi, interview with Nick Turse, January 22, 2008.

199. Earl Martin, *Reaching the Other Side: The Journal of an American Who Stayed to Witness Vietnam's Postwar Transition* (New York: Crown, 1978), 150.

200. Huynh Thi Hai, interview with Nick Turse, January 12, 2008.

201. "Report of Investigation Conducted by CDR H.A. Kusulos, USN Concerning Alleged Brutality by U.S. Navy Personnel," in Dinh Tuong—1969, in Record Group 472, MACV, MACIG, CORDS MR4, Office Dpty, CORDS, General Records, Box 12. Lieutenant Bishop was not found guilty of any

crime. For more on torture by SEALs, see Gregory L. Vistica, *The Education of Lieutenant Kerrey* (New York: St. Martin's Press, 2003), 235.

202. CID Report of Investigation, "Cruelty and Maltreatment" (November 4, 1970–June 23, 1971), Tufts; and memorandum for chief of staff (April 14, 1973), Herbert Controversy, 1970–73 Box 1.

203. Sworn statement of Anthony Herbert, in ibid., 13; Anthony Herbert and James T. Wooten, *Soldier* (New York: Dell, 1973), 381–83.

204. Sworn statement of Anthony Herbert, in CID Report of Investigation, "Cruelty and Maltreatment," 14; Herbert and Wooten, *Soldier*, 381–83.

205. Sworn statement of Anthony Herbert, in CID Report of Investigation, "Cruelty and Maltreatment," 14; Herbert and Wooten, *Soldier*, 421–22.

206. Deborah Nelson and Nick Turse, "A Tortured Past," *Los Angeles Times*, August 20, 2006.

207. Ibid.

208. CID Report of Investigation, "Cruelty and Maltreatment (WCI)."

209. Sworn statement of William O'Sullivan (December 9, 1970), in MIV-19-71, "Rpt. LTC Herbert's Charges against Joseph Franklin . . . ," Record Group 472, MACV, MACIG Investigative Division, ROI; CID Report of Investigation, "Cruelty and Maltreatment (WCI)."

210. Army documents, however, asserted "maltreatment was not established as the cause of death." Deborah Nelson and Nick Turse, "A Tortured Past."

211. CID Report of Investigation, "Cruelty and Maltreatment (WCI)."

212. Sworn statement of Stacy Peterson (December 19, 1970), in ibid.

213. Sworn statement of Willard McFalls (December 12, 1970), in MIV-19-71, "Rpt. LTC Herbert's Charges against Joseph Franklin . . ."

214. Statement of Larry B. Tackett [unsworn] (November? 1970), in MIV-19-71, "Rpt. LTC Herbert's Charges against Joseph Franklin . . ."; CID Report of Investigation, "Cruelty and Maltreatment (WCI)."

215. CID Report of Investigation, "Cruelty and Maltreatment (WCI)."

216. Murray W. Williams, "Allegations of War Crimes," in "Memorandum for: Chief of Staff, United States Army; Subject: 'Soldier' by Anthony Herbert" (January 29, 1973), Herbert Documents and Working Papers, January 1973, part 2 of 2, Records of the Army Staff, Office of the Deputy Chief of Staff, Vietnam War Crimes Working Group, LTC Herbert Controversy, 1970–73, Box 1.

217. David Carmon, electronic messages to Nick Turse, May 31, 2006, and June 4, 2006.

218. Quoted in Ronald Spector, *After Tet: The Bloodiest Year in Vietnam* (New York: Free Press, 1993), 203.

219. For examples, see Martha Hess, *Then the Americans Came* (New York and London: Four Walls Eight Windows, 1993), 140; Ebert, *A Life in a Year*, 355–57; Clodfelter, *Mad Minutes and Vietnam Months*, 263–64.

220. Abraham Cooke, sworn statement to CID investigator, "Callander Inci-

dent," Army Staff, Deputy Chief of Staff, Vietnam War Crimes Working Group, War Crimes Allegations Files, Box 20.

221. Concerned Sergeant, letter to William Westmoreland (May 25, 1970), "copy reproduced on 27 August 1971," in "Concerned Sergeant Allegation," War Crimes Allegations, Case Files, War Crimes Working Group, Record Group 319, NARA; "Hall Allegation," War Crimes Allegations, Case Summaries, Record Group 319, Records of the Army Staff, Office of the Deputy Chief of Staff for Personnel (ODSPER), Records of the Vietnam War Crimes Working Group; War Crimes Allegations, Case Studies, Box 1; Glaser, *365 Days*, 91; Hersh, *Cover-Up*, 24; Ebert, *A Life in a Year*, 354; "Report of Investigation Concerning Allegations Made Against 2LT Warren Ambrose, 561-60-8722, for Possible War Crimes," in "Ambrose Incident," Case 157, Army Staff, Deputy Chief of Staff, Vietnam War Crimes Working Group, War Crimes Allegations Files, Box 16; "Investigative Summarizes [*sic*]," SRAC, in Record Group 472, MACV, MACIG, Investigative Division, Miscellaneous Reports of Investigation, Box 10.

222. For more, see Philip Caputo, *A Rumor of War* (New York: Henry Holt, 1996), 229.

223. "Bonvillain Incident," War Crimes Allegations, Case Files, Record Group 319, Records of the Army Staff, NARA. For more, see "U.S. Officer Held in POW Death," *Washington Post*, November 27, 1969.

224. Calvin Mehlert, confidential memo to General [Edward] Lansdale (February 26, 1968), Edward Lansdale Papers, National Security Archive; "Current Intelligence Memorandum, Subject: Cast of Characters in South Vietnam" (August 28, 1963), Lansdale Papers.

225. "Green Beret Incident," War Crimes Allegations, Case Summary, Record Group 319, War Crimes Allegations Case Files, Box 16; Stein, *A Murder in Wartime*, 116–17, 180.

226. Stein, *A Murder in Wartime*, 117.

227. Homer Bigart, "Beret Affair: Step by Step," *New York Times*, October 6, 1969; Stein, *A Murder in Wartime*, 130.

228. McCoy, *A Question of Torture*, 63–64. Edmund R. Thompson, "Division G2 in Vietnam," COMUSAC, ca. 1969/1970, Viet Cong Captives Interrogation Reports, Miscellaneous file: Intelligence—VN (U.S. Army Military Institute, Carlisle Barracks). For more, see Valentine, *The Phoenix Program*.

229. Valentine, *The Phoenix Program*, 204, 289; Jack Shulimson et al., *U.S. Marines in Vietnam: The Defining Year, 1968* (Washington, D.C.: History and Museums Division, 1997), 603fn; Robert Gard, e-mails to Nick Turse, August 8, 2008, and August, 13, 2008; John Prados, *Vietnam: The History of an Unwinnable War, 1945–1975* (Lawrence: University Press of Kansas, 2009), 327.

230. In the years since the war, some authors have attempted to soften the

image of the Phoenix program or slough off blame for its worst abuses on the South Vietnamese (as if their effort was at all detached from that of the Americans) by casting different parts or components of Phoenix as separate and distinct. One notable example of this reinterpretation is Mark Moyar's *Phoenix and the Birds of Prey: The CIA's Secret Campaign to Destroy the Viet Cong* (Annapolis, Md.: Naval Institute Press, 1997). For more on the Phoenix program, see Kolko, *Anatomy of a War*, 330; Hersh, *Cover-Up*, 87–88; Willenson et al., *The Bad War*, 216; Trullinger, *Village at War*, 172–73; Valentine, *The Phoenix Program*, 190–92, 267, 309, 321.

231. Appy, *Patriots*, 361–62.

232. Transcript, William E. Colby, Oral History Interview 2 (March 1, 1982) by Ted Gittinger, Internet Copy, 7, LBJ Library; Thomas Thayer, ed. [Assistant Secretary of Defense (Systems Analysis), Southeast Asia Division], *Southeast Asia Analysis Report/A Systems Analysis View of the War in Vietnam, 1965–1972* (Washington, D.C. [?]:Assistant Secretary of Defense [Systems Analysis], Southeast Asia Division, 1975), vol. 10 (*Pacification and Civil Affairs*), 80 (15—dual numbering system); McCoy, *A Question of Torture*, 63–67. For more, see Valentine, *The Phoenix Program*, 170–71, 218–19, 264–65, 315; Balaban, *Remembering Heaven's Face*, 49–50.

233. McCoy, *A Question of Torture*, 67. See also Dale Andrade, *Ashes to Ashes: The Phoenix Program and the Vietnam War* (Lexington, Mass.: Lexington Books, 1990), appendix, table A-1.

234. Like Donald Duncan, Osborn said he was taught these "extralegal, illegal and covert" methods, stating he had learned them while training at the Army Intelligence School at Fort Holabird. Others echoed him. For example, Lieutenant Francis Reitemeyer recalled that, while at the Army Intelligence School at Fort Holabird, he was taught to use "the most extreme forms of torture." Douglas Robinson, "Army Intelligence School Silent as Sphinx at Door," *New York Times*, October 18, 1969. Colby stated that "various of the things that Mr. Osborn alleges might have happened" and admitted, "I knew there were people killed," but denied it was a "systematic program of assassination." Quoted in McCoy, *A Question of Torture*, 68–69.

6: THE BUMMER, THE "GOOK-HUNTING" GENERAL, AND THE BUTCHER OF THE DELTA

1. Sworn testimony of Jack Donovan, in Record of Trial of Roy E. Bumgarner (1969), 208–9; sworn testimony of Richard Childers, in Record of Trial of Roy E. Bumgarner, 301; Anthony Herbert and James T. Wooten, *Soldier* (New York: Dell, 1973), 244–45; sworn testimony of John Nicholson, in Record of Trial of Roy E. Bumgarner, 193.

2. Arthur Williams, statement to John M. Dove (March 4, 1968), author's collection.

3. Deborah Nelson and Nick Turse, "Lasting Pain, Minimal Punishment," *Los Angeles Times*, August 20, 2006.

4. Herbert and Wooten, *Soldier*, 242–45; Franklin Miller and Elwood Kureth, *Reflections of a Warrior* (New York: Pocket Books, 1992), 11–17, where he uses the pseudonym "Staff Sergeant Bumstaten" for "Bumgarner."

5. Nelson and Turse, "Lasting Pain, Minimal Punishment."

6. Huynh Thi Nay, interview with Nick Turse and Deborah Nelson, 2006; Phan Thi Dan, interview with Nick Turse and Deborah Nelson, 2006; Nelson and Turse, "Lasting Pain, Minimal Punishment."

7. Nelson and Turse, "Lasting Pain, Minimal Punishment"; "Statement of Rodarte" and "Statement of Charles H. Boss," in "Bumgarner Incident," Record Group 319, Records of the Army Staff, Office of the Deputy Chief of Staff for Personnel (ODSPER), Records of the Vietnam War Crimes Working Group; War Crimes Allegations, Case Files, Box 15.

8. "Statement of Charles H. Boss," and "Statement of James C. Rodarte," in "Bumgarner Incident," Record Group 319 NARA.

9. Peter Berenbak, e-mail to Nick Turse, 2006; Peter Berenbak, interview with Nick Turse, 2006.

10. That friend was Robert Stemme. "Statement of Charles H. Boss" and "Statement of Thomas F. Dvorak," both in "Bumgarner Incident"; Berenbak, e-mail to Nick Turse; Peter Berenbak, letter to the editor of the *New York Times* (April 1, 1972), Record Group 319, NARA.

11. "Statement of James C. Rodarte, in "Bumgarner Incident," Record Group, 319, NARA.

12. "Faces of Combat: His Fourth Asia War," *Army Digest*, August 1968, 61.

13. Sworn testimony of Roy Bumgarner, in Record of Trial of Roy E. Bumgarner, 231–32. Bumgarner joined the army National Guard in 1958 and the regular army the next year.

14. Record of Trial of Roy E. Bumgarner, 188–93, and Alex McVeigh, "Soldier Gets Silver Star 45 Years after Wartime Action," http://www.army.mil/article/29585/Soldier_gets_Silver_Star_45_years_after_wartime_action/.

15. Peter Berenbak, interview with Nick Turse, 2006; "Statement of James C. Rodarte," in "Bumgarner Incident"; and Record of Trial of Roy E. Bumgarner.

16. Berenbak, e-mail to Nick Turse.

17. Fox Butterfield, "For Handful of Americans, Vietnam Is Almost Home," *New York Times*, March 31, 1972; Peter Berenbak, e-mail to Nick Turse (2006); Peter Berenbak, letter to the editor of the *New York Times*.

18. George McArthur, "Only 5,000 U.S. Infantrymen Left in Vietnam," *Los Angeles Times*, March 28, 1972; and Roy Bumgarner, military personnel records.

19. "Bumgarner Incident," Record Group, 319; Peter Berenbak interview with Nick Turse.

20. Those in the army generally served twelve-month tours, while the marines' lasted thirteen months. James Westheider, *Fighting in Vietnam* (Mechanicsburg, Pa: Stackpole Books, 2011), 69.

21. Herbert and Wooten, *Soldier*, 387–88. See Brian Thomas, "Medal of Honor Recipient Visits Fort Bragg, Recounts Combat Experience," *ArmyLINK News*, http://www.dtic.mil/armylink/news/Aug1998/a19980804miller .html; Richard Goldstein, "Franklin D. Miller, 55, Hero as a Green Beret in Vietnam," *New York Times*, July 17, 2000; Miller, *Reflections of a Warrior*.

22. Sworn testimony of Roy Bumgarner, in Record of Trial of Roy E. Bumgarner, 234.

23. "Did This General Kill Civilians?" *Life*, June 25, 1971, 40–41; Maureen Mylander, *The Generals* (New York: Dial Press, 1974), 12.

24. Michael Uhl, *Vietnam Awakening* (Jefferson, N.C.: McFarland, 2007), 74–75.

25. John McNown Jr., interviews with Richard Verrone, December 16–18, 2003, and January 28–30, 2004, Texas Tech.

26. "Charge of a General," *Time*, June 14, 1971; fact sheet, Donaldson Case (April 29, 1971), NARA; fact sheet, Donaldson Case; CID-N, fact sheet, Donald Francis Hanson (May 22, 1971), University of Michigan.

27. Status of 70-CID011-00757, Donaldson, University of Michigan, and fact sheet, Donaldson Case.

28. Status of 70-CID011-00757.

29. Ibid.

30. Witness statement of Kenneth Grogan (September 1, 1971), in Seger Allegation, NARA.

31. Witness statement of Richard Cichowski (September 9, 1971), in ibid.

32. Witness statement of Kenneth Grogan (September 1, 1971), in ibid.

33. Status of 70-CID011-00757. Evidence indicates that Carver was never charged in connection with the killings.

34. Witness statement of John Donaldson (August 27, 1970), University of Michigan; OCINFO, Wire Service News (June 2, 1971); Mylander, *The Generals*, 12.

35. Seymour M. Hersh, *Cover-Up* (New York: Random House, 1972), 220–26.

36. Such a story was not surprising, given how many lieutenant colonels, full colonels, and generals reportedly "hunted" Vietnamese from their helicopters, setting the tone for the men under their command. Sir Robert Thompson, the British counterinsurgency expert who helped defeat the Communist insurgency in Malaysia in the 1950s and then advised on efforts in Vietnam, had earlier called attention to "one-star generals who regard their tour in Vietnam as an opportunity to indulge in a year's big-game shooting from their helicopter howdahs at government expense." He wasn't exaggerating.

The 1st Infantry Division's commanding general, James Hollingsworth, to cite one example, was recognized for his penchant for conducting "turkey shoot" missions, where he blazed away with his M-16 at fleeing Vietnamese. While being interviewed about his combat leadership experiences in Vietnam, a staff sergeant who served in the 2nd Battalion, 12th Infantry, 25th Infantry Division, told an officer that his battalion commander, Lieutenant Colonel Burton Walrath, ordered a helicopter pilot to gun down a Vietnamese seen working in a rice paddy in August or September 1968. During a resulting CID investigation, another allegation surfaced that Walrath had also ordered a helicopter pilot to shoot and kill a farmer in October or November 1969. (Walrath was never charged with any crime.) Similarly, Lieutenant Thomas Loflin recalled helicopter pilots bragging about killing civilians for sport. "You should've seen those goddamned slopes running around down there before everything went up in flames," Loflin recalled an officer saying. Thomas Loflin, "Slaughter of Vietnamese Civilians for Sport by U.S. Helicopter Pilots," *Avante Guard*, 1967; "Pilots Accused of Slaying Civilians," *Los Angeles Times*, November 29, 1969; "Crowe Allegation," War Crimes Allegations, Case Summaries, Record Group 319, Records of the Army Staff, Office of the Deputy Chief of Staff for Personnel (ODSPER), Records of the Vietnam War Crimes Working Group, War Crimes Allegations, Case Studies, Box 1. Quoted in Richard Armstrong, "'Believe Me, He Can Kill You,'" *Saturday Evening Post*, March 25, 1967, 32. Philip Knightly, *The First Casualty: From Crimea to Iraq; The War Correspondent as Hero, Propagandist and Myth Maker* (Baltimore: Johns Hopkins University Press, 2004), 425; TJAG/Military Justice Division, Talking Paper, Subject: BG Donaldson and McClosky Cases (June 14, 1971); Hersh, *Cover-Up*, 226.

37. Fact sheet, Donaldson Case.

38. "Did This General Kill Civilians?" 41.

39. Fact sheet, Donaldson Case.

40. "Night of the General," *Time*, May 10, 1971.

41. Michael Getler, "Murders Laid to General," *Washington Post*, June 3, 1971; Rudy Abramson, "General Charged in Slayings of Six Civilians in Vietnam," *Los Angeles Times*, June 3, 1971; William Beecher, "General, Ex-Aide Accused of Murdering Vietnamese," *New York Times*, June 3, 1971.

42. Beecher, "General, Ex-Aide Accused of Murdering Vietnamese"; Mylander, *The Generals*, 13.

43. Henry Tufts, memorandum for the record, subject: B. G. Donaldson (June 5, 1974), University of Michigan.

44. Charles Lane, "A Soldier's Story," *New Republic*, October 16, 1995, 20; Karen DeYoung, *Soldier: The Life of Colin Powell* (Random House Digital, 2006).

45. DeYoung, *Soldier*.

46. Douglas Robinson, "Army Drops Charges Against General Accused of Killing 6 South Vietnamese Civilians," *New York Times*, December 10, 1971.

47. For more on the Donaldson case, see Tony Swindell, "Our Descent into Hell Has Begun," Counterpunch.org, May 4, 2006, http://www.counter punch.org/swindell05042006.html; Robert Parry and Norman Solomon, "Behind Colin Powell's Legend—Pentagon Man," ConsortiumNews.com, http://www.consortiumnews.com/archive/colin4.html.

48. Robert Parry, "Colin Powell Skates Free on Torture," *In These Times*, May 26, 2009, http://www.inthesetimes.com/article/4447/colin_powell_skates_free_on_torture/.

49. Arnold Dibble, "Bombing Perils Saigon's Bid to Win Delta Loyalty," *Chicago Tribune*, March 10, 1968; Don Oberdorfer, *Tet: The Turning Point in the Vietnam War* (New York: Da Capo Press, 1985), 151; George O'Connor, Senior Officer Debriefing Report (February 25, 1968), 1; Victor Croziat, "Problems Relating to the Deployment of U.S. Ground Combat Forces to the Mekong Delta Area of South Vietnam," Rand Corporation (October 11, 1966), 10; David Elliott, *The Vietnamese War: Revolution and Social Change in the Mekong Delta, 1930–1975* (Armonk, N.Y.: M. E. Sharpe, 2007).

50. Much of the Plain of Reeds is located in Long An Province, the only portion of the Mekong Delta not in IV Corps. Daniel Ellsberg, *Secrets: A Memoir of Vietnam and the Pentagon Papers* (New York: Penguin, 2002), 136–37.

51. Charles Mohr, "Air Strikes Hit Vietcong—And South Vietnamese Civilians," *New York Times*, September 5, 1965.

52. "Yank Mistake Kills 31 Viets," *Chicago Tribune*, January 30, 1967; Tom Buckley, "Error in Vietnam Kills 31 Civilians," *New York Times*, January 30, 1967; "U.S. Copters Kill 31 Civilians in Sampans," *Los Angeles Times*, January 30, 1967.

53. The 9th Divison would serve until August 1969. Its 3rd Brigade remained in Vietnam, under command of the 25th Infantry Division, until October 1970. Joseph W. Callaway Jr., *Mekong First Light* (New York: Ballantine Books, 2004), 37–38; "U.S. Completes Its Build-Up in the Mekong Delta," *New York Times*, January 31, 1967; U.S. Army, "Old Reliables: 9th Infantry Division" (Fort Riley, Kans., 1966/1967?); Shelby Stanton, *Vietnam Order of Battle* (New York: Galahad Books, 1987 [1981]), 77–78.

54. Callaway, *Mekong First Light*, 87.

55. Ibid., 64–65.

56. Julian Ewell, interview with Ted Gittinger, November 7, 1985, LBJ Library, 1.

57. Julian Ewell and Ira A. Hunt, *Sharpening the Combat Edge: The Use of Analysis to Reinforce Military Judgment* (Washington, D.C.: Department of the Army, 1995), 16, 44–74, 128–34.

58. Ronald Dellums, *The Dellums Committee Hearings on War Crimes in Viet-*

nam: An Inquiry into Command Responsibility in Southeast Asia, eds. Citizens Commission of Inquiry (New York: Vintage Books, 1972), 65.

59. For more, see Andrew F. Krepinevich, *The Army and Vietnam* (Baltimore: Johns Hopkins University Press, 1986), 204; Christian Appy, *Patriots: The Vietnam War Remembered from All Sides* (New York: Viking, 2003), 323; William Taylor Jr., interview with Neil Sheehan, November 11, 1975, Neil Sheehan Papers.

60. William Taylor Jr., interview with Neil Sheehan, November 11, 1975.

61. William Taylor Jr., interview with Nick Turse, September 24, 2008.

62. Hackworth had founded the 101st Airborne's Tiger Force during an earlier tour in Vietnam. For more, see John Kifner, "Report on Brutal Vietnam Campaign Stirs Memories," *New York Times*, December 28, 2003; David Hackworth and Julie Sherman, *About Face: The Odyssey of an American Warrior* (New York: Touchstone, 1990), 485, 501; David Hackworth and Eilhys England, *Steel My Soldiers' Hearts* (New York: Rugged Land, 2002), 98.

63. Testimony of William Hauser (August 6, 1971), in Concerning David H. Hackworth, vol. 3 of 8 vols., part 2 of 2, in Record Group 472, MSCV, MACIG, Investigative Division, ROI, Box 121.

64. Testimony of John Hayes (August 9, 1971), in ibid., vol. 4, part 2.

65. Ewell was also known as "Bloody Ewell." For more, see Krepinevich, *The Army and Vietnam*, 203; Hackworth and England, *Steel My Soldiers' Hearts*, 99; Gloria Emerson, *Winners and Losers: Battles, Gains, Losses and Ruins from a Long War* (New York: Random House, 1976), 154; Keith Nolan, *House to House: Playing the Enemy's Game in Saigon, May 1968* (St. Paul, Minn.: Zenith Press, 2006), 156; Appy, *Patriots*, 323.

66. Lewis Lapham, "Military Theology," *Harper's*, July 1971, 74.

67. Testimony of James A. Musselman, 1742, in Concerning David H. Hackworth, vol. 4, part 2.

68. Quoted in Elliott, *The Vietnamese War*, concise edition, 346.

69. Robert Gard, interview with Nick Turse and Deborah Nelson, 2006.

70. Hackworth and England, *Steel My Soldiers' Hearts*, 99.

71. Thomas Thayer, ed. [Assistant Secretary of Defense (Systems Analysis), Southeast Asia Division], *Southeast Asia Analysis Report/A Systems Analysis View of the War in Vietnam, 1965–1972* (Washington, D.C. [?]: Assistant Secretary of Defense [Systems Analysis], Southeast Asia Division, 1975), vol. 4 (*Allied Ground and Naval Operations*), 157.

72. Hackworth and England, *Steel My Soldiers' Hearts*, 98–99. For more, see Hackworth and Sherman, *About Face*, 667–68.

73. Guenter Lewy, *America in Vietnam* (New York: Oxford University Press, 1981), 107.

74. Ewell and Hunt, *Sharpening the Combat Edge*, 134.

75. "Overview, Operation Speedy Express, IV Corps Tactical Zone," in MACV, MACIG, Investigative Division, ROI, Box 143.

76. Ewell and Hunt, *Sharpening the Combat Edge*, 16.

77. For an example of the gross disparities, see "Operation Speedy Express," ABC news segment, March 17, 1969, in which it was reported that U.S. forces had "killed more than 130 Viet Cong in the Mekong Delta over the weekend," but that no U.S. troops had been killed. Operation Speedy Express, Casualties by Week, in MACV, MACIG, Investigative Division, ROI, Box 143.

78. In 1967-68, two U.S. Marine Corps divisions in I Corps had accounted for 29-30 percent of enemy KIAs but had taken 35-38 percent of American KIAs. The 9th Division exceeded them in enemy KIAs but took just 15 percent of American KIAs. Thayer, *Southeast Asia Analysis Report*, vol. 4, 22, 156-57, 169, 189-91.

79. Ira Hunt, *The 9th Infantry Division in Vietnam: Unparalleled and Unequaled* (Lexington, Ky.: University Press of Kentucky, 2010), 45-46; Elliott, *The Vietnamese War*, 347-49; George McArthur, "Vietcong Scarecrows Disappear in Delta," *Tri-City Herald*, January 26, 1969.

80. Elliott, *The Vietnamese War*, 344-47; Operational Report of 9th Infantry Division for Period Ending April 30, 1969 (May 15, 1969), "Enemy Situation" slide.

81. Julian Ewell, Senior Officers Debriefing Program (U.S. Army Military Institute, 1979), 76.

82. Julian Ewell, "Senior Officer Debriefing Report: LTG Julian Ewell" (Department of the Army, 1969), 7-8.

83. Myra MacPherson, *Long Time Passing: Vietnam and the Haunted Generation*, new edition (Bloomington: Indiana University Press, 2001), 22.

84. Ewell, Senior Officers Debriefing Program, 65; Ewell and Hunt, *Sharpening the Combat Edge*, 129-31; David Farnham, interview with Neil Sheehan, October 15, 1975, Neil Sheehan Papers.

85. Julian Ewell, interview with Ted Gittinger, November 7, 1985, LBJ Library, 27-28.

86. When the letter was written, Komer was a consultant with the Rand Corporation. John Vann, letter to Robert W. Komer, May 5, 1971, Neil Sheehan Papers.

87. Record's superior, Peter Brownback, the senior province adviser of Bac Lieu, also saw the children and the water buffalo, with explosions (which he took to be rockets) impacting amid them. Brownback noted the water buffalo being hit by fire from the helicopters, but claimed not to have seen any dead children or heard later reports of dead children. According to a summary in U.S. Army documents, Major Le Van Sy, a South Vietnamese official in Bac Lieu, stated that "it was normal procedure to shoot livestock and personnel in the area as it was a 'free fire zone' during the period in question." "Record

Allegation," War Crimes Allegations, Case Summaries, Records of the Vietnam War Crimes Working Group, War Crimes Allegations, Case Studies, Box 1; and Jeffrey Record, "Maximizing Cobra Utilization," *Washington Monthly*, April 1971, 12.

88. Jeffrey Record, *The Wrong War: Why We Lost in Vietnam* (Annapolis: Naval Institute Press, 1998), 91.

89. Louis F. Janowski, "End of Tour Report" (ca. 1970), Neil Sheehan Papers.

90. William Taylor Jr., interview with Nick Turse, September 24, 2008.

91. Lady Borton, *After Sorrow: An American Among the Vietnamese* (New York: Kodansha International, 1995), 38–39.

92. Katsuichi Honda, "Terror for Helicopters," in Richard A. Falk, Gabriel Kolko, and Robert J. Lifton, eds., *Crimes of War* (New York: Random House, 1971), 357–59.

93. An NLF report put the figure at "over 3,000," including B-52 strikes, for Kien Hoa Province alone, during the first eleven months of 1969. One U.S. report put the number of sorties at 5,309. Committee to Denounce the U.S.-Puppets' War Crimes in South Viet Nam on the U.S.-Puppets' Savage Acts Against Patriots Detained by Them, "Appendix: U.S.-Puppet Massacres of the Population in South Vietnam (From 1965 to 1969)." Kevin Buckley, "Pacification's Deadly Price," *Newsweek*, June 19, 1972, 42; Phillip Stevens, letter to Kevin Buckley (December 14, 1971), author's collection; "Air Operations, 9th U.S. Division from ORLL," in "Operation Speedy Express—Allegations in Newsweek Article and Comments Concerning," in Allegations by Newsweek re: 9th Infantry Division and the Delta, in MACV, MACIG, Investigative Division, ROI, Box 143.

94. Quoted in Douglas Valentine, *The Phoenix Program* (New York: Morrow, 1990), 216.

95. Not surprisingly, a 1969 CIA and U.S. embassy assessment found that Vietnamese in the 9th Division's area of operations viewed U.S. firepower as a major threat. The assessment ranked U.S. firepower as comparable to "VC terror." Thayer, *Southeast Asia Analysis Report*, vol. 4, 27 [195—dual numbering system]. John Lichfield, "Verdun: Myths and Memories of the 'Lost Villages' of France," *Independent*, February 21, 2006; Julian Ewell, "Senior Officer Debriefing Report," 12.

96. Operational Report of 9th Infantry Division for Period Ending April 30, 1969 (May 15, 1969), 26.

97. Robert Gard, interview with Nick Turse and Deborah Nelson, 2006.

98. Edwin Deagle, interview with Nick Turse, September 13, 2008; Edwin Deagle, letter to Nick Turse, September 30, 2008.

99. Concerned Sergeant, letter to William Westmoreland (May 25, 1970), "copy reproduced on 27 August 1971," in "Concerned Sergeant Allegation," War Crimes Allegations, Case Files, War Crimes Working Group, Record Group 319, NARA.

100. Deagle, interview.

101. From January to April 1969, IV Corps accounted for a higher percentage of civilian war casualties than any other region. *Civilian Casualty, Social Welfare and Refugee Problems in South Vietnam*, part 1, Hearings before the Subcommittee on Refugees and Escapees, Senate Judiciary Committee (June 24–25, 1969), 23. "Civilian War Casualties, DMAC IV," Neil Sheehan Papers, Box 49, folder 3; George Eckhardt, Senior Officer Debriefing Report: Delta Military Assistance Command and Senior Advisor, IV CTZ, Period 15 January 1968 to 1 June 1969, Army Adjutant General's Office (June 16, 1969), 52.

102. *Civilian Casualty, Social Welfare, and Refugee Problems in South Vietnam*, part 1, 42, 56–57.

103. Concerned Sergeant, letter to William Westmoreland.

104. Concerned Sergeant, letter to Orwin Talbott (March 30, 1971), in Concerned Sergeant Allegation. Hackworth offers a similar portrait of Hunt, yelling and screaming in his chopper; see Hackworth and Sherman, *About Face*, 673.

105. Concerned Sergeant, letter to Orwin Talbott. The "Concerned Sergeant" often spelled phonetically, writing, for example, about "cashays"—that is, caches—of weapons. I standardized the spelling in his letters.

106. Concerned Sergeant, letter to William Westmoreland.

107. Concerned Sergeant, letter to Orwin Talbott.

108. Concerned Sergeant, letter to William Westmoreland.

109. Concerned Sergeant, letter to Orwin Talbott.

110. Concerned Sergeant, letter to William Westmoreland.

111. Orwin Talbott, who served as a division commander in Vietnam and eventually retired as a three-star general, told me that everyone knew these rumors about the 9th Division. "I can't believe that top headquarters in Saigon could not have heard the gossip," he said. Orwin Talbott, interview with Nick Turse and Deborah Nelson, 2006; Julian Ewell, interview with Ted Gittinger, 10.

112. Years later, neither Talbott nor Enemark—both of them previously top commanders in Vietnam—could recall receiving letters from the Concerned Sergeant. Talbott would later dismiss charges against two 9th Infantry Division officers charged with wounding and killing civilians in the Mekong Delta. "Army Clears 2 Officers in Fatal Viet Shooting," *Washington Post*, October 31, 1970; U.S. Army Command Information Fact Sheet: Incident at Son My, April 2, 1971; "Partial Text of Army's Fact Sheet on My Lai," *Washington Post*, April 4, 1971; Concerned Sergeant, letter to Orwin Talbott; Concerned Sergeant, letter to W. A. Enemark (July 30, 1971), in "Concerned Sergeant Allegation"; Orwin Talbott, interview with Nick Turse and Deborah Nelson, 2006; William Enemark, interview with Nick Turse and Deborah Nelson, 2006.

113. Dellums, *The Dellums Committee Hearings on War Crimes in Vietnam*; Concerned Sergeant, letter to W. A. Enemark.

114. George Lewis, Military Service Records, author's collection.

115. John Murchison, Memorandum for Record (September 7, 1971).

116. Talking Paper, Subject: David Hackworth (October 1, 1971), University of Michigan.

117. For examples, see Mark Lane, *Conversations with Americans* (New York: Simon and Schuster, 1970), 168–81; statement of James D. Henry, February 28, 1970, in CID Reports, "Henry Allegation," War Crimes Allegations, Case Files, Record Group 319, Records of the Army Staff, Office of the Deputy Chief of Staff for Personnel (ODSPER), Records of the Vietnam War Crimes Working Group, War Crimes Allegations, Case Studies, Case 32 (4), 1–10; King, "Who Needs West Point?"; Buckley, "Pacification's Deadly Price," 43; Nick Turse, "A My Lai a Month," *Nation*, December 1, 2008; "Abrams Is Cleared of Soldier's Charge," *New York Times*, December 5, 1970; "Sergeant in Songmy Case Says Westmoreland Must Take Blame," *New York Times*, September 10, 1970; "Westmoreland Order to Level Village Charged," *Los Angeles Times*, December 7, 1970.

118. King, "Who Needs West Point?"

7: WHERE HAVE ALL THE WAR CRIMES GONE?

1. *In the Name of America* (New York: Clergy and Laymen Concerned about Vietnam; Annandale, Va.: Turnpike Press, 1968); Neil Sheehan, "Should We Have War Crimes Trials?" *New York Times Book Review*, March 28, 1971.

2. Seymour Hersh, "My Lai, and Its Omens," *New York Times*, March 16, 1998.

3. Jeff Stein, *A Murder in Wartime: The Untold Spy Story That Changed the Course of the Vietnam War* (New York: St. Martin's Press, 1992), 324, 332–33.

4. Ward Just, "The Special Forces Six and the Shadow War," *Washington Post*, September 21, 1969; John Darnton, "Ex-Beret Says He Killed Agent on Orders of CIA," *New York Times*, April 4, 1971; Stein, *A Murder in Wartime*, 324.

5. "Text of Resor's Statement," *New York Times*, September 30, 1969; Stein, *A Murder in Wartime*, 360, 367, 374.

6. Philip Knightly, *The First Casualty: From Crimea to Iraq; The War Correspondent as Hero, Propagandist and Myth Maker* (Baltimore: Johns Hopkins University Press, 2004), 434; Normand Poirier, "An American Atrocity," *Esquire*, August 1969.

7. Sven Eriksson was a pseudonym. Daniel Lang, *Casualties of War* (New York: Pocket Books, 1989), 17, 55–77.

8. Morris K. Udall, letter to Stanley Resor, September 30, 1969, in Duffy-Lanasa Incident, Case 2 (4), Army Staff, Deputy Chief of Staff, Vietnam War Crimes Working Group, War Crimes Allegations Files, Box 3.

9. George D. Chunko, account of George D. Chunko (September 12, 1969), in ibid., Box 3, 2; Richard A. Falk, Gabriel Kolko, and Robert Jay Lifton, eds., *Crimes of War: A Legal, Political-Documentary, and Psychological Inquiry into the Responsibility of Leaders, Citizens, and Soldiers for Criminal Acts in Wars* (New York: Random House, 1971), 245.

10. George D. Chunko, account of George D. Chunko, Box 3, 3.

11. Ibid., Box 3, 3–4.

12. Ibid., Box 3, 4.

13. Ibid., Box 3, 6.

14. Ibid.

15. "VZCZCSD316 . . . DA for TAG and OTPMG and TJAGJ" (confidential backchannel communication), in Duffy-Lanasa Incident, Box 3, 2.

16. Falk, Kolko, and Lifton, *Crimes of War*, 245.

17. Raymond T. Reid, letter to Morris K. Udall, November 21, 1969, in Duffy-Lanasa Incident, Box 3.

18. *United States v. First Lieutenant James B. Duffy,* 569-70-4070, U.S. Army, Headquarters and Headquarters Company, 2nd Battalion (Mechanized), 47th Infantry, 3rd Brigade, 9th Infantry Division, APO San Francisco 96371, CM 424795, United States Army Court of Military Review, 47 C.M.R. 658, 1973 CMR LEXIS 697 (July 18, 1973). Philip Shabecoff, "6-Month Term Set in Vietnam Death," *New York Times*, April 1, 1970.

19. Shabecoff, "6-Month Term Set in Vietnam Death"; "Army Jury Has Second Thoughts," *Times* (London), March 30, 1970.

20. Philip Shabecoff, "Murder Verdict Eased in Vietnam," *New York Times*, March 31, 1970.

21. Michael Bilton and Kevin Sim, *Four Hours in My Lai* (New York: Penguin, 1993), 214–20, 382.

22. Ron Ridenhour, "My Lai and Why It Matters," speech (1998).

23. William M. Hammond, *Public Affairs: The Military and the Media, 1968–1973* (Washington, D.C.: Center of Military History, 1996), 223.

24. Knightly, *The First Casualty*, 429–30.

25. http://history.state.gov/historicaldocuments/frus1964-68v03/d105; Abe Peck, *Uncovering the Sixties: The Life and Times of the Underground Press* (New York: Citadel Press, 1991), 201; Tom Engelhardt, *The End of Victory Culture: Cold War America and the Disillusioning of a Generation* (New York: Basic Books, 1995), 219.

26. Knightly, *The First Casualty*, 392; Engelhardt, *The End of Victory Culture*, 219; Bilton and Sim, *Four Hours in My Lai*, 253–64.

27. "Transcript of Interview of Vietnam War Veteran on His Role in Alleged Massacre of Civilians at Songmy," *New York Times*, November 25, 1969.

28. Transcript of phone conversation between Henry Kissinger and Secretary of Defense Melvin Laird, November 21, 1969, 3:50 P.M., from Nixon Presidential Materials Project, Henry A. Kissinger Telephone Conversations Transcripts, Chronological File, Box 3, File 3, 083-084, National Security Archive. See also Elizabeth Becker, "Kissinger Tapes Describe Crises, War and Stark Photos of Abuse," *New York Times*, May 27, 2004.

29. Quoted in Hammond, *Public Affairs*, 231.

30. Joseph Goldstein, Burke Marshall, and Jack Schwartz, *The My Lai Massacre and Its Cover-Up: Beyond the Reach of Law? The Peers Commission Report with a Supplement and Introductory Essay on the Limits of Law* (New York: Free Press, 1976), 33.

31. Ibid., 45.

32. Ibid.

33. Ibid., 52.

34. Ibid., 52–56, 286, 320–29. (See http://law2.umkc.edu/faculty/projects/ftrials/mylai/suppression.html and http://law2.umkc.edu/faculty/projects/ftrials/mylai/Henderson.html.)

35. William Beecher, "Songmy Data Lag Laid to 2 Groups," *New York Times*, March 19, 1970.

36. United Press, "The Army's My Lai Report Is Released," *San Francisco Chronicle*, November 14, 1974; Bilton and Sim, *Four Hours in My Lai*, 308–9; Beecher, "Songmy Data Lag Laid to 2 Groups."

37. Bilton and Sim, *Four Hours in My Lai*, 309; Henry Tufts, transcript of interview with Dwight Oland, December 11, 1995, 36, 38, University of Michigan.

38. For more, see Nick Turse and Deborah Nelson, "Civilian Killings Went Unpunished," *Los Angeles Times*, August 6, 2006; Deborah Nelson, *The War Behind Me* (New York: Basic Books, 2008), 168–75.

39. Plenty of photos of homes being destroyed made it into print, too. For examples of the grim realities of war as shown in *Life*, see "The Air War," *Life*, September 9, 1966; "This Girl Tron," *Life*, November 8, 1968; "The Massacre at My Lai," *Life*, December 5, 1969.

40. Telford Taylor, *Nuremberg and Vietnam: An American Tragedy* (New York: Bantam/Books and New York Times, 1970); Kendrick Oliver, *The My Lai Massacre in American History and Memory* (Manchester: Manchester University Press, 2006), 112.

41. Neil Sheehan, "Taylor Says by Yamashita Ruling Westmoreland May Be Guilty," *New York Times*, January 9, 1971; Taylor, *Nuremberg and Vietnam*.

42. U.S. Army, *Final Report of the Research Project: Conduct of the War in Vietnam* (U.S. Army, May 1971), 1–3; Bernd Greiner, *War Without Fronts: The USA in Vietnam* (London: Bodley Head, 2009), 319; Guenter Lewy, *America in Vietnam* (New York: Oxford University Press, 1981), 239.

43. U.S. Army, *Final Report of the Research Project*, 3.

44. Ibid., 27, 2, 34–55, 3.

45. Ibid., 82–83.

46. Robert D. Heinl Jr., "The Collapse of the Armed Forces," *Armed Forces Journal*, June 7, 1971.

47. David Cortright, *Soldiers in Revolt* (Chicago: Haymarket, 2005), 55.

48. Gloria Emerson, *Winners and Losers: Battles, Gains, Losses and Ruins from a Long War* (New York: Random House, 1976), 330.

49. Ibid.

50. Andrew E. Hunt, *The Turning: A History of Vietnam Veterans Against the War* (New York: New York University Press, 1999), 45; James S. Kunen, *Standard Operating Procedure: Notes of a Draft-Age American* (New York: Avon, 1971), 21–27; Ronald Dellums, *The Dellums Committee Hearings on War Crimes in Vietnam: An Inquiry into Command Responsibility in Southeast Asia*, eds. Citizens Commission of Inquiry (New York: Vintage Books, 1972), viii.

51. Quoted in Kunen, *Standard Operating Procedure*, 182–83.

52. Hunt, *The Turning*, 1–2.

53. Christian Appy, *Working-Class War: American Combat Soldiers and Vietnam* (Chapel Hill: University of North Carolina Press, 1993), 60, 75.

54. Flyer reprinted in Jan Barry, ed., *Peace Is Our Profession* (Montclair, N.J.: East River Anthology, 1981), 141. See also Gerald Nicosia, *Home to War: A History of the Vietnam Veterans' Movement* (New York: Crown, 2001), 61.

55. Statement of James D. Henry, February 28, 1970, in CID Reports, "Henry Allegation," War Crimes Allegations, Case Files, Record Group 319, Records of the Army Staff, Office of the Deputy Chief of Staff for Personnel (ODSPER), Records of the Vietnam War Crimes Working Group, War Crimes Allegations, Case Studies, Case 32 (4), 1–10, NARA.

56. James Henry, interview with Nick Turse and Deborah Nelson, October 1, 2005; Mark Lane, *Conversations with Americans* (New York: Simon and Schuster, 1970), 168–81; Michael Learmonth, "Scanlan's Monthly (1970–1971)," *Folio*, May 1, 2003; James Henry, as told to Donald Duncan, "The Men of Company 'B,'" *Scanlan's Monthly*, March 1970, 26–31; statement of James D. Henry, in "Henry Allegation."

57. Henry, "The Men of Company 'B,'" 26–31.

58. "Ex-GI Claims Vietnam Atrocities Are Common," *Los Angeles Times*, February 28, 1968; Henry, interview; Turse and Nelson, "Civilian Killings Went Unpunished."

59. Jerry M. Flint, "Veterans Assess Atrocity Blame," *New York Times*, February 7, 1971; Nicosia, *Home to War*, 87; Hunt, *The Turning*, 66–73.

60. Winter Film Collective, director, *Winter Soldier* (Milliarium Zero, 1972). See also *The Winter Soldier Investigation: An Inquiry into American War Crimes* (Boston: Beacon Press, 1972), 43–45.

61. Sheehan, "Should We Have War Crimes Trials?"

62. LTC Schopper, "Talking Paper: Allegations of War Crimes Other Than Son May" (April 11, 1971), Procedures and Responsibilities for Monitoring War Crimes Allegations, Record Group 319, Records of the Army Staff, Office of the Deputy Chief of Staff for Personnel (ODSPER), Records of the Vietnam War Crimes Working Group, Vietnam War Crimes Working Group Central File, Box 3.

63. Daniel Ellsberg, *Secrets: A Memoir of Vietnam and the Pentagon Papers* (New York: Penguin, 2002), 289, 368–69; Engelhardt, *The End of Victory Culture*, 231.

64. Ibid., 385–410.

65. Frank Browning and Dorothy Forman, eds., *The Wasted Nations: Report of the International Commission of Enquiry into United States War Crimes in Indochina, June 20–25, 1971* (New York: Harper Colophon Books, 1972), 139–208.

66. Ibid., 335–40.

67. William Chapman, "Pentagon Can't Find Way to Prosecute Former Servicemen," *Washington Post*, April 9, 1971; William Westmoreland, *A Soldier Reports* (New York: Dell, 1980), 495; Bilton and Sim, *Four Hours in My Lai*, 323.

68. Robert Jordan, memorandum for the Assistant Attorney General: Trial of Discharged Servicemen for Violation of the Law of War (December 2, 1969); Turse and Nelson, "Civilian Killings Went Unpunished."

69. Robert Jordan, e-mail to Deborah Nelson, July 23, 2006; Robert Jordan, interview with Deborah Nelson, 2006.

70. "My Lai: A Question of Orders," *Time*, January 25, 1971; Bilton and Sim, *Four Hours in My Lai*, 325–31.

71. Goldstein, Marshall, and Schwartz, *The My Lai Massacre and Its Cover-Up*, 318; Michal Belknap, *The Vietnam War on Trial* (Lawrence: University Press of Kansas, 2002), 128–29; William Peers, *The My Lai Inquiry* (New York: W. W. Norton, 1979), 214–22, 225–26.

72. Bilton and Sim, *Four Hours in My Lai*, 308–9. The files have since been declassified.

73. Such actions may also help to explain the occasional discrepancies that occur in a fraction of the veterans' testimonies in War Crimes Working Group summary files. Scott Swett, "Newly Discovered Army Reports Discredit 'Winter Soldier' Claims," FrontPageMagazine.com, February 25, 2008. See also Henry, interview; Robert Stemme, interview with Nick Turse and Deborah Nelson, August 12, 2006; Michael Sallah and Mitch Weiss, *Tiger Force: A True Story of Men and War* (New York: Little, Brown, 2006), 268–69; Gary Kulik, *War Stories* (Dulles, Va.: Potomac Books, 2009), 103; Patty Henry, interview with Nick Turse and Deborah Nelson, October 1, 2005; Bud Schultz and Ruth Schultz, *It Did Happen Here: Recollections of Political Repression in America* (Berkeley: University of California Press, 1989), 319–34.

74. For more, see Sallah and Weiss, *Tiger Force*, 281–83.

75. Steven Chucala, interview with Deborah Nelson, 2006.

76. "Laird Tightening Pentagon Control of Army Investigators," *New York Times*, April 8, 1971.

77. Michael D. Sallah and Mitch Weiss, "Day 2: Inquiry Ended Without Justice: Army Substantiated Numerous Charges—Then Dropped Case of Vietnam War Crimes," *Toledo Blade*, October 20, 2003.

78. Statement of Robert Miller, August 5, 1972, "Henry Allegation"; Robert Miller, interview with Nick Turse and Deborah Nelson, 2006.

79. CID Report of Investigation, 70-CID 121-00805, author's collection.

80. William Westmoreland, memorandum for the Commanding Officer, U.S. Army CID Agency; Directive for Investigation (November 13, 1970), Colonel Henry Tufts Archive, Labadie Collection, University of Michigan Special Collections Library, Ann Arbor.

81. See: [John T.?] Paula, "Talking Paper," CID Herbert Task Force Talking Papers, May–July 1971, Records of the Army Staff, Office of the Deputy Chief of Staff for Personnel, Records of the Vietnam War Crimes Working Group, Records Pertaining to the LTC Herbert Controversy, 1970–73, Box 2.

82. CID Report of Investigation, Unidentified Vietnamese Government Forces, Tam Quan, Republic of Vietnam (November 4, 1970–February 24, 1971), University of Michigan; "Sworn Statement of Dolores Hensley," Herbert Talking Papers; William Legat, "Statement [re: Hensley, Carl E.]," Herbert Talking Papers, July 1971–January 1972, Record Group 319, Records of the Army Staff, Office of the Deputy Chief of Staff for Personnel, Records of the Vietnam War Crimes Working Group, Records Pertaining to the LTC Herbert Controversy, 1970–73, Box 1.

83. William Legat, interview with Nick Turse and Deborah Nelson, 2006.

84. Herbert does not give a specific date but notes the telephone conversation took place "shortly after" a meeting he had in "early April." Anthony Herbert and James T. Wooten, *Soldier* (New York: Dell, 1973), 467, 465.

85. "Sworn Statement of Dolores Hensley."

86. Karla Florhaug, interview with Deborah Nelson, February 7, 2006; Joanne Wright, interview with Deborah Nelson (2006).

87. Kenneth Reich, "Head of Army Atrocity Probe Called Suicide," *Los Angeles Times*, April 17, 1971.

88. Ira Greenberg, memorandum for Major Steven Chucala: The Hensley Matter (December 3, 1971), NARA.

89. Legat, interview; Murray W. Williams, "Selected Incidents that Reflect Unfavorably on the Army and Other U.S. Government Agencies," in "Memorandum for: Chief of Staff, United States Army; Subject: 'Soldier' by Anthony Herbert" (January 29, 1973), Herbert Documents and Working Papers, January 1973, part 2 of 2, Records of the Army Staff, Office of the Deputy Chief of Staff, Vietnam War Crimes Working Group, LTC Herbert Controversy, 1970–73, Box 1.

90. See Henry H. Tufts, "Memorandum for: Chief of Staff, United States Army; Subject: Herbert's *Soldier*" (ca. April 14, 1973), Herbert Documents and Working Papers, part 1, Box 1.

91. For more, see Deborah Nelson and Nick Turse, "A Tortured Past," *Los Angeles Times*, August 20, 2006.

92. Ellsberg, *Secrets*, 440, 372.

93. For more, see Knightly, *The First Casualty*, 438–39; Nick Turse, "The Vietnam Exposé that Wasn't," TheNation.com, November 13, 2008; Nick Turse, "A My Lai a Month," *Nation*, December 1, 2008.

94. Kevin Buckley, "Pacification's Deadly Price," *Newsweek*, June 19, 1972, 43; David Sigler, *Vietnam Battle Chronology: U.S. Army and Marine Corps Combat Operations, 1965–1973* (Jefferson, N.C.: McFarland, 1992), 84.

95. "Comparative Results" and "Casualties and Weapons," briefing slides, in "Allegations by Newsweek re: 9th Infantry Division and the Delta," in MACV, MACIG, Investigative Division, ROI, Box 143.

96. "Major Contacts, 9th Division" and "Casualties by Week," both in ibid.

97. Kevin Buckley and Alex Shimkin, "Speedy Express and Civilian Deaths," draft version of "Pacification's Deadly Price," January 17, 1972, author's collection; Buckley, "Pacification's Deadly Price," 42–43. One Western doctor who served in the Mekong Delta said it was commonly accepted that more than 50 percent of the seriously wounded people never reached the hospital. For more, see K. F. King, "Orthopaedic Aspects of War Wounds in South Vietnam," *Journal of Bone and Joint Surgery* 51 B, no. 1 (February 1969), 115; Frank Harvey, *Air War: Vietnam* (New York: Bantam Books, 1967), 74.

98. Buckley, "Pacification's Deadly Price"; Kevin Buckley, "Byliner advisory one norweek," draft version of "Pacification's Deadly Price," January 30, 1972, author's collection.

99. Kevin Buckley, letter to Phillip Stevens, November 27, 1971, author's collection.

100. Phillip Stevens, letter to Kevin Buckley, December 14, 1971, author's collection.

101. David Farnham, interview with Neil Sheehan, October 15, 1975, Neil Sheehan Papers.

102. Neil Sheehan, *A Bright and Shining Lie: John Paul Vann and America in Vietnam* (New York: Vintage Books, 1988), 733–52; Laura Wood, "Vann, John Paul," in Spencer Tucker, ed., *The Encyclopedia of the Vietnam War: A Political, Social and Military History* (New York: Oxford University Press, 1998), 440; Farnham, interview with Neil Sheehan.

103. Farnham recalled the meeting as occurring just before Buckley's article was published in June 1972. Vann's travel timeline, on the other hand, suggests that the meeting happened shortly before January 1972, when the

story would have been published if *Newsweek* had not held it up. Farnham, interview with Neil Sheehan.

104. In his memoir, Palmer would obliquely note "especially in the Delta, some units were . . . careless about avoiding civilian casualties." Bruce Palmer, *The 25-Year War: America's Military Role in Vietnam* (Lexington: University Press of Kentucky, 1984), 165.

105. Kevin Buckley, cable to Edward Klein, January 25, 1972, author's collection.

106. Buckley and Shimkin, "Speedy Express and Civilian Deaths."

107. Hebert Klein, cable to Kevin Buckley, January 24, 1972, author's collection.

108. Kevin Buckley, cable to Edward Klein, January 25, 1972.

109. Kevin Buckley, cables to Edward Klein, January 29, 1972, and January 30, 1972, author's collection.

110. Knightly, *The First Casualty*, 438–40; Turse, "The Vietnam Exposé that Wasn't"; Turse, "A My Lai a Month"; "Writer Says U.S. Troops Killed Civilians in Delta," *New York Times*, June 12, 1972.

111. Nick Proffitt, cable to Edward Klein and Kevin Buckley, June 21, 1972, author's collection.

112. The report used the word "casualties" to mean dead only, not wounded. "Operation Speedy Express—Allegations in Newsweek Article and Comments Concerning."

113. Ibid.

114. Dennis Doolin, letter to Harold Hughes, September 1972, author's collection.

115. Julian Ewell and Ira A. Hunt, *Sharpening the Combat Edge: The Use of Analysis to Reinforce Military Judgment* (Washington, D.C.: Department of the Army, 1995), 227–28.

116. Nick Turse, "Mortal Sins of Omission," TruthDig.com, March 18, 2011; Ira A. Hunt, *The 9th Infantry Division in Vietnam: Unparalleled and Unequaled* (Lexington: University Press of Kentucky, 2010).

117. Tom Bissell, *The Father of All Things* (New York: Pantheon Books, 2007), xi. According to Worldcat, almost one-third of these books were published between 1970 and 1972.

118. The documents used in this book have since been declassified.

EPILOGUE: WANDERING GHOSTS

1. James Henry, interview with Nick Turse and Deborah Nelson, October 1, 2005; James Henry, e-mail to Nick Turse, October 10, 2005.

2. Ho Thi A, interview with Nick Turse, January 24, 2008.

3. Heonik Kwon, *After the Massacre* (Los Angeles: University of California Press, 2006), 11–15.

ACKNOWLEDGMENTS

The research and writing of this book lasted more than a decade. I would never have completed it without the love and assistance of my family and friends, as well as the generosity and support of those I encountered during this long voyage. To those I'm unable to acknowledge by name, please know that you have my sincere appreciation.

For fellowships and grants that helped keep me financially afloat while working on this book, I thank Edward Hirsch and the John Simon Guggenheim Memorial Foundation; Marilyn Young, the late Michael Nash, and New York University's Center for the United States and the Cold War; Barbara Grosz, Judy Vichniac, and the Radcliffe Institute for Advanced Study; Ham Fish, Taya Kitman, Esther Kaplan, and the Nation Institute; and Sandy Bergo, the late John Hyde, and the Fund for Investigative Journalism.

I owe a great debt to more sources and interview subjects than I can possibly list—from those who opened their doors and homes or spent hours on the phone with me to those who provided leads, documents, and information. The list of American veterans of the war to whom I'm grateful would add another dozen pages to this book, so I'll name two to stand in for the many who helped me to make sense of the senseless and understand (to the extent it can be understood) the war. In many ways, this entire project began with

Jamie Henry. He was the one who really put the hook in me when it came to war crimes in Vietnam. He ultimately changed my life. I'm a better person for having met him and saddened that he didn't live to see the completion of this project.

As with Jamie, I first came to know Richard Brummett in print before "meeting" him via e-mail, and only later in person—in Saigon, fittingly enough. And, like Jamie, Richard had the moral compass and profound courage to speak out when so many stayed silent. All these years later, he's still taking action to better lives in Vietnam in ways heartening and inspiring. I'm grateful to Richard for providing me with information, photographs, and advice, but mostly for being a friend.

Gratitude doesn't begin to cover what I feel for my Vietnamese interviewees. In hamlet after hamlet, I was the first American to arrive since the war ended decades earlier. And I descended out of the blue, asking about murders, rapes, assaults, bombings, and massacres. I made elderly people dredge up their most painful memories and tell me in often excruciating detail about devastating traumas—and then I asked about them in another way and another to make sure I got the story straight. Elsewhere under similar circumstances, I suspect I would have been thrown out of house after house—and with good reason. In Vietnam, I was always thanked. I still haven't fully wrapped my head around that simple fact. I lack the space to recognize all the Vietnamese men and women to whom I'm forever indebted, but I especially want to thank Bui Thi Nhi, Ho Thi A, Le Thi Van, Le Thi Vang, Nguyen Thi Lam, Pham Thi Cuc, Pham Thi Luyen, Vi Thi Ngoi, Pham Thi Nien, Pham Thi Tay, Tran Thi Anh, Tran Thi Nhut, and Vo Thi Truong, among many other inspiring survivors of the war who opened their homes and their lives to an American stranger.

I could never have conducted my interviews without the expert assistance of Le Minh Tuan, a colleague on multiple research trips whose formidable translation skills and endless patience opened doors, smoothed the way, and enabled me to carry out my work in

Vietnam. It would be impossible to overstate how important his intelligence, dedication, skill, and empathy were to this project. Thanks also go to Nguyen Chung of Vietnam's Foreign Press Centre and to Hanh Tran of the South and Southeast Asian Studies Department at the University of California, Berkeley, who not only provided translations of numerous interviews but added nuance and depth to my understanding of them.

I'm also grateful to veteran Chuck Searcy of Project Renew and Major Ramon Osorio of the U.S. military's Joint POW/MIA Accounting Command, who helped immensely in coordinating a 2010 trip to Vietnam.

Thanks are due as well to another set of veterans of the war who proved immensely helpful to my efforts: reporters. In addition to their invaluable work decades earlier, which I drew upon extensively in writing this book, a host of talented correspondents, including Jonathan Schell and Judith Coburn, were more helpful than they could possibly know in furthering my research. Neil Sheehan did a great service to me, and the rest of the scholarly community, by donating his papers to the U.S. Library of Congress.

Another iconic correspondent, Gloria Emerson, witnessed only the first stages of this project before her death but aided me in inestimable ways, taught me so much, and will always have my deepest gratitude. Her final note to me informs my work daily.

Newsweek stringer Alex Shimkin passed away decades before I began this project—before I was born, in fact—but left behind work that was integral to my own. I was fortunate to have been able to draw upon his meticulous research, which came my way due to the generosity of his colleague Kevin Buckley, who shared his notes as well as Alex's materials (and other research documents) with me. Kevin's reporting from that now distant era was heroic and I consider myself extremely lucky to have come to call him a good friend. I am forever indebted to him for his kindness and wise counsel. Indeed, one of my great thrills as a writer was being awarded a James Aronson Award for Social Justice Journalism alongside Kevin for our work, decades apart, in exposing the horror of Operation Speedy Express.

Quite a few scholars aided my efforts along the way. Foremost among them is my longtime mentor and dissertation committee chairperson David Rosner, who not only took a chance on me for his new Center for the History and Ethics of Public Health at Columbia University, but quite literally launched me on the path that led to this book. Without him, I might never have pursued this line of research. There's no way I can ever convey the full extent of my gratitude to him for his generosity and support. He made this possible.

Another member of my dissertation committee, Chris Appy, was instrumental in my pursuing this topic and his guidance over the years was invaluable. I also owe a debt to my other committee members: Alan Brinkley, Eric Foner, Gerald Markowitz, and especially Amy Fairchild, who not only served as my dissertation sponsor but saw to it that I survived my doctoral studies and later had access to the scholarly resources necessary to complete this book. Additionally, I am grateful to my colleagues at the Center for the History and Ethics of Public Health for their support over the years.

It's my good fortune to have had the sage advice, counsel, and expertise of many colleagues over the last decade who gave freely of their time, contacts, leads, and research materials—among them Randy Fertel, Heonik Kwon, Milton Leitenberg, and John Prados. Hue-Tam Ho Tai was kind enough to read a few early, rough chapters, providing advice that improved the book significantly. I also benefited immensely from the guidance and advice of Marilyn Young, who waded through a desperately rough draft of this book.

The winding road that led to this book took me to the Radcliffe Institute, exposing me to a community of thinkers who changed my life in incalculable ways, especially Mignon Nixon, Anna Maria Hong, Taylor Davis, and Irene Lusztig. And then there's Ann Jones—an old friend who I'd somehow never met before. More than a just a wonderful fellow Fellow, she proved a kindred spirit, providing an ear when I needed to talk, advice when I was drowning, and hope when I most needed it. Somehow, she helped me get so much material out of my head and onto the page, making me a better writer in the process. My Radcliffe research partners Sharon Kim and Cerianne Robertson also provided valuable insights and wisdom beyond their years.

I'm grateful to Fanella Ferrato and Katherine Holden for making photographs by their father, the great photojournalist Philip Jones Griffiths, available to me, and to Michael Shulman and Magnum Photos for arranging use of these iconic, powerful images.

Financial support aside, winning a grant from the Fund for Investigative Journalism was particularly meaningful to me because FIJ had provided the initial funding, almost four decades earlier, that allowed Seymour Hersh to expose the My Lai massacre. I want to thank Sy for giving of his time, for opening his office to me, and for a couple of words one night at Harvard that meant a great deal.

Also meaningful was winning a Ridenhour Prize for my work on Speedy Express. There can be no higher distinction for a war crimes researcher than an award in the name of Ron Ridenhour, so I'm exceptionally grateful to the Nation Institute and the Fertel Foundation for the honor.

I'm thankful also to John Carroll and the *Los Angeles Times* for sending me to Vietnam for the first time, to Deborah Nelson for valuable lessons about investigative reporting and the limits of trust, and to Janet Lundblad, whose formidable research skills left me in awe and aided my work immensely.

I'm grateful to Esther Kaplan of the Nation Institute's Investigative Fund and Katrina vanden Heuvel, Roane Carey, and the *Nation* for taking a chance on historical investigative journalism and allowing me the opportunity to expose grave crimes that otherwise may have remained in history's dustbin.

If not for Bruce Dohrenwend, I would likely never have become a Vietnam War historian. To him and all my colleagues at Columbia University's Social Psychiatry Research Unit, I offer thanks for helping teach me about the war in ways I never could have learned from books alone.

My appreciation goes to the staff of the Columbia University Library system, especially the Lehman and Butler libraries and the men and women in the Inter-Library Loan (ILL) office, for their tireless efforts on my behalf, as well as librarians across the country and around the world who filled my many ILL requests. I also want to express my gratitude to Cliff Snyder, Rich Boylan, Jeannine Swift, and numerous archivists and other employees at the U.S. National Archives at College Park, Maryland, without whose work I would have been lost from the beginning.

I am similarly grateful to the dedicated staffs of the University of Michigan Special Collections Library, the National Security Archive, Rutgers University's Archibald S. Alexander Library, and the Manuscript Division at the U.S. Library of Congress, among other repositories, for their assistance. My thanks go as well to the staffs at the U.S. Army Crime Records Center and U.S. Navy's Office of the Judge Advocate General, for processing my many Freedom of Information Act requests. I also want to recognize the Vietnam Center and Archive at Texas Tech University's Virtual Vietnam Archive—an indispensable resource that should be a model for collections everywhere.

My agent Mel Flashman so ably took care of the tasks that make my head ache, fielded interminable e-mails on my behalf, and kept the faith through this long process.

I'm profoundly grateful that Sara Bershtel—publisher, editor, guardian angel—stuck with me on this long journey, despite so many delays, detours, and seeming dead ends. When I was in need, she was there. There are editors—and then there's Sara. All authors should be so lucky.

What did Grigory Tovbis ever do to deserve utter immersion in a world of atrocities? Whatever it was, I'm grateful for it. In addition to the scrupulous editing, thoughtful suggestions, and patient phone calls to make sure the changes worked and that my voice still rang true, I'm convinced he must have taken a degree in the history of the Vietnam War on the side. His devotion to the project was palpable. What more can any writer ask?

Where to begin with Tom Engelhardt? A mentor, colleague, and friend, he was there from the first pitch to the final read. To say this book wouldn't exist without him is an understatement. He walked some of the hardest roads of this project with me, and thanks are hardly enough.

My parents made much of my travel for this project possible and lent assistance in ways too numerous to count, as did my in-laws. Reading and writing integral to this book went on under their roofs. I owe Bailey a big thank-you too, for being a constant companion over the course of the project.

Some authors' spouses edit drafts or act as sounding boards. Some listen or provide advice. And then there are those who will walk side by side with you into a minefield. Literally. That's Tam. When we were standing near that M-79 round, I wondered: what kind of husband puts his wife in these situations? The real question is—what sort of wife will travel across the globe to brave unexploded ordnance, willingly immerse herself in the worst of traumas, and document people at their most vulnerable with sensitivity and aplomb? Quite simply, the best.

Tam believed in this project longer and more strongly than anyone, maybe even me, and sustained it in every way possible. From the lizard behind the picture in the delta to the cluster munitions in the brush near the DMZ, from the endless nights and weekends I was cooped up writing to the way I turned our home into an archive that often looked like it had been hit by a tornado, Tam braved it all, talked me through crises, and provided the love and the support I needed to press on. Her poignant photos put faces to victims and rescued survivors from anonymity. I'm awed by her work. It has made mine undeniably better.

INDEX

ABOUT THE AUTHOR

NICK TURSE, an award-winning journalist and historian, is the author of *The Complex: How the Military Invades Our Everyday Lives*, the managing editor for TomDispatch.com, and a fellow at the Nation Institute. His work has appeared in the *Los Angeles Times*, the *San Francisco Chronicle*, and the *Nation*, among other publications. Turse's investigations of U.S. war crimes in Vietnam have gained him a Ridenhour Prize for Reportorial Distinction, a Guggenheim Fellowship, and a fellowship at Harvard University's Radcliffe Institute for Advanced Study. He lives near New York City.

The American Empire Project

In an era of unprecedented military strength, leaders of the United States, the global hyperpower, have increasingly embraced imperial ambitions. How did this significant shift in purpose and policy come about? And what lies down the road?

The American Empire Project is a response to the changes that have occurred in American's strategic thinking as well as in its military and economic posture. Empire, long considered an offense against America's democratic heritage, now threatens to define the relationship between our country and the rest of the world. The American Empire Project publishes books that question this development, examine the origins of U.S. imperial aspirations, analyze their ramifications at home and abroad, and discuss alternatives to this dangerous trend.

The project was conceived by Tom Engelhardt and Steve Fraser, editors who are themselves historians and writers. Published by Metropolitan Books, an imprint of Henry Holt and Company, its titles include *Hegemony or Survival* and *Failed States* by Noam Chomsky, *The Limits of Power* and *Washington Rules* by Andrew Bacevich, *Blood and Oil* by Michael T. Klare, *A Question of Torture* by Alfred McCoy, *A People's History of American Empire* by Howard Zinn, and *Empire's Workshop* by Greg Grandin.

For more information about the American Empire Project and for a list of forthcoming titles, please visit americanempireproject.com.